Authors
AP® Writing Prompts

• • • • • • • • • • • • • • • • • • • •

W.H. Auden, "Musée des Beaux Arts" (p. 356)
Elizabeth Bishop, "One Art" (p. 258)
Elizabeth Bishop, "The Fish" (p. 307)
Elizabeth Bishop, "Manners" (p. 357)
Robert Browning, "Meeting at Night" (p. 58)
Robert Browning, "Parting at Morning" (p. 59)
Robert Browning, "Porphyria's Lover" (p. 224)
Robert Browning, "My Last Duchess" (p. 288)
Amy Clampitt "Witness" (p. 361)
Samuel Taylor Coleridge "Kubla Khan" (p. 363)
Billy Collins, "Sonnet" (p. 159)
Billy Collins, "Weighing the Dog" (p. 364)
Emily Dickinson, "A narrow Fellow in the Grass"
(p. 167)
Emily Dickinson, "I heard a Fly buzz—when I died"
(p. 237)
John Donne, "A Valediction: Forbidding Mourning"
(p. 86)
John Donne, "Batter my heart, three-personed God"
(p. 124)
Paul Laurence Dunbar, "We Wear the Mask" (p. 263)
T.S. Eliot "Journey of the Magi" (p. 145)
Robert Francis, "Pitcher" (p. 272)
Robert Frost, "After Apple Picking" (p. 65)
Robert Frost, "The Road Not Taken" (p. 91)
Robert Frost, "Stopping by Woods on a Snowy
Evening" (p. 153)
Robert Frost, "Birches" (p. 371)
Thomas Hardy, "The Man He Killed" (p. 24)
Thomas Hardy, "Channel Firing" (p. 376)
Robert Hayden, "Those Winter Sundays" (p. 66)
Seamus Heaney, "Digging" (p. 96)
Gerard Manley Hopkins, "Pied Beauty" (p. 272)
A.E. Housman, "Is my team plowing" (p. 29)
A.E. Housman, "Loveliest of Trees" (p. 152)
John Keats, "On the Sonnet" (p. 158)

John Keats, "La Belle Dame Sans Merci" (p. 388)
Philip Larkin, "Church Going" (p. 181)
Archibald MacLeish, "Ars Poetica" (p. 393)
Andrew Marvell "To His Coy Mistress" (p. 88)
Sharon Olds, "35/10" (p. 50)
Sharon Olds, "I Go Back to May 1937" (p. 402)
Mary Oliver, "Spring in the Classroom" (p. 44)
Mary Oliver, "Music Lessons" (p. 200)
Linda Pastan, "To a Daughter Leaving Home" (p. 223)
Marge Piercy, "Barbie Doll" (p. 119)
Edwin Arlington Robinson, "Richard Cory" (p. 17)
Edwin Arlington Robinson, "Miniver Cheevy"
(p. 143)
Theodore Roethke, "The Waking" (p. 189)
Christina Rossetti, "Up-Hill" (p. 408)
William Shakespeare, "Shall I compare thee to a sum-
mer's day" (p. 11)
William Shakespeare, "My mistress' eyes are nothing
like the sun" (p. 172)
Percy Bysshe Shelley, "Ozymandias" (p. 122)
Edmund Spenser, "One day I wrote her name upon
the strand" (p. 409)
Jonathan Swift, "A Description of the Morning"
(p. 410)
Alfred, Lord Tennyson, "Crossing the Bar" (p. 172)
Natasha Trethewey, "Southern History" (p. 160)
Walt Whitman, "A Noiseless Patient Spider" (p. 93)
Walt Whitman, "Had I the Choice" (p. 220)
William Carlos Williams, "The Widow's Lament in
Springtime" (p. 61)
William Wordsworth, "Composed upon Westminster
Bridge, September 3, 1802" (p. 275)
Thomas Wyatt, "My galley chargèd with forgetfulness"
(p. 416)
William Butler Yeats, "The Song of Wandering
Aengus" (p. 418)

AP® EDITION

PERRINE'S

SOUND
&
SENSE

True ease in writing comes from art, not chance,
As those move easiest who have learned to dance.
'Tis not enough no harshness gives offense,
The sound must seem an echo to the sense.

—ALEXANDER POPE

From *An Essay on Criticism*

AP® EDITION

PERRINE'S

SOUND
&
SENSE

AN INTRODUCTION TO POETRY
Fifteenth Edition

Greg Johnson
Kennesaw State University

Thomas R. Arp
Late, Southern Methodist University

CENGAGE
Learning·

Australia • Brazil • Mexico • Singapore • United Kingdom • United States

CENGAGE
Learning

AP® Edition of Perrine's Sound & Sense:
An Introduction to Poetry,
Fifteenth Edition
Greg Johnson / Thomas R. Arp

Product Director: Monica Eckman

Product Manager: Vanessa Coloura

Content Developer: Karl Yambert

Senior Content Developer: Kathy
    Sands-Boehmer

Associate Content Developer: Erin
    Bosco

Product Assistant: Claire Branman

Senior Marketing Manager: Kina Lara

Senior Content Project Manager:
    Michael Lepera

Senior Art Director: Marissa Falco

Manufacturing Planner: Betsy
    Donaghey

IP Analyst: Ann Hoffman

IP Project Manager: Betsy Hathaway

Production Service and Compositor:
    SPi Global

Text Designer: Anne Bell Carter, a bell
    design company

Cover Designer: Chen Design
    Associates

Product Manager, Advanced
    and Elective Products Program:
    Jeff Werle

Senior Content Developer, Advanced
    and Elective Products Program:
    Ashley Jack

Product Assistant, Advanced and
    Elective Products Program: Erica
    Pitcairn

For product information and technology assistance,
contact us at **Cengage Learning Customer & Sales
Support, 1-866-915-3276**

For permission to use material from this text or
product, submit all requests online at
www.cengage.com/permissions
Further permissions questions can be emailed to
permissionrequest@cengage.com

Library of Congress Control Number: 2016956507

AP® Edition:
ISBN-13: 978-1-337-10653-5

Cengage Learning
20 Channel Center Street
Boston, MA 02210
USA

Cengage Learning is a leading provider of customized
learning solutions with employees residing in nearly 40
different countries and sales in more than 125 countries
around the world. Find your local representative at
www.cengage.com.

Cengage Learning products are represented in Canada by
Nelson Education, Ltd.

For your course and learning solutions, visit
www.cengage.com.

To find online supplements and other instructional
support, please visit **www.cengagebrain.com.**

AP® is a trademark registered and/or owned by the College
Board, which was not involved in the production of, and
does not endorse, this product.

Printed in the United States of America
Print Number: 02   Print Year: 2017

CONTENTS

Preface   xx

Professional Acknowledgments   xxiv

Foreword to Students   xxv

Preparing to Succeed on the AP® English Literature
and Composition Examination   xxvii

PART ONE

The Elements of Poetry   1

CHAPTER ONE   What Is Poetry?   2

Alfred, Lord Tennyson   The Eagle   4
William Shakespeare   Winter   5
Wilfred Owen   Dulce et Decorum Est   6
Reviewing Chapter One   9
Understanding and Evaluating Poetry   10

William Shakespeare   Shall I compare thee to a summer's day?   11
Sylvia Plath   Black Rook in Rainy Weather   11
John Donne   The Triple Fool   13
Gwendolyn Brooks   The Bean Eaters   14
Louise Glück   Labor Day   14
William Carlos Williams   The Red Wheelbarrow   15
Elizabeth Bishop   Filling Station   16

Langston Hughes Suicide's Note   17
Edwin Arlington Robinson Richard Cory   17
Ben Jonson On My First Son   18
Billy Collins Introduction to Poetry   19
Suggestions for Writing   20
Practice AP® Writing Prompts   21

CHAPTER TWO Reading the Poem   22

Thomas Hardy The Man He Killed   24
Philip Larkin A Study of Reading Habits   25
A. E. Housman "Is my team plowing"   29
Reviewing Chapter Two   31

John Donne Break of Day   31
Emily Dickinson There's been a Death, in the Opposite House   32
Ted Hughes Hawk Roosting   33
John Keats Ode on Melancholy   34
Robert Herrick Upon Julia's Clothes   35
Sylvia Plath Mirror   36
Natasha Trethewey Collection Day   36
Walt Whitman The Dalliance of the Eagles   37
Adrienne Rich Storm Warnings   38
Suggestions for Writing   39
Practice AP® Writing Prompts   40

CHAPTER THREE Denotation and Connotation   41

Emily Dickinson There is no Frigate like a Book   42
William Shakespeare When my love swears that she is made of truth   43
Mary Oliver Spring in the Classroom   44
Exercises   46
Reviewing Chapter Three   47

Langston Hughes Cross   47
William Wordsworth The world is too much with us   48
Robert Frost Desert Places   48

Natasha Trethewey Accounting   49
Sharon Olds 35/10   50
J. D. McClatchy The Ledger   51
Julia Alvarez Dusting   51
Elizabeth Bishop In the Waiting Room   52
Wallace Stevens Disillusionment of Ten O'Clock   55
Suggestions for Writing   56
Practice AP® Writing Prompts   56

CHAPTER FOUR Imagery   57

Robert Browning Meeting at Night   58
Robert Browning Parting at Morning   59
Exercises   60
Reviewing Chapter Four   60

Gerard Manley Hopkins Spring   60
William Carlos Williams The Widow's Lament in Springtime   61
Emily Dickinson I felt a Funeral, in my Brain   62
Adrienne Rich Living in Sin   63
Seamus Heaney The Forge   64
Robert Frost After Apple-Picking   65
Robert Hayden Those Winter Sundays   66
Walt Whitman I saw in Louisiana a live-oak growing   67
Wallace Stevens The Snow Man   68
John Keats To Autumn   69
Suggestions for Writing   70
Practice AP® Writing Prompts   70

CHAPTER FIVE Figurative Language 1: Simile, Metaphor, Personification, Apostrophe, Metonymy   72

Langston Hughes Harlem   73
Emily Dickinson It sifts from Leaden Sieves   74
Anne Bradstreet The Author to Her Book   76
John Keats Bright Star   77
Exercise   80
Reviewing Chapter Five   81

Sylvia Plath Metaphors 81
Emily Dickinson I taste a liquor never brewed 82
Philip Larkin Toads 83
Ralph Waldo Emerson The Snowstorm 84
Rachel Hadas Ghost Yogurt 85
Billy Collins Divorce 86
John Donne A Valediction: Forbidding Mourning 86
Andrew Marvell To His Coy Mistress 88
Suggestions for Writing 90
Practice AP® Writing Prompts 90

CHAPTER SIX Figurative Language 2:
Symbol, Allegory 91

Robert Frost The Road Not Taken 91
Walt Whitman A Noiseless Patient Spider 93
William Blake The Sick Rose 95
Seamus Heaney Digging 96
Robert Herrick To the Virgins, to Make Much of Time 99
George Herbert Redemption 100
Exercises 101
Reviewing Chapter Six 102

Louise Glück Purple Bathing Suit 102
Clive James Whitman and the Moth 103
Archibald MacLeish You, Andrew Marvell 104
Robert Frost Fire and Ice 105
Emily Dickinson Because I could not stop for Death 106
John Donne Hymn to God, My God, in My Sickness 107
Sylvia Plath Spinster 109
Alfred, Lord Tennyson Ulysses 110
Suggestions for Writing 112
Practice AP® Writing Prompts 113

CHAPTER SEVEN Figurative Language 3:
Paradox, Overstatement, Understatement, Irony 114

Emily Dickinson Much Madness is divinest Sense 115
John Donne The Sun Rising 116
Marge Piercy Barbie Doll 119

William Blake   The Chimney Sweeper   120
Percy Bysshe Shelley   Ozymandias   122
Exercise   123
Reviewing Chapter Seven   123

William Wordsworth   A slumber did my spirit seal   124
John Donne   Batter my heart, three-personed God   124
Seamus Heaney   Mid-Term Break   125
W. H. Auden   The Unknown Citizen   126
Lucille Clifton   in the inner city   127
Emily Dickinson   What Soft—Cherubic Creatures   128
Theodore Roethke   My Papa's Waltz   128
Sylvia Plath   The Colossus   129
Robert Browning   Soliloquy of the Spanish Cloister   130
Suggestions for Writing   133
Practice AP® Writing Prompts   133

CHAPTER EIGHT   Allusion   135

Robert Frost   "Out, Out—"   136
William Shakespeare   from *Macbeth* ("She should have died hereafter")   137
Sylvia Plath   Wuthering Heights   139
Reviewing Chapter Eight   140

Louise Glück   Eurydice   140
e. e. cummings   in Just—   141
John Milton   On His Blindness   142
Edwin Arlington Robinson   Miniver Cheevy   143
Sharon Olds   My Son the Man   144
T. S. Eliot   Journey of the Magi   145
Billy Collins   Genesis   147
William Butler Yeats   Leda and the Swan   148
Emily Dickinson   A little East of Jordan   149
Suggestions for Writing   150
Practice AP® Writing Prompts   150

CHAPTER NINE   Meaning and Idea   151

A. E. Housman   Loveliest of Trees   152
Robert Frost   Stopping by Woods on a Snowy Evening   153
Reviewing Chapter Nine   155

Emily Dickinson   Four Trees—upon a solitary Acre   155
Robert Frost   Design   156
e. e. cummings   O sweet spontaneous   157
Walt Whitman   When I Heard the Learn'd Astronomer   158
John Keats   On the Sonnet   158
Billy Collins   Sonnet   159
Natasha Trethewey   Southern History   160
Carolyn Forché   The Colonel   161
William Blake   The Lamb   162
William Blake   The Tiger   162
Suggestions for Writing   163
Practice AP® Writing Prompts   164

CHAPTER TEN   Tone   165

Denise Levertov   To the Snake   167
Emily Dickinson   A narrow Fellow in the Grass   167
Michael Drayton   Since there's no help   169
Louise Glück   Lost Love   170
Reviewing Chapter Ten   171

William Shakespeare   My mistress' eyes   172
Alfred, Lord Tennyson   Crossing the Bar   172
Thomas Hardy   The Oxen   173
John Donne   The Flea   174
Sharon Olds   Bop After Hip Op   175
William Butler Yeats   Among School Children   176
Natasha Trethewey   History Lesson   179
Matthew Arnold   Dover Beach   179
Philip Larkin   Church Going   181
Alexander Pope   Engraved on the Collar of a Dog Which I Gave to His
                Royal Highness   183
Suggestions for Writing   184
Practice AP® Writing Prompts   184

CHAPTER ELEVEN   Musical Devices   186

W. H. Auden   That night when joy began   188
Theodore Roethke   The Waking   189
Gerard Manley Hopkins   God's Grandeur   191
Exercise   192
Reviewing Chapter Eleven   192

William Shakespeare Blow, blow, thou winter wind   193
Gwendolyn Brooks We Real Cool   193
Edna St. Vincent Millay Counting-Out Rhyme   194
Edgar Allan Poe The Bells   195
Sylvia Plath Morning Song   198
Sharon Olds Rite of Passage   199
Mary Oliver Music Lessons   200
William Stafford Traveling through the dark   201
Robert Frost Nothing Gold Can Stay   202
Suggestions for Writing   202
Practice AP® Writing Prompts   203

CHAPTER TWELVE Rhythm and Meter   204

George Herbert Virtue   209
Exercises   218
Reviewing Chapter Twelve   219

William Blake "Introduction" to *Songs of Innocence*   219
Walt Whitman Had I the Choice   220
George Gordon, Lord Byron Stanzas   221
Elizabeth Bishop Insomnia   221
Sylvia Plath Old Ladies' Home   222
Linda Pastan To a Daughter Leaving Home   223
Robert Browning Porphyria's Lover   224
Alfred, Lord Tennyson Break, break, break   226
Edgar Allan Poe Annabel Lee   227
Suggestions for Writing   228
Practice AP® Writing Prompts   229

CHAPTER THIRTEEN Sound and Meaning   230

Anonymous Pease Porridge Hot   230
A. E. Housman Eight O'Clock   232
Alexander Pope Sound and Sense   233
Emily Dickinson I heard a Fly buzz—when I died   237
Exercises   239
Reviewing Chapter Thirteen   241

Wilfred Owen Anthem for Doomed Youth   241
Sylvia Plath Suicide off Egg Rock   242

Pattiann Rogers   Night and the Creation of Geography   243
Adrienne Rich   Aunt Jennifer's Tigers   244
Galway Kinnell   Blackberry Eating   244
Seamus Heaney   The Skunk   245
Dylan Thomas   Fern Hill   246
William Carlos Williams   The Dance   248
Suggestions for Writing   248
Practice AP® Writing Prompts   249

CHAPTER FOURTEEN   Pattern   250

George Herbert   The Pulley   251
John Keats   On First Looking into Chapman's Homer   253
William Shakespeare   That time of year   254
Dylan Thomas   Do Not Go Gentle into That Good Night   255
Exercises   257
Reviewing Chapter Fourteen   257

Elizabeth Bishop   One Art   258
Sylvia Plath   Mad Girl's Love Song   259
William Shakespeare   From *Romeo and Juliet*   260
John Donne   Death, be not proud   260
William Butler Yeats   The Folly of Being Comforted   261
Claude McKay   The White City   262
Billy Collins   Villanelle   262
Paul Laurence Dunbar   We Wear the Mask   263
Robert Frost   Acquainted with the Night   264
Seamus Heaney   Villanelle for an Anniversary   265
Robert Herrick   Delight in Disorder   266
Suggestions for Writing   267
Practice AP® Writing Prompts   267

CHAPTER FIFTEEN   Evaluating Poetry 1:
**Sentimental, Rhetorical,
Didactic Verse**   268

Reviewing Chapter Fifteen   271

God's Will for You and Me   271
Pied Beauty   272
Pitcher   272

The Old-Fashioned Pitcher   272
A Poison Tree   273
The Most Vital Thing in Life   273
Lower New York: At Dawn   274
Composed upon Westminster Bridge, September 3, 1802   275
Piano   275
The Days Gone By   276
I would not paint—a picture   276
If I can stop one Heart from breaking   277
When I have fears that I may cease to be   278
O Solitude!   278
Suggestions for Writing   279
Practice AP® Writing Prompts   279

CHAPTER SIXTEEN Evaluating Poetry 2:
Poetic Excellence   280

John Donne The Canonization   281
Percy Bysshe Shelley Ode to the West Wind   283
John Keats Ode on a Grecian Urn   286
Robert Browning My Last Duchess   288
Emily Dickinson There's a certain Slant of light   290
Robert Frost Home Burial   291
T. S. Eliot The Love Song of J. Alfred Prufrock   295
William Butler Yeats Sailing to Byzantium   300
Wallace Stevens Sunday Morning   301
Langston Hughes The Weary Blues   305
Elizabeth Bishop The Fish   307
Sylvia Plath Lady Lazarus   309
Practice AP® Writing Prompts   312

FEATURED POETS

The following poems appear as illustrations in various chapters of the book, but these five poets are represented by a sufficient number of poems to warrant studying them as individual artists. Approaches to analysis and writing are suggested on page 317 of Part Two of this book.

Emily Dickinson
A little East of Jordan   149
A narrow Fellow in the Grass   167
Because I could not stop for Death   106

Four Trees—upon a solitary Acre   155
I died for Beauty—but was scarce   367
I felt a Funeral, in my Brain   62
I heard a Fly buzz—when I died   237
I taste a liquor never brewed   82
I would not paint—a picture   276
If I can stop one Heart from breaking   277
It sifts from Leaden Sieves   74
Much Madness is divinest Sense   115
There is no Frigate like a Book   42
There's a certain Slant of light   290
There's been a Death, in the Opposite House   32
What Soft—Cherubic Creatures   128

John Donne

A Valediction: Forbidding Mourning   86
Batter my heart, three-personed God   124
Break of Day   31
Death, be not proud   260
Hymn to God, My God, in My Sickness   107
Song: Go and catch a falling star   367
The Apparition   368
The Canonization   281
The Flea   174
The Good-Morrow   369
The Sun Rising   116
The Triple Fool   13

Robert Frost

Acquainted with the Night   264
After Apple-Picking   65
Birches   371
Desert Places   48
Design   156
Fire and Ice   105
Home Burial   291
Mending Wall   373
Nothing Gold Can Stay   202
"Out, Out—"   136
Stopping by Woods on a Snowy Evening   153
The Road Not Taken   91

John Keats

Bright Star   77
La Belle Dame sans Merci   388
O Solitude!   278
Ode on a Grecian Urn   286
Ode on Melancholy   34
Ode to a Nightingale   390
On First Looking into Chapman's Homer   253
On the Sonnet   158
This living hand   392
To Autumn   69
To Sleep   392
When I have fears that I may cease to be   278

Sylvia Plath

Black Rook in Rainy Weather   11
Lady Lazarus   309
Mad Girl's Love Song   259
Metaphors   81
Mirror   36
Morning Song   198
Old Ladies' Home   222
Spinster   109
Suicide off Egg Rock   242
The Colossus   129
Wuthering Heights   139

A CONTEMPORARY COLLECTION

These five contemporary poets are represented by six or seven poems each, included at various points in the book. They offer students the opportunity to sample at greater lengths the works of poets of their own time. Approaches to analysis and writing are suggested on page 317 of Part Two of this book.

Billy Collins

Divorce   86
Genesis   147
Introduction to Poetry   19
Sonnet   159
The Dead   364
Villanelle   262
Weighing the Dog   364

Louise Glück
Cousins   374
Eurydice   140
Labor Day   14
Lost Love   170
Primavera   375
Purple Bathing Suit   102

Seamus Heaney
Digging   96
Follower   380
Mid-Term Break   125
The Forge   64
The Skunk   245
Villanelle for an Anniversary   265

Sharon Olds
Bop After Hip Op   175
I Go Back to May 1937   402
My Son the Man   144
Rite of Passage   199
The Connoisseuse of Slugs   402
35/10   50

Natasha Trethewey
Accounting   49
Blond   411
Collection Day   36
History Lesson   179
Miscegenation   412
Southern History   160

PART TWO

Writing about Poetry 313

I.   Why Write about Literature?   315
II.   For Whom Do You Write?   315
III.   Two Basic Approaches   317
    1. Explication   317
    2. Analysis   318

IV.   Choosing a Topic   318
  1. Essays That Focus on a Single Poem   319
  2. Essays of Comparison and Contrast   319
  3. Essays on a Number of Poems by a Single Author   320
  4. Essays on a Number of Poems with Some Feature Other than Authorship in Common   322
V.   Proving Your Point   322
VI.   Writing the Essay   324
VII.   Introducing Quotations (Q1-Q11)   326
VIII.   Documentation   332
  1. Textual Documentation (TD1-TD5)   333
  2. Parenthetical Documentation (PD1-PD5)   335
  3. Documentation by Works Cited   336
  4. Documentation of Electronic Sources   339
IX.   Stance and Style (S1–S6)   341
X.   Grammar, Punctuation, and Usage: Common Problems   344
  1. Grammar (G1–G2)   344
  2. Punctuation (P1–P5)   344
  3. Usage (U1–U2)   346
XI.   Writing Samples   349
  1. Explication: "A Study of Reading Habits"   349
  2. Analysis: Diction in "Spring in the Classroom"   351

PART THREE

Poems for Further Reading   355

Kim Addonizio   Sonnenizio on a Line from Drayton   356
W. H. Auden   Musée des Beaux Arts   356
Aphra Behn   On Her Loving Two Equally   357
Elizabeth Bishop   Manners   357
William Blake   The Garden of Love   359
Gwendolyn Brooks   a song in the front yard   359
Gwendolyn Brooks   Sadie and Maud   360
George Gordon, Lord Byron   She Walks in Beauty   360
Amy Clampitt   Witness   361
Lucille Clifton   good times   362
Henri Cole   Mask   362

Samuel Taylor Coleridge   Kubla Khan   363
Billy Collins   The Dead   364
Billy Collins   Weighing the Dog   364
Stephen Crane   War Is Kind   365
e. e. cummings   Buffalo Bill's defunct   366
e. e. cummings   the Cambridge ladies who live in furnished souls   366
Emily Dickinson   I died for Beauty—but was scarce   367
John Donne   Song: Go and catch a falling star   367
John Donne   The Apparition   368
John Donne   The Good-Morrow   369
Mark Doty   Pescadero   369
Paul Laurence Dunbar   Sympathy   370
Alice Moore Dunbar-Nelson   I Sit and Sew   371
Robert Frost   Birches   371
Robert Frost   Mending Wall   373
Louise Glück   Cousins   374
Louise Glück   Primavera   375
Thomas Hardy   "Ah, Are You Digging on My Grave?"   375
Thomas Hardy   Channel Firing   376
Thomas Hardy   Hap   378
Thomas Hardy   The Darkling Thrush   378
Thomas Hardy   The Ruined Maid   379
Seamus Heaney   Follower   380
George Herbert   Love   381
George Herbert   Peace   381
A. E. Housman   "Terence, this is stupid stuff"   383
A. E. Housman   To an Athlete Dying Young   385
Langston Hughes   Theme for English B   386
Randall Jarrell   The Death of the Ball Turret Gunner   387
Ben Jonson   Still to be neat   387
Ben Jonson   To Celia   388
John Keats   La Belle Dame sans Merci   388
John Keats   Ode to a Nightingale   390
John Keats   This living hand   392
John Keats   To Sleep   392
Galway Kinnell   After Making Love We Hear Footsteps   393
Archibald MacLeish   Ars Poetica   393
Christopher Marlowe   The Passionate Shepherd to His Love   394
Cleopatra Mathis   Survival: A Guide   395
Judson Mitcham   Story   396
Judson Mitcham   Stroke   396
Meghan O'Rourke   Apartment Living   397

Joyce Carol Oates   Bloodline, Elegy: Su Qijian Family, Beijing   397
Joyce Carol Oates   Playlet for Voices   400
Sharon Olds   I Go Back to May 1937   402
Sharon Olds   The Connoisseuse of Slugs   402
Katha Pollitt   Moth   403
Alexander Pope   Ode on Solitude   404
Edwin Arlington Robinson   Eros Turannos   405
Edwin Arlington Robinson   Mr. Flood's Party   406
Christina Rossetti   Song   408
Christina Rossetti   Up-Hill   408
William Shakespeare   Let me not to the marriage of true minds   409
Edmund Spenser   One day I wrote her name upon the strand   409
Wallace Stevens   Anecdote of the Jar   410
Jonathan Swift   A Description of the Morning   410
Natasha Trethewey   Blond   411
Natasha Trethewey   Miscegenation   412
Walt Whitman   A sight in camp in the daybreak gray and dim   412
Walt Whitman   Hours continuing long, sore and heavy-hearted   413
William Wordsworth   I wandered lonely as a cloud   414
William Wordsworth   My heart leaps up when I behold   415
William Wordsworth   The Solitary Reaper   415
Thomas Wyatt   My galley chargèd with forgetfulness   416
William Butler Yeats   The Lake Isle of Innisfree   416
William Butler Yeats   The Second Coming   417
William Butler Yeats   The Song of Wandering Aengus   418
William Butler Yeats   The Wild Swans at Coole   418
Practice AP® Writing Prompts   420
Practice AP® Multiple-Choice Questions   423
Answers for the Practice AP® Multiple-Choice Questions   434

Glossary and Index of Literary Terms   435

Copyrights and Acknowledgments   444

Index of Authors, Titles, and First Lines   453

PREFACE

In preparing this fifteenth edition of *Perrine's Sound & Sense*, I have striven to be true to the principles established by Laurence Perrine more than sixty years ago while also acknowledging the evolving nature of poetry. I have been guided not only by my own experience but also by the rich legacy of Thomas R. Arp, who joined Perrine in 1979, and by the helpful suggestions of many teachers who have contributed the results of their classroom experience. Many of them are identified in the "Professional Acknowledgments" listed here. They have helped me in revising the text and in replacing more than twenty-five percent of the poems printed in the previous edition.

Here I must comment briefly on the contribution of Thomas R. Arp, who passed away in 2015 but whose work on *Sound & Sense* for more than thirty-five years has left an indelible and invaluable imprint. Professor Arp's depth of knowledge and experience with the book as a whole, combined with his perspicacity in choosing poems to illustrate the principles of each chapter, has been a source of inspiration to me during the many years I worked with him, and here I wish to salute his achievement. Though any faults in this new edition are mine alone, I continued to benefit from his wisdom and insight in his last years, since he graciously consented to serve in a consulting role as I wrote the book. Thus his name, I am happy to say, continues to grace the cover of the book, a fitting reminder of his past contributions and his recent involvement.

In keeping with Perrine's and Arp's shared principles, this book works to balance the classic with the contemporary, to represent a wide diversity of poets, and to emphasize the importance of the close reading of poetry as the avenue to enjoy and appreciate it. Although there are many flourishing approaches to poetry and its effects, all three of us have believed that the initial step must be understanding the elements through which poetry presents itself.

The book is addressed to the student who is beginning a serious investigation of poetry. I have attempted to offer that student a sufficient grasp of the nature and variety of poetry, some reasonable means for reading it with appreciative understanding, and a few primary ideas on how to evaluate it. One important principle established in the earliest editions of the book is the need for conciseness and compactness, so that the book will have a friendly, welcoming appeal and will not seem daunting in its comprehensiveness. In matters of theory, some issues are undoubtedly simplified for the purposes of an introductory textbook, but none I hope seriously so, and some more sophisticated theoretical approaches have had to be excluded in the interests of space. Classroom teachers of course will supplement the basic materials here with their own insights.

Another principle is that the elements of poetry are presented in a progression in which each new topic builds on what preceded it. The separate chapters gradually introduce the student to the elements of poetry, putting the emphasis always on *how* and *why*. *How* can the reader use these elements to get at the total meaning of the poem, to interpret it sensibly, and to respond to it adequately? *Why* does the poet use these elements? What values have they for the poet and the reader?

The organization and structure of the book reinforce the step-by-step approach to understanding poetry. Part One consists of sixteen chapters of definition and discussion. Most of the chapters contain two parts: (1) a discussion of the topic indicated by the chapter title, with illustrative poems, and (2) a relevant selection of additional poems with study questions for further illustration of the topic. A heavy line in the text and in the table of contents indicates the division between the two parts of each chapter. Also in these chapters I have included a list of review topics for the materials, and a list of suggestions for writing about those materials as they are illustrated elsewhere in the book.

The presentation of poetry in the whole book is similarly divided into two parts: Part One consists of the sixteen discussion chapters; Part Three contains a selection of poems for further reading, without study questions.

Part Two, "Writing about Poetry," embraces the important assumption that the fullest understanding and appreciation of a poem arises from a reader's ability to express in language its meaning and emotional effects. The process of finding the right words to make these clear, and the additional clarity that results from the correct and effective presentation of these materials, is a significant part of making a poem part of one's experience.

Although the book emphasizes the study of poems, not poets, I have continued the practice of representing some poets with a sufficient number of poems in the chapters and in Part Three to support the study of them as individual poets. This edition includes five "Featured Poets": John Donne from the Renaissance, John Keats and Emily Dickinson from the nineteenth century, and Robert Frost and Sylvia Plath from the twentieth century. The table of contents gathers the titles of their poems in a boxed format for easy reference.

This edition also continues the presentation of a "Contemporary Collection," a gathering of some of the best work from five contemporary poets. Each of these poets is represented by six or seven poems each, placed throughout the text. These too are identified in a boxed format in the table of contents. Among them for the first time is Pulitzer Prize–winning poet Louise Glück. Also, a special effort has been made, in response to users' requests, to include a number of poems written in the twenty-first century.

Finally, to provide an introduction to the further works of individual poets, the book contains at least three poems each by more than two dozen additional poets, both classic and contemporary. These poems can easily be referenced in the index of the book.

An Instructor's Manual has again been prepared to accompany this book, available to all teachers who adopt the book for their classes. The manual contains an analytical essay on every poem, suggesting approaches to interpretation and some information that places the poems in their contexts. Some of these essays are the work of the author who prepared this edition, but many were written by the man who originated the first edition, Laurence Perrine, and by his successor, Thomas R. Arp.

Through the fifteen editions of a book that originated in the middle of the twentieth century, *Sound & Sense* has evolved in many ways, responding to shifts in interest, concern, and taste expressed by its users. However, certain abiding principles remain as relevant to the twenty-first century as they were in the last. Among these are the conviction that the close reading of a text is basic to the understanding and appreciation of poetry; that to understand the means by which a poem achieves its ends is an essential part of experiencing it fully; and that reading poetry is important to the development of the whole person.

AP® Edition

This AP® edition contains helpful features for students preparing for the AP® English Literature and Composition Examination. There are more than 50 AP® practice prompts akin to the poetry essay question, prose essay question, and open essay question students will find on the AP® Literature and Composition Exam. There is also an introduction to the AP® course and exam that offers strategies students can use both in preparing for the exam and taking it. Finally, writers who appear in the College Board's list of representative authors are indicated in the table of contents.

AP® Teacher Support

For this edition, there is a corresponding *Instructors Manual* which includes information and lesson suggestions for teaching the course. Additionally, teachers who adopt the book can request *Classroom Practice Exercises*, which includes a set of additional multiple-choice questions in AP® format.

AP® Student Support

Fast Track to a 5: Preparing for the AP® English Literature and Composition Examination is a test-preparation manual that includes an introduction for students about the exam, chapters on each type of question, and two complete practice tests. It can be purchased either with the text or separately.

AP® Contributors

Robert Brown Rob Brown teaches AP® English and leads the English Department at Rice Memorial High School in South Burlington, Vermont, where he has taught for more than 35 years. A nationally-recognized consultant, Rob has presented numerous workshops and institutes, and has served for many years as an AP® Reader.

Donna Carlson Tanzer A former AP® Literature teacher for the West Allis, Wisconsin, school district, Donna Tanzer teaches writing and humanities at the Milwaukee Institute of Art and Design and has taught at Marian University. She coauthored *Interpreting Poetry* with Martin Beller, with whom she has presented at several AP® Annual Conferences and NCTE national conventions. She has been an AP® Reader since 2004.

Martin Beller Martin Beller is a Visiting Professor in the English Department at Texas Southern University. Dr. Beller is co-author, with Donna Tanzer, of *Interpreting Poetry*, a text for AP® and pre-AP® classes, and has presented workshops on teaching poetry, with Ms. Tanzer, at AP® Annual Conferences and at annual meetings of the NCTE. He taught both AP® English courses during ten years as a high school teacher, and has served as an AP® Reader since 2006.

Suzanne Loosen Suzanne Loosen has been teaching AP® English Literature and Composition since she was a first year teacher at Milwaukee School of Languages. In 2011, she was honored as a "Teacher of the Year" by the Milwaukee Metropolitan Alliance of Black School Educators.

PROFESSIONAL ACKNOWLEDGMENTS

The following instructors have offered helpful reactions and suggestions for this fifteenth edition of *Perrine's Sound & Sense:*

Paul Almonte
St. Peter's University

Paulette Bane
University of Florida

Chere Blair
Southwestern Assemblies of God University

Eileen G'Sell
Washington University, St. Louis

Ellen Gil-Gomez
California State University, San Bernardino

Jesse Graves
East Tennessee State University

Christine Grogan
University of South Florida

Rod Hernandez
California State University, Dominguez Hills

Geri Jacobs
Jackson College

Rebecca Macijeski
University of Nebraska

Kathleen Mayberry
Lehigh Carbon Community College

Susan Mayberry
Alfred University

Kathleen Monahan
St. Peter's University

Patrick O'Connell
Gannon University

Kelly Seufert
Queens College, CUNY

Tyrone Williams
Xavier University

Dominika Wrozynski
Manhattan College

FOREWORD TO STUDENTS

"I've never been good at poetry." Most teachers have heard this statement repeatedly from students as they begin a course in the serious study of poetry. The patient teacher knows what students mean—that there is something apparently mysterious or even intimidating about trying to experience the full range of what a poem can mean or be. And the teacher believes them, because reading poetry is a learned skill and they may not have had the practice or opportunity to learn that skill, just as they might not have mastered the skills necessary to bake a pie or dive off the 10-meter platform or win at poker.

If this is your situation, this book is for you.

On the other hand, you may feel that your experience with poems has developed for you the sensitivity to respond fully and to live vicariously within the world that a poem represents.

If this is your situation, this book is for you, too.

Here's why: both the beginner and the more experienced reader of poems can profit from a book that provides a step-by-step method for understanding how a poem does what it does and of judging its accomplishment. All of us—teachers, beginners, experienced students—know how we feel when we first read through a poem. We probably start by thinking "I like this" or "This poem doesn't say much to me" or "What in the world is this supposed to mean?" Under normal circumstances, if you could, you'd either act on your first reaction and read the poem again, or you'd attempt to discover its meaning, or you'd drop it and go on to do something more pleasurable.

However, you're in a special situation. You're taking a course (either by your own choice or because you're required to), and one of the rules of the game is that you're supposed to move from your initial reaction to some sort of "serious" response that will satisfy your teacher. If you like the poem and want to reread it, your teacher will pester you with wanting to know *why* you liked it, and might even insist that you offer reasons why other people should like it, too. If you are only a little bit curious about it or think that it is a waste of time, your teacher will lead (or nudge, or bash) you into finding things in the poem that might change your initial opinion. In any case, the terms of your special situation, as a student in a course with a grade on the horizon, make it necessary for you to have more than an initial reaction. You'll need to develop an understanding of the poem, and you'll need to show in discussion or writing both what you understand and how the poem led you to that understanding.

That's where this book will help. In addition to a systematic guide for discovering how and what a poem means, we've provided, at the ends of the chapters, suggestions for writing, and we've presented standards for your written work in Part Two of the book.

Why is writing important? It's the most straightforward way of sorting out your feelings and ideas, putting them into shape, and nailing down your own experience. All writing about literature has a double motive—it sharpens your grasp of the work, and it helps you to lead other people to share your experience. Writing about literature is writing persuasively, and persuading others to see what you see helps you to see it more clearly.

So, at the most basic level, we want this book (and your course) to help you with reading and writing. However, you have every right to ask, "Why read and write about poetry?" That's a good question, because in our world there are so many ways of gaining experience and insight into our lives and the lives of others that focusing on one resource based on the spoken and written word may seem narrow and old-fashioned. We're willing to grant that, and we'll go even further: in a sense, literary study is elitist, and turning to poetry as a source of experience will set you apart from the majority of people.

As you'll see as you proceed through this book, poetry is the most compact and emotionally stimulating of literary experiences. It has the ability to deliver the most insight in the smallest amount of space, and it is a richly powerful way into the hearts and minds of many different kinds of people in many different situations. We challenge you to hold it up to the several other sources of insight into human behavior with which you might be familiar—films, television drama, radio and television talk shows, courses in psychology or sociology, eavesdropping on other people, or quarreling and making up with people who mean something to you. All of these have limitations when you compare them with the compacted experience and wisdom of poetry. Poets are experts in seeing, feeling, understanding, and expressing. In ages before literacy, poets were the only means to truths beyond individual experience, and they can still help us enlarge our limited lives.

You can understand and benefit from poetry, and you can learn to express your thoughts and feelings about the experience it conveys by writing persuasively about it. In short, you can be "good at poetry." Turn to Chapter 1 to begin.

PREPARING TO SUCCEED ON THE AP® ENGLISH LITERATURE AND COMPOSITION EXAMINATION

Advanced Placement® courses can be both challenging and stimulating. The rigor of an AP® course, whether you are taking it at your high school or through distance education, will help you prepare for the challenges of college course work. AP® English Literature and Composition focuses on two skills: critical and analytical reading, and clear and coherent writing about what you have read. Unlike AP® Language and Composition, which concentrates on nonfiction, AP® Literature and Composition draws on imaginative literature for its texts. As you explore the expanse and variety of literature, you will develop close reading skills that enable you to see how writers of literature use structure and style, along with figurative language, imagery, symbolism, and tone, to convey meaning.

The AP® English Literature and Composition exam is also a writing exam in that it tests your ability to write clearly and coherently about the details and meaning of a poetry or prose selection. It is in the essay portion of the exam that you can show off your skills as a writer. When scoring essays, readers look for variety in sentence structure, sophisticated vocabulary, logical organization of ideas, and balance between the general meaning of the selection and the specific elements by which the overall meaning is developed. Don't think of the exam as something designed to trip you up; it is an opportunity to demonstrate how well you have honed your reading and writing skills.

Before the AP® Exam

If you have been steadily doing your homework and keeping up with the course work, you should be in good shape.

The evening before the exam is not the time to cram. If you'd like, briefly review the terminology or take a quick look through class notes or your textbook, but avoid getting caught up in small details. Do get a good night's sleep. And on the day of the examination, be sure to eat breakfast—fuel for the brain. Then go get a 5.

Taking the AP® English Literature and Composition Exam

The purpose of the Advanced Placement® Program hasn't changed since 1955, when it was introduced: It was designed to give students an opportunity to extend their knowledge with meaningful and engaging college-level course work. Each year hundreds of thousands of students take the AP® English Literature and Composition exam! Students value the abilities to read critically, to make insightful connections between what they read and the larger world, and to write cogently about ideas. Those abilities enrich the individual. They are also the foundation for a free-thinking society.

About the Exam

If you are enrolled in an English Literature and Composition (or English IV AP®) course, you are being given a year's instruction in the skills necessary for success on the AP® exam. Most students who take the class will take the test—many took the AP® English Language and Composition exam the year before. Many schools require students in AP® classes to take the exam. Keep in mind that a formal year-long course is not a necessity. Any high school student may take any AP® examination. Our advice to students in an AP® course is always to take the test. Even if you don't get a high grade, you will have grown as a thinker and a writer. AP® makes you far better prepared for college courses.

To take the test, you need to sign up with your teacher or the designated AP® coordinator at your high school. There is a charge for each test. However, many states and districts offer a variety of financial incentives for taking the tests, so you may not be charged the full amount.

The AP® exams are given during May at high schools worldwide. The methods of scoring and grading will be discussed in detail later, but for now know that the exams are scored in June by AP® teachers and college instructors. Students receive their grades at the beginning of July. You can have the College Board send your grades directly to the colleges of your choice. If you are not yet ready to apply to a college, you can have your scores "banked," to be sent at a later date.

Examination Day

The AP® English Literature and Composition exam is nearly always given in the morning and lasts approximately three and half hours. Bring a form of identification (usually your driver's license or school ID card is sufficient). In addition, you should have two well-sharpened pencils with erasers and a dark-blue or black pen. Wear comfortable clothes. We recommend layering your clothing in case the heat or air-conditioning is erratic. There is nothing worse than roasting or freezing while you are trying to concentrate on writing! It's a good idea to wear a watch so you can keep track of the time. Letting go of your cell phone can be like saying goodbye to a best friend, but they are not permitted in the testing room. In addition, no food or bottles of water are permitted in the testing room at any time.

Once you are in your seat, the proctor will take attendance, check IDs if that hasn't already been done, and give general directions. If your school has not had you provide the necessary demographic information at an earlier time, you will bubble in those sheets at this point. The proctor will then pass out a test booklet and read through the directions on filling out the answer sheet.

You will be allowed a ten-minute bathroom and water break after the multiple-choice section. If possible, get some fresh air and stretch.

Once you are back in your seat, the proctor will hand out the essay materials. The format of those materials has been changing in recent years. You will probably be given one booklet with three essay questions in it. Make your annotations in that booklet. You will get a separate booklet with lined pages for writing your essays. Each page in that booklet has a box in the upper right-hand corner where you should indicate which essay question—1, 2, or 3—you are answering. You don't have to write the essays in any particular order. If you forget to put the essay number in the box, don't worry. AP® readers are trained to leave no page unturned in a student test booklet. They will read all the pages in the booklet in order to find your essay. You will not be penalized for that error.

There are three essay questions on the AP® exam. One is based on poetry; another is based on a prose or drama passage; a third asks you to respond to a general statement or question, making reference to a work of literature of your own choosing. You have two hours to work on the three essay questions. All are of the same value, so it is suggested that you spend equal time—forty minutes—on each.

Writing the three essays will feel like a purging of your brain cells! It is in this section that many students begin to panic. If you feel that happening, resist it. The key to this portion of the test is managing your time. You may find yourself spending much more time on one of the essays than on the others. Rather than leaving the third essay blank and polishing the second essay to try to attain a higher score, it's better to stop where you are and focus on a response to the third essay prompt. Why? Even if you were able to raise the score on the second essay by a point, you would lose valuable time for your third essay, costing you much more than a single point. AP® readers know that you don't have enough time to "polish" an essay. When you complete an essay, take a minute or two to look it over for any glaring mistakes such as omitted words or wrong names. Proctors may periodically announce how much time is left. If you have time after you've finished your final essay, go back and check all of the essays again, this time more slowly. Use any free time to check for major flaws in wording and to edit your writing where necessary.

To help stay focused on the task at hand, keep your booklet with the essay prompts in your line of sight. Seeing your notes and annotations of the essay passages can spur you on. Don't agonize over the spelling of words or capitalization rules. Some wording problems can be dismissed as well. AP® readers evaluate the essays as rough drafts. Continue to write your ideas.

Quality is far more important than quantity. Many students think they must write an essay of many pages in order to earn a high score. That is not true. First, forty minutes is not enough time to write a lengthy essay. The exam is designed to evaluate your abilities to understand what the prompt is asking, and you are expected to respond with accuracy, insight, and stylistic maturity. The short time forces you to pull your thoughts together quickly and write concisely. Readers don't expect the essays to be polished, but they do expect them to present a credible thesis and demonstrate the student's control of standard written English.

At the conclusion of the two hours, you will turn in to the proctor both the booklet with your essays and the booklet with the prompts. Now you can breathe a sigh of relief. It's over! You will no doubt be exhausted, and may feel like your brain has been drained of every fact it ever possessed. Very rarely does a student think the test was easy. Take pride in the fact that you made it through a challenging exam, and give yourself a pat on the back for a job well done!

About Scores and Grades

The multiple-choice section of the exam counts for 45 percent of your total score. The College Board tallies the number of correct answers—incorrect answers and questions you skip are not counted—for the multiple-choice score. This means that you should answer every question, even if you have to guess. If you can even narrow down the possible answers, you will be ahead. That number is then multiplied by a number found by dividing the 67.5 possible points on the multiple-choice section by the number of multiple-choice questions on the test. Because the test normally has fifty-five multiple-choice questions, the multiplier is usually about 1.23. Continuing with the example above, your multiple-choice score would be about 28 × 1.23, or 34.

The three essays together count for 55 percent of your total score on the test. Each of your essays is scored on the basis of scoring guidelines that range from 1 to 9. Essays with scores of 1 to 4 are considered weak. Scores of 5 to 9 are given for essays that are acceptable to excellent. You will find detailed scoring guidelines explaining what each of these numbers means in the chapters on essay questions and in the diagnostic and practice tests. Each essay score is multiplied by 3.05. For example, if you score a 4, a 6, and a 7 on the three essays, your total score for the essay section would be approximately 52. Added to the multiple-choice score of 34, your composite score would be 86. At the end of the diagnostic and practice tests, you will find worksheets for calculating your exam scores and final AP grade.

Composite scores range from zero to a high of 150. Each year all of the composite scores are broken into five ranges, one for each final AP® grade. Each final AP® grade represents a level of qualification about your skills:

- a 5 means you are exceptionally well qualified;
- a 4 means you are well qualified;
- a 3 means you are qualified;
- a 2 means you are possibly qualified;
- a 1 means no recommendation.

This is very approximate, but generally, a score in the mid-70s produces a final AP® grade of 3, a score in the mid-90s produces a final AP® grade of 4, and a score above about 110 produces a final AP® grade of 5. If you can correctly answer more than half the multiple-choice questions and earn an average of 5 on your essays, you should perform well on the exam, with a final grade of 3 or better.

When you receive notice of your final AP® grade, it will be reported to you as a 1, 2, 3, 4, or 5. The notice doesn't show the scores on the two separate sections—the multiple-choice section and the essay section—of the test.

Your Turn

It's now time for you to get ready for the exam. A diagnostic test awaits you on the next page. You may not feel ready to take an AP® exam in a timed environment, but if you feel fairly confident, by all means put the pressure on and see how well you do when faced with the mighty clock. Remember that the purpose of the diagnostic test is to help you spot both your weaknesses and your strengths. That way you will know where to focus your attention in preparation for the real deal. Be sure to check your answers carefully and read the explanation that goes with each test question. Good luck and happy testing!

PART ONE

The Elements
of Poetry

CHAPTER ONE

What Is Poetry?

Poetry is as universal as language and almost as ancient. The most primitive peoples have used it, and the most civilized have cultivated it. In all ages and in all countries, poetry has been written, and eagerly read or listened to, by all kinds and conditions of people—by soldiers, legislators, lawyers, homemakers, farmers, doctors, scientists, clergy, philosophers, kings, and queens. In all ages, it has been especially the concern of the educated, the intelligent, and the sensitive, yet it has appealed, in its simpler forms, to the uneducated and to children. Why? Because it has given pleasure. People have read it, listened to it, or recited it because they liked it—because it gave them enjoyment. But this is not the whole answer. Poetry in all ages has been regarded as important, not simply as one of several alternative forms of amusement, as one person might choose video games, another chess, and another poetry. Rather, it has been regarded as something central to existence, something having unique value to the fully realized life, something that we are better off for having and without which we are spiritually impoverished. To understand the reasons for this, we need to have at least a provisional understanding of what poetry is—provisional, because people have always been more successful at appreciating poetry than at defining it.

Initially, poetry might be defined as a kind of language that says *more* and says it *more intensely* than does ordinary language. To understand this fully, we need to understand what poetry "says." After all, language is employed on different occasions to say quite different kinds of things; in other words, language has different uses.

Perhaps the most common use of language is to communicate *information*. We say that it is nine o'clock, that we liked a certain movie, that George Washington was the first president of the United States, that bromine and iodine are members of the halogen group of chemical elements.

This we might call the *practical* use of language; it helps us with the ordinary business of living.

But it is not primarily to communicate information that novels, short stories, plays, and poems are written. These exist to bring us a sense and a perception of life, to widen and sharpen our contacts with existence. Their concern is with *experience.* We all have an inner need to live more deeply and fully and with greater awareness, to know the experience of others, and to understand our own experience better. Poets, from their own store of felt, observed, or imagined experiences, select, combine, and reorganize. They create significant new experiences for their readers—significant because the language is focused and formed—in which readers can participate and from which they may gain a greater awareness and understanding of their world. Literature, in other words, can be used as a function for stepping up the intensity and increasing the range of our experience, and as a glass for clarifying it. This is the *literary* use of language, for literature is not only an aid to living but a means of living.

In advertisements, sermons, political speeches, and even some poems, we find a third use of language: as an instrument of *persuasion,* or argument. But the distinctions among these three uses—the practical, the literary, and the argumentative—are not always clear-cut, since some written language simultaneously performs two or even all three functions. For example, an excellent poem we consider "literary" may convey information, and may also try to persuade us to share a particular point of view. Effectiveness in communicating experience, however, is the one essential criterion for any poem aspiring to the condition of literature.

Suppose, for instance, that we are interested in eagles. If we want simply to acquire information about eagles, we may turn to Google.com, a book of natural history, or Wikipedia. We would find that there are about fifty-five species of eagles and that most have hooked bills, curved claws, broad wings, and powerfully developed breast muscles. We would also learn that eagles vary in length from about sixteen inches to as long as forty inches; that most hunt while flying, though some await their prey on a high perch; that they nest in tall trees or on inaccessible cliffs; that they lay only one or two eggs; and that for human beings eagles "symbolize power, courage, freedom, and immortality and have long been used as national, military, and heraldic emblems and as symbols in religion."*

But unless we are interested in this information only for practical purposes, we are likely to feel a little disappointed, as though we had grasped the feathers of the eagle but not its soul. True, we have learned many facts

*Encyclopedia Americana, International Edition, Vol. 9 (1995): 520–22.

about the eagle, but we have missed somehow its lonely majesty, its power, and the wild grandeur of its surroundings that would make the eagle a living creature rather than a mere museum specimen, and that would inspire the potent symbolic image of eagles. For the living eagle we must turn to literature.

The Eagle

He clasps the crag with crooked hands;
Close to the sun in lonely lands,
Ringed with the azure world, he stands.

The wrinkled sea beneath him crawls;
He watches from his mountain walls,   5
And like a thunderbolt he falls.

—ALFRED, LORD TENNYSON (1809–1892)

QUESTIONS

1. What is peculiarly effective about the expressions "crooked hands," "Close to the sun," "Ringed with the azure world," "wrinkled," "crawls," and "like a thunderbolt"?
2. Notice the formal pattern of the poem, particularly the contrast of "he stands" in the first stanza and "he falls" in the second. Is there any other contrast between the two stanzas?

When "The Eagle" has been read well, readers will feel that they have enjoyed a significant experience and understand eagles better, though in a different way, than they did from the Wikipedia article alone. Although the article *analyzes* our experience of eagles, the poem in some sense *synthesizes* such an experience. Indeed, we may say the two approaches to experience—the scientific and the literary—complement each other, and we may contend that the kind of understanding we get from the second is at least as valuable as the kind we get from the first.

Literature, then, exists to communicate significant experience—significant because it is concentrated and organized. Its function is not to tell us *about* experience but to allow us imaginatively to *participate* in it. It is a means of allowing us, through the imagination, to live more fully, more deeply, more richly, and with greater awareness. It can do this in two ways: by *broadening* our experience—that is, by making us acquainted with a range of experience with which in the ordinary course of events we might have no contact—or by *deepening* our experience—that is, by making us feel more poignantly and more understandingly the everyday experiences all of us have. It enlarges our perspectives and breaks down some of the limits we may feel.

We can avoid two limiting approaches to poetry if we keep this conception of literature firmly in mind. The first approach always looks for a lesson or a bit of moral instruction. The second expects to find poetry always beautiful. Let us consider one of the songs from Shakespeare's *Love's Labor's Lost* (Act 5, scene 2).

Winter

When icicles hang by the wall,
And Dick the shepherd blows his nail,
And Tom bears logs into the hall,
And milk comes frozen home in pail,
When blood is nipped and ways be foul,   5
Then nightly sings the staring owl,
"Tu-whit, tu-who!"
    A merry note,
    While greasy Joan doth keel° the pot.   skim

When all aloud the wind doth blow,   10
And coughing drowns the parson's saw,
And birds sit brooding in the snow,
And Marian's nose looks red and raw,
When roasted crabs° hiss in the bowl,   crab apples
Then nightly sings the staring owl,   15
"Tu-whit, tu-who!"
    A merry note,
    While greasy Joan doth keel the pot.

—WILLIAM SHAKESPEARE (1564–1616)

QUESTIONS

1. Vocabulary: *saw* (11), *brooding* (12).
2. Is the owl's cry really a "merry" note? How are this adjective and the verb "sings" employed?
3. In what way does the owl's cry contrast with the other details of the poem?

In this poem, Shakespeare communicates the quality of winter life around a sixteenth-century English country house. But he does not do so by telling us flatly that winter in such surroundings is cold and in many respects unpleasant, though with some pleasant features too (the adjectives *cold, unpleasant,* and *pleasant* are not even used in the poem). Instead, he provides a series of concrete, rather dismal details that suggest these qualities and enable us, imaginatively, to experience this winter life ourselves. The shepherd blows on his fingernails to warm his hands; the milk freezes in the pail between the cowshed and the kitchen; the cook is slovenly and unclean, "greasy" either from spattered cooking fat or from her own sweat as she leans over the hot fire; the roads are muddy; the folk listening to the parson have colds; the birds "sit brooding in the snow"; and the servant girl's nose is raw from cold. But pleasant things are in prospect. Tom is bringing in logs for the fire, the hot cider or ale with its roasted crab apples is ready for drinking, and the soup or stew will soon be ready. In contrast to all these familiar details of country life is the mournful and eerie note of the owl.

Obviously the poem contains no moral. If we limit ourselves to looking in poetry for some lesson, message, or noble truth about life, we are bound to be disappointed. This limited approach sees poetry as a kind of sugarcoated pill—a wholesome truth or lesson made palatable by being put into pretty words. What this narrow approach really wants is a sermon—not a poem, but something inspirational. Yet "Winter," which has appealed to readers for more than four centuries, is not inspirational and contains no moral preachment.

Nor is the poem "Winter" beautiful. Though it is appealing in its way and contains elements of beauty, there is little that is really beautiful in red, raw noses, coughing in chapel, nipped blood, foul roads, and greasy cooks. Yet the second limiting approach may lead us to feel that poetry deals exclusively with beauty—with sunsets, flowers, butterflies, love, God—and that the one appropriate response to any poem is, after a moment of awed silence, "Isn't that beautiful!" But this narrow approach excludes a large proportion of poetry. The function of poetry is sometimes to be ugly rather than beautiful. And poetry may deal with common colds and greasy cooks as legitimately as with sunsets and flowers. Consider another example:

Dulce et Decorum Est

Bent double, like old beggars under sacks,
Knock-kneed, coughing like hags, we cursed through sludge,
Till on the haunting flares we turned our backs,
And towards our distant rest began to trudge.
Men marched asleep. Many had lost their boots,   5
But limped on, blood-shod. All went lame, all blind;
Drunk with fatigue; deaf even to the hoots
Of gas-shells dropping softly behind.

Gas! GAS! Quick, boys!—An ecstasy of fumbling,
Fitting the clumsy helmets just in time,   10
But someone still was yelling out and stumbling
And flound'ring like a man in fire or lime.—
Dim through the misty panes and thick green light,
As under a green sea, I saw him drowning.
In all my dreams before my helpless sight   15
He plunges at me, guttering, choking, drowning. —

If in some smothering dreams, you too could pace
Behind the wagon that we flung him in,
And watch the white eyes writhing in his face,
His hanging face, like a devil's sick of sin,—   20
If you could hear, at every jolt, the blood
Come gargling from the froth-corrupted lungs
Bitter as the cud
Of vile, incurable sores on innocent tongues,—
My friend, you would not tell with such high zest   25
To children ardent for some desperate glory,
The old lie: *Dulce et decorum est*
Pro patria mori.

—WILFRED OWEN (1893–1918)

QUESTIONS

1. Vocabulary: *lime* (12).
2. The Latin quotation (27–28), from the Roman poet Horace, means "It is sweet and becoming to die for one's country." What is the poem's comment on this statement?
3. List the elements of the poem that seem not beautiful and therefore "unpoetic." Are there any elements of beauty in the poem?
4. How do the comparisons in lines 1, 14, 20, and 23–24 contribute to the effectiveness of the poem?
5. What does the poem gain by moving from plural pronouns and the past tense to singular pronouns and the present tense? What does the poem gain by moving from first person (plural, then singular) to second person?

MindTap° Read, highlight, and take notes online.

Poetry takes all life as its province. Its primary concern is not with beauty, not with philosophical truth, not with persuasion, but with experience. Beauty and philosophical truth are aspects of experience, and the poet is often engaged with them. But poetry as a whole is concerned with all kinds of experience—beautiful or ugly, strange or common, noble or ignoble, actual or imaginary. Paradoxically, an artist can transform even the most unpleasant or painful experiences into works of great beauty and emotional power. Encountered in real life, pain and death are not pleasurable for most people; but we might read and reread poems about these subjects because of their ability to enlighten and move us. A real-life experience that makes us cry is usually an unhappy one; but if we cry while reading a great novel or poem it is because we are deeply moved, our humanity affirmed. Similarly, we do not ordinarily like to be frightened in real life, but we sometimes seek out books or movies that will terrify us. Works of art focus and organize experiences of all kinds, conveying the broad spectrum of human life and evoking a full range of emotional and intellectual responses. Even the most tragic literature, through its artistry of language, can help us see and feel the significance of life, appealing to our essential humanity in a way that can be intensely pleasurable and affirming.

There is no sharp distinction between poetry and other forms of imaginative literature. Although some readers may believe that poetry can be recognized by the arrangement of its lines on the page or by its use of rhyme and meter, such superficial signs are of little worth. The book of Job in the Bible and Melville's *Moby-Dick* are highly poetical, but the familiar verse that begins "Thirty days hath September, / April, June, and November . . ." is not. The difference between poetry and other literature is one of degree. Poetry is the most condensed and concentrated form of literature. It is language whose individual lines, either because of their own brilliance or because they focus so powerfully on what has gone before, have a higher voltage than most language. It is language that grows frequently incandescent, giving off both light and heat.

Ultimately, then, poetry can be recognized only by the response made to it by a practiced reader, someone who has acquired some sensitivity to poetry. But there is a catch here. We are not all equally experienced readers. To some readers, poetry may often seem dull and boring, a fancy way of writing something that could be said more simply. So might a color-blind person deny that there is such a thing as color.

The act of communication involved in reading poetry is like the act of communication involved in receiving a message by radio. Two devices are required: a transmitting station and a receiving set. The completeness of the communication depends on both the power and clarity of the transmitter and the sensitivity and tuning of the receiver. When a person reads a poem and no experience is received, either the poem is not a good poem or the reader is not properly tuned. With new poetry, we cannot always be sure which is at fault. With older poetry, if it has acquired critical acceptance—has been enjoyed and admired by generations of readers—we may assume that the receiving set is at fault. Fortunately, the fault is not irremediable. Though we cannot all become expert readers, we can become good enough to find both pleasure and value in much good poetry, or we can increase the amount of pleasure we already find in poetry and the number of kinds of poetry in which we find it. The purpose of this book is to help you increase your sensitivity and range as a receiving set.

Poetry, finally, is a kind of multidimensional language. Ordinary language—the kind that we use to communicate information—is one-dimensional. It is directed at only part of the listener, the understanding. Its one dimension is intellectual. Poetry, which is language used to communicate experience, has at least four dimensions. If it is to communicate experience, it must be directed at the *whole* person, not just at one's understanding. It must involve not only our intelligence but also our senses, emotions, and imagination. To the intellectual dimension, poetry adds a sensuous dimension, an emotional dimension, and an imaginative dimension.

Poetry achieves its extra dimensions—its greater pressure per word and its greater tension per poem—by drawing more fully and more consistently than does ordinary language on a number of language resources, none of which is peculiar to poetry. These various resources form the subjects of a number of the following chapters. Among them are connotation, imagery, metaphor, symbol, paradox, irony, allusion, sound repetition, rhythm, and pattern. Using these resources and the materials of life, the poet shapes and makes a poem. Successful poetry is never effusive language. If it is to come alive, it must be as cunningly put together and as efficiently organized as a tree. It must be an organism whose every part serves a useful purpose and cooperates with every other part to preserve and express the life that is within it.

REVIEWING CHAPTER ONE

1. Differentiate between ordinary language and poetic language.
2. Describe the uses of language: information, experience, persuasion.
3. Consider how looking for moral instruction or beauty are limiting approaches.
4. Explain the distinctions between poetry and other imaginative literature.
5. Review the four dimensions of experience that poetry involves.
6. Determine which ideas in this chapter are exemplified in the following poems.

UNDERSTANDING AND EVALUATING POETRY

Most of the poems in this book are accompanied by study questions that are by no means exhaustive. The following is a list of questions and analytical exercises that you may apply to any poem. You may be unable to answer many of them until you have read further into the book.

1. Who is the speaker? What kind of person is the speaker?
2. Is there an identifiable audience for the speaker? What can we know about it (her, him, or them)?
3. What is the occasion?
4. What is the setting in time (hour, season, century, and so on)?
5. What is the setting in place (indoors or out, city or country, land or sea, region, nation, hemisphere)?
6. What is the central purpose of the poem?
7. State the central idea or theme of the poem in a sentence.
8. a. Outline the poem to show its structure and development, or
   b. Summarize the events of the poem.
9. Paraphrase the poem.
10. Discuss the diction of the poem. Point out words that are particularly well chosen and explain why.
11. Discuss the imagery of the poem. What kinds of imagery are used? Is there a structure of imagery?
12. Point out examples of metaphor, simile, personification, and metonymy, and explain their appropriateness.
13. Point out and explain any symbols. If the poem is allegorical, explain the allegory.
14. Point out and explain examples of paradox, overstatement, understatement, and irony. What is their function?
15. Point out and explain any allusions. What is their function?
16. What is the tone of the poem? How is it achieved?
17. Point out significant examples of sound repetition and explain their function.
18. a. What is the meter of the poem?
    b. Copy the poem and mark its scansion.
19. Discuss the adaptation of sound to sense.
20. Describe the form or pattern of the poem.
21. Criticize and evaluate the poem.

Shall I compare thee to a summer's day?*

Shall I compare thee to a summer's day?
Thou art more lovely and more temperate:
Rough winds do shake the darling buds of May,
And summer's lease hath all too short a date.
Sometimes too hot the eye of heaven shines,   5
And often is his gold complexion dimmed;
And every fair° from fair sometimes declines   beauty
By chance of nature's changing course untrimmed°;   stripped bare
But thy eternal summer shall not fade
Nor lose possession of that fair thou ow'st°,   own 10
Nor shall death brag thou wand'rest in his shade
When in eternal lines to time thou grow'st.
So long as men can breathe or eyes can see,
So long lives this°, and this gives life to thee.   this poem

—WILLIAM SHAKESPEARE (1564–1616)

QUESTIONS

1. Vocabulary: *temperate* (2), *shade* (11). What different meanings does "temperate" have when used to describe a person or "a summer's day"?
2. What details show that "a summer's day" is lacking in loveliness and is intemperate?
3. What are "the eye of heaven" (5) and "his gold complexion" (6)?
4. The poem begins more or less literally comparing the person being addressed to "a summer's day," but at line 9 it departs from what is literally possible into what is impossible. What does the poem gain by this shift in meaning?
5. Explain the logic behind lines 13–14. Is this a valid proof? Why or why not?

Black Rook in Rainy Weather

On the stiff twig up there
Hunches a wet black rook
Arranging and rearranging its feathers in the rain.
I do not expect a miracle
Or an accident   5

*Whenever a heading duplicates the first line of the poem or a substantial portion thereof, with typically only the first word capitalized, it is probable that the poet left the poem untitled and that the anthologist has substituted the first line or part of it as an editorial convenience. Such a heading is not referred to as the title of the poem.

To set the sight on fire
In my eye, nor seek
Any more in the desultory weather some design,
But let spotted leaves fall as they fall,
Without ceremony, or portent.   10

Although, I admit, I desire,
Occasionally, some backtalk
From the mute sky, I can't honestly complain:
A certain minor light may still
Lean incandescent   15

Out of kitchen table or chair
As if a celestial burning took
Possession of the most obtuse objects now and then—
Thus hallowing an interval
Otherwise inconsequent   20

By bestowing largesse, honor,
One might say love. At any rate, I now walk
Wary (for it could happen
Even in this dull, ruinous landscape); skeptical,
Yet politic; ignorant   25

Of whatever angel may choose to flare
Suddenly at my elbow. I only know that a rook
Ordering its black feathers can so shine
As to seize my senses, haul
My eyelids up, and grant   30

A brief respite from fear
Of total neutrality. With luck,
Trekking stubborn through this season
Of fatigue, I shall
Patch together a content   35

Of sorts. Miracles occur,
If you care to call those spasmodic
Tricks of radiance miracles. The wait's begun again,
The long wait for the angel,
For that rare, random descent.   40

—SYLVIA PLATH (1932–1963)

QUESTIONS

1. Vocabulary; *Rook* (title), *desultory* (8), *portent* (10), *incandescent* (15), *obtuse* (18), *hallowing* (19), *largesse* (21), *politic* (25).
2. What are the negative associations the speaker gives to the rook? Are there any affirmative associations? Overall, is her watching the rook a negative or affirmative experience?
3. What aspect of this experience makes the speaker "Wary" (23)?

The Triple Fool

I am two fools, I know,
For loving, and for saying so
In whining poetry.
But where's the wiseman that would not be I
If she would not deny?   5
Then, as the earth's inward, narrow, crooked lanes
Do purge sea water's fretful salt away,
I thought if I could draw my pains
Through rhyme's vexations, I should them allay.
Grief brought to numbers° cannot be so fierce,   verse 10
For he tames it that fetters it in verse.

But when I have done so,
Some man, his art and voice to show,
Doth set and sing my pain,
And by delighting many, frees again   15
Grief, which verse did restrain
To love and grief tribute of verse belongs,
But not of such as pleases when 'tis read°;   read aloud
Both are increasèd by such songs,
For both their triumphs so are publishèd.   20
And I, which was two fools, do so grow three.
Who are a little wise, the best fools be.

—JOHN DONNE (1572–1631)

QUESTIONS

1. Vocabulary; *allay* (9), *fetters* (11).
2. The speaker first says he is "two fools" (1), but the title is "The Triple Fool." How does he progress from double to triple?
3. Discuss the paradox embodied in the final line (22). What is the relationship implied here between wisdom and foolishness?

The Bean Eaters

They eat beans mostly, this old yellow pair.
Dinner is a casual affair.
Plain chipware on a plain and creaking wood,
Tin flatware.

Two who are Mostly Good.   5
Two who have lived their day,
But keep on putting on their clothes
And putting things away.

And remembering . . .
Remembering, with twinklings and twinges,   10
As they lean over the beans in their rented back room that
    is full of beads and receipts and dolls and cloths, tobacco
    crumbs, vases and fringes.

—GWENDOLYN BROOKS (1917–2000)

QUESTIONS

1. What details in the poem suggest that these old people are poor?
2. What details suggest that they have overcome their poverty emotionally?
3. What is the poet's attitude toward them? Is it pity? Is it admiration?

Labor Day

It's a year exactly since my father died.
Last year was hot. At the funeral, people talked about the weather.
How hot it was for September. How unseasonable.

This year, it's cold.
There's just us now, the immediate family.   5
In the flower beds,
shreds of bronze, of copper.

Out front, my sister's daughter rides her bicycle
the way she did last year,
up and down the sidewalk. What she wants is   10
to make time pass.

While to the rest of us
a whole lifetime is nothing

One day, you're a blond boy with a tooth missing;
the next, an old man gasping for air.   15
Its comes to nothing, really, hardly
a moment on earth.
Not a sentence, but a breath, a caesura.

—LOUISE GLÜCK (B. 1943)

QUESTIONS

1. Vocabulary: *caesura* (18)
2. Discuss the significance of the weather in the first two stanzas. Why is the weather the focus of these stanzas?
3. In the third stanza, the speaker imagines that her sister's daughter by riding her bicycle wants "to make time pass" (11). Is this true, or is it merely a fantasy of the speaker's?
4. Discuss the meaning of the final word, "caesura." This word is most commonly used in the context of disscussing poetic technique. Why is it the appropriate word here?

The Red Wheelbarrow

so much depends
upon

a red wheel
barrow

glazed with rain   5
water

beside the white
chickens.

—WILLIAM CARLOS WILLIAMS (1883–1963)

QUESTIONS

1. The speaker asserts that "so much depends upon" the objects he refers to, leading the reader to ask: *How much* and *why?* This glimpse of a farm scene implies one kind of answer. What is the importance of the wheelbarrow, rain, and chicken to a farmer? To all of us?
2. What further importance can you infer from the references to color, shape, texture, and the juxtaposition of objects? Does the poem itself have a shape? What two ways of observing and valuing the world does the poem imply?
3. What are the possible reasons for "experimental" qualities in this poem—for instance, its lack of capitalization, its very short lines, and its plain, even homely, images? Do these qualities give the poem a greater emotional power than a more conventional and decorative poem on the same topic might have achieved?

Filling Station

Oh, but it is dirty!
—this little filling station,
oil-soaked, oil-permeated
to a disturbing, over-all
black translucency.   5
Be careful with that match!

Father wears a dirty,
oil-soaked monkey suit
that cuts him under the arms,
and several quick and saucy   10
and greasy sons assist him
(it's a family filling station),
all quite thoroughly dirty.

Do they live in the station?
It has a cement porch   15
behind the pumps, and on it
a set of crushed and grease-
impregnated wickerwork;
on the wicker sofa
a dirty dog, quite comfy.   20

Some comic books provide
the only note of color—
of certain color. They lie
upon a big dim doily
draping a taboret   25
(part of the set), beside
a big hirsute begonia.

Why the extraneous plant?
Why the taboret?
Why, oh why, the doily?   30
(Embroidered in daisy stitch
with marguerites, I think,
and heavy with gray crochet.)

Somebody embroidered the doily.
Somebody waters the plant,   35

or oils it, maybe. Somebody
arranges the rows of cans
so that they softly say:
ESSO—SO—SO—SO
to high-strung automobiles.   40
Somebody loves us all.

—ELIZABETH BISHOP (1911–1979)

QUESTIONS

1. Vocabulary: *taboret* (25), *hirsute* (27), *marguerites* (32). The brand name "ESSO" (39) is the former name of the Exxon Mobil Oil Company.
2. What is the speaker's attitude toward the filling station? Is her physical description of the station affectionate or critical? Can it be both?
3. Discuss the rhetorical questions beginning in line 28. What are the implied answers to these questions?
4. Analyze the final stanza. Why does the speaker stress that somebody takes care of and decorates the filling station? What is the significance of the final line?

Suicide's Note

The calm,
Cool face of the river
Asked me for a kiss.

—LANGSTON HUGHES (1902–1967)

QUESTIONS

1. How is the speaker's desire for death like the desire expressed in the comparison of the river to a person? How are they unlike? Explore the frame of mind that would create this comparison.
2. Does the repeated "k" sound seem beautiful to you? Can you explain the repetition in terms that reflect the speaker's frame of mind?

Richard Cory

Whenever Richard Cory went down town,
We people on the pavement looked at him:
He was a gentleman from sole to crown,
Clean favored, and imperially slim.

And he was always quietly arrayed,   5
And he was always human when he talked;
But still he fluttered pulses when he said,
"Good-morning," and he glittered when he walked.

And he was rich—yes, richer than a king—
And admirably schooled in every grace: 10
In fine, we thought that he was everything
To make us wish that we were in his place.

So on we worked, and waited for the light,
And went without the meat, and cursed the bread;
And Richard Cory, one calm summer night,   15
Went home and put a bullet through his head.

—EDWIN ARLINGTON ROBINSON (1869–1935)

QUESTIONS

1. In how many senses is Richard Cory a gentleman?
2. The word *crown* (3), meaning the top of the head, is familiar to you from "Jack and Jill," but why does Robinson use the unusual phrase "from sole to crown" instead of the common "from head to foot" or "from top to toe"?
3. List the words in the poem that express or suggest the idea of aristocracy or royalty.
4. Try to explain why the poet chose his wording rather than the following alternatives: *sidewalk* for *pavement* (2), *good-looking* for *clean favored* (4), *thin* for *slim* (4), *dressed* for *arrayed* (5), *courteous* for *human* (6), *wonderfully* for *admirably* (10), *trained* for *schooled* (10), *manners* for *every grace* (10), *in short* for *in fine* (11). What other examples of effective diction do you find in the poem?
5. Why is "Richard Cory" a good name for the character in this poem?
6. This poem is a good example of how ironic contrast (see Chapter 7) generates meaning. The poem makes no direct statement about life; it simply relates an incident. What larger meanings about life does it suggest?

On My First Son

Farewell, thou child of my right hand, and joy.
My sin was too much hope of thee, loved boy.
Seven years thou wert lent to me, and I thee pay,
Exacted by thy fate, on the just day.
O could I lose all father° now! For why   fatherhood 5
Will man lament the state he should envy,
To have so soon 'scaped world's and flesh's rage,
And if no other misery, yet age?

Rest in soft peace, and asked, say, "Here doth lie
Ben Jonson his best piece of poetry,"   10
For whose sake henceforth all his vows be such
As what he loves may never like too much

—BEN JONSON (1573–1637)

QUESTIONS

1. "[C]hild of my right hand" (1) is a literal translation of the Hebrew "Benjamin," the name given to the poet's son, who died of plague on his seventh birthday in 1603. What are the connotations of "right hand"? Explore the denotations of "Exacted" and "just" (4). In what sense might a son's life and death be compared to a loan that falls due?
2. "Jonson his" (10) is an older form of the possessive "Jonson's"; what in the etymology of poet/poetry justifies calling his son a "piece of poetry"?
3. The Christian cardinal virtues are faith, hope, and love (or charity). How can "hope" be interpreted a "sin" (2)?

Introduction to Poetry

I ask them to take a poem
and hold it up to the light
like a color slide

or press an ear against its hive.

I say drop a mouse into a poem   5
and watch him probe his way out,

or walk inside the poem's room
and feel the walls for a light switch.

I want them to water-ski
across the surface of a poem   10
waving at the author's name on the shore.

But all they want to do
is tie the poem to a chair with rope
and torture a confession out of it.

They begin beating it with a hose   15
to find out what it really means.

—BILLY COLLINS (B. 1941)

QUESTIONS

1. What is the basic situation of the poem? Who are "I" (I) and "them" (I)?
2. Explain the simile in line 3. From that point onward through line II, the speaker invents a series of metaphors. For each of them, define what a poem is being compared to and how the metaphor expresses some characteristic quality of poetry. For example, how is a poem like a "hive" (4) full of buzzing bees?
3. The last five lines present a single extended metaphor to express what "they want to do" when they encounter a poem. What are "they" and "the poem" compared to, and how do these comparisons reflect a different attitude toward poetry from the ones expressed in the first eleven lines? What, ultimately, does this poem express about poetry and its readers?

SUGGESTIONS FOR WRITING

"Writing about Poetry," Part Two of this book, offers practical advice about the formal requirements and style that are usually expected in student papers. Although many of the suggestions presented there may be familiar to you, reviewing them when you prepare to complete these writing assignments should help you to write more effectively.

1. The following pairs of poems deal with similar subject matter treated in very different ways. Yet in each case the two poems employ the multidimensional language that is one criterion of poetic excellence. Choose one pair and discuss the ways in which both poems qualify as poetry, even though they take different approaches to similar topics.
   a. Tennyson, "The Eagle" (page 4) and Hughes, "Hawk Roosting" (page 33).
   b. Owen, "Dulce et Decorum Est" (page 6) and Whitman, "A sight in camp in the daybreak gray and dim" (page 412).
   c. Hopkins, "Spring" (page 60) and Oliver, "Spring in the Classroom" (page 44).
   d. Plath, "Black Rook in Rainy Weather" (page II) and Keats, "Ode to a Nightingale" (page 390).
   e. Robinson, "Richard Cory" (page 17) and Plath, "Suicide off Egg Rock" (page 242).
   f. Hayden, "Those Winter Sundays" (page 66) and Roethke, "My Papa's Waltz" (page 128).
2. According to "Ars Poetica" by Archibald MacLeish (page 393), "A poem should not mean / But be" (23–24). Relate this assertion to one or more of the following:
   a. Williams, "The Red Wheelbarrow" (page 15).
   b. Keats, "Ode on a Grecian Urn" (page 286).
   c. Blake, "The Tiger" (page 162).
   d. cummings, "Buffalo Bill's defunct" (page 366).
   e. Stevens, "Disillusionment of Ten O'Clock" (page 55).
   f. Glück, "Purple Bathing Suit" (page 102).
   g. Wordsworth, "I wandered lonely as a cloud" (page 414).

PRACTICE AP® WRITING PROMPTS

Edwin Arlington Robinson, "Richard Cory" (pp. 17–18)

Read "Richard Cory" carefully. Then write an essay in which you analyze the speaker's complex attitude toward Richard Cory's suicide. You may choose to consider such elements as tone, point of view, and structure.

....

William Shakespeare, "Shall I compare thee to a summer's day" (p. 11)

Carefully read the sonnet "Shall I compare thee to a summer's day." Focusing on imagery and figurative language, analyze the speaker's strategy used to achieve the poem's emotional and artistic purposes.

....

CHAPTER TWO

Reading the Poem

How can you develop your understanding and appreciation of poetry? Here are some preliminary suggestions:

1. Read a poem more than once. A good poem will no more yield its full meaning on a single reading than will a Beethoven symphony on a single hearing. Two readings may be necessary simply to let you get your bearings. And if the poem is a work of art, it will repay repeated and prolonged examination. One does not listen to a good piece of music once and forget it; one does not look at a good painting once and throw it away. A poem is not like a website, to be hastily read and forgotten. It is to be hung on the wall of one's mind.

2. Get in the habit of using an online dictionary. It is futile to try to understand poetry without knowing the meanings of the words of which it is composed. You might as well attempt to play tennis without a ball. One of the benefits of studying literature is an enlarged vocabulary, and the study of poetry offers an excellent opportunity. Other references also will be invaluable, particularly online articles on mythology and various online translations of the Bible.

3. Read so that you hear the sounds of the words in your mind. Poetry is written to be heard: its meanings are conveyed through sound as well as through print. Every word is therefore important. The best way to read a poem may be just the opposite of the best way to read a newspaper. One might read a website article rapidly, and probably only once; but a poem should be read slowly, and most poems must be read many times before their full complexity and meaning can be experienced. When you cannot read a poem aloud so as to hear its sounds, lip-read it: form the words with your tongue and mouth even though you do not utter sounds. With ordinary reading material, lip-reading is a bad habit; with poetry, it is a good habit.

4. Always pay careful attention to what the poem is saying. Although you should be conscious of the sounds of the poem, you should never be so exclusively conscious of them that you pay no attention to what the poem means. For some readers, reading a poem is like getting on board a rhythmical roller coaster. The car starts and off they go, up and down, paying no attention to the landscape flashing past them, arriving at the end of the poem breathless, with no idea of what it has been about. This is the wrong way to read a poem. One should make the utmost effort to follow the thought continuously and to grasp the full implications and suggestions. Because a poem says so much, several readings may be necessary, but on the very first reading you should determine the subjects of the verbs, the antecedents of the pronouns, and other normal grammatical facts.

5. Practice reading poems aloud. When you find one you especially like, have friends listen to your reading of it. Try to read it to them in such a way that they will like it too. (a) Read it affectionately, but not affectedly. The two extremes that oral readers often fall into are equally deadly: one is to read as if one were reading a tax report or a train schedule, unexpressively, in a monotone; the other is to elocute, with artificial flourishes and vocal histrionics. It is not necessary to put emotion into reading a poem. The emotion is already there. It wants only a fair chance to get out. It will express *itself* if the poem is read naturally and sensitively. (b) Of the two extremes, reading too fast offers greater danger than reading too slow. Read slowly enough that each word is clear and distinct and that the meaning has time to sink in. Remember that your friends do not have the advantage, as you do, of having the text before them. Your ordinary rate of reading will probably be too fast. (c) Read the poem so that the rhythmical pattern is felt but not exaggerated. Remember that poetry, with few exceptions, is written in sentences, just as prose is, and that punctuation is a signal as to how it should be read. Give all grammatical pauses their full due. Do not distort the natural pronunciation of words or a normal accentuation of the sentence to fit into what you have decided is its metrical pattern. One of the worst ways to read a poem is to read it ta-DUM ta-DUM ta-DUM, with an exaggerated emphasis on every other syllable. On the other hand, it should not be read as if it were prose. An important test of your reading will be how you handle the end of a line that lacks line-ending punctuation. A frequent mistake of the beginning reader is to treat each line as if it were a complete thought, whether grammatically complete or not, and to drop the voice at the end of it. A frequent mistake of the sophisticated reader is to take a running start when approaching the end of a line and fly over it as if it were not there. The line is a rhythmical unit, and its end should be observed whether there is punctuation or not. If there is

no punctuation, you ordinarily should observe the end of the line by the slightest of pauses or by holding on to the last word in the line just a little longer than usual, without dropping your voice. In line 12 of the following poem, you should hold on to the word "although" longer than if it occurred elsewhere in the line. But do not lower your voice on it: it is part of the clause that follows in the next stanza.

The Man He Killed

     Had he and I but met
     By some old ancient inn,
We should have sat us down to wet
     Right many a nipperkin!°   half-pint cup

     But ranged as infantry,   5
     And staring face to face,
I shot at him as he at me,
     And killed him in his place.

     I shot him dead because—
     Because he was my foe,   10
Just so: my foe of course he was;
     That's clear enough; although

     He thought he'd 'list, perhaps,
     Off-hand-like—just as I—
Was out of work—had sold his traps°—   belongings 15
     No other reason why.

     Yes; quaint and curious war is!
     You shoot a fellow down
You'd treat, if met where any bar is,
     Or help to half-a-crown.   20

—THOMAS HARDY (1840–1928)

QUESTIONS

1. Vocabulary: *half-a-crown* (20).
2. In informational prose, the repetition of a word like "because" (9–10) would be an error. What purpose does the repetition serve here? Why does the speaker repeat to himself his "clear" reason for killing a man (10–11)? The word "although" (12) gets more emphasis than it would ordinarily because it comes not only at the

end of a line but at the end of a stanza. What purpose does this emphasis serve? Can the redundancy of "old ancient" (2) be poetically justified?
3. Poetry has been defined as "the expression of elevated thought in elevated language." Comment on the adequacy of this definition in the light of Hardy's poem.

MindTap® Read, highlight, and take notes online.

One starting point for understanding a poem at the simplest level, and for clearing up misunderstanding, is to paraphrase its content or part of its content. To **paraphrase** a poem means to restate it in different language, so as to make its prose sense as plain as possible. The paraphrase may be longer or shorter than the poem, but it should contain all the ideas in the poem in such a way as to make them clear and to make the central idea, or **theme,** of the poem more accessible.

A Study of Reading Habits

When getting my nose in a book
Cured most things short of school,
It was worth ruining my eyes
To know I could still keep cool,
And deal out the old right hook   5
To dirty dogs twice my size.

Later, with inch-thick specs,
Evil was just my lark:
Me and my cloak and fangs
Had ripping times in the dark.   10
The women I clubbed with sex!
I broke them up like meringues.

Don't read much now: the dude
Who lets the girl down before
The hero arrives, the chap   15
Who's yellow and keeps the store,
Seem far too familiar. Get stewed:
Books are a load of crap.

—PHILIP LARKIN (1922–1985)

QUESTIONS
1. The three stanzas delineate three stages in the speaker's life. Describe each.
2. What kind of person is the speaker? What kinds of books does he read? May we identify him with the poet?

Larkin's poem may be paraphrased as follows:

There was a time when reading was one way I could avoid almost all my troubles—except for school. It seemed worth the danger of ruining my eyes to read stories in which I could imagine myself maintaining my poise in the face of threats and having the boxing skill and experience needed to defeat bullies who were twice my size.

Later, already having to wear thick glasses because my eyesight had become so poor, I found my delight in stories of sex and evil: imagining myself with Dracula cloak and fangs, I relished vicious nocturnal adventures. I identified myself with sexual marauders whose inexhaustible potency was like a weapon wielded against women who were sweet and fragile.

I don't read much anymore because now I can identify myself only with the flawed secondary characters, such as the flashy dresser who wins the heroine's confidence and then betrays her in a moment of crisis before the cowboy hero comes to her rescue, or the cowardly storekeeper who cringes behind the counter at the first sign of danger. Getting drunk is better than reading—books are just full of useless lies.

Notice that in a paraphrase, figurative language gives way to literal language (similes replace metaphors) and normal word order supplants inverted syntax. But a paraphrase retains the speaker's use of first, second, and third person, and the tenses of verbs. Although it is neither necessary nor possible to avoid using some of the words found in the original, a paraphrase should strive for plain, direct diction. And since a paraphrase is prose, it does not maintain the length and position of poetic lines.

A paraphrase is useful only if you understand that it is the barest, most inadequate approximation of what the poem really "says" and is no more equivalent to the poem than a corpse is to a person. After you have paraphrased a poem, you should endeavor to see how far short of the poem it falls, and why. In what respects does Larkin's poem say more, and say it more memorably, than the paraphrase? Does the phrase "full of useless lies" in the paraphrase capture the impact of "a load of crap"? Furthermore, a paraphrase may fall far short of revealing the theme of a poem. "A Study of Reading Habits" represents a man summing up his reading experience and evaluating it—but in turn the poem itself evaluates *him* and his defects. A statement of the theme of the poem might be this:

> A person who turns to books as a source of self-gratifying fantasies may, in the course of time, discover that escapist reading no longer protects him from his awareness of his own reality, and he may out of habit have to find other, more potent, and perhaps more self-destructive means of escaping.

Notice that in stating a theme, we should be careful not to phrase it as a moral or lesson—not "you shouldn't" but "a person may."

To aid us in the understanding of a poem, we may ask ourselves a number of questions about it. Two of the most important are *Who is the speaker?* and *What is the occasion?* A cardinal error of some readers is to assume that a speaker who uses the first-person pronouns (*I, my, mine, me*) is always the poet. A less risky course would be to assume always that the speaker is someone other than the poet. Poems, like short stories, novels, and plays, belong to the world of fiction, an imaginatively conceived world that at its best is "truer" than the factually "real" world that it reflects. When poets put themselves or their thoughts into a poem, they present a *version* of themselves; that is, they present a person who in many ways is *like* themselves but who, consciously or unconsciously, is shaped to fit the needs of the poem. We must therefore be very careful about identifying anything in a poem with the biography of the poet.

However, caution is not prohibition. Sometimes events or ideas in a poem will help us understand some episodes in the poet's life. More importantly for us, knowledge of the poet's life may help us understand a poem. There can be little doubt, when all the evidence is in, that "Terence, this is stupid stuff" (page 383) is Housman's defense of the kind of poetry he writes, and that the six lines in which Terence sums up his beliefs about life and the function of poetry closely echo Housman's own beliefs. On the other hand, it would be folly to suppose that Housman ever got drunk at "Ludlow fair" and once lay down in "lovely muck" and slept all night in a roadside ditch. It may seem paradoxical that Philip Larkin, a poet and novelist and for many years the chief administrator of a university library, would end a poem with the line, "Books are a load of crap." But poems often feature a persona, or speaker, who expresses a viewpoint the poet presumably does not share.

We may therefore well think of every poem as being to some degree *dramatic*—that is, the utterance not of the person who wrote the poem but of a fictional character in a particular situation that may be inferred. Many poems are expressly dramatic.

In "The Man He Killed," the speaker is a soldier; the occasion is his having been in battle and killed a man—obviously for the first time in his life. We can tell a good deal about him. He is not a career soldier: he enlisted only because he was out of work. He is a working-class man: he speaks a simple and colloquial language ("nipperkin," "'list," "off-hand-like," "traps"). He is a friendly, kindly sort who enjoys a neighborly drink of ale in a bar and will gladly lend a friend a half-a-crown when he has it. He has known what it is to be poor. In any other circumstances he would have been horrified at taking a human life. It gives him pause even now. He is trying to figure it out. But he is not a deep thinker and thinks he has supplied a reason when he has only supplied a name: "I killed the man . . . because he was my foe." The critical question, of course, is *why* was the man his "foe"? Even the speaker is left unsatisfied by his answer, though he is not analytical enough to know what is wrong with it. Obviously this poem is expressly dramatic. We need know nothing about Thomas Hardy's life (he was never a soldier and never killed a man) to realize that the poem is dramatic. The internal evidence of the poem tells us so.

A third important question that we should ask ourselves upon reading any poem is *What is the central purpose of the poem?** The purpose may be to tell a story, to reveal human character, to impart a vivid impression of a scene, to express a mood or an emotion, or to convey vividly some idea or attitude. Whatever the purpose is, we must determine it for ourselves and define it mentally as precisely as possible. Only by relating the various details in the poem to the central purpose or theme can we fully understand their function and meaning. Only then can we begin to assess the value of the poem and determine whether it is a good one or a poor one. In "The Man He Killed," the central purpose is quite clear: it is to make us realize more keenly the irrationality of war. The puzzlement of the speaker may be our puzzlement. But even if we are able to give a more sophisticated answer than his as to why men kill each other, we ought still to have a greater awareness, after reading the poem, of the fundamental irrationality in war that makes men kill who have no grudge against each other and who might under different circumstances show each other considerable kindness.

---

*Our only reliable evidence of the poem's purpose, of course, is the poem itself. External evidence, when it exists, though often helpful, may also be misleading. Some critics have objected to the use of such terms as "purpose" and "intention" altogether; we cannot know, they maintain, what was *attempted* in the poem; we can only know what was *done*. We are concerned, however, not with the *poet's* purpose, but with the *poem's* purpose; that is, with the theme (if it has one), and this is determinable from the poem itself.

"Is my team plowing"

"Is my team plowing,
That I was used to drive
And hear the harness jingle
When I was man alive?"

Aye, the horses trample,   5
The harness jingles now;
No change though you lie under
The land you used to plow.

"Is football playing
Along the river shore,   10
With lads to chase the leather,
Now I stand up no more?"

Aye, the ball is flying,
The lads play heart and soul;
The goal stands up, the keeper   15
Stands up to keep the goal.

"Is my girl happy,
That I thought hard to leave,
And has she tired of weeping
As she lies down at eve?"   20

Aye, she lies down lightly,
She lies not down to weep:
Your girl is well contented.
Be still, my lad, and sleep.

"Is my friend hearty,   25
Now I am thin and pine;
And has he found to sleep in
A better bed than mine?"

Yes, lad, I lie easy,
I lie as lads would choose;   30
I cheer a dead man's sweetheart,
Never ask me whose.

—A. E. HOUSMAN (1859–1936)

QUESTIONS

1. How many actual speakers are there in this poem? What is meant by "whose" in line 32?
2. Is this poem cynical in its observation of human nature?
3. The word "sleep" (24, 27) in the concluding stanzas suggests three different meanings. What are they? How many meanings are suggested by the word *bed*?

After we have answered the question *What is the central purpose of the poem?* we can consider another question, equally important to full understanding: *By what means is that purpose achieved?* It is important to distinguish means from ends. A student on an examination once used the poem "Is my team plowing" as evidence that A. E. Housman believed in immortality because in it a man speaks from the grave. This is as much a misconstruction as to say that Thomas Hardy joined the army because he was out of work. The purpose of Housman's poem is to communicate poignantly a certain truth about human life: life goes on after our deaths pretty much as it did before—our dying does not disturb the universe. Further, it dramatizes that irrational sense of betrayal and guilt that may follow the death of a friend. The poem achieves this purpose by means of a fanciful **dramatic framework** in which a dead man converses with his still-living friend. The framework tells us nothing about whether Housman believed in immortality (as a matter of fact, he did not). It is simply an effective means by which we *can* learn how Housman felt a man's death affected the life he left behind. The question *By what means is that purpose achieved?* is partially answered by describing the poem's dramatic framework, if it has any. The complete answer requires an accounting of various resources of communication that we will discuss in this book.

The most important preliminary advice we can give for reading poetry is to maintain always, while reading it, the utmost mental alertness. The most harmful idea one can get about poetry is that its purpose is to soothe and relax and that the best place to read it is lying in a hammock with a cool drink while low music plays in the background. You *can* read poetry lying in a hammock, but only if you refuse to put your mind in the same attitude as your body. Its purpose is not to soothe and relax but to arouse and awake, to shock us into life, to make us more alive.

An analogy can be drawn between reading poetry and playing tennis. Both offer great enjoyment if the game is played hard. Good tennis players must be constantly on the tips of their toes, concentrating on their opponent's every move. They must be ready for a drive to the right or left, a lob overhead, or a drop shot barely over the net. They must be ready for topspin or underspin, a ball that bounces crazily to the left or the right. They must jump for the high ones and run for the long ones. And they will enjoy the game almost exactly in proportion to the effort they put into it. The same is true of reading poetry. Great enjoyment is there, but this enjoyment demands a mental effort equivalent to the physical effort one puts into tennis.

The reader of poetry has one advantage over the tennis player: poets are not trying to win matches. They may expect the reader to stretch for their shots, but they *want* the reader to return them.

REVIEWING CHAPTER TWO

1. Review the five preliminary suggestions for reading poems.
2. List steps in paraphrasing, and create paraphrases of several poems, showing how paraphrase helps to clarify the theme.
3. Explain how identifying the speaker and the occasion of the poem shows the dramatic quality of poetry.
4. Explore the concept of a "central purpose" of a poem.
5. Consider the difference between the means and the ends in determining the central purpose of a poem.
6. Determine which ideas in this chapter are exemplified in the following poems.

Break of Day

'Tis true, 'tis day; what though it be?
Oh, wilt thou therefore rise from me?
Why should we rise because 'tis light?
Did we lie down because 'twas night?
Love which in spite of darkness brought us hither   5
Should, in despite of light, keep us together.

Light hath no tongue, but is all eye;
If it could speak as well as spy,
This were the worst that it could say:
That, being well, I fain would stay,   10
And that I loved my heart and honor so,
That I would not from him that had them go.

Must business thee from hence remove?
Oh, that's the worst disease of love;
The poor, the foul, the false, love can   15
Admit, but not the busied man.
He which hath business and makes love, doth do
Such wrong as when a married man doth woo.

—JOHN DONNE (1572–1631)

QUESTIONS

1. Vocabulary: *fain* (10).
2. Who is the speaker? Who is addressed? What is the situation? Can the speaker be identified with the poet?
3. Explain the comparison in line 7. To whom does "I" (10–12) refer? Is "love" (15–16) the subject or object of "can admit"?
4. Summarize the arguments used by the speaker to keep the person addressed from leaving. What does the speaker value most?
5. Are the two persons married or unmarried? Justify your answer.

There's been a Death,
in the Opposite House

There's been a Death, in the Opposite House,
As lately as Today—
I know it, by the numb look
Such Houses have—alway—

The Neighbors rustle in and out—   5
The Doctor—drives away—
A Window opens like a Pod—
Abrupt—mechanically—

Somebody flings a Mattress out—
The Children hurry by—   10
They wonder if it died—on that—
I used to—when a Boy—

The Minister—goes stiffly in—
As if the House were His—
And He owned all the Mourners—now—   15
And little Boys—besides—

And then the Milliner—and the Man
Of the Appalling Trade—
To take the measure of the House—

There'll be that Dark Parade—   20

Of Tassels—and of Coaches—soon—
It's easy as a Sign—
The Intuition of the News—
In just a Country Town—

—EMILY DICKINSON (1830–1886)

QUESTIONS

1. What can we know about the speaker in the poem?
2. By what signs does the speaker "intuit" that a death has occurred? Explain them
   stanza by stanza. What does it mean that the speaker must intuit rather than simply
   know that death has taken place?
3. Comment on the words "Appalling" (18) and "Dark" (20).
4. What shift in the poem is signaled by the separation of line 20 from the end of
   stanza 5?
5. What is the speaker's attitude toward death?

Hawk Roosting

I sit in the top of the wood, my eyes closed.
Inaction, no falsifying dream
Between my hooked head and hooked feet:
Or in sleep rehearse perfect kills and eat.

The convenience of the high trees!   5
The air's buoyancy and the sun's ray
Are of advantage to me;
And the earth's face upward for my inspection.

My feet are locked upon the rough bark.
It took the whole of Creation   10
To produce my foot, my each feather:
Now I hold Creation in my foot

Or fly up, and revolve it all slowly—
I kill where I please because it is all mine.
There is no sophistry in my body: 15
My manners are tearing off heads—

The allotment of death.
For the one path of my flight is direct
Through the bones of the living.
No arguments assert my right: 20

The sun is behind me.
Nothing has changed since I began.
My eye has permitted no change.
I am going to keep things like this.

—TED HUGHES (1930–1998)

QUESTIONS

1. Vocabulary: *sophistry* (15).
2. Who is the speaker of this poem? Characterize his "personality." What do his errors in summing up his situation contribute to your characterization?
3. What are the similarities and differences between this poem and "The Eagle" (page 4)?

Ode on Melancholy

No, no, go not to Lethe, neither twist
    Wolf's-bane, tight-rooted, for its poisonous wine;
Nor suffer thy pale forehead to be kissed
    By nightshade, ruby grape of Proserpine;
Make not your rosary of yew-berries,   5
        Nor let the beetle, nor the death-moth be
        Your mournful Psyche, nor the downy owl
A partner in your sorrow's mysteries;
        For shade to shade will come too drowsily,
            And drown the wakeful anguish of the soul.   10

But when the melancholy fit shall fall
    Sudden from heaven like a weeping cloud,
That fosters the droop-headed flowers all,
    And hides the green hill in an April shroud;
Then glut thy sorrow on a morning rose,   15
        Or on the rainbow of the salt sand-wave,
        Or on the wealth of globèd peonies;
Or if thy mistress some rich anger shows,
        Emprison her soft hand, and let her rave,
            And feed deep, deep upon her peerless eyes.   20

She dwells with Beauty—Beauty that must die;
   And Joy, whose hand is ever at his lips
Bidding adieu; and aching Pleasure nigh,
   Turning to Poison while the bee-mouth sips:
Ay, in the very temple of delight   25
   Veiled Melancholy has her sovereign shrine,
      Though seen of none save him whose strenuous tongue
Can burst Joy's grape against his palate fine;
   His soul shall taste the sadness of her might,
      And be among her cloudy trophies hung.   30

—JOHN KEATS (1795–1821)

QUESTIONS

1. Using a good book on Greek mythology or an Internet search, find out the meaning of the following mythical references: *Lethe* (1); *Wolf's-bane* (2); *nightshade, Proserpine* (4); *Psyche* (7).
2. In the second stanza, the speaker gives advice on how to endure a "fit" (11) of melancholy. What is the essence of his advice?
3. According to the third stanza, what is the root cause of human melancholy (today we would simply call it "depression")? What kind of person is most susceptible to experiencing melancholy?

Upon Julia's Clothes

Whenas in silks my Julia goes
Then, then, methinks, how sweetly flows
That liquefaction of her clothes.

Next, when I cast mine eyes, and see
That brave vibration, each way free,   5
O, how that glittering taketh me!

—ROBERT HERRICK (1591–1674)

QUESTIONS

1. Vocabulary: *methinks* (2), *liquefaction* (3).
2. What is the speaker's attitude toward Julia? Does he have any particular emotion toward her?
3. Why does he focus on her clothes? What is the "brave vibration" described in line 5?

Mirror

I am silver and exact. I have no preconceptions.
Whatever I see I swallow immediately
Just as it is, unmisted by love or dislike.
I am not cruel, only truthful—
The eye of a little god, four-cornered.   5
Most of the time I meditate on the opposite wall.
It is pink, with speckles. I have looked at it so long
I think it is a part of my heart. But it flickers.
Faces and darkness separate us over and over.

Now I am a lake. A woman bends over me,   10
Searching my reaches for what she really is.
Then she turns to those liars, the candles or the moon.
I see her back, and reflect it faithfully.
She rewards me with tears and an agitation of hands.
I am important to her. She comes and goes.   15
Each morning it is her face that replaces the darkness.
In me she has drowned a young girl, and in me an old woman
Rises toward her day after day, like a terrible fish.

—SYLVIA PLATH (1932–1963)

QUESTIONS

1. Who is the speaker? What is the central purpose of the poem, and by what means is it achieved?
2. In what ways is the mirror like and unlike a person (stanza 1)? In what ways is it like a lake (stanza 2)?
3. What is the meaning of the last two lines?

Collection Day

Saturday morning, Motown
forty-fives and thick seventy-eights
on the phonograph, window fans
turning light into our rooms,
we clean house to a spiral groove,   5
sorting through our dailiness—
washtubs of boiled-white linens,
lima beans soaking, green as luck,
trash heaped out back for burning—
everything we can't keep,   10
make new with thread or glue.

Beside the stove, a picture calendar
of the seasons, daily scripture,
compliments of the Everlast Interment
Company, one day each month marked   15
in red—PREMIUM DUE—collection visit
from the insurance man, his black suits
worn to a shine. In our living room
he'll pull out photos of our tiny plot,
show us the slight eastward slope,   20
all the flowers in bloom now, how neat
the shrubs are trimmed, and *See here,*
the trees we planted are coming up fine.

We look out for him all day, listen
for the turn-stop of wheels   25
and rocks crunching underfoot.
Mama leafs through the Bible
for our payment card—June 1969,
the month he'll stamp PAID
in bright green letters, putting us   30
one step closer to what we'll own,
something to last: patch of earth,
view of sky.

—Natasha Trethewey (b. 1966)

QUESTIONS

1. The poem recounts a fact of life for poor African American families early in the twentieth century: they were sold insurance, often at usurious rates, to assure themselves a burial plot. What is the speaker's attitude toward her memory of the insurance man's visits and her mother's participation in the insurance program? Is she bitter, angry, resigned, or a combination of all these?
2. Find details in the poem that help clarify the time and place being described.
3. Focus on the last few lines. What do the images tell us about the speaker's mother's motivation for continuing to pay the monthly fee for her insurance?

The Dalliance of the Eagles

Skirting the river road, (my forenoon walk, my rest,)
Skyward in air a sudden muffled sound, the dalliance of
    the eagles,
The rushing amorous contact high in space together,

The clinching interlocking claws, a living, fierce,
    gyrating wheel,
Four beating wings, two beaks, a swirling mass tight
    grappling,   5
In tumbling turning clustering loops, straight downward
    falling,
Till o'er the river pois'd, the twain yet one, a moment's
    lull,
A motionless still balance in the air, then parting, talons
    loosing,
Upward again on slow-firm pinions slanting, their
    separate diverse flight,
She hers, he his, pursuing.   10

—WALT WHITMAN (1819–1892)

QUESTIONS

1. Vocabulary: *Dalliance* (title), *gyrating* (4), *pinions* (9).
2. What is being depicted from the speaker's viewpoint?
3. Is the speaker completely objective in reporting what he sees, or does the tone of the poem suggest a degree of emotion?

Storm Warnings

The glass has been falling all the afternoon,
And knowing better than the instrument
What winds are walking overhead, what zone
Of gray unrest is moving across the land,
I leave the book upon a pillowed chair   5
And walk from window to closed window, watching
Boughs strain against the sky

And think again, as often when the air
Moves inward toward a silent core of waiting,
How with a single purpose time has traveled   10
By secret currents of the undiscerned
Into this polar realm. Weather abroad
And weather in the heart alike come on
Regardless of prediction.

Between foreseeing and averting change   15
Lies all the mastery of elements
Which clocks and weatherglasses cannot alter.

Time in the hand is not control of time,
Nor shattered fragments of an instrument
A proof against the wind; the wind will rise,   20
We can only close the shutters.

I draw the curtains as the sky goes black
And set a match to candles sheathed in glass
Against the keyhole draught, the insistent whine
Of weather through the unsealed aperture.   25
This is our sole defense against the season;
These are the things that we have learned to do
Who live in troubled regions.

—ADRIENNE RICH (1929–2012)

SUGGESTIONS FOR WRITING

1. Here are four definitions of poetry, all framed by poets themselves. Which definition best fits the poems you have so far read?
   a. I wish our clever young poets would remember my homely definitions of prose
      and poetry: that is, prose = words in their best order; poetry = the best words
      in the best order.   *Samuel Taylor Coleridge*
   b. It is not meters, but a meter-making argument, that makes a poem—a thought
      so passionate and alive that, like the spirit of a plant or an animal, it has an
      architecture of its own, and adorns nature with a new thing.
                                                                 Ralph Waldo Emerson
   c. If I read a book and it makes my whole body so cold no fire can warm me,
      I know that is poetry. If I feel physically as if the top of my head were taken
      off, I know that is poetry. These are the only ways I know it. Is there any other
      way?   *Emily Dickinson*
   d. A poem begins in delight, it inclines to the impulse, it assumes a direction with
      the first line laid down, it runs a course of lucky events, and ends in a clarifi-
      cation of life—not necessarily a great clarification, such as sects and cults are
      founded on, but in a momentary stay against confusion.
                                                                 Robert Frost
2. Using two or three poems from this chapter, or poems from the following list,
   write an essay that supports the definition you have chosen.
   a. Plath, "Black Rook in Rainy Weather" (page 11).
   b. Clifton, "good times" (page 362).
   c. Dickinson, "A narrow Fellow in the Grass" (page 167).
   d. Donne, "Song: Go and catch a falling star" (page 367).
   e. Keats, "Ode on Melancholy" (page 34).
   f. Glück, "Labor Day" (page 14).

PRACTICE AP® WRITING PROMPTS

Thomas Hardy, "The Man He Killed" (pp. 24–25)

Read "The Man He Killed" carefully. Then write a well-organized essay in which you analyze the speaker's complex view of war. Pay attention to literary techniques such as irony, point of view, and diction.

A.E. Housman, "Is my team plowing" (pp. 29–30)

Read "Is my team plowing" carefully. Then write a well-organized essay in which you explain how the speakers in the poem convey a nuanced perspective on life, death, and human nature. Refer to specific elements such as point of view, tone, and diction in your analysis.

CHAPTER THREE

Denotation
and Connotation

A primary distinction between the practical use of language and the literary use is that in literature, especially in poetry, a *fuller* use is made of individual words. To understand this, we need to examine the composition of a word.

The average word has three component parts: sound, denotation, and connotation. Words begin with sound—a combination of tones and noises, uttered by the lips, tongue, and throat, for which the written word is a notation. But it differs from a musical tone or a noise in that it has a meaning attached to it. The basic part of this meaning is its **denotations**; that is, the dictionary meaning of the word. Beyond its denotations, a word may also have connotations. The **connotations** are what the word suggests beyond what it expresses—its overtones of meaning. It acquires these connotations from its past history and associations, from the way and the circumstances in which it has been used. The word *home,* for instance, by denotation means only a place where one lives, but by connotation it suggests security, love, comfort, and family. The words *childlike* and *childish* both mean "characteristic of a child," but *childlike* suggests meekness, innocence, and wide-eyed wonder, whereas *childish* suggests pettiness, willfulness, and temper tantrums. If we list the names of different coins—nickel, peso, euro, sen, doubloon—the word *doubloon,* to four out of five readers, immediately will suggest pirates, yet a dictionary definition includes nothing about pirates. Pirates are part of its connotation.

Connotation is very important in poetry, for it is one of the means by which the poet can concentrate or enrich meaning—say more in fewer words. Consider, for instance, the following short poem:

There is no Frigate like a Book

There is no Frigate like a Book
To take us Lands away
Nor any Coursers like a Page
Of prancing Poetry—
This Traverse may the poorest take   5
Without oppress of Toll—
How frugal is the Chariot
That bears the Human soul.

—EMILY DICKINSON (1830–1886)

This poem considers the power of a book or of poetry to carry us away, to take us from our immediate surroundings into a world of the imagination. To do this it compares literature to various means of transportation: a boat, a team of horses, a wheeled land vehicle. But the poet has been careful to choose kinds of transportation and names for them that have romantic connotations. "Frigate" suggests exploration and adventure; "coursers," beauty, spirit, and speed; "chariot," speed and the ability to go through the air as well as on land. (Compare "Swing Low, Sweet Chariot" and the myth of Phaëthon, who tried to drive the chariot of Apollo, and Guido Reni's famous painting of Aurora with her horses.) How much of the meaning of the poem comes from this selection of vehicles and words is apparent if we substitute *cruise ship* for "frigate," *horses* for "coursers," and *bus* for "chariot."

QUESTIONS

1. What is lost if *miles* is substituted for "Lands" (2) or *cheap* for "frugal" (7)?
2. How is "prancing" (4) peculiarly appropriate to poetry as well as to coursers? Could the poet without loss have compared a book to coursers and poetry to a frigate?
3. Is this account appropriate to all kinds of poetry or just to certain kinds? That is, was the poet thinking of poems like Wilfred Owen's "Dulce et Decorum Est" (page 6) or of poems like Coleridge's "Kubla Khan" (page 363) and Keats's "La Belle Dame sans Merci" (page 388)?

Just as a word has a variety of connotations, so may it have more than one denotation. If we look up the word *spring* in the dictionary, for instance, we will find that it has between twenty-five and thirty distinguishable meanings:

it may mean (1) a pounce or leap, (2) a season of the year, (3) a natural source of water, (4) a coiled elastic wire, and so forth. This variety of denotation, complicated by additional tones of connotation, makes language confusing and difficult to use. Any person using words must be careful to define precisely by context the denotation that is intended. But the difference between the writer using language to communicate and the poet is this: the practical writer will usually attempt to confine words to one denotation at a time; the poet will often take advantage of the fact that the word has more than one meaning by using it to mean more than one thing at the same time. Thus, when Edith Sitwell in one of her poems writes, "this is the time of the wild spring and the mating of the tigers,"* she uses the word "spring" to denote both a season of the year and a sudden leap (and she uses the word "tigers" rather than *deer* or *birds* because it has a connotation of fierceness and wildness that the others lack). The two denotations of "spring" are also appropriately possessed of contrasting connotations: the season is positive in its implications, whereas a sudden leap in a line that includes "tigers" may connote the pouncing of a beast of prey. Similarly, in "Mirror" (page 36), the word "swallow" in line 2 denotes both accepting without question and consuming or devouring, and so connotes both an inability to think and an obliteration or destruction.

When my love swears that she is made of truth

When my love swears that she is made of truth,
I do believe her, though I know she lies,
That she might think me some untutored youth,
Unlearnèd in the world's false subtleties.
Thus vainly thinking that she thinks me young,   5
Although she knows my days are past the best,
Simply I credit her false-speaking tongue;
On both sides thus is simple truth supprest.
But wherefore says she not she is unjust?°   unfaithful
And wherefore say not I that I am old?   10
Oh, love's best habit is in seeming trust,
And age in love loves not to have years told:
Therefore I lie with her and she with me,
And in our faults by lies we flattered be.

—WILLIAM SHAKESPEARE (1564–1616)

* *Collected Poems* (New York: Vanguard, 1968): 392.

QUESTIONS

1. How old is the speaker? How old is his beloved? What is the nature of their relationship?
2. How is the contradiction in line 2 to be resolved? In lines 5–6? Who is lying to whom?
3. How do "simply" (7) and "simple" (8) differ in meaning? The words "vainly" (5), "habit" (11), "told" (12), and "lie" (13) all have double denotative meanings. What are they?
4. What is the tone of the poem—that is, the attitude of the speaker toward his situation? Should line 11 be taken as an expression of (a) wisdom, (b) conscious rationalization, or (c) self-deception? In answering these questions, consider both the situation and the connotations of all the important words beginning with "swears" (1) and ending with "flattered" (14).

A frequent misconception of poetic language is that poets seek always the most beautiful or noble-sounding words. What they really seek are the most *meaningful* words, and these vary from one context to another. Language has many levels and varieties, and poets may choose from all of them. Their words may be grandiose or humble, fanciful or matter-of-fact, romantic or realistic, archaic or modern, technical or everyday, monosyllabic or polysyllabic. Usually a poem will be pitched pretty much in one key: the words in Emily Dickinson's "There is no Frigate like a Book" (page 42) and those in Thomas Hardy's "The Man He Killed" (page 24) are chosen from quite different areas of language, but both poets have chosen the words most meaningful for their own poetic context. It is always important to determine the level of diction employed in a poem, for it may provide clear insight into the purpose of the poem by helping to characterize the speaker. Sometimes a poet may import a word from one level or area of language into a poem composed mostly of words from a different level or area. If this is done clumsily, the result will be incongruous and sloppy; if it is done skillfully, the result will be a shock of surprise and an increment of meaning for the reader. In fact, the many varieties of language open to poets provide their richest resource. Their task is one of constant exploration and discovery. They search always for the secret affinities of words that allow them to be brought together with soft explosions of meaning.

Spring in the Classroom

Elbows on dry books, we dreamed
Past Miss Willow Bangs, and lessons, and windows,
To catch all day glimpses and guesses of the greening
  woodlot,

Its secrets and increases,
Its hidden nests and kind.   5
And what warmed in us was no book-learning,
But the old mud blood murmuring,
Loosening like petals from bone sleep.
So spring surrounded the classroom, and we suffered to be
    kept indoors,
Droned through lessons, carved when we could with
    jackknives   10
Our pulsing initials into the desks, and grew
Angry to be held so, without pity and beyond reason,
By Miss Willow Bangs, her eyes two stones behind glass,
Her legs thick, her heart
In love with pencils and arithmetic.   15

So it went—one gorgeous day lost after another
While we sat like captives and breathed the chalky air
And the leaves thickened and birds called
From the edge of the world—till it grew easy to hate,
To plot mutiny, even murder. Oh, we had her in chains,   20
We had her hanged and cold, in our longing to be gone!
And then one day, Miss Willow Bangs, we saw you
As we ran wild in our three o'clock escape
Past the abandoned swings; you were leaning
All furry and blooming against the old brick wall   25
In the Art Teacher's arms.

—MARY OLIVER (B.1935)

QUESTIONS

1. The poem juxtaposes two contrasted concepts, "Spring" and "Classroom." What are the connotations of the two words?
2. Based on their connotations, show how the following words support one or the other of those concepts: "dry" (1), "greening" (3), "petals" and "bone" (8), "droned" (10), "pulsing" (11), "chalky" (17), "wild" (23), "furry," "blooming," and "brick" (25).
3. How does the surprise ending contribute to the characterization of the speaker?

People using language only to convey information are usually indifferent to the sounds of the words and may feel frustrated by their connotations and multiple denotations. They would rather confine each word to a single, exact meaning. They use, one might say, a fraction of the word and throw away the rest. Poets, on the other hand, use as much of the word as possible. They are interested in connotation and use it to enrich and convey meaning. And they may rely on more than one denotation.

Perhaps the purest form of practical language is scientific language. Scientists need an exact language to convey information precisely. The existence of multiple denotations and various overtones of meaning may interfere with this purpose. As a result of this, scientists have even devised special "languages" such as the following:

$$SO_2 + H_2O = H_2SO_3$$

In such a statement the symbols are entirely unambiguous; they have been stripped of all connotation and of all denotations but one. The word *sulfurous,* if it occurred in poetry, might have all kinds of connotations: fire, smoke, brimstone, hell, damnation. But H_2SO_3 means one thing and one thing only: sulfurous acid.

The ambiguity and multiplicity of meanings possessed by words might be an obstacle to the scientist, but they are an advantage for the poet who seeks richness of meaning. One resource for that is a multidimensional language using a multidimensional vocabulary, in which the dimensions of connotation and sound are added to the dimension of denotation.

The poet, we may say, plays on a many-stringed instrument and sounds more than one note at a time.

Thus, the first task in reading poetry, as in reading any kind of literature, is to develop a sense of language, a feeling for words. One needs to become acquainted with their shape, their color, and their flavor. Two of the ways of doing this are extensive use of the dictionary and extensive reading.

EXERCISES

1. Which word in each group has the most "romantic" connotations: (a) horse, steed, nag; (b) king, ruler, tyrant, autocrat; (c) Chicago, Pittsburgh, Samarkand, Detroit?
2. Which word in each group is the most emotionally connotative: (a) female parent, mother, dam; (b) offspring, children, progeny; (c) brother, sibling?
3. Arrange the words in each of the following groups from most positive to most negative in connotation: (a) skinny, thin, gaunt, slender; (b) prosperous, loaded, moneyed, affluent; (c) brainy, intelligent, eggheaded, smart.
4. Of the following, which should you be less offended at being accused of: (a) having acted foolishly, (b) having acted like a fool?
5. In any competent piece of writing, the possible multiple denotations and connotations of the words used are controlled by context. The context screens out irrelevant meanings while allowing the relevant meanings to pass through. What denotation has the word *fast* in the following contexts: fast runner, fast color, fast living, fast day? What are the varying connotations of these four denotations of *fast*?

6. Explain how in the following examples the denotation of the word *white* remains the same, but the connotations differ: (a) The young princess had blue eyes, golden hair, and a breast as white as snow; (b) Confronted with the evidence, the false princess turned as white as a sheet.

REVIEWING CHAPTER THREE

1. Distinguish between connotation and denotation as components of words.
2. Explain how words accumulate their connotations.
3. Explore the ways in which a word may have multiple denotations, and multiple connotations, showing that different denotations may have different connotations.
4. Explore the ways in which the context will determine which denotations and which connotations are relevant in a poem.
5. Show how levels of diction may characterize the speaker in a poem.

Cross

My old man's a white old man
And my old mother's black.
If ever I cursed my white old man
I take my curses back.

If ever I cursed my black old mother   5
And wished she were in hell,
I'm sorry for that evil wish
And now I wish her well.

My old man died in a fine big house.
My ma died in a shack.   10
I wonder where I'm gonna die,
Being neither white nor black?

—LANGSTON HUGHES (1902–1967)

QUESTIONS

1. What different denotations does the title have? What connotations are linked to each of them?

2. The language in this poem, such as "old man" (1, 3, 9), "ma" (10), and "gonna" (11), is plain, and even colloquial. Is it appropriate to the subject? Why or why not?

The world is too much with us

The world is too much with us; late and soon,
Getting and spending, we lay waste our powers:
Little we see in nature that is ours;
We have given our hearts away, a sordid boon!
This sea that bares her bosom to the moon,   5
The winds that will be howling at all hours,
And are up-gathered now like sleeping flowers,
For this, for everything, we are out of tune;
It moves us not. —Great God! I'd rather be
A pagan suckled in a creed outworn;   10
So might I, standing on this pleasant lea,
Have glimpses that would make me less forlorn;
Have sight of Proteus rising from the sea;
Or hear old Triton blow his wreathèd horn.

—WILLIAM WORDSWORTH (1770–1850)

QUESTIONS

1. Vocabulary: *boon* (4), *Proteus* (13), *Triton* (14). What two relevant denotations has "wreathèd" (14)?
2. Explain why the poet's words are more effective than these possible alternatives: *earth* for "world" (1); *selling and buying* for "getting and spending" (2); *exposes* for "bares" (5); *dozing* for "sleeping" (7); *posies* for "flowers" (7); *nourished* for "suckled" (10); *visions* for "glimpses" (12); *sound* for "blow" (14).
3. Is "Great God!" (9) a vocative (term of address) or an expletive (exclamation)? Or something of both?
4. State the theme (central idea) of the poem in a sentence.

MindTap® Read, highlight, and take notes online.

Desert Places

Snow falling and night falling fast, oh, fast
In a field I looked into going past,
And the ground almost covered smooth in snow,
But a few weeds and stubble showing last.

The woods around it have it—it is theirs.   5
All animals are smothered in their lairs.

I am too absent-spirited to count;
The loneliness includes me unawares.

And lonely as it is that loneliness
Will be more lonely ere it will be less—   10
A blanker whiteness of benighted snow
With no expression, nothing to express.

They cannot scare me with their empty spaces
Between stars—on stars where no human race is.
I have it in me so much nearer home   15
To scare myself with my own desert places.

—Robert Frost (1874–1963)

QUESTIONS

1. Examine the poem for examples of words or phrases with negative or positive connotations. Which stanza is most negative? Considering its possible synonyms, how emotionally powerful is the word "scare" (13 and 16)?
2. What multiple denotations of the word "benighted" (11) are functional in the poem? How does the etymology of "blanker" (11) add to its force in this context?
3. "Absent-spirited" (7) is coined from the common word *absent-minded*. What denotations of "spirit" are relevant here?
4. Who are "They" (13) who can create fear by talking about the emptiness of space? Fear of what? What are the "desert places" (16) within the speaker that may be compared to literal emptiness of space?
5. In the first publication of the poem, line 14 concluded "on stars void of human races." Frost's final version calls attention to the potentially comic effect of rhyming *spaces/race is/places,* a device called feminine rhyme often used in humorous verse (see pages 188, 192). Is the speaker feeling comical? Can you relate this effect to what you determined about the word "scare" in question 1?

Accounting

Nights too warm for TV
we're flung outdoors to the porch,
citronella candles scenting the space
between us, our faces aglow
in gold light. She crowds the card table   5
with coin banks, an abacus,
five and ten dollar rolling paper,
our tidy ledger.

I count, line the coins in neat rows,
the abacus clicking out our worth,   10
how much we can save, stack up
against the seasons—winter coming,
her tightly braided hair turning white;
her hands quick, filling the paper casings
like homemade sausage.   15

There's money in the bank downtown,
but this we'll keep at home
buried in jars beneath the house,
the crawl space filling up, packed solid
as any foundation.   20

—NATASHA TRETHEWEY (B. 1966)

QUESTIONS

1. Vocabulary: *citronella* (3), *abacus* (6).
2. Discuss the connotations of "worth" in the phrase "the abacus clicking out our worth" (10). Is the speaker referring only to financial worth, or to something more as well?
3. Why do the speaker and her mother keep money "buried in jars beneath the house" (18) when, as she says, they have money in a downtown bank? Is there an emotional or psychological reason for hoarding the coins at home?
4. Consider the connotations of the word "foundation" (20), which concludes the poem.

35/10

Brushing out our daughter's brown
silken hair before the mirror
I see the grey gleaming on my head,
the silver-haired servant behind her. Why is it
just as we begin to go   5
they begin to arrive, the fold in my neck
clarifying as the fine bones of her
hips sharpen? As my skin shows
its dry pitting, she opens like a moist
precise flower on the tip of a cactus;   10
as my last chances to bear a child
are falling through my body, the duds among them,
her full purse of eggs, round and
firm as hard-boiled yolks, is about

to snap its clasp. I brush her tangled   15
fragrant hair at bedtime. It's an old
story—the oldest we have on our planet—
the story of replacement.

—SHARON OLDS (B. 1942)

QUESTIONS

1. What does the title mean?
2. Much of the poem consists of contrasts between physical characteristics of the mother and daughter. What connotations give emotional weight to these contrasts?
3. Is the last sentence (16–18) regretful or resigned, or can it be seen to be positive?

The Ledger

Love is injustice, said Camus.
We want to be loved. What's still more true?
Each wants most to be preferred,
And listens for those redeeming words
Better than X, more than Y—   5
Enough to quiet the child's cry,
The bridegroom's nerves, the patient's
Reluctant belief in providence.
Break what you can, hurt whom you will,
Humiliate the others until   10
Someone takes a long, hard look.
Oh Love, put down your balance book.

—J. D. MCCLATCHY (B. 1945)

QUESTIONS

1. Look up the French novelist Albert Camus (1913–1960) online. Why is the quotation from Camus in line 1 relevant to this poem?
2. According to the poem, why is love "unjust"?
3. Why does the speaker tell "Love" to "put down your balance book"?
4. Discuss the title. To what "Ledger" is it referring?
5. Discuss the connotations of the phrase "balance book" (12).

Dusting

Each morning I wrote my name
On the dusty cabinet, then crossed

The dining table in script, scrawled
In capitals on the backs of chairs,
Practicing signatures like scales   5
While mother followed, squirting
Linseed from a burping can
Into a crumpled-up flannel.

She erased my fingerprints
From the bookshelf and rocker,   10
Polished mirrors on the desk
Scribbled with my alphabets.
My name was swallowed in the towel
With which she jeweled the table tops.
The grain surfaced in the oak   15
And the pine grew luminous.
But I refused with every mark

To be like her, anonymous.

—JULIA ALVAREZ (B. 1950)

QUESTIONS

1. Vocabulary: *linseed* (7).
2. What is the situation in this poem? Who are the speaker and her mother?
3. Why is the speaker writing in the dust? What does it suggest about her future?
4. Why, at the end of the poem, does the speaker refuse to be "anonymous"?
5. Discuss the connotations of the words "scales" (5), "erased" (9), and "mark" (17).

In the Waiting Room

In Worcester, Massachusetts,
I went with Aunt Consuelo
to keep her dentist's appointment
and sat and waited for her
in the dentist's waiting room.   5
It was winter. It got dark
early. The waiting room
was full of grown-up people,
arctics and overcoats,
lamps and magazines.   10
My aunt was inside

what seemed like a long time
and while I waited I read
the *National Geographic*
(I could read) and carefully   15
studied the photographs:
the inside of a volcano,
black, and full of ashes;
then it was spilling over
in rivulets of fire.   20
Osa and Martin Johnson
dressed in riding breeches,
laced boots, and pith helmets.
A dead man slung on a pole
—"Long Pig," the caption said.   25
Babies with pointed heads
wound round and round with string;
black, naked women with necks
wound round and round with wire
like the necks of light bulbs.   30
Their breasts were horrifying.
I read it right straight through.
I was too shy to stop.
And then I looked at the cover:
the yellow margins, the date.   35
Suddenly, from inside,
came an *oh!* of pain
—Aunt Consuelo's voice—
not very loud or long.
I wasn't at all surprised;   40
even then I knew she was
a foolish, timid woman.
I might have been embarrassed,
but wasn't. What took me
completely by surprise   45
was that it was *me:*
my voice, in my mouth.
Without thinking at all
I was my foolish aunt,
I—we—were falling, falling,   50
our eyes glued to the cover
of the *National Geographic,*
February, 1918.

I said to myself: three days
and you'll be seven years old.   55
I was saying it to stop
the sensation of falling off
the round, turning world
into cold, blue-black space.
But I felt: you are an *I*,   60
you are an *Elizabeth*,
you are one of *them*.
Why should you be one, too?
I scarcely dared to look
to see what it was I was.   65
I gave a sidelong glance
—I couldn't look any higher—
at shadowy gray knees,
trousers and skirts and boots
and different pairs of hands   70
lying under the lamps.
I knew that nothing stranger
had ever happened, that nothing
stranger could ever happen.

Why should I be my aunt,   75
or me, or anyone?
What similarities—
boots, hands, the family voice
I felt in my throat, or even
the *National Geographic*   80
and those awful hanging breasts—
held us all together
or made us all just one?
How—I didn't know any
word for it—how "unlikely". . .   85
How had I come to be here,
like them, and overhear
a cry of pain that could have
got loud and worse but hadn't?

The waiting room was bright   90
and too hot. It was sliding
beneath a big black wave,
another, and another.

Then I was back in it.
The War was on. Outside,   95
in Worcester, Massachusetts,
were night and slush and cold,
and it was still the fifth
of February, 1918.

—ELIZABETH BISHOP (1911–1979)

QUESTIONS

1. Vocabulary: *arctics* (9); *pith helmets* (23). Osa and Martin Johnson (21) were early twentieth-century explorers and documentary filmmakers.
2. The poem situates the speaker very specifically in time and place. Why is this important, given the theme of the poem?
3. The speaker, almost seven years old, is in a dentist's waiting room. In what sense is this setting a metaphor for a different kind of waiting?
4. Reread lines 60–74. In what sense had "nothing stranger" ever happened to the speaker before? What *has* happened to her?
5. Discuss the significance of the final stanza, with its reiteration of the poem's time and place. Why is this an effective ending to the poem?
6. Explore the uses of connotation in the poem. Which phrases have connotative richness that adds to the poem's meaning?

Disillusionment of Ten O'Clock

The houses are haunted
By white night-gowns.
None are green,
Or purple with green rings,
Or green with yellow rings,   5
Or yellow with blue rings.
None of them are strange,
With socks of lace
And beaded ceintures.°   sashes
People are not going   10
To dream of baboons and periwinkles.
Only, here and there, an old sailor,
Drunk and asleep in his boots,
Catches tigers
In red weather.   15

—WALLACE STEVENS (1879–1955)

QUESTIONS

1. Vocabulary: *periwinkles* (11).
2. What is the "Disillusionment" to which the title refers?
3. What connotations do the various colors have in lines 2–6?
4. Why does the sailor in lines 11–15 live in "red weather" (15)?
5. What is the connotation of "red" (15)?

SUGGESTIONS FOR WRITING

Consider the denotative meaning(s) of the following titles. Then read each poem carefully and note the multiple connotations that attach to the title phrase as the poem progresses. Choose two or three titles, then write a short essay comparing the denotative and connotative meanings of each.

1. Williams, "The Red Wheelbarrow" (page 15).
2. Frost, "Fire and Ice" (page 105).
3. Piercy, "Barbie Doll" (page 119).
4. Plath, "The Colossus" (page 129).
5. Donne, "The Good-Morrow" (page 369).
6. Mitcham, "Stroke" (page 396).
7. Roethke, "My Papa's Waltz" (page 128).
8. Yeats, "The Second Coming" (page 417).

PRACTICE AP® WRITING PROMPTS

Mary Oliver, "Spring in the Classroom" (pp. 44–45)

Read "Spring in the Classroom" carefully, paying close attention to Mary Oliver's characterization of the teacher and her students. Write an essay in which you analyze these character portraits, showing how such literary elements as figurative language, tone, and irony contribute to meaning.

....

Sharon Olds, "35/10" (pp. 50–51)

Contemporary poet Sharon Olds has written many poems about her feelings and experiences as a parent. Read carefully "35/10." In a well-organized essay, analyze the speaker's complex reaction to seeing her daughter grow up. Show how diction, structure, and figurative language contribute to the poem's meaning.

....

CHAPTER FOUR

Imagery

Experience comes to us largely through the senses. Our experiences of a spring day, for instance, may consist partly of certain emotions we feel and partly of certain thoughts we think, but most of it will be a cluster of sense impressions. It will consist of *seeing* blue sky and white clouds, budding leaves and daffodils; of *hearing* robins and bluebirds singing in the early morning; of *smelling* damp earth and blossoming hyacinths; and of *feeling* a fresh wind against our cheek. A poet seeking to express the experience of a spring day therefore provides a selection of sense impressions. Similarly, to present a winter day (page 5), Shakespeare gives us hanging "icicles," milk "frozen," blood "nipped," and Marian's "red and raw" nose, as well as the melancholy "'Tu-whit, tu-who'" of the owl. Had he not done so, he might have failed to evoke the emotions that accompany these sensations. The poet's language, then, is more *sensuous* than ordinary language. It is richer in imagery.

Imagery may be defined as the representation through language of sense experience. Poetry appeals directly to our senses, of course, through its music and rhythms, which we actually hear when it is read aloud. But indirectly it appeals to our senses through imagery, the representation to the imagination of sense experience. The word *image* perhaps most often suggests a mental picture, something seen in the mind's eye—and *visual imagery* is the kind of imagery that occurs most frequently in poetry. But an image may also represent a sound (*auditory imagery*); a smell (*olfactory imagery*); a taste (*gustatory imagery*); touch, such as hardness, softness, wetness, or heat and cold (*tactile imagery*); an internal sensation, such as hunger, thirst, fatigue, or nausea (*organic imagery*); or movement or tension in the muscles or joints (*kinesthetic imagery*). If we wish to be scientific, we could extend this list further, for psychologists no longer confine themselves to five or even six senses, but for purposes of discussing poetry the preceding classification should ordinarily be sufficient.

Meeting at Night

The gray sea and the long black land;
And the yellow half-moon large and low;
And the startled little waves that leap
In fiery ringlets from their sleep,
As I gain the cove with pushing prow,   5
And quench its speed i' the slushy sand.

Then a mile of warm sea-scented beach;
Three fields to cross till a farm appears;
A tap at the pane, the quick sharp scratch
And blue spurt of a lighted match,   10
And a voice less loud, through its joys and fears,
Than the two hearts beating each to each!

—ROBERT BROWNING (1812–1889)

"Meeting at Night" is a poem about love. One might say that it makes a number of statements about love: being in love is a sweet and exciting experience; when one is in love everything seems beautiful, and the most trivial things become significant; when one is in love, one's beloved seems the most important thing in the world. But the poet actually *tells* us none of these things directly. He does not even use the word *love* in his poem. His business is to communicate experience, not information. He does this largely in two ways. First, he presents us with a specific situation, in which a lover goes to meet his love. Second, he describes the lover's journey so vividly in terms of sense impressions that the reader virtually sees and hears what the lover saw and heard and seems to share his anticipation and excitement.

Every line in the poem contains some image, some appeal to the senses: the gray sea, the long black land, the yellow half-moon, the startled little waves with their fiery ringlets, the blue spurt of the lighted match—all appeal to our sense of sight and convey not only shape but also color and motion. The warm sea-scented beach appeals to the senses of both smell and touch. The pushing prow of the boat on the slushy sand, the tap at the pane, the quick scratch of the match, the low speech of the lovers, and the sound of their hearts beating—all appeal to the sense of hearing.

Parting at Morning

Round the cape of a sudden came the sea,
And the sun looked over the mountain's rim:
And straight was a path of gold for him,
And the need of a world of men for me.

—ROBERT BROWNING (1812–1889)

QUESTIONS

1. This poem is a sequel to "Meeting at Night." "[H]im" (3) refers to the sun. Does the last line mean that the lover needs the world of men or that the world of men needs the lover? Or both?
2. Does the sea *actually* come suddenly around the cape or *appear* to? Why does Browning mention the *effect* before its *cause* (the sun looking over the mountain's rim)?
3. Do these two poems, taken together, suggest any larger truths about love? Browning, in answer to a question, said that the second poem is the man's confession of "how fleeting is the belief (implied in the first part) that such raptures are self-sufficient and enduring—as for the time they appear."

The sharpness and vividness of any image will ordinarily depend on how specific it is and on the poet's use of effective detail. The word *hummingbird,* for instance, conveys a more definite image than does *bird,* and *ruby-throated hummingbird* is sharper and more specific still. However, to represent something vividly, a poet need not describe it completely. One or two especially sharp and representative details will often serve, inviting the reader's imagination to fill in the rest. Tennyson in "The Eagle" (page 4) gives only one visual detail about the eagle itself—that he clasps the crag with "crooked hands"—but this detail is an effective and memorable one. Oliver in "Spring in the Classroom" (page 44) does not state why the students grow to hate their teacher but through the series of contrasted images leads us to feel their frustration and desire. Browning, in "Meeting at Night," calls up a whole scene with "A tap at the pane, the quick sharp scratch / And blue spurt of a lighted match."

Since imagery is a peculiarly effective way of evoking vivid experience, and since it may be used to convey emotion and suggest ideas as well as to cause a mental reproduction of sensations, it is an invaluable resource for the poet. In general, the poet will seek concrete or image-bearing words in preference to abstract or non–image-bearing words. We cannot evaluate a poem, however, by the amount or quality of its imagery alone. Sense impression is only one of the elements of experience. Poetry may attain its ends by other means. We should never judge any single element of a poem except in reference to the total intent of that poem.

EXERCISES

In the following images, what sense is being evoked, and what does the image contribute to its context?

1. "Dulce et Decorum Est" (page 6):"deaf even to the hoots / Of gas-shells" (7–8); "He plunges at me, guttering, choking, drowning" (16);"gargling from the froth-corrupted lungs" (22).
2. "Shall I compare thee to a summer's day?" (page 11):"Rough winds do shake the darling buds of May" (3);"Sometimes too hot the eye of heaven shines" (5); "often is his gold complexion dimmed" (6).
3. "Spring in the Classroom" (page 44):"mud blood murmuring" (7);"Droned through lessons" (10);"the chalky air" (18);"All furry and blooming" (25).

REVIEWING CHAPTER FOUR

1. State the definition of *poetic imagery.*
2. Relate imagery to its uses in conveying emotion, suggesting ideas, and mentally evoking sense experience.
3. Select individual images that demonstrate these three uses of imagery, and explain how they work.
4. Show that specificity in an image contributes to its sharpness and vividness.
5. Explain the distinction between abstract statements and concrete, image-bearing statements, providing examples.
6. Demonstrate that ambiguity and multiplicity of meanings contribute to the richness of poetic language.

Spring

Nothing is so beautiful as spring—
When weeds, in wheels, shoot long and lovely and lush;
Thrush's eggs look little low heavens, and thrush
Through the echoing timber does so rinse and wring

The ear, it strikes like lightnings to hear him sing;   5
    The glassy peartree leaves and blooms, they brush
    The descending blue; that blue is all in a rush
With richness; the racing lambs too have fair their fling.

What is all this juice and all this joy?
    A strain of the earth's sweet being in the beginning   10
In Eden garden.——Have, get, before it cloy,
    Before it cloud, Christ, lord, and sour with sinning,
Innocent mind and Mayday in girl and boy,
    Most, O maid's child, thy choice and worthy the winning.

—GERARD MANLEY HOPKINS (1844–1889)

QUESTIONS

1. The first line makes an abstract statement. How is this statement brought to carry conviction?
2. The sky is described as being "all in a rush / With richness" (7–8). In what other respects is the poem "rich"?
3. To what two things does the speaker compare the spring in lines 9–14? In what ways are the comparisons appropriate?
4. Lines 11–14 might be made clearer by paraphrasing them thus: "Christ, lord, child of the Virgin: save the innocent mind of girl and boy before sin taints it, since it is most like yours and worth saving." Why are Hopkins's lines more effective, both in imagery and in syntax?

The Widow's Lament in Springtime

Sorrow is my own yard
where the new grass
flames as it has flamed
often before but not
with the cold fire   5
that closes round me this year.
Thirtyfive years
I lived with my husband.
The plumtree is white today
with masses of flowers.   10
Masses of flowers
load the cherry branches
and color some bushes
yellow and some red

but the grief in my heart   15
is stronger than they
for though they were my joy
formerly, today I notice them
and turned away forgetting.
Today my son told me   20
that in the meadows,
at the edge of the heavy woods
in the distance, he saw
trees of white flowers.
I feel that I would like   25
to go there
and fall into those flowers
and sink into the marsh near them.

—WILLIAM CARLOS WILLIAMS (1883–1963)

QUESTIONS

1. Why is springtime so poignant a time for this lament? What has been the speaker's previous experience at this time of year?
2. Why does the speaker's son tell her of the flowering trees "in the distance" (23)? What does he want her to do? Contrast the two locations in the poem—"yard" versus "meadows" (21), "woods" (22), and "marsh" (28). What does the widow desire?
3. Imagery may have degrees of vividness, depending on its particularity, concreteness, and specific detail. What is the result of the contrast between the vividness of lines 2–3 and the relative flatness of lines 13–14? How does the fact that "masses" (10, 11) appeals to two senses relate to the speaker's emotional condition?

I felt a Funeral, in my Brain

I felt a Funeral, in my Brain,
And Mourners to and fro
Kept treading—treading—till it seemed
That Sense was breaking through—

And when they all were seated,   5
A Service, like a Drum—
Kept beating—beating—till I thought
My Mind was going numb—

And then I heard them lift a Box
And creak across my Soul   10

With those same Boots of Lead, again,
Then Space—began to toll,

As all the Heavens were a Bell,
And Being, but an Ear,
And I, and Silence, some strange Race   15
Wrecked, solitary, here—

And then a Plank in Reason, broke,
And I dropped down, and down—
And hit a World, at every plunge,
And Finished knowing—then—   20

—EMILY DICKINSON (1830–1886)

QUESTIONS

1. What senses are being evoked by the imagery? Can you account for the fact that one important sense is absent from the poem?
2. In sequence, what aspects of a funeral and burial are represented in the poem? Is it possible to define the sequence of mental events that are being compared to them?
3. With respect to the funeral activities in stanzas 1–3, where is the speaker imaginatively located?
4. What finally happens to the speaker?

Living in Sin

She had thought the studio would keep itself,
no dust upon the furniture of love.
Half heresy, to wish the taps less vocal,
the panes relieved of grime. A plate of pears,
a piano with a Persian shawl, a cat   5
stalking the picturesque amusing mouse
had risen at his urging.
Not that at five each separate stair would writhe
under the milkman's tramp; that morning light
so coldly would delineate the scraps   10
of last night's cheese and three sepulchral bottles;
that on the kitchen shelf among the saucers
a pair of beetle-eyes would fix her own—
envoy from some village in the moldings . . .
Meanwhile, he, with a yawn,   15
sounded a dozen notes upon the keyboard,

declared it out of tune, shrugged at the mirror,
rubbed at his beard, went out for cigarettes;
while she, jeered by the minor demons,
pulled back the sheets and made the bed and found   20
a towel to dust the table-top,
and let the coffee-pot boil over on the stove.
By evening she was back in love again,
though not so wholly but throughout the night
she woke sometimes to feel the daylight coming   25
like a relentless milkman up the stairs.

—ADRIENNE RICH (1929–2012)

The Forge

All I know is a door into the dark.
Outside, old axles and iron hoops rusting;
Inside, the hammered anvil's short-pitched ring,
The unpredictable fantail of sparks
Or hiss when a new shoe toughens in water.   5
The anvil must be somewhere in the center,
Horned as a unicorn, at one end square,
Set there immovable: an altar
Where he expends himself in shape and music.
Sometimes, leather-aproned, hairs in his nose,   10
He leans out on the jamb, recalls a clatter
Of hoofs where traffic is flashing in rows;
Then grunts and goes in, with a slam and flick
To beat real iron out, to work the bellows.

—SEAMUS HEANEY (1939–2013)

QUESTIONS

1. What does the speaker mean when he says that "all" he knows is "a door into the dark" (1)? What more does he know, and how does he make his knowledge evident?
2. How do the images describing the blacksmith (10–11) relate to his attitude toward his work and toward the changing times?
3. The speaker summarizes the smith's world as "shape and music" (9), terms that suggest visual and auditory imagery. What do the contrasts between visual images contribute? The contrasts between auditory images?

After Apple-Picking

My long two-pointed ladder's sticking through a tree
Toward heaven still,
And there's a barrel that I didn't fill
Beside it, and there may be two or three
Apples I didn't pick upon some bough.   5
But I am done with apple-picking now.
Essence of winter sleep is on the night,
The scent of apples: I am drowsing off.
I cannot rub the strangeness from my sight
I got from looking through a pane of glass   10
I skimmed this morning from the drinking trough
And held against the world of hoary grass.
It melted, and I let it fall and break.
But I was well
Upon my way to sleep before it fell,   15
And I could tell
What form my dreaming was about to take.
Magnified apples appear and disappear,
Stem end and blossom end,
And every fleck of russet showing clear.   20
My instep arch not only keeps the ache,
It keeps the pressure of a ladder-round.
I feel the ladder sway as the boughs bend.
And I keep hearing from the cellar bin
The rumbling sound   25
Of load on load of apples coming in.
For I have had too much
Of apple-picking: I am overtired
Of the great harvest I myself desired.
There were ten thousand thousand fruit to touch,   30
Cherish in hand, lift down, and not let fall.
For all
That struck the earth,
No matter if not bruised or spiked with stubble,
Went surely to the cider-apple heap   35
As of no worth.
One can see what will trouble
This sleep of mine, whatever sleep it is.
Were he not gone,

The woodchuck could say whether it's like his   40
Long sleep, as I describe its coming on,
Or just some human sleep.

—ROBERT FROST (1874–1963)

QUESTIONS

1. How does the poet convey so vividly the experience of "apple-picking"? Point out effective examples of each kind of imagery used. What emotional responses do the images evoke?
2. How does the speaker regard his work? Has he done it well or poorly? Does he find it enjoyable or tedious? Is he dissatisfied with its results?
3. The speaker predicts what he will dream about in his sleep. Why does he shift to the present tense (18) when he begins describing a dream he has not yet had? How sharply are real experience and dream experience differentiated in the poem?
4. The poem uses the word *sleep* six times. Does it, through repetition, come to suggest a meaning beyond the purely literal? If so, what attitude does the speaker take toward this second signification? Does he fear it? Does he look forward to it? What does he expect of it?
5. If sleep is symbolic (both literal and metaphorical), other details also may take on additional meaning. If so, how would you interpret (a) the ladder, (b) the season of the year, (c) the harvesting, (d) the "pane of glass" (10)? What denotations has the word "Essence" (7)?
6. How does the woodchuck's sleep differ from "just some human sleep" (42)?

Those Winter Sundays

Sundays too my father got up early
and put his clothes on in the blueblack cold,
then with cracked hands that ached
from labor in the weekday weather made
banked fires blaze. No one ever thanked him.   5

I'd wake and hear the cold splintering, breaking.
When the rooms were warm, he'd call,
and slowly I would rise and dress,
fearing the chronic angers of that house,

Speaking indifferently to him,   10
who had driven out the cold
and polished my good shoes as well.

What did I know, what did I know
of love's austere and lonely offices?

—ROBERT HAYDEN (1913–1980)

QUESTIONS

1. Vocabulary: *offices* (14).
2. What kind of imagery is central to the poem? How is this imagery related to the emotional concerns of the poem?
3. How do the subsidiary images relate to the central images?
4. From what point in time does the speaker view the subject matter of the poem? What has happened to him in the interval?

I saw in Louisiana a live-oak growing

I saw in Louisiana a live-oak growing,
All alone stood it and the moss hung down from the
    branches,
Without any companion it grew there uttering joyous
    leaves of dark green,
And its look, rude, unbending, lusty, made me think of
    myself,
But I wonder'd how it could utter joyous leaves standing
    alone there without its friend near, for I knew
    I could not,   5
And I broke off a twig with a certain number of leaves
    upon it, and twined around it a little moss,
And brought it away, and I have placed it in sight in my
    room,
It is not needed to remind me as of my own dear
    friends,
(For I believe lately I think of little else than of them,)
Yet it remains to me a curious token, it makes me think
    of manly love;   10
For all that, and though the live-oak glistens there in
    Louisiana solitary in a wide flat space,
Uttering joyous leaves all its life without a friend a lover
    near,
I know very well I could not.

—WALT WHITMAN (1819–1892)

QUESTIONS

1. To the speaker, what is the most distinctive characteristic of the oak tree?
2. When the speaker breaks off the twig, why does he twine some moss around it?
3. What does the speaker find in the tree that is similar to himself? Different from himself?
4. What images does Whitman choose to evoke a tree? What are their specific connotations?

MindTap® Read, highlight, and take notes online.

The Snow Man

One must have a mind of winter
To regard the frost and the boughs
Of the pine-trees crusted with snow;

And have been cold a long time
To behold the junipers shagged with ice,   5
The spruces rough in the distant glitter

Of the January sun; and not to think
Of any misery in the sound of the wind,
In the sound of a few leaves,

Which is the sound of the land   10
Full of the same wind
That is blowing in the same bare place

For the listener, who listens in the snow,
And, nothing himself, beholds
Nothing that is not there and the nothing that is.   15

—WALLACE STEVENS (1879–1955)

QUESTIONS

1. The poem presents two kinds of "mind"—one that is cold and unmoved, the other emotional and responsive. What advantages does each of them have? Does the poem promote one or the other?
2. What emotional meanings are presented in the visual imagery in lines 2–3 and 5–7?
3. What emotional meanings are presented in the auditory imagery in lines 8–11?
4. How is the snow man "nothing himself" (14)? What is the meaning of what he "beholds" (14–15)? Paraphrase the poem.

To Autumn

Season of mists and mellow fruitfulness,
   Close bosom-friend of the maturing sun;
Conspiring with him how to load and bless
   With fruit the vines that round the thatch-eaves run;
To bend with apples the mossed cottage-trees,   5
   And fill all fruit with ripeness to the core;
     To swell the gourd, and plump the hazel shells
With a sweet kernel; to set budding more,
   And still more, later flowers for the bees,
Until they think warm days will never cease,   10
   For summer has o'er-brimmed their clammy cells.

Who hath not seen thee oft amid thy store?
   Sometimes whoever seeks abroad may find
Thee sitting careless on a granary floor,
   Thy hair soft-lifted by the winnowing wind;   15
Or on a half-reaped furrow sound asleep,
   Drowsed with the fume of poppies, while thy hook
     Spares the next swath and all its twinèd flowers:
And sometimes like a gleaner thou dost keep
   Steady thy laden head across a brook;   20
Or by a cider-press, with patient look,
   Thou watchest the last oozings hours by hours.

Where are the songs of spring? Ay, where are they?
   Think not of them, thou hast thy music too,—
While barred clouds bloom the soft-dying day,   25
   And touch the stubble-plains with rosy hue;
Then in a wailful choir the small gnats mourn
   Among the river sallows, borne aloft
     Or sinking as the light wind lives or dies;
And full-grown lambs loud bleat from hilly bourn;   30
   Hedge-crickets sing; and now with treble soft
   The red-breast whistles from a garden-croft;
   And gathering swallows twitter in the skies.

—JOHN KEATS (1795–1821)

QUESTIONS

1. Vocabulary: *hook* (17), *barred* (25), *sallows* (28), *bourn* (30), *croft* (32).
2. How many kinds of imagery do you find in the poem? Give examples of each.
3. Are the images arranged haphazardly or are they carefully organized? In answering this question, consider (a) what aspect of autumn each stanza particularly concerns, (b) what kind of imagery dominates each stanza, and (c) what time of the season each stanza presents. Is there any progression in time of day?
4. What is autumn personified as in stanza 2? Is there any suggestion of personification in the other two stanzas?
5. Although the poem is primarily descriptive, what attitude toward transience and passing beauty is implicit in it?

SUGGESTIONS FOR WRITING

Analyze the imagery in one of the following poems, drawing some conclusions as to whether individual images function primarily to evoke vivid experience, convey emotion, or suggest ideas (see page 57). Be sure in each case to identify the sense reference of the imagery—visual, auditory, and so forth.

1. Dickinson, "A narrow Fellow in the Grass" (page 167).
2. Oates, "Playlet for Voices" (page 400).
3. Plath, "Lady Lazarus" (page 309).
4. Roethke, "My Papa's Waltz" (page 128).
5. Rogers, "Night and the Creation of Geography" (page 243).
6. Stevens, "Sunday Morning" (page 301).
7. Glück, "Purple Bathing Suit" (page 102).
8. Yeats, "The Wild Swans at Coole" (page 418).

PRACTICE AP® WRITING PROMPTS

Robert Browning, "Meeting at Night" (p. 58) and "Parting at Morning" (p. 59)

Robert Browning's "Parting at Morning" was written as a sequel to "Meeting at Night." Read both poems carefully and write an essay in which you explain how the two poems, taken together, suggest the roles of love and "the world of men" in the speaker's life. Explain how literary devices such as imagery, personification, and point of view convey Browning's theme.

William Carlos Williams, "The Widow's Lament in Springtime" (pp. 61–62)

"The Widow's Lament in Springtime" juxtaposes a widow's grief against the vividness of spring. Read the poem carefully. Then write an essay in which you show how poetic techniques such as imagery, metaphor, and concrete detail combine to illustrate the speaker's response to the coming of spring.

Robert Frost, "After Apple-Picking" (pp. 65–66)

Read "After Apple-Picking" carefully, paying close attention to imagery and to the intensity of the experience described in the poem. Then write a well-organized essay in which you show how the speaker links the literal experience of picking apples to a deeper, more abstract meaning.

Robert Hayden, "Those Winter Sundays" (pp. 66–67)

Read "Those Winter Sundays" carefully. Then write an essay in which you analyze how the author combines childhood memory and adult reflection to arrive at a moment of deep feeling. You may wish to consider literary elements such as imagery, rhythm, and detail.

CHAPTER FIVE

Figurative Language I

Simile, Metaphor, Personification, Apostrophe, Metonymy

> *Poetry provides the one permissible way of saying one thing and meaning another.*
>
> —Robert Frost

Let us assume that your brother has just come in out of a rainstorm and you say to him, "Well, you're a pretty sight! Got slightly wet, didn't you?" And he replies, "Wet? I'm drowned! It's raining cats and dogs, and my raincoat's like a sieve!"

You and your brother probably understand each other well enough; yet if you examine this conversation literally, that is to say unimaginatively, you will find that you have been speaking nonsense. Actually you have been speaking figuratively. You have been saying less than what you mean, or more than what you mean, or the opposite of what you mean, or something other than what you mean. You did not mean that your brother was a pretty sight but that he was a wretched sight. You did not mean that he got slightly wet but that he got very wet. Your brother did not mean that he got drowned but that he got drenched. It was not raining cats and dogs; it was raining water. And your brother's raincoat is so unlike a sieve that not even a child would confuse them.

On first examination, it might seem absurd to say one thing and mean another. But we all do it—and with good reason. We do it because we can say what we want to say more vividly and forcefully by figures of speech than we can by saying it directly. And we can say more by figurative statements than we can by literal statements. Figures of speech offer another way of adding extra dimensions to language.

Broadly defined, a **figure of speech** is any way of saying something other than the ordinary way; some rhetoricians have classified as many as 250 separate figures. For our purposes, however, a figure of speech is more narrowly definable as a way of saying one thing and meaning another, and we need to be concerned with no more than a dozen. **Figurative language**—language using figures of speech—is language that cannot be taken literally (or should not be taken literally only).

Simile and **metaphor** are both used as a means of comparing things that are essentially unlike. The only distinction between them is that in simile, the comparison is *expressed* by the use of some word or phrase, such as *like, as, than, similar to, resembles,* or *seems*; in metaphor, the comparison is not expressed but is created when a figurative term is *substituted for* or *identified with* the literal term.

Harlem

What happens to a dream deferred?

Does it dry up
like a raisin in the sun?
Or fester like a sore—
And then run?   5
Does it stink like rotten meat?
Or crust and sugar over—
like a syrupy sweet?

Maybe it just sags
like a heavy load.   10

Or does it explode?

—LANGSTON HUGHES (1902–1967)

QUESTIONS

1. Of the six images, five are similes. Which is a metaphor? Comment on its position and effectiveness.
2. What specific denotation has the word "dream" (1)? Since the poem does not reveal the contents of the dream, the poem is general in its implication. What

happens to your understanding of it on learning that the poet was an African American?

Metaphors may take one of four forms, depending on whether the literal and figurative terms are respectively *named* or *implied*. In the first form of metaphor, as in simile, *both* the literal and figurative terms are *named*. In Williams's "The Widow's Lament in Springtime" (page 61), for example, the literal term is "sorrow" and the figurative term is "yard." In the second form, shown in Hughes's "Harlem," the literal term "dream" is *named* and the figurative term, "bomb," is *implied*.

In the third form of metaphor, the literal term is *implied* and the figurative term is *named*. In the fourth form, *both* the literal *and* figurative terms are *implied*. The following poem exemplifies both forms:

It sifts from Leaden Sieves

It sifts from Leaden Sieves—
It powders all the Wood.
It fills with Alabaster Wool
The Wrinkles of the Road—

It makes an Even Face   5
Of Mountain, and of Plain—
Unbroken Forehead from the East
Unto the East again—

It reaches to the Fence—
It wraps it Rail by Rail   10
Till it is lost in Fleeces—
It deals Celestial Veil

To Stump, and Stack—and Stem—
A Summer's empty Room—
Acres of Joints, where Harvests were,   15
Recordless,° but for them—   unrecorded

It Ruffles Wrists of Posts
As Ankles of a Queen—
Then stills its Artisans—like Ghosts—
Denying they have been—   20

—EMILY DICKINSON (1830–1886)

QUESTIONS

1. This poem consists essentially of a series of metaphors with the same literal term identified only as "It." What is "It"?
2. In several of these metaphors the figurative term is named—"Alabaster Wool" (3), "Fleeces" (11), "Celestial Veil" (12). In two of them, however, the figurative term as well as the literal term is left unnamed. To what is "It" compared in lines 1–2? In lines 17–18?
3. Comment on the additional metaphorical expressions or complications contained in "Leaden Sieves" (1), "Alabaster Wool" (3), "Even Face" (5), "Unbroken Forehead" (7), "A Summer's empty Room" (14), "Artisans" (19).

Metaphors of the fourth form, as one might guess, are comparatively rare.

Using some examples from the poems discussed in this and the preceding chapters, this chart provides a visual demonstration of the figures of comparison (simile and the four forms of metaphor).

	Poet	Literal Term	Figurative Term
Similes (*like, as, seems,* etc.)	Hughes	named dream	named raisin
Metaphors (*is, are,* etc.) Form 1	Williams	named sorrow	named yard
Form 2	Hughes	named dream	implied bomb
Form 3	Dickinson	implied it [snow]	named wool
Form 4	Dickinson	implied it [snow]	implied [flour] sifts

Personification consists of giving the attributes of a human being to an animal, an object, or a concept. It is really a subtype of metaphor, an implied comparison in which the figurative term of the comparison is always a human being. When Sylvia Plath makes a mirror speak and think (page 36), she is personifying an object. When Keats describes autumn as a harvester "sitting careless on a granary floor" or "on a half-reaped furrow sound asleep" (page 69), he is personifying a season. Personifications differ in the degree to which they ask the reader actually to visualize the literal term in human form. In Keats's comparison, we are asked to make a complete identification of autumn with a human being. In Plath's, although the mirror speaks and thinks, we continue to visualize it as a mirror. In Browning's reference to "the startled little waves" (page 58), a personification is barely suggested;

we would make a mistake if we tried to visualize the waves in human form or even, really, to think of them as having human emotions.

The Author to Her Book

Thou ill-formed offspring of my feeble brain,
Who after birth did'st by my side remain,
Till snatched from thence by friends, less wise than true,
Who thee abroad exposed to public view;
Made thee in rags, halting, to the press to trudge,   5
Where errors were not lessened, all may judge.
At thy return my blushing was not small,
My rambling brat (in print) should mother call;
I cast thee by as one unfit for light,
Thy visage was so irksome in my sight;   10
Yet being mine own, at length affection would
Thy blemishes amend, if so I could:
I washed thy face, but more defects I saw,
And rubbing off a spot, still made a flaw.
I stretched thy joints to make thee even feet,   15
Yet still thou run'st more hobbling than is meet;
In better dress to trim thee was my mind,
But nought save homespun cloth in the house I find.
In this array, 'mongst vulgars may'st thou roam;
In critics' hands beware thou dost not come;   20
And take thy way where yet thou are not known.
If for thy Father asked, say thou had'st none;
And for thy Mother, she alas is poor,
Which caused her thus to send thee out of door.

—ANNE BRADSTREET (1612?–1672)

QUESTIONS

1. Vocabulary: *halting* (5), *feet* (15), *meet* (16), *vulgars* (19). Lines 3–4 refer to the fact that Bradstreet's book *The Tenth Muse* was published in 1650 without her permission.
2. The poem is an extended personification addressing Bradstreet's book as a child. What similarities does the speaker find between a child and a book of poems? What does she plan to do now that her child has been put on public display?
3. Trace the developing attitudes of the speaker toward the child/book. Why does she instruct the child to deny it has a father (22)?

MindTap® Read, highlight, and take notes online.

The various figures of speech blend into each other, and it is sometimes difficult to classify a specific example as definitely metaphor or simile, symbol or allegory, understatement or irony, irony or paradox (some of these topics will be examined in the next two chapters). Often, a given example may exemplify two or more figures at once. In Wordsworth's "The world is too much with us" (page 48), when the winds are described as calm, "like sleeping flowers," the flowers function as part of a simile and are also personified as something that can sleep. The important consideration in reading poetry is not that we classify figures but that we construe them correctly.

Closely related to personification is **apostrophe,** which consists of addressing someone absent or dead or something nonhuman as if that person or thing were present and alive and could reply to what is being said. The speaker in A. E. Housman's "To an Athlete Dying Young" (page 385) apostrophizes a dead runner. William Blake apostrophizes a tiger throughout his famous poem (page 162) but does not otherwise personify it. In his poem "Bright Star," Keats apostrophizes *and* personifies a star, as he does with autumn in "To Autumn" (page 69).

Personification and apostrophe are both ways of giving life and immediacy to one's language, but since neither requires great imaginative power on the part of the poet—apostrophe especially does not—they may degenerate into mere mannerisms and occur as often in bad and mediocre poetry as in good—a fact that Shakespeare parodies in Bottom's apostrophe to night in *A Midsummer Night's Dream* (Act 5, scene 1):

O grim-looked night! O night with hue so black!
O night, which ever art when day is not!
O night, O night! Alack, alack, alack.

We need to distinguish between their effective use and their merely conventional use.

Bright Star

Bright star, would I were steadfast as thou art—
    Not in lone splendor hung aloft the night,
And watching, with eternal lids apart,
    Like nature's patient, sleepless Eremite,°   hermit
The moving waters at their priestlike task   5
    Of pure ablution° round earth's human shores,   cleansing
Or gazing on the new soft fallen mask
    Of snow upon the mountains and the moors—

No—yet still steadfast, still unchangeable,
    Pillowed upon my fair love's ripening breast,   10
To feel forever its soft fall and swell,
    Awake forever in a sweet unrest,
Still, still to hear her tender-taken breath,
And so live ever—or else swoon to death.

—JOHN KEATS (1795–1821)

QUESTIONS

1. The speaker longs to be as "steadfast" (1) as the star, yet lines 2–8 express his wish to be unlike the star in important ways. What are the qualities of the star that he would not want to emulate? Why would these be wrong for him in his situation?
2. Explore the apparent contradictions in the phrase "sweet unrest" (12). How do the contradictions anticipate the final line?
3. The speaker repeats "still" (13). What relevant denotations does the word evoke, and how does the repetition add intensity and meaning to this apostrophe?
4. Why is an apostrophe more effective here than a description of the star that does not address it?

In contrast to the preceding figures that compare *unlike* things are two figures that rest on congruences or correspondences. **Synecdoche** (the use of the part for the whole) and **metonymy** (the use of something closely related for the thing actually meant) are alike in that both substitute some significant detail or quality of an experience for the experience itself. Housman's Terence uses synecdoche when he declares that "malt does more than Milton can / To justify God's ways to man" (page 383), for "malt" means beer or ale, of which malt is an essential ingredient. On the other hand, when Terence advises "fellows whom it hurts to think" to "Look into the pewter pot / To see the world as the world's not," he is using metonymy, for by "pewter pot" he means the ale *in* the pot, not the pot itself, and by "world" he means human life and the conditions under which it is lived. Robert Frost uses metonymy in "'Out, Out—'" (page 136) when he describes an injured boy holding up his cut hand "as if to keep / The life from spilling," for literally he means to keep the blood from spilling. In each case, however, the poem gains in compactness, vividness, or meaning. Frost tells us both that the boy's hand is bleeding and that his life is in danger.

Many synecdoches and metonymies, of course, like many metaphors, have become so much a part of the language that they no longer strike us as figurative; this is the case with *redhead* for a red-haired person, *hands* for manual workers, *highbrow* for a sophisticate, *tongues* for languages, and a boiling *kettle* for the water *in* the kettle. Such figures are often called *dead metaphors* (where the word *metaphor* is itself a metonymy for all figurative speech). Synecdoche and metonymy are so much alike that it is hardly worthwhile to distinguish between them, and the latter term is increasingly used for both. In this book, *metonymy* will be used for both figures—that is, for any figure in which a part or something closely related is substituted for the thing literally meant.

Recall from the beginning of this chapter you learned that figurative language often provides a more effective means of saying what we mean than does direct statement. What are some of the reasons for that effectiveness?

First, figurative language affords us imaginative pleasure. Imagination might be described in one sense as that faculty or ability of the mind that proceeds by sudden leaps from one point to another, that goes up a stair by leaping in one jump from the bottom to the top rather than by climbing up one step at a time.* The mind takes delight in these sudden leaps, in seeing likenesses between unlike things. We have all probably taken pleasure in staring into a fire and seeing castles and cities and armies in it, or in looking into the clouds and shaping them into animals or faces, or in seeing a man in the moon. We name our plants and flowers after fancied resemblances: jack-in-the-pulpit, baby's breath, Queen Anne's lace. Figures of speech are therefore satisfying in themselves, providing us with a source of pleasure in the exercise of the imagination.

Second, figures of speech are a way of bringing additional imagery into verse, of making the abstract concrete, of making poetry more sensuous. When Tennyson's eagle falls "like a thunderbolt" (page 4), his swooping down for his prey is charged with energy, speed, and power; the simile also recalls that the Greek god Zeus was accompanied by an eagle and armed with lightning. When Emily Dickinson compares poetry to prancing coursers (page 42), she objectifies imaginative and rhythmical qualities by presenting them in visual terms. When Robert Browning compares the crisping waves to "fiery ringlets" (page 58), he starts with one image and transforms it into three. Figurative language is a way of augmenting the sense appeal of poetry.

Third, figures of speech are a way of adding emotional intensity to otherwise merely informative statements and of conveying attitudes along with information. If we say, "So-and-so is a jerk" or "My feet are killing me," our meaning is as much emotional as informative. When Philip Larkin's pathetic

---

*It is also the faculty of mind that is able to "picture" or "image" absent objects as if they were present. It was with imagination in this sense that the authors were concerned in the chapter on imagery.

escapist metaphorically compares books to "a load of crap" (page 25), the vulgar language not only expresses his distaste for reading, but intensifies the characterization of him as a man whose intellectual growth was stunted. As this example shows, the use of figures may be a poet's means of revealing the characteristics of a speaker—*how* he or she expresses a thought will define the attitudes or qualities as much as *what* that thought is. When Wilfred Owen compares a soldier caught in a gas attack to a man drowning under a green sea (page 7), he conveys a feeling of despair and suffocation as well as a visual image.

Fourth, figures of speech are an effective means of concentration, a way of saying much in brief compass. Like words, they may be multidimensional. Consider, for instance, the merits of comparing life to a candle, as Shakespeare does in a passage from *Macbeth* (pages 137–138). Life is like a candle in that it begins and ends in darkness; in that while it burns, it gives off light and energy, is active and colorful; in that it gradually consumes itself, gets shorter and shorter; in that it can be snuffed out at any moment; in that it is brief at best, burning only for a short duration. Possibly your imagination can suggest other similarities. But at any rate, Macbeth's compact, metaphorical description of life as a "brief candle" suggests certain truths about life that would require dozens of words to state in literal language. At the same time it makes the abstract concrete, provides imaginative pleasure, and adds a degree of emotional intensity.

It is as important, when analyzing and discussing a poem, to decide what it is that the figures accomplish as it is to identify them. Seeing a personification or a simile should lead to analytical questions: *What use is being made of this figure? How does it contribute to the experience of the poem?*

If we are to read poetry well, we must be able to respond to figurative language. Every use of figurative language involves a risk of misinterpretation, although the risk is well worth taking. For the person who can interpret the figure, the dividends are immense. Fortunately, all people have imagination to some degree, and imagination can be cultivated. Through practice, one's ability to interpret figures of speech can be enhanced.

EXERCISE

Decide whether the following quotations are literal or figurative. If figurative, identify the figure, explain what is being compared to what, and explain the appropriateness of the comparison. EXAMPLE: "Talent is a cistern; genius is a fountain." ANSWER: Metaphor. Talent = cistern; genius = fountain. Talent exists in finite supply, and can be used up. Genius is inexhaustible, ever renewing.

1. O tenderly the haughty day
   Fills his blue urn with fire.   —RALPH WALDO EMERSON

2. It is with words as with sunbeams—the more
   they are condensed, the deeper they burn. —ROBERT SOUTHEY
3. Joy and Temperance and Repose
   Slam the door on the doctor's nose. —ANONYMOUS
4. The pen is mightier than the sword. —EDWARD BULWER-LYTTON
5. The strongest oaths are straw
   To the fire i' the blood. —WILLIAM SHAKESPEARE
6. The Cambridge ladies . . . live in furnished souls. —e. e. cummings
7. Dorothy's eyes, with their long brown lashes,
   looked very much like her mother's. —LAETITIA JOHNSON
8. The tawny-hided desert crouches watching her. —FRANCIS THOMPSON
9. Let us eat and drink, for tomorrow we shall die. —ISAIAH 22:13
10. Let us eat and drink, for tomorrow
    we may die. —COMMON MISQUOTATION OF THE ABOVE

REVIEWING CHAPTER FIVE

1. Distinguish between language used literally and language used figuratively, and consider why poetry is often figurative.

2. Define the figures of comparison (simile and metaphor, personification and apostrophe), and rank them in order of their emotional effectiveness.

3. Define the figures of congruence or correspondence (synecdoche and metonymy).

4. Review the four major contributions of figurative language.

Metaphors

I'm a riddle in nine syllables,
An elephant, a ponderous house,
A melon strolling on two tendrils.
O red fruit, ivory, fine timbers!
This loaf's big with its yeasty rising.   5
Money's new-minted in this fat purse.
I'm a means, a stage, a cow in calf.
I've eaten a bag of green apples,
Boarded the train there's no getting off.

—SYLVIA PLATH (1932–1963)

QUESTIONS

1. Like its first metaphor, this poem is a riddle to be solved by identifying the literal terms of its metaphors. After you have identified the speaker ("riddle," "elephant," "house," "melon," "stage," "cow"), identify the literal meanings of the related metaphors ("syllables," "tendrils," "fruit," "ivory," "timbers," "loaf," "yeasty rising," "money," "purse," "train"). How do you interpret line 8?
2. How does the form of the poem relate to its content? Is this poem a complaint?

I taste a liquor never brewed

I taste a liquor never brewed—
From Tankards scooped in Pearl—
Not all the Vats upon the Rhine
Yield such an Alcohol!

Inebriate of Air—am I—   5
And Debauchee of Dew—
Reeling—thro endless summer days—
From inns of Molten Blue—

When "Landlords" turn the drunken Bee
Out of the Foxglove's door—   10
When Butterflies—renounce their "drams"—
I shall but drink the more!

Till Seraphs swing their snowy Hats—
And Saints—to windows run—
To see the little Tippler   15
Leaning against the—Sun—

—EMILY DICKINSON (1830–1886)

QUESTIONS

1. Vocabulary: *Debauchee* (6), *Foxglove* (10).
2. In this **extended metaphor,** what is being compared to alcoholic intoxication? The clues are given in the variety of "liquors" named or implied—"Air" (5), "Dew" (6), and the nectar upon which bees and butterflies feed.
3. What figurative meanings have the following details: "Tankards scooped in Pearl" (2), "inns of Molten Blue" (8), "snowy Hats" (13)?
4. The last stanza creates a stereotypical street scene in which neighbors observe the behavior of a drunkard. What do comic drunks lean against in the street? What unexpected attitude do the seraphs and saints display?

Toads

Why should I let the toad *work*
    Squat on my life?
Can't I use my wit as a pitchfork
    And drive the brute off?

Six days of the week it soils   5
    With its sickening poison—
Just for paying a few bills!
    That's out of proportion.

Lots of folk live on their wits:
    Lecturers, lispers,   10
Losels,° loblolly-men,° louts—   scoundrels; bumpkins
    They don't end as paupers;

Lots of folk live up lanes
    With fires in a bucket,
Eat windfalls and tinned sardines—   15
    They seem to like it.

Their nippers° have got bare feet,   children
    Their unspeakable wives
Are skinny as whippets—and yet
    No one actually *starves*.   20

Ah, were I courageous enough
    To shout *Stuff your pension!*
But I know, all too well, that's the stuff
    That dreams are made on;

For something sufficiently toad-like   25
    Squats in me, too;
Its hunkers° are heavy as hard luck,   haunches
    And cold as snow,

And will never allow me to blarney
    My way to getting   30
The fame and the girl and the money
    All at one sitting.

I don't say, one bodies the other
    One's spiritual truth;
But I do say it's hard to lose either,   35
    When you have both.

—PHILIP LARKIN (1922–1985)

QUESTIONS

1. The poem describes two "toads." Where is each located? How are they described? What are the antecedents of the pronouns "one" and "the other / One's" (33–34) respectively?
2. What characteristics in common have the people mentioned in lines 9–12? Those mentioned in lines 13–20?
3. Explain the pun in lines 22–23 and the literary allusion it leads into. (If you don't recognize the allusion, check Shakespeare's *The Tempest,* Act 4, scene 1, lines 156–158.)
4. The first "toad" is explicitly identified as "work" (1). The literal term for the second "toad" is not named. Why not? What do you take it to be?
5. What kind of person is the speaker? What are his attitudes toward work?

The Snowstorm

Announced by all the trumpets of the sky,
Arrives the snow, and, driving o'er the fields,
Seems nowhere to alight: the whited air
Hides hills and woods, the river, and the heaven,
And veils the farmhouse at the garden's end.   5
The sled and traveler stopped, the courier's feet
Delayed, all friends shut out, the housemates sit
Around the radiant fireplace, enclosed
In a tumultuous privacy of storm.
    Come see the north wind's masonry.   10
Out of an unseen quarry evermore
Furnished with tile, the fierce artificer
Curves his white bastions with projected roof
Round every windward stake, or tree, or door.
Speeding, the myriad-handed, his wild work   15
So fanciful, so savage, nought cares he
For number or proportion. Mockingly,
On coop or kennel he hangs Parian wreaths;
A swan-like form invests the hidden thorn;
Fills up the farmer's lane from wall to wall,   20

Maugre the farmer's sighs; and, at the gate,
A tapering turret overtops the work.
And when his hours are numbered and the world
Is all his own, retiring as he were not,
Leaves, when the sun appears, astonished Art   25
To mimic in slow structures, stone by stone,
Built in an age, the mad wind's night-work,
The frolic architecture of the snow.

—RALPH WALDO EMERSON (1803–1882)

QUESTIONS

1. Vocabulary: *Parian* (18); *thorn* (19); *Maugre* (21); "as he were not" (24) means "as if he had not existed."
2. From line 10 the poem presents an extended metaphor in the form of a personification. As what is the snowstorm personified? How do subsidiary metaphors support that personification (e.g., explain how "quarry" and "tile" [11–12] are used)?
3. The last sentence (23–28) has "he" as an understood subject, and introduces a second personification, "Art." Paraphrase the sentence and discuss how it extends the meaning of this descriptive poem.
4. The poem contains no end rhyme, but compensates with a richness of alliteration, assonance, consonance, and internal rhyme. Find as many examples as you can.

Ghost Yogurt

Line a deep bowl with cheesecloth—or in my
kitchen, with a pillowcase worn thin,
    threadbare as gauze. Dump in
a quart or so of yogurt. Let it strain.
    As the whey   5
drips through the sheer fabric, let it pool
    in the bowl awhile
and then discard. What yogurt will remain
is denser, more acerbic, almost dry.
    Less is more: a mere   10
spoonful of it now goes a long way.
    And we?
Are years the cheesecloth, so we drip and drain,
ourselves the milky residue we toss?
    Or is it time   15
that hour by day by year is strained through us,
steadily reduced to more itself,

stronger, purer, more distilled from less?
The either and the or: they both are true.
    We fall through time; it passes through   20
us. Therefore,
    both are less, both more,
nourished by refuse, by what we refuse,
    enriched by waste and loss.
The survivor is victorious.   25

—RACHEL HADAS (B. 1948)

QUESTIONS

1. Vocabulary: *cheesecloth* (1), *acerbic* (9).
2. Discuss the metaphor of the cheesecloth and the yogurt. What do they represent? Does their meaning change in the course of the poem?
3. Focus on the last line. Why is the "survivor" described as being "victorious"? Does this constitute an affirmative ending to the poem?

Divorce

Once, two spoons in bed,
now tined forks

across a granite table
and the knives they have hired.

—BILLY COLLINS (B. 1941)

QUESTIONS

1. Why is the domestic metaphor of cutlery appropriate here?
2. Discuss the double meaning of "spoons" (1).
3. What is the significance of the table at which they are sitting being made of "granite" (3)?
4. Who or what are "the knives they have hired" (4)?

A Valediction: Forbidding Mourning

As virtuous men pass mildly away,
    And whisper to their souls to go,
While some of their sad friends do say,
    The breath goes now, and some say, no:

So let us melt, and make no noise,   5
    No tear-floods, nor sigh-tempests move;
'Twere profanation of our joys
    To tell the laity our love.

Moving of th' earth brings harms and fears,
    Men reckon what it did and meant,   10
But trepidation of the spheres,
    Though greater far, is innocent.

Dull sublunary lovers' love
    (Whose soul is sense) cannot admit
Absence, because it doth remove   15
    Those things which elemented it.

But we by a love so much refined,
    That ourselves know not what it is,
Inter-assurèd of the mind,
    Care less, eyes, lips, and hands to miss.   20

Our two souls therefore, which are one,
    Though I must go, endure not yet
A breach, but an expansion,
    Like gold to airy thinness beat.

If they be two, they are two so   25
    As stiff twin compasses are two;
Thy soul, the fixed foot, makes no show
    To move, but doth, if th' other do.

And though it in the center sit,
    Yet when the other far doth roam,   30
It leans, and hearkens after it,
    And grows erect, as that comes home.

Such wilt thou be to me, who must
    Like th' other foot, obliquely run;
Thy firmness makes my circle just,   35
    And makes me end, where I begun.

— JOHN DONNE (1572–1631)

QUESTIONS

1. Vocabulary: *valediction* (title), *mourning* (title), *profanation* (7), *laity* (8), *trepidation* (11), *innocent* (12), *sublunary* (13), *elemented* (16). Line 11 is a reference to the spheres of the Ptolemaic cosmology, whose movements caused no such disturbance as does a movement of the earth—that is, an earthquake.
2. Is the speaker in the poem about to die? Or about to leave on a journey? (The answer may be found in a careful analysis of the simile in the last three stanzas and by noticing that the idea of dying in stanza 1 is introduced in a simile.)
3. The poem is organized around a contrast of two kinds of lovers: the "laity" (8) and, as their implied opposite, the priesthood. Are these terms literal or metaphorical? What is the essential difference between their two kinds of love? How, according to the speaker, does their behavior differ when they must separate from each other? What is the motivation of the speaker in this "valediction"?
4. Find and explain three similes and one metaphor used to describe the parting of true lovers. The figure in the last three stanzas is one of the most famous in English literature. Demonstrate its appropriateness by obtaining a drawing compass or by using two pencils to imitate the two legs.

To His Coy Mistress

Had we but world enough, and time,
This coyness, lady, were no crime.
We would sit down, and think which way
To walk, and pass our long love's day.
Thou by the Indian Ganges' side   5
Shouldst rubies find; I by the tide
Of Humber would complain. I would
Love you ten years before the Flood,
And you should, if you please, refuse
Till the conversion of the Jews.   10
My vegetable love should grow
Vaster than empires, and more slow;
An hundred years should go to praise
Thine eyes, and on thy forehead gaze;
Two hundred to adore each breast,   15
But thirty thousand to the rest;
An age at least to every part,
And the last age should show your heart.
For, lady, you deserve this state,
Nor would I love at lower rate.   20

But at my back I always hear
Time's wingèd chariot hurrying near;
And yonder all before us lie
Deserts of vast eternity.
Thy beauty shall no more be found,   25
Nor, in thy marble vault, shall sound
My echoing song; then worms shall try
That long-preserved virginity,
And your quaint honor turn to dust,
And into ashes all my lust: 30
The grave's a fine and private place,
But none, I think, do there embrace.
    Now therefore, while the youthful hue
Sits on thy skin like morning dew,
And while thy willing soul transpires   35
At every pore with instant fires,
Now let us sport us while we may,
And now, like amorous birds of prey,
Rather at once our time devour
Than languish in his slow-chapped power.   40
Let us roll all our strength and all
Our sweetness up into one ball,
And tear our pleasures with rough strife
Thorough° the iron gates of life.   through
Thus, though we cannot make our sun   45
Stand still, yet we will make him run.

—ANDREW MARVELL (1621–1678)

QUESTIONS

1. Vocabulary: *coy* (title), *Humber* (7), *transpires* (35). "Mistress" (title) has the now archaic meaning of *sweetheart;* "slow-chapped" (40) derives from *chap,* meaning *jaw.*
2. What is the speaker urging his sweetheart to do? Why is she being "coy"?
3. Outline the speaker's argument in three sentences that begin with the words *If, But,* and *Therefore.* Is the argument valid?
4. Explain the appropriateness of "vegetable love" (11). What simile in the third section contrasts with it and how? What image in the third section contrasts with the distance between the Ganges and the Humber? Of what would the speaker be "complaining" by the Humber (7)?
5. Explain the figures in lines 22, 24, and 40 and their implications.
6. Explain the last two lines. For what is "sun" a metonymy?
7. Is this poem principally about love or about time? If the latter, what might making love represent? What philosophy is the poet advancing here?

SUGGESTIONS FOR WRITING

1. Robert Frost has said that "poetry is what evaporates from all translations." Why might this be true? How much of a word can be translated?
2. Ezra Pound has defined great literature as "simply language charged with meaning to the utmost possible degree." Would this be a good definition of poetry? The word "charged" is roughly equivalent to *filled*. Why is "charged" a better word in Pound's definition?
3. In each of the following, the title announces a metaphor that dominates the poem. Write an essay describing the pair of objects and/or concepts compared in one of these poems. How does the figurative language help to communicate an idea with greater vividness or force than an ordinary, prosaic description could have achieved?
   a. Stevens, "The Snow Man" (page 68).
   b. Glück, "Labor Day" (page 14).
   c. Larkin, "Toads" (page 83).
   d. Herbert, "The Pulley" (page 251).
   e. Plath, "Lady Lazarus" (page 309).
   f. Trethewey, "Miscegenation" (page 412).

PRACTICE AP® WRITING PROMPTS

John Donne, "A Valediction: Forbidding Mourning" (pp. 86–87)

John Donne's "A Valediction: Forbidding Mourning" attempts to define true love. Read the poem carefully. Then write an essay in which you analyze how the author uses poetry itself to develop ideas about love. You may wish to focus on such elements as figurative language, poetic form, and word choice.

....

Andrew Marvell, "To His Coy Mistress" (pp. 88–89)

Andrew Marvell's "To His Coy Mistress" is a well-known Epicurean, or *carpe diem* ("seize the day"), poem, in which the speaker tries to seduce a woman to whom the poem is addressed. Read the poem carefully. Then write a well-organized essay in which you analyze the speaker's argument, showing how he employs such literary elements as simile, allusion, and hyperbole to help support his case.

....

CHAPTER SIX

Figurative Language 2
Symbol, Allegory

The Road Not Taken

Two roads diverged in a yellow wood,
And sorry I could not travel both
And be one traveler, long I stood
And looked down one as far as I could
To where it bent in the undergrowth;   5

Then took the other, as just as fair,
And having perhaps the better claim,
Because it was grassy and wanted wear;
Though as for that the passing there
Had worn them really about the same,   10

And both that morning equally lay
In leaves no step had trodden black.
Oh, I kept the first for another day!
Yet knowing how way leads on to way,
I doubted if I should ever come back.   15

I shall be telling this with a sigh
Somewhere ages and ages hence:
Two roads diverged in a wood, and I—

I took the one less traveled by,
And that has made all the difference.   20

—ROBERT FROST (1874–1963)

QUESTIONS

1. Does the speaker feel that he has made the wrong choice in taking the road "less traveled by" (19)? If not, why will he "sigh" (16)? What does he regret?
2. Why will the choice between two roads that seem very much alike make such a big difference many years later?

A **symbol** may be roughly defined as something that means *more* than what it is. "The Road Not Taken," for instance, concerns a choice made between two roads by a person out walking in the woods. He would like to explore both roads. He tells himself that he will explore one and then come back and explore the other, but he knows that he will probably be unable to do so. By the last stanza, however, we realize that the poem is about something more than the choice of paths in a wood, for that choice would be relatively unimportant, whereas this choice, the speaker believes, is one that will make a great difference in his life and is one that he will remember "with a sigh . . . ages and ages hence." We must interpret his choice of a road as a symbol for any choice in life between alternatives that appear almost equally attractive but will result through the years in a large difference in the kind of experience one knows.

Image, metaphor, and symbol shade into each other and are sometimes difficult to distinguish. In general, however, an image means only what it is; the figurative term in a metaphor means something other than what it is; and a symbol means what it is and something more, too. A symbol, that is, functions literally and figuratively at the same time.* If I say that a shaggy brown dog was rubbing its back against a white picket fence, I am talking about nothing but a dog (and a picket fence) and am therefore presenting an image. If I say, "Some dirty dog stole my wallet at the party," I am not talking about a dog at all and am therefore using a metaphor. But if I say, "You can't teach an old dog new tricks," I am talking not only about dogs but about living creatures of any species and am therefore speaking symbolically. Images, of course, do not cease to be images when they become incorporated in metaphors or symbols. If we are discussing

---

* This account does not hold for nonliterary symbols such as the letters of the alphabet and algebraic signs (the symbol ∞ for infinity or = for equals). With these, the symbol is meaningless except as it stands for something else, and the connection between the sign and what it stands for is purely arbitrary.

the sensuous qualities of "The Road Not Taken," we should refer to the two leaf-strewn roads in the yellow wood as an image; if we are discussing the significance of the poem, we talk about the roads as symbols.

The symbol is the richest and, at the same time, the most difficult of the poetic figures. Both its richness and its difficulty result from its imprecision. Although the poet may pin down the meaning of a symbol to something fairly definite and precise, more often the symbol is so general in its meaning that it can suggest a great variety of specific meanings. It is like an opal that flashes out different colors when slowly turned in the light. "The Road Not Taken," for instance, concerns some choice in life, but what choice? Was it a choice of profession? A choice of residence? A choice of mate? It might be any, all, or none of these. We cannot determine what particular choice the poet had in mind, if any, and it is not important that we do so. It is enough if we see in the poem an expression of regret that the possibilities of life experience are so sharply limited. The speaker in the poem would have liked to explore both roads, but he could explore only one. The person with a craving for life, whether satisfied or dissatisfied with the choices he has made, will always long for the realms of experience that he had to forgo. Because the symbol is a rich one, the poem suggests other meanings too. It affirms a belief in the possibility of choice and says something about the nature of choice—how each choice narrows the range of possible future choices, so that we make our lives as we go, both freely choosing and being determined by past choices. Although not a philosophical poem, it obliquely comments on the issue of free will and determinism and indicates the poet's own position. It can do all these things, concretely and compactly, by its use of an effective symbol.

Symbols vary in the degree of identification and definition given them by their authors. In this poem Frost forces us to interpret the choice of roads symbolically by the degree of importance he gives it in the last stanza. Sometimes poets are much more specific in identifying their symbols. Sometimes they do not identify them at all. Consider, for instance, the next two poems.

A Noiseless Patient Spider

A noiseless patient spider,
I marked where on a little promontory it stood isolated,
Marked how to explore the vacant vast surrounding,
It launched forth filament, filament, filament, out of itself,
Ever unreeling them, ever tirelessly speeding them.   5

And you, O my soul where you stand,
Surrounded, detached, in measureless oceans of space,
Ceaselessly musing, venturing, throwing, seeking the spheres
    to connect them,
Till the bridge you will need be formed, till the ductile
    anchor hold,
Till the gossamer thread you fling catch somewhere,
    O my soul.   10

—WALT WHITMAN (1819–1892)

In the first stanza, the speaker describes a spider's apparently tireless effort to attach its thread to some substantial support so that it can begin constructing a web. The speaker reveals his attentive interest by the hinted personification of the spider, and his sympathy with it is expressed in the overstatement of size and distance—he is trying to perceive the world as a spider sees it from a "promontory" surrounded by vast space. He even attributes a human motive to the spider: exploration, rather than instinctive web-building. Nevertheless, the first stanza is essentially literal—the close observation of an actual spider at its task. In the second stanza the speaker explicitly interprets the symbolic meaning of what he has observed: his soul (personified by apostrophe and by the capabilities assigned to it) is like the spider in its constant striving. But the soul's purpose is to find spiritual or intellectual certainties in the vast universe it inhabits. The symbolic meaning is richer than a mere comparison; although a spider's actual purpose is limited to its instinctive drives, the human soul strives for much more, in a much more complex "surrounding." And, of course, the result of the soul's symbolized striving is much more open-ended than is the attempt of a spider to spin a web, as the paradoxical language ("Surrounded, detached," "ductile anchor") implies. *Can* the human soul connect the celestial spheres?

QUESTIONS

1. In "Harlem" (page 73) Langston Hughes compares a frustrated dream to a bomb. Whitman compares the striving human soul to a spider. Why is Hughes's comparison a metaphor and Whitman's a symbol? What additional comparison does Whitman make to the soul's quest? What figure of speech is it?
2. In what ways are the spider and the soul contrasted? What do the contrasts contribute to the meaning of the symbol?
3. Can the questing soul represent human actions other than the search for spiritual certainties?

The Sick Rose

O Rose, thou art sick!
The invisible worm
That flies in the night,
In the howling storm,
Has found out thy bed   5
Of crimson joy,
And his dark secret love
Does thy life destroy.

—WILLIAM BLAKE (1757–1827)

QUESTIONS

1. What figures of speech do you find in the poem in addition to symbol? How do they contribute to its force or meaning?
2. Several symbolic interpretations of this poem are given next. Can you think of others?
3. Should symbolic meanings be sought for the night and the storm? If so, what meanings would you suggest?

In "A Noiseless Patient Spider" the symbolic meaning of the spider is identified and named. By contrast, in "The Sick Rose" no meanings are explicitly indicated for the rose and the worm. Indeed, we are not *compelled* to assign them specific meanings. The poem might literally be read as being about a rose that has been attacked on a stormy night by a cankerworm.

The organization of "The Sick Rose" is so rich, however, and its language so powerful that the rose and the worm refuse to remain *merely* a flower and an insect. The rose, apostrophized and personified in the first line, has traditionally been a symbol of feminine beauty and love, as well as of sensual pleasures. "Bed" can refer to a woman's bed as well as to a flower bed. "Crimson joy" suggests the intense pleasure of passionate lovemaking as well as the brilliant beauty of a red flower. The "dark secret love" of the "invisible worm" is more strongly suggestive of a concealed or illicit love affair than of the feeding of a cankerworm on a plant, though it fits that too. For all these reasons the rose almost immediately suggests a woman and the worm her secret lover—and the poem suggests the corruption of innocent but physical love by concealment and deceit.

But the possibilities do not stop there. The worm is a common symbol or metonymy for death; and for readers steeped in Milton (as Blake was) it recalls the "undying worm" of *Paradise Lost*, Milton's metaphor for the snake (or Satan in the form of a snake) that tempted Eve. Meanings multiply also for the reader who is familiar with Blake's other writings.

Thus, "The Sick Rose" has been variously interpreted as referring to the destruction of joyous physical love by jealousy, deceit, concealment, or the possessive instinct; of innocence by experience; of humanity by Satan; of imagination and joy by analytic reason; of life by death. We cannot say what specifically the poet had in mind, nor need we do so. A symbol defines an *area* of meaning, and any interpretation that falls within that area is permissible. In Blake's poem the rose stands for something beautiful, or desirable, or good. The worm stands for some corrupting agent. Within these limits, the meaning is largely "open." And because the meaning is open, the reader is justified in bringing personal experience to its interpretation. Blake's poem, for instance, might remind someone of a gifted friend whose promise has been destroyed by drug addiction.

Between the extremes exemplified by "A Noiseless Patient Spider" and "The Sick Rose," a poem may exercise all degrees of control over the range and meaning of its symbolism. Consider another example:

Digging

Between my finger and my thumb
The squat pen rests; snug as a gun.

Under my window, a clean rasping sound
When the spade sinks into gravelly ground:
My father, digging. I look down   5

Till his straining rump among the flowerbeds
Bends low, comes up twenty years away
Stooping in rhythm through potato drills
Where he was digging.

The coarse boot nestled on the lug, the shaft   10
Against the inside knee was levered firmly.
He rooted out tall tops, buried the bright edge deep
To scatter new potatoes that we picked
Loving their cool hardness in our hands.

By God, the old man could handle a spade.   15
Just like his old man.

My grandfather cut more turf in a day
Than any other man on Toner's bog.

Once I carried him milk in a bottle
Corked sloppily with paper. He straightened up   20
To drink it, then fell to right away
Nicking and slicing neatly, heaving sods
Over his shoulder, going down and down
For the good turf. Digging.

The cold smell of potato mould, the squelch and slap   25
Of soggy peat, the curt cuts of an edge
Through living roots awaken in my head.
But I've no spade to follow men like them.

Between my finger and my thumb
The squat pen rests.   30
I'll dig with it.

—SEAMUS HEANEY (1939–2013)

QUESTIONS

1. Vocabulary: *drills* (8), *fell to* (21). In Ireland, "turf" (17) is a block of peat dug from a bog; when dried, it is used as fuel.
2. What emotional responses are evoked by the imagery?

On the literal level, this poem presents a writer who interrupts himself to have a look at his father digging in a flower garden below his window. He is reminded of his father twenty years earlier digging potatoes for harvesting, and by that memory he is drawn farther back to his grandfather digging peat from a bog for fuel. The memories are vivid and appealing and rich in imagery, but the writer is not like his forebears; he has "no spade to follow" their examples. And so, with a trace of regret, he decides that his writing will have to be his substitute for their manual tasks.

But the title and the emphasis on varieties of the same task carried out in several different ways over a span of generations alert the reader to the need to discover the further significance of this literal statement. The last line is metaphorical, comparing digging to writing (and thus is itself not symbolic, for on a literal level one cannot dig with a pen). The metaphor, however, suggesting that the writer will commit himself to exploring the kinds of memories in this poem, invites an interpretation of the literal forms of digging. We notice then that the father has been involved in two sorts—the practical, backbreaking task of digging up potatoes to be gathered by the children, and twenty years later the relatively easy chore of digging in flowerbeds so as to encourage the growth of ornamental plants.

There is a progression represented in the father's activities, from the necessary and arduous earlier life to the leisurely growing of flowers. Farther back in time, the grandfather's labors were deeper, heavier, and more essential, cutting and digging the material that would be used for heating and cooking—cooking potatoes, we should assume. The grandfather digs deeper and deeper, always in quest of the best peat, "the good turf."

Symbolically, then, digging has meanings that relate to basic needs—for warmth, for sustenance, for beauty, and for the personal satisfaction of doing a job well. In the concluding metaphor, another basic need is implied: the need to remember and confront one's origins, to find oneself in a continuum of meaningful activities, to assert the relevance and importance of one's vocation. And it is not coincidental that an Irish poet should find symbolic meanings in a confluence of Irish materials—from peat bogs to potatoes to poets and writers, that long-beleaguered island has asserted its special and distinct identity. Nor is it coincidental that Heaney selected this to be the opening poem in his first book of poetry: "Digging" is what his poetry does.

Meanings ray out from a symbol, like the corona around the sun or like connotations around a richly suggestive word. But the very fact that a symbol may be so rich in meanings requires that we use the greatest tact in its interpretation. Although Blake's "The Sick Rose" might, because of personal association, remind us of a friend destroyed by drug addiction, it would be unwise to say that Blake uses the rose to symbolize a gifted person succumbing to drug addiction, for this interpretation is private, idiosyncratic, and narrow. The poem allows it, but does not itself suggest it.

Moreover, we should never assume that because the meaning of a symbol is more or less open, we may make it mean anything we choose. We would be wrong, for instance, in interpreting the choice in "The Road Not Taken" as some choice between good and evil, for the poem tells us that the two roads are much alike and that both lie "In leaves no step had trodden black." Whatever the choice is, it is a choice between two goods. Whatever our interpretation of a symbolic poem, it must be tied firmly to the facts of the poem. We must not let loose of the string and let our imaginations go ballooning up among the clouds. Because the symbol is capable of adding so many dimensions to a poem, it is a peculiarly effective resource for the poet, but it is also peculiarly susceptible to misinterpretation by the incautious reader.

Accurate interpretation of the symbol requires delicacy, tact, and good sense. The reader must maintain balance while walking a tightrope between too little and too much—between underinterpretation and overinterpretation. If the reader falls off, however, it is much more desirable to fall off on the side of too little. Someone who reads "The Road Not

Taken" as being only about a choice between two roads in a wood has at least understood part of the experience that the poem communicates, but the reader who reads into it anything imaginable might as well discard the poem and simply daydream.

Above all, we should avoid the tendency to indulge in symbol-hunting and to see virtually anything in a poem as symbolic. It is preferable to miss a symbol than to try to find one in every line of a poem.

To the Virgins, to Make Much of Time

Gather ye rosebuds while ye may,
    Old Time is still a-flying;
And this same flower that smiles today
    Tomorrow will be dying.

The glorious lamp of heaven, the Sun,   5
    The higher he's a-getting,
The sooner will his race be run,
    And nearer he's to setting.

That age is best which is the first,
    When youth and blood are warmer;   10
But being spent, the worse, and worst
    Times still succeed the former.

Then be not coy, but use your time;
    And while ye may, go marry;
For having lost but once your prime,   15
    You may forever tarry.

—ROBERT HERRICK (1591–1674)

QUESTIONS

1. The first two stanzas might be interpreted literally if the third and fourth stanzas did not force us to interpret them symbolically. What do the "rosebuds" symbolize (stanza 1)? What does the course of a day symbolize (stanza 2)? Does the poet narrow the meaning of the rosebud symbol in the last stanza or merely name *one* of its specific meanings?
2. How does the title help us interpret the meaning of the symbol? Why is "virgins" a more meaningful word than, for example, *maidens*?
3. Why is such haste necessary in gathering the rosebuds? True, the blossoms die quickly, but others will replace them. Who *really* is dying?

4. What are "the worse, and worst" times (11)? Why?
5. Why is the wording of the poem better than these possible alternatives: *blooms* for "smiles" (3); *course* for "race" (7); *used* for "spent" (11); *spend* for "use" (13)?

Allegory is a narrative or description that has a second meaning beneath the surface. Although the surface story or description may have its own interest, the author's major interest is in the ulterior meaning. When Pharoah in the Bible, for instance, has a dream in which seven fat kine (cattle) are devoured by seven lean kine, the story does not really become significant until Joseph interprets its allegorical meaning: that Egypt is to enjoy seven years of fruitfulness and prosperity followed by seven years of famine. Allegory has been defined sometimes as an extended metaphor and sometimes as a series of related symbols. But it is usually distinguishable from both of these. It is unlike extended metaphor in that it involves a *system* of related comparisons rather than one comparison drawn out. It differs from symbolism in that it puts less emphasis on the images for their own sake and more on their ulterior meanings. Also, these meanings are more fixed. In allegory there is usually a one-to-one correspondence between the details and a single set of ulterior meanings. In complex allegories the details may have more than one meaning, but these meanings tend to be definite. Meanings do not ray out from allegory as they do from a symbol.

Allegory is less popular in modern literature than it was in medieval and Renaissance writing, and it is much less often found in short poems than in long narrative works such as *The Faerie Queene*, *Everyman*, and *Pilgrim's Progress*. It has sometimes, especially with political allegory, been used to disguise meaning rather than reveal it (or, rather, to disguise it from some people while revealing it to others). Although less rich than the symbol, allegory is an effective way of making the abstract concrete and has occasionally been used effectively even in fairly short poems.

Redemption

Having been tenant long to a rich Lord,
Not thriving, I resolvèd to be bold,
And make a suit unto him, to afford
A new small-rented lease and cancel the old.
In heaven at his manor I him sought: 5
They told me there that he was lately gone
About some land which he had dearly bought
Long since on earth, to take possession.
I straight returned, and knowing his great birth,

Sought him accordingly in great resorts;   10
In cities, theaters, gardens, parks, and courts:
At length I heard a ragged noise and mirth
Of thieves and murderers; there I him espied,
Who straight, "Your suit is granted," said, and died.

—GEORGE HERBERT (1593–1633)

QUESTIONS

1. Vocabulary: suit (3, 14), *afford* (3), *dearly* (7).
2. On the surface this poem tells about a business negotiation between a tenant landholder and his landlord. What clues indicate that the poem really concerns something deeper?
3. Who is the "rich Lord"? Who is the tenant? What is the old lease? What is the new one? Where does the tenant find his Lord? What is the significance of his suit being granted just as the landlord dies?
4. What are the implications of the landlord's having gone to take possession of some land which he "had dearly bought / Long since on earth"? In what senses (on both levels of meaning) is the landlord of "great birth"? What is "a ragged noise and mirth / Of thieves and murderers"?

MindTap® Read, highlight, and take notes online.

EXERCISES

1. Determine whether "sleep" in the following poems is literal, a symbol, or a metaphor (or simile).
    a. "Stopping by Woods on a Snowy Evening" (page 153).
    b. "The Chimney Sweeper" (page 120).
    c. "Is my team plowing" (page 29).
    d. "The Second Coming" (page 417).
2. Donne's "The Flea" (page 174) and Dickinson's "I heard a Fly buzz—when I died" (page 237) deal with common insect pests. Which of them is symbolic? Explain your choice.
3. What do Blake's lamb and tiger symbolize (page 162)?
4. Determine whether the following poems are predominantly symbolic or literal.
    a. "Because I could not stop for Death" (page 106).
    b. "The Snow Man" (page 68).
    c. "Song: Go and catch a falling star" (page 367).
    d. "Blackberry Eating" (page 244).
    e. "Musée des Beaux Arts" (page 356).
    f. "Richard Cory" (page 17).
    g. "The Wild Swans at Coole" (page 418).
    h. "Desert Places" (page 48).

REVIEWING CHAPTER SIX

1. Using examples from the poems that follow, explore how symbols must read both literally and figuratively.
2. Show that the context of a poem determines the limits of its symbolic meanings. (As an exercise, you might want to examine the multiple possible meanings of a particular symbol, and eliminate those that are ruled out by the context.)
3. Discuss the difference between symbol and allegory, if possible accounting for the fact that allegory is no longer as popular a figure as it once was.

Purple Bathing Suit

I like watching you garden
with your back to me in your purple bathing suit:
your back is my favorite part of you,
the part furthest away from your mouth.

You might give some thought to that mouth.   5
Also to the way you weed, breaking
the grass off at ground level
when you should pull it up by the roots.

How many times do I have to tell you
how the grass spreads, your little   10
pile notwithstanding, in a dark mass which
by smoothing over the surface you have finally
fully obscured? Watching you

stare into space in the tidy
rows of the vegetable garden, ostensibly   15
working hard while actually
doing the worst job possible, I think

you are a small irritating purple thing
and I would like to see you walk off the face of the earth
because you are all that's wrong with my life   20
and I need you and I claim you.

—LOUISE GLÜCK (B. 1943)

QUESTIONS

1. Vocabulary: *notwithstanding* (11), *ostensibly* (15).
2. Is the speaker in this poem a man or a woman? How can you tell?
3. Is the person in the purple bathing suit a man or a woman? How can you tell?
4. Is the purple bathing suit symbolic? If so, of what?
5. Why does the speaker call the individual in the bathing suit "a small irritating purple thing" (18)?
6. Discuss the seeming contradiction in the last two lines. What do they suggest about the relationship?

Whitman and the Moth

Van Wyck Brooks tells us Whitman in old age
Sat by a pond in nothing but his hat,
Crowding his final notebooks page by page
With names of trees, birds, bugs, and things like that.

The war could never break him, though he'd seen   5
Horrors in hospitals to chill the soul.
But now, preserved, the Union had turned mean:
Evangelizing greed was in control.

Good reason to despair, yet grief was purged
By tracing how creation reigned supreme.   10
A pupa cracked, a butterfly emerged:
America, still unfolding from its dream.

Sometimes he rose and waded in the pond,
Soothing his aching feet in the sweet mud.
A moth he knew, of which he had grown fond,   15
Perched on his hand as if to draw his blood.

But they were joined by what each couldn't do,
The meeting point where great art comes to pass—
Whitman, who danced and sang but never flew,
The moth, which had not written "Leaves of Grass,"   20

Composed a picture of the interchange
Between the mind and all that it transcends
Yet must stay near. No, there was nothing strange
In how he put his hand out to make friends

With such a fragile creature, soft as dust.   25
Feeling the pond cool as the light grew dim,
He blessed new life, though it had only just
Arrived in time to see the end of him.

—CLIVE JAMES (B. 1939)

QUESTIONS

1. Van Wyck Brooks (1886–1963) was a biographer of Walt Whitman and other American writers. Vocabulary: *pupa* (11).
2. Analyze the symbol of the moth. What connotations are attached to this particular insect?
3. What contrast does the poem highlight between Walt Whitman, a human being, and a mere moth? What is the significance of their "meeting point" in line 18?

You, Andrew Marvell

And here face down beneath the sun
And here upon earth's noonward height
To feel the always coming on
The always rising of the night:

To feel creep up the curving east   5
The earthly chill of dusk and slow
Upon those under lands the vast
And ever-climbing shadow grow

And strange at Ecbatan the trees
Take leaf by leaf the evening strange   10
The flooding dark about their knees
The mountains over Persia change

And now at Kermanshah the gate
Dark empty and the withered grass
And through the twilight now the late   15
Few travelers in the westward pass

And Baghdad darken and the bridge
Across the silent river gone
And through Arabia the edge
Of evening widen and steal on   20

And deepen on Palmyra's street
The wheel rut in the ruined stone
And Lebanon fade out and Crete
High through the clouds and overblown

And over Sicily the air   25
Still flashing with the landward gulls
And loom and slowly disappear
The sails above the shadowy hulls

And Spain go under and the shore
Of Africa the gilded sand   30
And evening vanish and no more
The low pale light across that land

Nor now the long light on the sea:
And here face downward in the sun
To feel how swift how secretly   35
The shadow of the night comes on ...

—ARCHIBALD MACLEISH (1892–1982)

QUESTIONS

1. We ordinarily speak of *nightfall*; why does MacLeish speak of the *rising* of the night? What implicit metaphorical comparison is suggested by phrases like "rising of the night" (4), "the flooding dark" (11), "the bridge / Across the silent river gone" (17–18), "deepen on Palmyra's street" (21), "Spain go under" (29), and so on?
2. Does the comparative lack of punctuation serve any function? What is the effect of the repetition of *and* throughout the poem?
3. Ecbatan (9) was founded in 700 B.C. and is associated in history with Cyrus the Great, founder of the Persian Empire, and with Alexander the Great. It and Kermanshah were ancient cities of Persia. Where are Baghdad, Palmyra, Lebanon, and Crete?

Fire and Ice

Some say the world will end in fire,
Some say in ice.
From what I've tasted of desire
I hold with those who favor fire.
But if it had to perish twice,   5

I think I know enough of hate
To say that for destruction ice
Is also great
And would suffice.

—ROBERT FROST (1874–1963)

QUESTIONS

1. Who are "Some" (1–2)? To which two theories do lines 1–2 refer? (In answering, it might help you to know that the poem was published in 1920.)
2. What do "fire" and "ice," respectively, symbolize? What two meanings has "the world"?
3. The poem ends with an *understatement* (see Chapter 7). How does it affect the tone of the poem?

Because I could not stop for Death

Because I could not stop for Death—
He kindly stopped for me—
The Carriage held but just Ourselves—
And Immortality.

We slowly drove—He knew no haste   5
And I had put away
My labor and my leisure too,
For His Civility—

We passed the School, where Children strove
At Recess—in the Ring—   10
We passed the Fields of Gazing Grain—
We passed the Setting Sun—

Or rather—He passed Us—
The Dews drew quivering and chill—
For only Gossamer, my Gown—   15
My Tippet—only Tulle—

We paused before a House that seemed
A Swelling of the Ground—
The Roof was scarcely visible—
The Cornice—in the Ground—   20

Since then—'tis Centuries—and yet
Feels shorter than the Day
I first surmised the Horses' Heads
Were toward Eternity—

—EMILY DICKINSON (1830–1886)

QUESTIONS

1. Vocabulary: *Gossamer* (15); *Tippet, Tulle* (16); *surmised* (23).
2. Define the stages of this journey—where it begins, what events occur on the way, and its destination. Where is the speaker *now*? What is her present emotional condition?
3. To what is "Death" (1) being compared?
4. Identify the allegorical implications of the events. For example, what aspects of human life are implied by the three items that are "passed" in stanza 3? What is the "House" (17) before which the carriage pauses, and why does it pause there?
5. Explore the three time references in the concluding stanza. Can you explain why the passage of "Centuries ... Feels shorter than the Day" the speaker guessed that her journey was proceeding "toward Eternity"? For what is "Eternity" a metonymy? Has the carriage reached that destination yet?

Hymn to God, My God, in My Sickness

Since I am coming to that holy room
    Where, with thy choir of saints for evermore,
I shall be made thy music, as I come
    I tune the instrument here at the door,
    And what I must do then, think now before.   5

Whilst my physicians by their love are grown
    Cosmographers, and I their map, who lie
Flat on this bed, that by them may be shown
    That this is my southwest discovery,
    Per fretum febris,° by these straits to die,   through the 10
                                      raging of fever

I joy that in these straits I see my west;
    For though those currents yield return to none,
What shall my west hurt me? As west and east
    In all flat maps (and I am one) are one,
    So death doth touch the resurrection.   15

Is the Pacific Sea my home? Or are
    The eastern riches? Is Jerusalem?
Anyan° and Magellan and Gibraltar,   Bering Strait
    All straits, and none but straits, are ways to them,
    Whether where Japhet dwelt, or Cham, or Shem.   20

We think that Paradise and Calvary,
    Christ's cross and Adam's tree, stood in one place;
Look, Lord, and find both Adams met in me;
    As the first Adam's sweat surrounds my face,
    May the last Adam's blood my soul embrace.   25

So, in his purple wrapped receive me, Lord;
    By these his thorns give me his other crown;
And as to others' souls I preached thy word,
    Be this my text, my sermon to mine own:
    Therefore that he may raise, the Lord throws down.   30

—JOHN DONNE (1572–1631)

QUESTIONS

1. Vocabulary: *Cosmographers* (7).
2. What is the speaker doing in stanza 1? What are "that holy room" (1) and "the instrument" (4)? For what is the speaker preparing himself?
3. In Donne's time, explorers were seeking a Northwest Passage to Asia to match discovery of a southwest passage, the Straits of Magellan. Why is "southwest" more appropriate to the speaker's condition than "northwest"? In what ways is his fever like a strait? What denotations of "straits" (10) are relevant? What do the straits symbolize?
4. In what ways does the speaker's body resemble a map? Although the map is meta-phorical, its parts are symbolic. What do west and east symbolize? Explain how the west and east "are one" (14).
5. Japhet, Cham (or Ham), and Shem (20)—sons of Noah—were in Christian legend the ancestors of the races of man, roughly identified as European, African, and Asian. In what ways are the Pacific Ocean, the East Indies, and Jerusalem (16–17) fitting symbols for the speaker's destination?
6. According to early Christian thinking, the Garden of Eden and Calvary were located in the same place. How does this tie in with the poem's geographical symbolism? Because Adam is said to prefigure Christ (Romans 5:12–21), Christ is called the second Adam. What connection is there between Adam's "sweat" (24) and Christ's "blood" (25)? How do the two Adams meet in the speaker? What do blood and sweat (together and separately) symbolize?

7. For what are "eastern riches" (17), "his purple" (26), and "his thorns" (27) metonymies? What do "purple" and "thorns" symbolize? What is Christ's "other crown" (27)?
8. How does this poem explain human suffering and give it meaning?

Spinster

Now this particular girl
During a ceremonious April walk
With her latest suitor
Found herself, of a sudden, intolerably struck
By the birds' irregular babel   5
And the leaves' litter.

By this tumult afflicted, she
Observed her lover's gestures unbalance the air,
His gait stray uneven
Through a rank wilderness of fern and flower.   10
She judged petals in disarray,
The whole season, sloven.

How she longed for winter then!—
Scrupulously austere in its order
Of white and black   15
Ice and rock, each sentiment within border,
And heart's frosty discipline
Exact as a snowflake.

But here—a burgeoning
Unruly enough to pitch her five queenly wits   20
Into vulgar motley—
A treason not to be borne. Let idiots
Reel giddy in bedlam spring:
She withdrew neatly.

And round her house she set   25
Such a barricade of barb and check
Against mutinous weather
As no mere insurgent man could hope to break
With curse, fist, threat
Or love, either.   30

—SYLVIA PLATH (1932–1963)

QUESTIONS

1. Vocabulary: *babel* (5), *tumult* (7), *sloven* (12), *burgeoning* (19), *motley* (21).
2. Discuss the contrast as presented here between spring and winter. Which does the "particular girl" (1) seem to prefer?
3. Why does the woman in the poem become a spinster?
4. What is the woman's attitude toward romantic love?

Ulysses

It little profits that an idle king,
By this still hearth, among these barren crags,
Matched with an agèd wife, I mete and dole
Unequal laws unto a savage race,
That hoard, and sleep, and feed, and know not me.   5
I cannot rest from travel; I will drink
Life to the lees. All times I have enjoyed
Greatly, have suffered greatly, both with those
That loved me, and alone; on shore, and when
Through scudding drifts the rainy Hyades   10
Vext the dim sea. I am become a name;
For always roaming with a hungry heart
Much have I seen and known,—cities of men,
And manners, climates, councils, governments,
Myself not least, but honored of them all;   15
And drunk delight of battle with my peers,
Far on the ringing plains of windy Troy.
I am a part of all that I have met;
Yet all experience is an arch wherethrough
Gleams that untraveled world, whose margin fades   20
For ever and for ever when I move.
How dull it is to pause, to make an end,
To rust unburnished, not to shine in use!
As though to breathe were life! Life piled on life
Were all too little, and of one to me   25
Little remains; but every hour is saved
From that eternal silence, something more,
A bringer of new things; and vile it were
For some three suns to store and hoard myself,
And this gray spirit yearning in desire   30
To follow knowledge like a sinking star,
Beyond the utmost bound of human thought.

This is my son, mine own Telemachus,
To whom I leave the scepter and the isle—
Well-loved of me, discerning to fulfill   35
This labor, by slow prudence to make mild
A rugged people, and through soft degrees
Subdue them to the useful and the good.
Most blameless is he, centered in the sphere
Of common duties, decent not to fail   40
In offices of tenderness, and pay
Meet adoration to my household gods,
When I am gone. He works his work, I mine.

There lies the port; the vessel puffs her sail:
There gloom the dark, broad seas. My mariners,   45
Souls that have toiled, and wrought, and thought with me—
That ever with a frolic welcome took
The thunder and the sunshine, and opposed
Free hearts, free foreheads—you and I are old;
Old age hath yet his honor and his toil.   50
Death closes all; but something ere the end,
Some work of noble note, may yet be done,
Not unbecoming men that strove with Gods.
The lights begin to twinkle from the rocks;
The long day wanes; the slow moon climbs; the deep   55
Moans round with many voices. Come, my friends,
'Tis not too late to seek a newer world.
Push off, and sitting well in order smite
The sounding furrows; for my purpose holds
To sail beyond the sunset, and the baths   60
Of all the western stars, until I die.
It may be that the gulfs will wash us down;
It may be we shall touch the Happy Isles,
And see the great Achilles, whom we knew.
Though much is taken, much abides; and though   65
We are not now that strength which in old days
Moved earth and heaven, that which we are, we are:
One equal temper of heroic hearts,
Made weak by time and fate, but strong in will
To strive, to seek, to find, and not to yield.   70

—ALFRED, LORD TENNYSON (1809–1892)

QUESTIONS

1. Vocabulary: *lees* (7), *Hyades* (10), *meet* (42).
2. Ulysses, king of Ithaca, is a legendary Greek hero, a major figure in Homer's *Iliad,* the hero of Homer's *Odyssey,* and a minor figure in Dante's *Divine Comedy.* After ten years at the siege of Troy, Ulysses set sail for home but, having incurred the wrath of the god of the sea, he was subjected to storms and vicissitudes and was forced to wander for another ten years, having many adventures and seeing most of the Mediterranean world before again reaching Ithaca, his wife, and his son. Once back home, according to Dante, he still wished to travel and "to follow virtue and knowledge." In Tennyson's poem, Ulysses is represented as about to set sail on a final voyage from which he will not return. Locate Ithaca on a map. Where exactly, in geographical terms, does Ulysses intend to sail (59–64)? (The Happy Isles were the Elysian fields, or Greek paradise; Achilles was another Greek prince, the hero of the *Iliad,* who was killed at the siege of Troy.)
3. Ulysses's speech is divided into three sections, beginning at lines 1, 33, and 44. What is the topic or purpose of each section? To whom, specifically, is the third section addressed? To whom, would you infer, are sections 1 and 2 addressed? Where do you visualize Ulysses as standing during his speech?
4. Characterize Ulysses. What kind of person is he as Tennyson represents him?
5. What way of life is symbolized by Ulysses? Find as many evidences as you can that Ulysses's desire for travel represents something more than mere wanderlust and wish for adventure.
6. Give two symbolic implications of the westward direction of Ulysses's journey.
7. Interpret lines 18–21 and 26–29. What metaphor is implied in line 23? What is symbolized by "The thunder and the sunshine" (48)? What do the two metonymies in line 49 stand for?

SUGGESTIONS FOR WRITING

The following poems may be regarded as character sketches, but in each case the richness and suggestiveness of the presentation refer to the symbolic nature of the sketch. Of what are the characters symbolic, and what clues does the poem present that make a symbolic presentation valid?

1. Oliver, "Spring in the Classroom" (page 44).
2. Frost, "After Apple-Picking" (page 65).
3. Shelley, "Ozymandias" (page 122).
4. Hardy, "The Ruined Maid" (page 379).
5. Marlowe, "The Passionate Shepherd to His Love" (page 394).
6. Robinson, "Eros Turannos" (page 405).

PRACTICE AP® WRITING PROMPTS

Seamus Heaney, "Digging" (pp. 96–97)

Carefully read the poem "Digging." In a well-written essay, analyze the speaker's complex attitude toward his father by examining how Heaney employs figurative language to develop a nuanced comparison between his father and himself.

Robert Frost, "The Road Not Taken" (pp. 91–92)

In his poem "Directive," Robert Frost likens himself to a mischievous guide "Who only has at heart your getting lost." Writing to his friend Louis Untermeyer in 1915, Frost made the unguarded remark, "I'll bet not half a dozen people can tell who was hit and where he was hit by my road not taken," perhaps the most authoritative evidence that this poem holds some intentional misdirection, a gesture that Frost often referred to broadly as his "kind of fooling." Carefully examine "The Road Not Taken" and write an essay in which you analyze the author's "fooling," showing how such tricks of language contribute to the overall meaning of the poem.

Walt Whitman, "A Noiseless Patient Spider" (pp. 93–94)

Read "A Noiseless Patient Spider" carefully. In a well-organized essay, demonstrate how Whitman's diction and concrete details develop the literal and symbolic meanings of the spider's activity.

CHAPTER SEVEN

Figurative Language 3

Paradox, Overstatement,
Understatement, Irony

Aesop tells the tale of a traveler who sought refuge with a Satyr on a bitter winter night. On entering the Satyr's lodging, he blew on his fingers, and was asked by the Satyr why he did it. "To warm them up," he explained. Later, on being served a piping-hot bowl of porridge, he blew also on it, and again was asked why he did it. "To cool it off," he explained. The Satyr thereupon thrust him out of doors, for he would have nothing to do with a man who could blow hot and cold with the same breath.

A **paradox** is an apparent contradiction that is nevertheless somehow true. It may be either a situation or a statement. Aesop's tale of the traveler illustrates a **paradoxical situation**. As a figure of speech, paradox is a statement. When Alexander Pope wrote that a literary critic of his time would "damn with faint praise," he was using a **verbal paradox,** for how can a man damn by praising?

When we understand all the conditions and circumstances involved in a paradox, we find that what at first seemed impossible is actually entirely plausible and not strange at all. The paradox of the cold hands and hot porridge is not strange to anyone who knows that a stream of air directed upon an object of different temperature will tend to bring that object closer to its own temperature. And Pope's paradox is not strange when we realize that *damn* is being used figuratively, and that Pope means only that a too reserved praise may damage an author with the public almost as much as adverse criticism. In a **paradoxical statement** the contradiction usually stems from one of the words being used figuratively or with more than one denotation.

The value of paradox is its shock value. Its seeming impossibility startles the reader into attention and, by the fact of its apparent absurdity, underscores the truth of what is being said.

Much Madness is divinest Sense

Much Madness is divinest Sense—
To a discerning Eye—
Much Sense—the starkest Madness—
'Tis the Majority
In this, as All, prevail—   5
Assent—and you are sane—
Demur—you're straightway dangerous—
And handled with a Chain—

—EMILY DICKINSON (1830–1886)

QUESTIONS

1. This poem presents the two sides of a paradoxical proposition: that insanity is good sense, and that good sense is insane. How do the concepts implied by the words "discerning" (2) and "Majority" (4) provide the resolution of this paradox?
2. How do we know that the speaker does not believe that the majority is correct? How do the last five lines extend the subject beyond a contrast between sanity and insanity?

Overstatement, understatement, and verbal irony form a continuous series, for they consist, respectively, of saying more, saying less, and saying the opposite of what one really means.

Overstatement, or *hyperbole,* is simply exaggeration, but exaggeration in the service of truth. It is not the same as a fish story. If you say, "I'm starved!" or "You could have knocked me over with a feather!" or "I'll die if I don't pass this course!" you do not expect to be taken literally; you are merely adding emphasis to what you really mean. (And if you say, "There were literally millions of people at the beach!" you are merely piling one overstatement on top of another, for you really mean, "There were figuratively millions of people at the beach," or, literally, "The beach was very crowded.") Like all figures of speech, overstatement may be used with a variety of effects. It may be humorous or grave, fanciful or restrained, convincing or unconvincing. When Tennyson says of his eagle (page 4) that it is *"Close to the sun in lonely lands,"* he says what appears to be literally true, though we know from our study of astronomy that it is not. When Frost says, at the conclusion of "The Road Not Taken" (page 91),

> I shall be telling this with a sigh
> Somewhere *ages and ages hence*

we are scarcely aware of the overstatement, so quietly is the assertion made. Unskillfully used, however, overstatement may seem strained and ridiculous, leading us to react as Gertrude does to the player-queen's speeches in *Hamlet:* "The lady doth protest too much."

It is paradoxical that one can emphasize a truth either by overstating it or by understating it. **Understatement,** or saying less than one means, may exist in what one says or merely in how one says it. If, for instance, upon sitting down to a loaded dinner plate, you say, "This looks like a nice snack," you are actually stating less than the truth; but if you say, with the humorist Artemus Ward, that a man who holds his hand for half an hour in a lighted fire will experience "a sensation of excessive and disagreeable warmth," you are stating what is literally true but with a good deal less force than the situation warrants.

The Sun Rising

> Busy old fool, unruly sun,
>   Why dost thou thus
> Through windows and through curtains call on us?
> Must to thy motions lovers' seasons run?
>   Saucy pedantic wretch, go chide   5
>   Late schoolboys and sour 'prentices,
>   Go tell court-huntsmen that the king will ride,
>   Call country ants to harvest offices;
> Love, all alike, no season knows, nor clime,
> Nor hours, days, months, which are the rags of time.   10
>
>   Thy beams so reverend and strong
>   Why shouldst thou think?
> I could eclipse and cloud them with a wink,
> But that I would not lose her sight so long;
>   If her eyes have not blinded thine,   15
>   Look, and tomorrow late tell me
>   Whether both th' Indias of spice and mine
>   Be where thou left'st them, or lie here with me.

Ask for those kings whom thou saw'st yesterday,
And thou shalt hear, "All here in one bed lay."   20

   She's all states, and all princes I;
   Nothing else is.
Princes do but play us; compared to this,
All honor's mimic, all wealth alchemy.
      Thou, sun, art half as happy as we,   25
         In that the world's contracted thus;
      Thine age asks ease, and since thy duties be
      To warm the world, that's done in warming us.
Shine here to us, and thou art everywhere;
This bed thy center is, these walls thy sphere.   30

—JOHN DONNE (1572–1631)

QUESTIONS

1. Vocabulary: *offices* (8), *alchemy* (24).
2. As precisely as possible, identify the time of day and the locale. What three "persons" does the poem involve?
3. What is the speaker's attitude toward the sun in stanzas 1 and 2? How and why does it change in stanza 3?
4. Does the speaker understate or overstate the actual qualities of the sun? Point out specific examples. Identify the overstatements in lines 9–10, 13, 15, 16–20, 21–24, 29–30. What do these overstatements achieve?
5. Line 17 introduces a geographical image referring to the East and West Indies, sources respectively of spices and gold. What relationship between the lovers and the rest of the world is expressed in lines 15–22?
6. Who is actually the intended listener for this extended apostrophe? What is the speaker's purpose? What is the poem's purpose?

   Like paradox, **irony** has meanings that extend beyond its use merely as a figure of speech.
   Verbal irony, saying the opposite of what one means, is often confused with sarcasm and with satire, and for that reason it may be well to look at the meanings of all three terms. Sarcasm and satire both imply ridicule, one on the colloquial level, the other on the literary level. **Sarcasm** is simply bitter or cutting speech, intended to wound the feelings (it comes from a Greek word meaning to tear flesh). **Satire** is a more formal term, usually applied to written literature rather than to speech and ordinarily implying a higher motive: it is ridicule (either bitter or gentle) of human folly or vice, with the purpose of bringing about reform or at least of keeping other people from falling into similar folly or vice. Irony, on the other hand, is a

literary device or figure that may be used in the service of sarcasm or ridicule or may not. It is popularly confused with sarcasm and satire because it is so often used as their tool; but irony may be used without either sarcastic or satirical intent, and sarcasm and satire may exist (though they do not usually) without irony.

If, for instance, one of the members of your class raises his hand on the discussion of this point and says, "I don't understand," and your instructor replies, with a tone of heavy disgust in his voice, "Well, I wouldn't expect *you* to," he is being sarcastic but not ironic; he means exactly what he says. But if, after you have done particularly well on an examination, your instructor brings your test papers into the classroom saying, "Here's some *bad* news for you: you all got A's and B's!" he is being ironic but not sarcastic. Sarcasm, we may say, is cruel, as a bully is cruel: it intends to give hurt. Satire is both cruel and kind, as a surgeon is cruel and kind: it gives hurt in the interest of the patient or of society. Irony is neither cruel nor kind: it is simply a device, like a surgeon's scalpel, for performing any operation more skillfully.

Although verbal irony always implies the opposite of what is said, it has many gradations, and only in its simplest forms does it mean *only* the opposite of what is said. In more complex forms it means both what is said and the opposite of what is said, at once, though in different ways and with different degrees of emphasis. When Terence's critic, in Housman's "Terence, this is stupid stuff" (page 383) says, "'*Pretty* friendship 'tis to rhyme / Your friends to death before their time'" (11–12), we may substitute the literal *sorry* for the ironic "pretty" with little or no loss of meaning. When Terence speaks in reply, however, of the pleasure of drunkenness—"And down in *lovely* muck I've lain, / Happy till I woke again" (35–36)—we cannot substitute *loathsome* for "lovely" without considerable loss of meaning, for while muck is actually extremely unpleasant to lie in, it may *seem* lovely to an intoxicated person. Thus, two meanings—one the opposite of the other—operate at once.

Like all figures of speech, verbal irony runs the danger of being misunderstood. With irony, the risks are perhaps greater than with other figures, for if metaphor is misunderstood, the result may be simply bewilderment; but if irony is misunderstood, the reader goes away with an idea exactly the opposite of what the user meant to convey. The results of misunderstanding if, for instance, you ironically called someone a numbskull might be calamitous. For this reason the user of irony must be very skillful in its use, conveying by an altered tone, or by a wink of the eye or pen, that irony is intended; and the reader of literature must be always alert to recognize the subtle signs of irony.

No matter how broad or obvious the irony, a number of people in any large audience always will misunderstand. Artemus Ward used to protect himself against these people by writing at the bottom of his newspaper column, "This is writ ironical." But irony is most delightful and most effective when it is subtlest. It sets up a special understanding between writer and reader that may add either grace or force. If irony is too obvious, it sometimes seems merely crude. But if effectively used, like all figurative language, it is capable of adding extra dimensions to meaning.

Barbie Doll

This girlchild was born as usual
and presented dolls that did pee-pee
and miniature GE stoves and irons
and wee lipsticks the color of cherry candy.
Then in the magic of puberty, a classmate said: 5
You have a great big nose and fat legs.

She was healthy, tested intelligent,
possessed strong arms and back,
abundant sexual drive and manual dexterity.
She went to and fro apologizing.   10
Everyone saw a fat nose on thick legs.

She was advised to play coy,
exhorted to come on hearty,
exercise, diet, smile and wheedle.
Her good nature wore out   15
like a fan belt.
So she cut off her nose and her legs
and offered them up.

In the casket displayed on satin she lay
with the undertaker's cosmetics painted on,   20
a turned-up putty nose,
dressed in a pink and white nightie.
Doesn't she look pretty? everyone said.
Consummation at last.
To every woman a happy ending.   25

—MARGE PIERCY (B. 1936)

QUESTIONS

1. In what ways is the girl described in this poem different from a Barbie doll? Discuss the poem's contrast of the living girl, a human being with intelligence and healthy appetites, and the doll, an inanimate object.
2. The poem contains a surprising but apt simile: "Her good nature wore out / like a fan belt" (15–16). Why is the image of the fan belt appropriate here?
3. Why does the speaker mention the girl's "strong arms and back" (8) and her "manual dexterity" (9)? How do these qualities contribute to her fate?
4. Discuss the verbal irony in the phrase "the magic of puberty" (5) and in the last three lines. What is the target of this satire?

The term *irony* always implies some sort of discrepancy or incongruity. In verbal irony, the discrepancy is between what is said and what is meant. In other forms, the discrepancy may be between appearance and reality or between expectation and fulfillment. These other forms of irony are, on the whole, more important resources for the poet than is verbal irony. Two types are especially important.

In **dramatic irony,** the discrepancy is not between what the speaker says and what the speaker means but between what the speaker says and what the poem means. The speaker's words may be perfectly straightforward, but the author, by putting these words in a particular speaker's mouth, may be indicating to the reader ideas or attitudes quite opposed to those the speaker is voicing. This form of irony is more complex than verbal irony and demands a more complex response from the reader. It may be used not only to convey attitudes but also to illuminate character, for the author who uses it is indirectly commenting not only upon the value of the ideas uttered but also upon the nature of the person who utters them. Such comment may be harsh, gently mocking, or sympathetic.

The Chimney Sweeper

When my mother died I was very young,
And my father sold me while yet my tongue
Could scarcely cry "'weep! 'weep! 'weep! 'weep!"
So your chimneys I sweep, and in soot I sleep.

There's little Tom Dacre, who cried when his head,   5
That curled like a lamb's back, was shaved; so I said,
"Hush, Tom! never mind it, for, when your head's bare,
You know that the soot cannot spoil your white hair."

And so he was quiet, and that very night,
As Tom was asleeping, he had such a sight!   10
That thousands of sweepers, Dick, Joe, Ned, and Jack,
Were all of them locked up in coffins of black.

And by came an Angel who had a bright key,
And he opened the coffins and set them all free;
Then down a green plain leaping, laughing, they run,   15
And wash in a river, and shine in the sun.

Then naked and white, all their bags left behind,
They rise upon clouds and sport in the wind;
And the Angel told Tom, if he'd be a good boy,
He'd have God for his father, and never want joy.   20

And so Tom awoke, and we rose in the dark,
And got with our bags and our brushes to work.
Though the morning was cold, Tom was happy and warm;
So if all do their duty they need not fear harm.

—WILLIAM BLAKE (1757–1827)

QUESTIONS

1. In the eighteenth century, small boys, sometimes no more than four or five years old, were employed to climb up the narrow chimney flues and clean them, collecting the soot in bags. Such boys, sometimes sold to the master sweepers by their parents, were miserably treated by their masters and often suffered disease and physical deformity. Characterize the boy who speaks in this poem. How do his and the poet's attitudes toward his lot in life differ? How, especially, are the meanings of the poet and the speaker different in lines 3, 7–8, and 24?

2. The dream in lines 11–20, besides being a happy dream, can be interpreted allegorically. Point out possible significances of the sweepers' being "locked up in coffins of black" (12) and the Angel's releasing them with a bright key to play upon green plains.

A third type of irony, **irony of situation,** occurs when a discrepancy exists between the actual circumstances and those that would seem appropriate or between what one anticipates and what actually comes to pass. If a man and his second wife, on the first night of their honeymoon, are accidentally seated at the theater next to the man's first wife, we should call the situation ironic. When, in O. Henry's famous short story "The Gift of the Magi," a poor young husband pawns his gold watch, in order to buy his wife a set of combs for her hair for Christmas, and his wife sells her long brown hair, in order to buy a fob for her husband's watch, the situation is ironic. When King Midas in the famous fable is granted his wish that anything he touch turn to gold, and then finds that he cannot eat because even his food turns to gold, the situation is ironic. When Coleridge's Ancient Mariner finds himself in the middle of the ocean with "Water, water, everywhere" but not a "drop to drink," the situation is ironic. In each case the circumstances are not what would seem appropriate or what we would expect.

Dramatic irony and irony of situation are powerful devices for poetry, for, like symbol, they enable a poem to suggest meanings without stating them—to communicate a great deal more than is said. One effective use of irony of situation is in "The Widow's Lament in Springtime" (page 61); Another is in "Ozymandias," which follows.

Ozymandias

I met a traveler from an antique land
Who said: Two vast and trunkless legs of stone
Stand in the desert . . . Near them, on the sand,
Half sunk, a shattered visage lies, whose frown,
And wrinkled lip, and sneer of cold command, 5
Tell that its sculptor well those passions read
Which yet survive, stamped on these lifeless things,
The hand that mocked them, and the heart that fed;
And on the pedestal these words appear:
"My name is Ozymandias, king of kings; 10
Look on my works, ye Mighty, and despair!"
Nothing beside remains. Round the decay
Of that colossal wreck, boundless and bare
The lone and level sands stretch far away.

—PERCY BYSSHE SHELLEY (1792–1822)

QUESTIONS

1. "[S]urvive" (7) is a transitive verb with "hand" and "heart" as direct objects. Whose hand? Whose heart? What figure of speech is exemplified in "hand" and "heart"?
2. Characterize Ozymandias.
3. Ozymandias was an ancient Egyptian tyrant. This poem was first published in 1817. Of what is Ozymandias a *symbol*? What contemporary reference might the poem have had in Shelley's time?
4. What is the theme of the poem and how is it "stated"?

MindTap Read, highlight, and take notes online.

Irony and paradox may be trivial or powerful devices, depending on their use. At their worst they may degenerate into mere mannerism and mental habit. At their best they may greatly extend the dimensions of meaning in a work of literature. Because irony and paradox demand an exercise of critical intelligence, they are particularly valuable as safeguards against sentimentality.

EXERCISE

Identify the figure in each of the following quotations as paradox, overstatement, understatement, or irony—and explain the use to which the figure is put (emotional emphasis, humor, satire, etc.).

1. Poetry is a language that tells us, through a more or less emotional reaction, something that cannot be said.   —EDWIN ARLINGTON ROBINSON
2. Christians have burnt each other, quite persuaded / That all the Apostles would have done as they did.   —LORD BYRON
3. A man who could make so vile a pun would not scruple to pick a pocket.
   —JOHN DENNIS
4. Last week I saw a woman flayed, and you will hardly believe how much it altered her person for the worse.   —JONATHAN SWIFT
5. Where ignorance is bliss, / 'Tis folly to be wise.   —THOMAS GRAY
6. All night I made my bed to swim; with my tears
   I dissolved my couch.   —PSALMS 6:6
7. Believe him, he has known the world too long / And seen the death of much immortal song.   —ALEXANDER POPE
8. Cowards die many times before their deaths;
   The valiant never taste of death but once.   —WILLIAM SHAKESPEARE
9. All men would be cowards if they durst.   —JOHN WILMOT, EARL OF ROCHESTER

REVIEWING CHAPTER SEVEN

1. Distinguish between paradoxical actions and paradoxical statements, and explain how paradoxical statements may usually be resolved— that is, how their underlying validity is determined.
2. Define overstatement and understatement, and draw the distinction between stating what is less than is true and underemphasizing what is true.
3. Review the definitions of sarcasm and satire.
4. Using examples from the poems that follow in this chapter, define the three principal forms of irony and demonstrate how the ironies contribute meaning or forcefulness to the poems.

A slumber did my spirit seal

A slumber did my spirit seal;
   I had no human fears:
She seemed a thing that could not feel
   The touch of earthly years.

No motion has she now, no force;   5
   She neither hears nor sees;
Rolled round in earth's diurnal course,
   With rocks, and stones, and trees.

—WILLIAM WORDSWORTH (1770–1850)

QUESTIONS

1. Vocabulary: *diurnal* (7).
2. What frame of mind does the first line exhibit? How does it justify the second line?
3. Explain the situational irony. How is the phrase "could not feel" (3) an example of dramatic irony?

Batter my heart, three-personed God

Batter my heart, three-personed God; for you
As yet but knock, breathe, shine, and seek to mend;
That I may rise and stand, o'erthrow me, and bend
Your force to break, blow, burn, and make me new.
I, like an usurped town, to another due,   5
Labor to admit you, but oh, to no end;
Reason, your viceroy in me, me should defend,
But is captived, and proves weak or untrue.
Yet dearly I love you and would be lovèd fain,°   gladly
But am betrothed unto your enemy;   10
Divorce me, untie or break that knot again,
Take me to you, imprison me, for I,
Except° you enthrall me, never shall be free,   unless
Nor ever chaste, except you ravish me.

—JOHN DONNE (1572–1631)

QUESTIONS

1. In this sonnet (one in a group called "Holy Sonnets") the speaker addresses God in a series of metaphors and paradoxes. What is the paradox in the first quatrain? To what is the "three-personed God" metaphorically compared? To what is the speaker compared? Can the first three verbs of the parallel lines 2 and 4 be

taken as addressed to specific "persons" of the Trinity (Father, Son, Holy Spirit)? If so, to which are "knock" and "break" addressed? "breathe" and "blow"? "shine" and "burn"? (What concealed pun helps in the attribution of the last pair? What etymological pun in the attribution of the second pair?)

2. To what does the speaker compare himself in the second quatrain? To what is God compared? Who is the usurper? What role does "Reason" (7) play in this political metaphor, and why is it a weak one?

3. To what does the speaker compare himself in the sestet (lines 9–14)? To what does he compare God? Who is the "enemy" (10)? Resolve the paradox in lines 12–13 by explaining the double meaning of "enthrall." Resolve the paradox in line 14 by explaining the double meaning of "ravish."

Mid-Term Break

I sat all morning in the college sick bay
Counting bells knelling classes to a close.
At two o'clock our neighbors drove me home.

In the porch I met my father crying—
He had always taken funerals in stride—   5
And Big Jim Evans saying it was a hard blow.

The baby cooed and laughed and rocked the pram
When I came in, and I was embarrassed
By old men standing up to shake my hand

And tell me they were 'sorry for my trouble.'   10
Whispers informed strangers I was the eldest,
Away at school, as my mother held my hand

In hers and coughed out angry tearless sighs.
At ten o'clock the ambulance arrived
With the corpse, stanched and bandaged by the nurses.   15

Next morning I went up into the room. Snowdrops
And candles soothed the bedside; I saw him
For the first time in six weeks. Paler now,

Wearing a poppy bruise on his left temple,
He lay in the four-foot box as in his cot.   20
No gaudy scars, the bumper knocked him clear.

A four-foot box, a foot for every year.

—SEAMUS HEANEY (B. 1939–2013)

QUESTIONS

1. Vocabulary: *knelling* (2), *stanched* (15), *Snowdrops* (16).
2. Describe in your own words the "story" being told in this narrative poem. Who is the speaker, and what is his attitude toward this event of his distant past?
3. How would you describe the general tone of the poem? Is the speaker making use of understatement or overstatement in conveying his emotion?
4. Discuss the impact of the final line. Why is the line set off in a separate stanza by itself?

The Unknown Citizen

(To JS/07/M/378 This Marble Monument Is Erected by the State)

He was found by the Bureau of Statistics to be
One against whom there was no official complaint,
And all the reports on his conduct agree
That, in the modern sense of an old-fashioned word, he was
    a saint,
For in everything he did he served the Greater Community.   5
Except for the War till the day he retired
He worked in a factory and never got fired,
But satisfied his employers, Fudge Motors Inc.
Yet he wasn't a scab or odd in his views,
For his Union reports that he paid his dues   10
(Our report on his Union shows it was sound),
And our Social Psychology workers found
That he was popular with his mates and liked a drink.
The Press are convinced that he bought a paper every day
And that his reactions to advertisements were normal in
    every way.   15
Policies taken out in his name prove that he was fully
    insured,
And his Health-card shows he was once in hospital but left it
    cured.
Both Producers Research and High-Grade Living declare
He was fully sensible to the advantages of the Installment
    Plan
And had everything necessary to the Modern Man,   20
A phonograph, a radio, a car and a frigidaire.
Our researchers into Public Opinion are content
That he held the proper opinions for the time of year;
When there was peace, he was for peace; when there was
    war, he went.

He was married and added five children to the population,   25
Which our Eugenist says was the right number for a parent
    of his generation,
And our teachers report that he never interfered with their
    education.
Was he free? Was he happy? The question is absurd:
Had anything been wrong, we should certainly have heard.

—W. H. AUDEN (1907–1973)

QUESTIONS

1. Vocabulary: *scab* (9), *Eugenist* (26).
2. Explain the allusion and the irony in the title. Why was the citizen "unknown"?
3. This obituary of an unknown state "hero" was apparently prepared by a functionary of the state. Give an account of the citizen's life and character from Auden's own point of view.
4. What trends in modern life and social organization does the poem satirize?

in the inner city

in the inner city
or
like we call it
home
we think a lot about uptown   5
and the silent nights
and the houses straight as
dead men
and the pastel lights
and we hang on to our no place   10
happy to be alive
and in the inner city
or
like we call it
home   15

—LUCILLE CLIFTON (1936–2010)

QUESTIONS

1. In what contexts is the term "inner city" most often used, and what is it usually meant to imply?

2. What are the connotations of "silent nights" (6), "straight as / dead men" (7–8), and "pastel lights" (9)? By implication, what contrasting qualities might be found in the life of the inner city?
3. Is the irony in this poem verbal or dramatic?

What Soft—Cherubic Creatures

What Soft—Cherubic Creatures—
These Gentlewomen are—
One would as soon assault a Plush—
Or violate a Star—

Such Dimity Convictions—   5
A Horror so refined
Of freckled Human Nature—
Of Deity—ashamed—

It's such a common—Glory—
A Fisherman's—Degree—   10
Redemption—Brittle Lady—
Be so—ashamed of Thee—

—EMILY DICKINSON (1830–1886)

QUESTIONS

1. Vocabulary: Cherubic (1), Plush (3), Dimity (5).
2. What is the speaker's attitude toward the "Gentlewomen" (2) described in the first stanza? Why does she have this attitude?
3. Why is "Human Nature" (7) described as "freckled"? Is human nature seen here as positive or negative?
4. Discuss the Christian imagery in the final stanza. How does this imagery broaden the poem's meaning?

My Papa's Waltz

The whiskey on your breath
Could make a small boy dizzy;
But I hung on like death:
Such waltzing was not easy.

We romped until the pans   5
Slid from the kitchen shelf;

My mother's countenance
Could not unfrown itself.

The hand that held my wrist
Was battered on one knuckle;   10
At every step you missed
My right ear scraped a buckle.

You beat time on my head
With a palm caked hard by dirt,
Then waltzed me off to bed   15
Still clinging to your shirt.

—THEODORE ROETHKE (1908–1963)

QUESTIONS

1. What type of dance is the "Waltz" (title)? Is it ironic that the speaker has chosen waltzing to describe his "dance" with his father?
2. Roughly what age is the little boy described in the poem? Is the dance he conducts with his father a pleasant or unpleasant one?
3. What assertions in the poem could be described as examples of ironic understatement?
4. Is the mature speaker recalling his boy's experience with his father with love or with disdain? Would you describe his feelings toward his father as ambivalent?

The Colossus

I shall never get you put together entirely,
Pieced, glued, and properly jointed.
Mule-bray, pig-grunt and bawdy cackles
Proceed from your great lips.
It's worse than a barnyard.   5

Perhaps you consider yourself an oracle,
Mouthpiece of the dead, or of some god or other.
Thirty years now I have labored
To dredge the silt from your throat.
I am none the wiser.   10

Scaling little ladders with gluepots and pails of Lysol
I crawl like an ant in mourning
Over the weedy acres of your brow

To mend the immense skull-plates and clear
The bald, white tumuli of your eyes.   15

A blue sky out of the Oresteia
Arches above us. O father, all by yourself
You are pithy and historical as the Roman Forum.
I open my lunch on a hill of black cypress.
Your fluted bones and acanthine hair are littered   20

In their old anarchy to the horizon-line.
It would take more than a lightning-stroke
To create such a ruin.
Nights, I squat in the cornucopia
Of your left ear, out of the wind,   25

Counting the red stars and those of plum-color.
The sun rises under the pillar of your tongue.
My hours are married to shadow.
No longer do I listen for the scrape of a keel
On the blank stones of the landing.   30

—SYLVIA PLATH (1932–1963)

QUESTIONS

1. Vocabulary: Colossus (title), oracle (6), dredge (9), silt (9), tumuli (15), Oresteia (16), acanthine (20), keel (29).
2. Why does the speaker refer to her father as a "Colossus"? Is this a flattering or critical image?
3. How does the speaker view herself in the poem? What do the images imply about the speaker's relationship with her father?
4. Describe the poem's humor. Why is the humor appropriate?
5. Analyze the final stanza closely. What is the implication of the final two lines?

Soliloquy of the Spanish Cloister

Gr-r-r—there go, my heart's abhorrence!
    Water your damned flower-pots, do!
If hate killed men, Brother Lawrence,
    God's blood, would not mine kill you!
What? your myrtle-bush wants trimming?   5
    Oh, that rose has prior claims—

Needs its leaden vase filled brimming?
    Hell dry you up with its flames!

At the meal we sit together:
    Salve tibi! I must hear   10
Wise talk of the kind of weather,
    Sort of season, time of year:
Not a plenteous cork-crop: scarcely
    Dare we hope oak-galls, I doubt:
What's the Latin name for "parsley"?   15
    What's the Greek name for Swine's Snout?

Whew! We'll have our platter burnished,
    Laid with care on our own shelf!
With a fire-new spoon we're furnished,
    And a goblet for ourself,   20
Rinsed like something sacrificial
    Ere 'tis fit to touch our chaps—
Marked with L. for our initial!
    (He-he! There his lily snaps!)

Saint, forsooth! While brown Dolores   25
    —Squats outside the Convent bank
With Sanchicha, telling stories,
    Steeping tresses in the tank,
Blue-black, lustrous, thick like horsehairs,
    —Can't I see his dead eye glow,   30
Bright as 'twere a Barbary corsair's?
    (That is, if he'd let it show!)

When he finishes refection,
    Knife and fork he never lays
Cross-wise, to my recollection,   35
    As do I, in Jesu's praise.
I the Trinity illustrate,
    Drinking watered orange-pulp—
In three sips the Arian frustrate;
    —While he drains his at one gulp.   40

Oh, those melons? If he's able
    We're to have a feast! so nice!

One goes to the Abbot's table,
    All of us get each a slice.
How go on your flowers? None double?   45
    Not one fruit-sort can you spy?
Strange!—And I, too, at such trouble,
    —Keep them close-nipped on the sly!

There's a great text in Galatians,
    Once you trip on it, entails   50
Twenty-nine distinct damnations,
    One sure, if another fails:
If I trip him just a-dying,
    Sure of heaven as sure can be,
Spin him round and send him flying   55
    Off to hell, a Manichee?

Or, my scrofulous French novel
    On gray paper with blunt type!
Simply glance at it, you grovel
    Hand and foot in Belial's gripe: 60
If I double down its pages
    At the woeful sixteenth print,
When he gathers his greengages,
    Ope a sieve and slip it in't?

Or, there's Satan!—one might venture   65
    Pledge one's soul to him, yet leave
Such a flaw in the indenture
    —As he'd miss till, past retrieve,
Blasted lay that rose-acacia
    We're so proud of! *Hy, Zy, Hine* ...   70
'St, there's Vespers! *Plena gratiâ*
    Ave, Virgo. Gr-r-r—you swine!

—ROBERT BROWNING (1812–1889)

QUESTIONS

1. The speaker is a Spanish cloistered monk who is observing a hated colleague, Brother Lawrence. The Latin phrases translate as follows: *Salve Tibi* (10), "Hail to Thee"; *Plena gratia / Ave, Virgo* (71-72), "Hail, Virgin, full of grace". The phrase *Hy, Zy, Hine* (70) is obscure and of uncertain meaning.

2. Vocabulary: *oak-galls* (14), *Barbary corsair's* (31), *Arian* (39), *Galatians* (49), *Manichee* (56), *scrofulous* (57), *Belial's* (60), *greengages* (63), *indenture* (67).

3. Is there a reason given for the speaker's feelings toward Brother Lawrence? Why or why not?
4. Can you find examples of ironic overstatement in the poem?
5. What is the significance of "brown Dolores" (25)? To use contemporary terminology, is the speaker "projecting" his own lust onto Brother Lawrence?
6. In the end, how is the reader meant to view the speaker? Brother Lawrence?

SUGGESTIONS FOR WRITING

1. Discuss the irony in one of the following poems. Does the poem employ verbal irony, dramatic irony, or irony of situation? How does the ironic content of the poem heighten its impact?
   a. Byron, "Stanzas" (page 221).
   b. Jonson, "Still to be neat" (page 387).
   c. Browning, "My Last Duchess" (page 288).
   d. Dickinson, "I died for Beauty—but was scarce" (page 367).
   e. Oates, "Playlet for Voices" (page 400).
2. Each of the following poems deals, at least in part, with the relationship between the individual human being and a society that imposes a dehumanizing conformity. Choose any two of the poems and compare their use(s) of irony in conveying this theme.
   a. Dickinson, "Much Madness is divinest Sense" (page 115).
   b. Piercy, "Barbie Doll" (page 119).
   c. Auden, "The Unknown Citizen" (page 126).
   d. Hughes, "Theme for English B" (page 386).

PRACTICE AP® WRITING PROMPTS

Marge Piercy, "Barbie Doll" (pp. 119–120)

Carefully read "Barbie Doll," paying close attention to the poem's diction, selection of detail, and tone. In a well-written essay, analyze the ways in which the author employs the resources of language to express a satiric point.

Percy Bysshe Shelley, "Ozymandias" (p. 122)

The sonnet "Ozymandias" turns on the words inscribed on the base of the ruined statue. If we examine the poem closely, we can identify as many as five distinct voices in the narrative, five separate persons who may have some stake in the language of the inscription: the ancient king, the unknown sculptor, the "traveler from an antique land," the narrative "I," and perhaps Shelley himself. Write an essay in which you describe the differences among these distinct voices, focusing especially on the quoted words in lines 10 and 11. Explore the motivation and attitude that might be ascribed to each voice, and show how the voices interact to produce the poem's ironic effect.

....

John Donne, "Batter my heart, three-personed God" (pp. 124–125)

Carefully read John Donne's "Batter my heart, three-personed God." Write an essay in which you examine the speaker's ambivalent feelings and attitudes toward God. In your analysis, you may choose to refer to such elements as metaphor, paradox, and poetic form.

....

CHAPTER EIGHT

Allusion

The famous English diplomat and letter writer Lord Chesterfield once was invited to a great dinner given by the Spanish ambassador. At the conclusion of the meal the host rose and proposed a toast to his master, the king of Spain, whom he compared to the sun. The French ambassador followed with a toast to the health of the king of France, whom he likened to the moon. It was then Lord Chesterfield's turn. "Your excellencies have taken from me," he said, "all the greatest luminaries of heaven, and the stars are too small for me to make a comparison of my royal master; I therefore beg leave to give your excellencies—Joshua!"*

A reader familiar with the Bible—that is, one who recognizes the biblical allusion—will recognize the witty point of Lord Chesterfield's story. For an **allusion**—a reference to something in history or previous literature—is, like a richly connotative word or a symbol, a means of suggesting far more than it says. The one word "Joshua," in the context of Chesterfield's toast, calls up in the reader's mind the whole biblical story of how the Israelite captain stopped the sun and the moon in order that the Israelites might finish a battle and conquer their enemies before nightfall (Joshua 10:12–14). The force of the toast lies in its extreme economy; it says so much in so little, and it exercises the mind of the reader to make the connection for himself.

The effect of Chesterfield's allusion is chiefly humorous or witty, but allusions also may have a powerful emotional effect. The essayist William Hazlitt writes of addressing a fashionable audience about the lexicographer Samuel Johnson. Speaking of Johnson's great heart and of his charity to the unfortunate, Hazlitt recounted how, finding a drunken prostitute lying in Fleet Street late at night, Johnson carried her on his broad back to the

*Samuel Shellabarger, *Lord Chesterfield and His World* (Boston: Little, Brown, 1951): 132.

address she managed to give him. The audience, unable to face the picture
of the famous dictionary-maker doing such a thing, broke out in titters
and expostulations, whereupon Hazlitt simply said: "I remind you, ladies
and gentlemen, of the parable of the Good Samaritan." The audience was
promptly silenced.*

Allusions are a means of reinforcing the emotion or the ideas of one's
own work with the emotion or ideas of another work or occasion. Because
they may compact so much meaning in so small a space, they are extremely
useful to the poet.

"Out, Out—"

The buzz-saw snarled and rattled in the yard
And made dust and dropped stove-length sticks of wood,
Sweet-scented stuff when the breeze drew across it.
And from there those that lifted eyes could count
Five mountain ranges one behind the other   5
Under the sunset far into Vermont.
And the saw snarled and rattled, snarled and rattled,
As it ran light, or had to bear a load.
And nothing happened: day was all but done.
Call it a day, I wish they might have said   10
To please the boy by giving him the half hour
That a boy counts so much when saved from work.
His sister stood beside them in her apron
To tell them "Supper." At the word, the saw,
As if to prove saws knew what supper meant,   15
Leaped out at the boy's hand, or seemed to leap—
He must have given the hand. However it was,
Neither refused the meeting. But the hand!
The boy's first outcry was a rueful laugh,
As he swung toward them holding up the hand   20
Half in appeal, but half as if to keep
The life from spilling. Then the boy saw all—
Since he was old enough to know, big boy
Doing a man's work, though a child at heart—
He saw all spoiled. "Don't let him cut my hand off—   25
The doctor, when he comes. Don't let him, sister!"
So. But the hand was gone already.

*Jacques Barzun, *Teacher in America* (Boston: Little, Brown, 1945): 160.

The doctor put him in the dark of ether.
He lay and puffed his lips out with his breath.
And then—the watcher at his pulse took fright.   30
No one believed. They listened at his heart.
Little—less—nothing!—and that ended it.
No more to build on there. And they, since they
Were not the one dead, turned to their affairs.

—ROBERT FROST (1874–1963)

QUESTIONS

1. How does this poem differ from a newspaper account that might have dealt with the same incident?
2. To whom does "they" (33) refer? The boy's family? The doctor and medical attendants? Casual onlookers? Need we assume that all these people—whoever they are—turned immediately "to their affairs" (34)? Does the ending of this poem seem to you callous or merely realistic? Would a more tearful and sentimental ending have made the poem better or worse?
3. What is the figure of speech in lines 21–22?

Allusions vary widely in the burden put on them by the poet to convey meaning. Lord Chesterfield risked his whole meaning on his listeners' recognizing his allusion. Robert Frost in " 'Out, Out—' " makes his meaning entirely clear even for the reader who does not recognize the allusion contained in the poem's title. His theme is the uncertainty and unpredictability of life, which may end accidentally at any moment, and the tragic waste of human potentiality that takes place when such premature deaths occur. A boy who is already "Doing a man's work" and gives every promise of having a useful life ahead of him is suddenly wiped out. There seems no rational explanation for either the accident or the death. The only comment to be made is, "No more to build on there."

Frost's title, however, is an allusion to one of the most famous passages in all English literature, and it offers a good illustration of how a poet may use allusion not only to reinforce emotion but also to help define his theme. The passage is that in *Macbeth* in which Macbeth has just been informed of his wife's death. A good many readers will recall the key phrase, "Out, out, brief candle!" with its underscoring of the tragic brevity and uncertainty of life. For some readers, however, the allusion will summon up the whole passage in Act 5, scene 5, in which Macbeth uses this phrase:

She should have died hereafter;
There would have been a time for such a word.
Tomorrow, and tomorrow, and tomorrow
Creeps in this petty pace from day to day

To the last syllable of recorded time;   5
And all our yesterdays have lighted fools
The way to dusty death. Out, out, brief candle!
Life's but a walking shadow, a poor player,
That struts and frets his hour upon the stage
And then is heard no more. It is a tale   10
Told by an idiot, full of sound and fury,
Signifying nothing.

—WILLIAM SHAKESPEARE (1564–1616)

QUESTION

Examine Macbeth's speech for examples of personification, apostrophe, and metonymy. How many metaphors for an individual human life does it present?

Macbeth's first words underscore the theme of premature death. The boy also "should have died hereafter." The rest of the passage, with its marvelous evocation of the vanity and meaninglessness of life, expresses neither Shakespeare's philosophy nor, ultimately, Frost's, but it is Macbeth's philosophy at the time of his bereavement, and it is likely to express the feelings of us all when such tragic accidents occur. Life does indeed seem cruel and meaningless, "a tale / Told by an idiot, . . . / Signifying nothing," when human life and potentiality are thus without explanation so suddenly ended.

Allusions also vary widely in the number of readers to whom they will be familiar. Poets, in using an allusion, as in using a figure of speech, are always in danger of being misunderstood. What appeals powerfully to one reader may lose another reader altogether. But poets must assume a certain fund of common experience in readers. They could not even write about the ocean unless they could assume that readers have seen the ocean or pictures of it. In the same way, poets assume a certain common fund of literary experience, most frequently of classical mythology, Shakespeare, or the Bible—particularly the King James Version. Poets are often justified in expecting a rather wide range of literary experience in readers, for the people who read poetry for pleasure are generally intelligent and well-read. But, obviously, beginning readers will not have this range, just as they will not know the meanings of as many words as will more experienced readers. Students should therefore be prepared to look up certain allusions, just as they should look up in their dictionaries the meanings of unfamiliar words. They will find that every increase in knowledge broadens their base for understanding both literature and life.

Wuthering Heights

The horizons ring me like faggots,
Tilted and disparate, and always unstable.
Touched by a match, they might warm me,
And their fine lines singe
The air to orange   5
Before the distances they pin evaporate,
Weighting the pale sky with a solider color.
But they only dissolve and dissolve
Like a series of promises, as I step forward.

There is no life higher than the grasstops   10
Or the hearts of sheep, and the wind
Pours by like destiny, bending
Everything in one direction.
I can feel it trying
To funnel my heat away.   15
If I pay the roots of the heather
Too close attention, they will invite me
To whiten my bones among them.

The sheep know where they are,
Browsing in their dirty wool-clouds,   20
Gray as the weather.
The black slots of their pupils take me in.
It is like being mailed into space,
A thin, silly message.
They stand about in grandmotherly disguise,   25
All wig curls and yellow teeth
And hard, marbly baas.

I come to wheel ruts, and water
Limpid as the solitudes
That flee through my fingers.   30
Hollow doorsteps go from grass to grass;
Lintel and sill have unhinged themselves.
Of people the air only
Remembers a few odd syllables.
It rehearses them moaningly: 35
Black stone, black stone.

The sky leans on me, me, the one upright
Among all horizontals.
The grass is beating its head distractedly.
It is too delicate   40
For a life in such company;
Darkness terrifies it.
Now, in valleys narrow
And black as purses, the house lights
Gleam like small change.   45

—SYLVIA PLATH (1932–1963)

QUESTIONS

1. Vocabulary: *faggots* (1), *disparate* (2), *limpid* (29), *Lintel* (32).
2. If you have not read Emily Brontë's *Wuthering Heights* (1847), do some research into the novel. What is it about? What kind of setting does it have? To what does the title refer?
3. What kind of landscape is described in this poem? What are some of the key images associated with the landscape?
4. How does the poem gain from its allusion to the novel?
5. What is the speaker's relationship to the landscape? Does she find it nurturing or threatening?
6. Discuss the double meaning of the final simile, "Gleam like small change." Why is this an appropriate ending to the poem?

REVIEWING CHAPTER EIGHT

1. Show how allusion is similar in its effect to connotative language as well as to symbolism.

2. Using examples from the poems that follow in this chapter, draw clear distinctions between allusions that reinforce the ideas in a poem and allusions that intensify the emotions being expressed—and note those allusions that carry both intellectual and emotional meanings.

Eurydice

Eurydice went back to hell.
What was difficult
was the travel, which,
on arrival, is forgotten.

Transition   5
is difficult.
And moving between two worlds
especially so;
the tension is very great.

A passage   10
filled with regret, with longing,
to which we have, in the world,
some slight access or memory.

Only for a moment
when the dark of the underworld   15
settled around her again
(gentle, respectful),
only for a moment could
an image of earth's beauty
reach her again, beauty   20
for which she grieved.

But to live with human faithlessness
is another matter.

—LOUISE GLÜCK (B. 1943)

QUESTIONS

1. Look up "Eurydice" on the Internet or in a book about Greek mythology. Who was she? What was her fate?
2. Discuss the double meaning of the word "passage" in line 10.
3. Does the speaker in this poem sympathize with Eurydice? How can you tell?
4. Analyze the meaning of the last two lines.

in Just—

in Just—
spring   when the world is mud-
luscious the little
lame balloonman

whistles   far   and wee   5

and eddieandbill come
running from marbles and
piracies and it's
spring

when the world is puddle-wonderful   10

the queer
old balloonman whistles
far   and   wee
and bettyandisbel come dancing

from hop-scotch and jump-rope and   15

it's
spring
and
      the
            goat-footed   20

balloonMan   whistles
far
and
wee

—e. e. cummings (1894–1962)

QUESTION

Why is the balloonman called "goat-footed" (20)? How does the identification made
by this mythological allusion enrich the meaning of the poem?

On His Blindness

When I consider how my light is spent
    Ere half my days in this dark world and wide,
    And that one talent which is death to hide
    Lodged with me useless, though my soul more bent
To serve therewith my Maker, and present   5
    My true account, lest he returning chide:
    "Doth God exact day-labor, light denied?"
    I fondly ask. But Patience, to prevent

That murmur, soon replies, "God doth not need
  Either man's work or his own gifts. Who best   10
  Bear his mild yoke, they serve him best. His state
Is kingly: thousands at his bidding speed,
  And post o'er land and ocean without rest;
  They also serve who only stand and wait."

—JOHN MILTON (1608–1674)

QUESTIONS

1. Vocabulary: *spent* (1), *fondly* (8), *prevent* (8), *post* (13).
2. What two meanings has "talent" (3)? What is Milton's "one talent"?
3. The poem is unified and expanded in its dimensions by a biblical allusion that Milton's original readers would have recognized immediately. What is it? If you do not know, look up Matthew 25:14–30. In what ways is the situation in the poem similar to that in the parable? In what ways is it different?
4. What is the point of the poem?

MindTap® Read, highlight, and take notes online.

Miniver Cheevy

Miniver Cheevy, child of scorn,
  Grew lean while he assailed the seasons;
He wept that he was ever born,
  And he had reasons.

Miniver loved the days of old   5
  When swords were bright and steeds were prancing;
The vision of a warrior bold
  Would set him dancing.

Miniver sighed for what was not,
  And dreamed, and rested from his labors;   10
He dreamed of Thebes and Camelot,
  And Priam's neighbors.

Miniver mourned the ripe renown
  That made so many a name so fragrant;
He mourned Romance, now on the town,   15
  And Art, a vagrant.

Miniver loved the Medici,
  Albeit he had never seen one;

He would have sinned incessantly
    Could he have been one.   20

Miniver cursed the commonplace
    And eyed a khaki suit with loathing;
He missed the medieval grace
    Of iron clothing.

Miniver scorned the gold he sought,   25
    But sore annoyed was he without it;
Miniver thought, and thought, and thought,
    And thought about it.

Miniver Cheevy, born too late,
    Scratched his head and kept on thinking;   30
Miniver coughed, and called it fate,
    And kept on drinking.

—EDWIN ARLINGTON ROBINSON (1869–1935)

QUESTIONS

1. Vocabulary: *khaki* (22). The phrase "on the town" (15) means "on charity" or "down and out."
2. Identify Thebes (11), Camelot (11), Priam (12), and the Medici (17). What names and what sort of life does each call up? What does Miniver's love of these names tell about him?
3. Discuss the phrase "child of scorn" (1). What does it mean? In how many ways is it applicable to Miniver?
4. What is Miniver's attitude toward material wealth?
5. The phrase "rested from his labors" (10) alludes to the Bible *and* to Greek mythology. Explore the ironic effect of comparing Miniver to the Creator (Genesis 2:2) and to Hercules. Point out other examples of irony in the poem and discuss their importance.
6. Can we call this a poem about a man whose "fate" was to be "born too late"? Explain your answer.

My Son the Man

Suddenly his shoulders get a lot wider,
the way Houdini would expand his body
while people were putting him in chains. It seems
no time since I would help him put on his sleeper,
guide his calves into the shadowy interior,   5

zip him up and toss him up and
catch his weight. I cannot imagine him
no longer a child, and I know I must get ready,
get over my fear of men now my son
is going to be one. This was not   10
what I had in mind when he pressed up through me like a
sealed trunk through the ice of the Hudson,
snapped the padlock, unsnaked the chains,
appeared in my arms. Now he looks at me
the way Houdini studied a box   15
to learn the way out, then smiled and let himself be
    manacled.

—SHARON OLDS (B. 1942)

QUESTIONS

1. "Harry Houdini" was the stage name of Erich Weiss (1874–1926), an escape artist whose most famous stunt was freeing himself after being chained, sealed in a padlocked trunk, and dropped into deep water.
2. To what event does the speaker compare Houdini's escape?
3. How does this allusion express the speaker's feelings about her son? Are they mixed feelings?

Journey of the Magi

"A cold coming we had of it,
Just the worst time of the year
For a journey, and such a long journey:
The ways deep and the weather sharp,
The very dead of winter."   5
And the camels galled, sore-footed, refractory,
Lying down in the melting snow.
There were times we regretted
The summer palaces on slopes, the terraces,
And the silken girls bringing sherbet.   10
Then the camel men cursing and grumbling
And running away, and wanting their liquor and women,
And the night-fires going out, and the lack of shelters,
And the cities hostile and the towns unfriendly
And the villages dirty and charging high prices: 15
A hard time we had of it.
At the end we preferred to travel all night,

Sleeping in snatches,
With the voices singing in our ears, saying
That this was all folly.   20

Then at dawn we came down to a temperate valley,
Wet, below the snow line, smelling of vegetation;
With a running stream and a water-mill beating the darkness,
And three trees on the low sky,
And an old white horse galloped away in the meadow.   25
Then we came to a tavern with vine-leaves over the lintel,
Six hands at an open door dicing for pieces of silver,
And feet kicking the empty wine-skins.
But there was no information, and so we continued
And arrived at evening, not a moment too soon   30
Finding the place; it was (you may say) satisfactory.

All this was a long time ago, I remember,
And I would do it again, but set down
This set down
This: were we led all that way for   35
Birth or Death? There was a Birth, certainly,
We had evidence and no doubt. I had seen birth and death,
But had thought they were different; this Birth was
Hard and bitter agony for us, like Death, our death.
We returned to our places, these Kingdoms,   40
But no longer at ease here, in the old dispensation,
With an alien people clutching their gods.
I should be glad of another death.

                                                        —T. S. ELIOT (1888–1965)

QUESTIONS

1. The biblical account of the journey of the Magi, or wise men, to Bethlehem is given in Matthew 2:1–12 and has since been elaborated by numerous legendary accretions. It has been made familiar through countless pageants and Christmas cards. How does this account differ from the familiar one? Compare it with the biblical account. What has been added? What has been left out? What is the poet doing? (Lines 1–5 are in quotation marks because they are taken, with very slight modification, from a Christmas sermon [1622] by the Anglican bishop Lancelot Andrewes.)
2. Who is the speaker? Where and when is he speaking? What is the "old dispensation" (41) to which he refers, and why are the people "alien" (42)? Why does he speak of the "Birth" (38) as being "like Death" (39)? Of whose "Birth" and "Death" is he speaking? How does his life differ from the life he lived before his journey? What does he mean by saying that he would be "glad of another death" (43)?

3. This poem was written while the poet was undergoing religious conversion. (Eliot published it in 1927, the year he was confirmed in the Anglican Church.) Could the poem be considered a parable of the conversion experience? If so, how does this account differ from popular conceptions of this experience?
4. How do the images in the second section differ from those of the first? Do any of them suggest connections with the life of Christ?

Genesis

It was late, of course,
just the two of us still at the table
working on a second bottle of wine

when you speculated that maybe Eve came first
and Adam began as a rib   5
that leaped out of her side one paradisal afternoon.

Could be, I remember saying,
because much was possible back then,
and I mentioned the talking snake
and the giraffes sticking their necks out of the ark,   10
their noses up in the pouring Old Testament rain.

I like a man with a flexible mind, you said then,
lifting your candle-lit glass to me
and I raised mine to you and began to wonder

what life would be like as one of your ribs—   15
to be with you all the time,
riding under your blouse and skin,
caged under the soft weight of your breasts,

your favorite rib, I am assuming,
if you ever bothered to stop and count them   20
which is just what I did later that night
after you had fallen asleep
and we were fitted tightly back to front,
your long legs against the length of mine,
my fingers doing the crazy numbering that comes of love.   25

—BILLY COLLINS (B. 1941)

QUESTIONS

1. Find the passages in the book of Genesis to which this poem alludes. Would you call the allusions serious or playful, or both?
2. Describe the relationship between the speaker and his partner.
3. Most of this poem about the romantic relationship is set in the past. Why is this appropriate?

Leda and the Swan

A sudden blow: the great wings beating still
Above the staggering girl, her thighs caressed
By the dark webs, her nape caught in his bill,
He holds her helpless breast upon his breast.

How can those terrified vague fingers push   5
The feathered glory from her loosening thighs?
And how can body, laid in that white rush,
But feel the strange heart beating where it lies?

A shudder in the loins engenders there
The broken wall, the burning roof and tower   10
And Agamemnon dead.
                                 Being so caught up,
So mastered by the brute blood of the air,
Did she put on his knowledge with his power
Before the indifferent beak could let her drop?

—WILLIAM BUTLER YEATS (1865–1939)

QUESTIONS

1. What is the connection between Leda and "The broken wall, the burning roof and tower / And Agamemnon dead" (10–11)? If you do not know, look up the myth of Leda and the story of Agamemnon.
2. How does this poem do more than evoke an episode out of mythology? What is the significance of the question asked in the last two lines? How would you answer it?

A little East of Jordan

A little East of Jordan,
Evangelists record,
A Gymnast and an Angel
Did wrestle long and hard—

Till morning touching mountain—   5
And Jacob, waxing strong,
The Angel begged permission
To Breakfast—to return—

Not so, said cunning Jacob!
"I will not let thee go   10
Except thou bless me"—Stranger!
The which acceded to—

Light swung the silver fleeces
"Peniel" Hills beyond,
And the bewildered Gymnast   15
Found he had worsted God!

—EMILY DICKINSON (1830–1886)

QUESTIONS

1. Discuss the biblical allusion in this poem. Does Dickinson hold fast to the biblical account or does she use it for her own purposes?
2. In what sense has the "Gymnast" (15) "worsted God" (16)?
3. Is the poem lighthearted or serious, or somewhere in between?

SUGGESTIONS FOR WRITING

An allusion may present a comparison or parallel, or it may create an ironic contrast. Choosing one or more of the following examples, write an essay demonstrating that the poem(s) use allusion positively, to enrich the theme, or, ironically, to undercut the speaker's ideas.

1. Larkin, "A Study of Reading Habits" (page 25; allusions to types of cheap fiction).
2. Keats, "On the Sonnet" (page 158; allusions to Andromeda and Midas).
3. Collins, "Sonnet" (page 159; allusions to Petrarch and Laura).
4. Keats, "Ode to a Nightingale" (page 390; allusion to the book of Ruth).
5. Yeats, "The Song of Wandering Aengus" (page 418; allusion to Irish mythology).

PRACTICE AP® WRITING PROMPTS

Edwin Arlington Robinson, "Miniver Cheevy" (pp. 143–144)

Read "Miniver Cheevy" with care. Then in a well-written essay analyze how the author employs selection of detail, diction, syntax, and allusion to characterize Miniver Cheevy.

T. S. Eliot, "Journey of the Magi" (pp. 145–146)

Read "The Journey of the Magi." Then write an essay in which you analyze how repetition, allusion, and detail enable the speaker to express his complex attitude toward his spiritual journey.

CHAPTER NINE

Meaning and Idea

The meaning of a poem is the experience it expresses—nothing less. But readers who, baffled by a particular poem, ask perplexedly, "What does it *mean?*" are usually after something more specific than this. They want something they can grasp entirely with their minds. We may therefore find it useful to distinguish the **total meaning** of a poem—the experience it communicates (and which can be communicated in no other way)—from its **prose meaning**—the ingredient that can be separated out in the form of a prose paraphrase (see Chapter 2). If we make this distinction, however, we must be careful not to confuse the two kinds of meaning. The prose meaning is no more the poem than a plum is a pie or a prune is a plum.

The prose meaning will not necessarily or perhaps even usually be an idea. It may be a story, a description, a statement of emotion, a presentation of human character, or some combination of these. "Porphyria's Lover" (page 224) tells a story; "The Eagle" (page 4) is primarily descriptive; "The Widow's Lament in Springtime" (page 61) is an expression of emotion; "My Last Duchess" (page 288) is an account of human character. None of these poems is directly concerned with ideas. Message-hunters will be baffled and disappointed by poetry of this kind because they will not find what they are looking for, and they may attempt to read some idea into the poem that is really not there. Yet ideas are also part of human experience, and therefore many poems are concerned, at least partially, with presenting ideas. But with these poems message-hunting is an even more dangerous activity, for the message-hunters are likely to think that the whole object of reading the poem is to find the message—that the idea is really the only important thing in it. Like Little Jack Horner, they will reach in and pluck out the idea and say, "What a good boy am I!" as if the pie existed for the plum.

The idea in a poem is only part of the total experience that it communicates. The value and worth of the poem are determined by the value of the total experience, not by the truth or the nobility of the idea itself. This is not to say that the truth of the idea is unimportant, or that its validity should not be examined and appraised. But a good idea alone will not make a good poem, nor will an idea with which the reader does not agree ruin one. Readers of poetry are receptive to all kinds of experiences. They are able to make that "willing suspension of disbelief" that Coleridge characterized as constituting poetic faith. When one attends a performance of *Hamlet,* one is willing to forget for the time being that such a person as Hamlet never existed and that the events on the stage are fictions. Likewise, poetry readers should be willing to entertain imaginatively, for the time being, ideas they objectively regard as untrue. It is one way of better understanding these ideas and of enlarging the reader's own experience. The person who believes in God should be able to enjoy a good poem expressing atheistic ideas, just as the atheist should be able to appreciate a good poem in praise of God. The optimist should be able to find pleasure in pessimistic poetry, and the pessimist in optimistic poetry. The teetotaler should be able to enjoy *The Rubáiyát of Omar Khayyám,* and the winebibber a good poem in praise of abstinence.

The primary value of a poem depends not so much on the truth of the idea presented as on the power with which it is communicated and on its being made a convincing part of a meaningful total experience. We must feel that the idea has been truly and deeply *felt* by the poet, and that the poet is doing something more than merely moralizing. The plum must be made part of a pie. If the plum is properly combined with other ingredients and if the pie is well baked, it should be enjoyable even for persons who do not care for the type of plums from which it is made. Consider, for instance, the following two poems.

Loveliest of Trees

Loveliest of trees, the cherry now
Is hung with bloom along the bough,
And stands about the woodland ride
Wearing white for Eastertide.

Now, of my threescore years and ten,   5
Twenty will not come again,
And take from seventy springs a score,
It only leaves me fifty more.

And since to look at things in bloom
Fifty springs are little room,   10

About the woodlands I will go
To see the cherry hung with snow.

—A. E. HOUSMAN (1859–1936)

QUESTIONS

1. Very briefly, this poem presents a philosophy of life. In a sentence, what is it?
2. How old is the speaker? Why does he assume that his life will be seventy years in length? What is surprising about the words "only" (8) and "little" (10)?
3. A good deal of ink has been spilt over whether "snow" (12) is literal or figurative. What do you say? Justify your answer.

Stopping by Woods on a Snowy Evening

Whose woods these are I think I know.
His house is in the village though;
He will not see me stopping here
To watch his woods fill up with snow.

My little horse must think it queer   5
To stop without a farmhouse near
Between the woods and frozen lake
The darkest evening of the year.

He gives his harness bells a shake
To ask if there is some mistake.   10
The only other sound's the sweep
Of easy wind and downy flake.

The woods are lovely, dark and deep,
But I have promises to keep,
And miles to go before I sleep,   15
And miles to go before I sleep.

—ROBERT FROST (1874–1963)

QUESTIONS

1. How do these two poems differ in idea?
2. What contrasts are suggested between the speaker in the second poem and (a) his horse and (b) the owner of the woods?

Both of these poems present ideas, the first more or less explicitly, the second symbolically. Perhaps the best way to get at the idea of the second poem is to ask two questions. First, why does the speaker stop? Second, why does he go on? He stops, we answer, to watch the woods fill up with snow—to observe a scene of natural beauty. He goes on, we answer, because he has "promises to keep"—that is, he has obligations to fulfill. He is momentarily torn between his love of beauty and these other various and complex claims that life has upon him. The small conflict in the poem is symbolic of a larger conflict in life. One part of the sensitive, thinking person would like to give up his life to the enjoyment of beauty and art. But another part is aware of larger duties and responsibilities—responsibilities owed, at least in part, to other human beings. The speaker in the poem would like to satisfy both impulses. But when the two conflict, he seems to suggest, the "promises" must take precedence.

The first poem also presents a philosophy but it is an opposing one. For the twenty-year-old speaker, the appreciation of beauty is of such importance that he will make it his lifelong dedication, filling his time with enjoying whatever the seasons bring. The metaphor comparing white cherry blossoms to snow suggests that each season has its own special beauty, though the immediate season is spring. In a limited life, one should seek out and delight in whatever beauty is present. Thoughtful readers will have to choose between these two philosophies—to commit themselves to one or the other—but this commitment should not destroy for them their enjoyment of either poem. If it does, they are reading for plums and not for pies.

Nothing we have said so far in this chapter should be construed as meaning that the truth or falsity of the idea in a poem is a matter of no importance. *Other things being equal,* good readers naturally will, and properly should, value more highly the poem whose idea they feel to be more mature and nearer to the heart of human experience. Some ideas, moreover, may seem so vicious or so foolish or so beyond the pale of normal human decency as to discredit *by themselves* the poems in which they are found. A rotten plum may spoil a pie. But good readers strive for intellectual flexibility and tolerance, and are able to entertain sympathetically ideas other than their own. They often will like a poem whose idea they disagree with better than one with an idea they accept. And, above all, they will not confuse the prose meaning of any poem with its total meaning. They will not mistake plums for pies.

REVIEWING CHAPTER NINE

1. The second paragraph of this chapter identifies four poems as not being "directly concerned with ideas"; examine those poems and demonstrate that although that statement is true of the prose meaning of each, the total meaning does in fact express an idea.

2. Explain how a poem that expresses an idea with which you do not agree may, nevertheless, be a source of appreciation and enjoyment.

3. The poems that follow in this chapter are paired in terms of their contrasted ideas; as you read them, practice discriminating between their ideas as we have done with the pair of poems by Housman and Frost, and determine which of the contrasted ideas more closely reflects your own beliefs.

4. Having determined where your beliefs are reflected, explain how the contrasting poem nevertheless has qualities you can admire.

Four Trees—upon a solitary Acre

Four Trees—upon a solitary Acre—
Without Design
Or Order, or Apparent Action—
Maintain—

The Sun—upon a Morning meets them—   5
The Wind—
No nearer Neighbor—have they—
But God—

The Acre gives them—Place—
They—Him—Attention of Passer by—   10
Of Shadow, or of Squirrel, haply—
Or Boy—

What Deed is Theirs unto the General Nature—
What Plan
They severally—retard—or further—   15
Unknown—

—EMILY DICKINSON (1830–1886)

QUESTIONS

1. Vocabulary: *haply* (11).
2. Discuss the major images in this poem. What do they imply about the landscape being described?
3. Is the landscape appealing or forbidding to the speaker? How can you tell?
4. Does the poem argue for a coherent design in the universe, or against such a notion?

Design

I found a dimpled spider, fat and white,
On a white heal-all, holding up a moth
Like a white piece of rigid satin cloth—
Assorted characters of death and blight
Mixed ready to begin the morning right,   5
Like the ingredients of a witches' broth—
A snow-drop spider, a flower like a froth,
And dead wings carried like a paper kite.

What had that flower to do with being white,
The wayside blue and innocent heal-all?   10
What brought the kindred spider to that height,
Then steered the white moth thither in the night?
What but design of darkness to appall?—
If design govern in a thing so small.

—ROBERT FROST (1874–1963)

QUESTIONS

1. Vocabulary: *characters* (4), *snow-drop* (7).
2. The heal-all is a wildflower, usually blue or violet but occasionally white, found blooming along roadsides in the summer. It was once supposed to have healing qualities, hence its name. Of what significance, scientific and poetic, is the fact that the spider, the heal-all, and the moth are all white? Of what poetic significance is the fact that the spider is "dimpled" and "fat" and like a "snow-drop," and that the flower is "innocent" and named "heal-all"?
3. The "argument from design"—that the manifest existence of design in the universe implies the existence of a Great Designer—was a favorite eighteenth-century argument for the existence of God. What twist does Frost give the argument? What answer does he suggest to the question in lines 11–12? How comforting is the apparent concession in line 14?

O sweet spontaneous

O sweet spontaneous
earth how often have
the
doting

      fingers of   5
prurient philosophers pinched
and
poked

thee
,has the naughty thumb   10
of science prodded
thy

      beauty   .how
often have religions taken
thee upon their scraggy knees   15
squeezing and

buffeting thee that thou mightest conceive
gods
   (but
true   20

to the incomparable
couch of death thy
rhythmic
lover

     thou answerest   25

them only with

       spring)

—e. e. cummings (1894–1962)

QUESTIONS

1. What metaphorical context is created by such words as *doting, prurient, naughty, conceive* (4, 6, 10, 17) and others? What have the philosophers attempted to do, and to what purpose?

2. Explain "the incomparable / couch of death" (21–22) and the "rhythmic / lover" (23–24).
3. How is "spring" (27) a response to the philosophers' attempts?

When I Heard the Learn'd Astronomer

When I heard the learn'd astronomer,
When the proofs, the figures, were ranged in columns
   before me,
When I was shown the charts and diagrams, to add, divide,
   and measure them,
When I sitting heard the astronomer where he lectured
   with much applause in the lecture-room,
How soon unaccountable I became tired and sick,   5
Till rising and gliding out I wandered off by myself,
In the mystical moist night-air, and from time to time,
Looked up in perfect silence at the stars.

—WALT WHITMAN (1819–1892)

QUESTIONS
1. What is it that makes the speaker "tired and sick" (5)?
2. Explain how "gliding" and "wandered off" (6) are contrasted to the astronomer's lecture. How is the phrase "from time to time" (7) a denial of the validity of the scientific approach to the universe? What attitude is expressed by the speaker's "perfect silence" (8)?
3. Both Whitman and cummings present emotional objections to science and scientific attempts to explain nature. How are these poems different in tone (see page 165)?

On the Sonnet

If by dull rhymes our English must be chained,
And like Andromeda, the sonnet sweet
Fettered, in spite of painéd loveliness,
Let us find, if we must be constrained,
Sandals more interwoven and complete   5
To fit the naked foot of Poesy:
Let us inspect the lyre, and weigh the stress
Of every chord, and see what may be gained
By ear industrious, and attention meet;

Misers of sound and syllable, no less   10
Than Midas of his coinage, let us be
Jealous of dead leaves in the bay-wreath crown;
So, if we may not let the Muse be free,
She will be bound with garlands of her own.

—JOHN KEATS (1795–1821)

QUESTIONS

1. Vocabulary: *Andromeda* (2), *meet* (9), *Midas* (11).
2. The poem prescribes a specific approach to writing sonnets. What qualities does the speaker suggest a good sonnet should have?
3. The speaker compares poetry to a foot and the sonnet form to a sandal. What does he mean by suggesting that the sonnet-sandals should be "more interwoven and complete" (5)?
4. What negative qualities does the poem imply that bad sonnets display?

MindTap Read, highlight, and take notes online.

Sonnet

All we need is fourteen lines, well, thirteen now,
and after this one just a dozen
to launch a little ship on love's storm-tossed seas,
then only ten more left like rows of beans.
How easily it goes unless you get Elizabethan   5
and insist the iambic bongos must be played
and rhymes positioned at the ends of lines,
one for every station of the cross.
But hang on here while we make the turn
into the final six where all will be resolved,   10
where longing and heartache will find an end,
where Laura will tell Petrarch to put down his pen,
take off those crazy medieval tights,
blow out the lights, and come at last to bed.

—BILLY COLLINS (B. 1941)

QUESTIONS

1. In line 12, "Laura will tell Petrarch to put down his pen," the poem alludes to the Italian poet Francesco Petrarch (1304–1374), who wrote a sequence of sonnets to his idealized lady-love, Laura. What attitude does the speaker take toward Petrarch and the Petrarchan sonnet?

2. The phrase "love's storm-tossed seas" (3) is a deliberate cliché. Why is the cliché appropriate here?
3. What is the effect of images such as "rows of beans" (4) and "iambic bongos" (6)? How do they help create the speaker's distinctive voice?
4. Although this and the preceding poem differ greatly in language and emotion, they may be compared as statements about the sonnet. What are their essential ideas about this poetic form?

Southern History

Before the war, they were happy, he said,
quoting our textbook. (This was senior-year

history class.) The slaves were clothed, fed,
and better off under a master's care.

I watched the words blur on the page. No one   5
raised a hand, disagreed. Not even me.

It was late; we still had Reconstruction
to cover before the test, and—luckily—

three hours of watching Gone with the Wind.
History, the teacher said, of the old South—   10

a true account of how things were back then.
On screen a slave stood big as life: big mouth,

bucked eyes, our textbook's grinning proof—a lie
my teacher guarded. Silent, so did I.

—NATASHA TRETHEWEY (B. 1966)

QUESTIONS

1. Is the history teacher African American? Is he presenting his own attitudes or those he is expected to teach? If the speaker can detect a lie in the lesson, can the teacher?
2. Why do none of the students disagree with the lesson? How does the speaker feel about herself? How does she feel about the teacher?

The Colonel

What you have heard is true. I was in his house. His wife carried a tray of coffee and sugar. His daughter filed her nails, his son went out for the night. There were daily papers, pet dogs, a pistol on the cushion beside him. The moon swung bare on its black cord over the house. On the television was a cop show. It was in English. Broken bottles were embedded in the walls around the house to scoop the kneecaps from a man's legs or cut his hands to lace. On the windows there were gratings like those in liquor stores. We had dinner, rack of lamb, good wine, a gold bell was on the table for calling the maid. The maid brought green mangoes, salt, a type of bread. I was asked how I enjoyed the country. There was a brief commercial in Spanish. His wife took everything away. There was some talk then of how difficult it had become to govern. The parrot said hello on the terrace. The colonel told it to shut up, and pushed himself from the table. My friend said to me with his eyes: say nothing. The colonel returned with a sack used to bring groceries home. He spilled many human ears on the table. They were like dried peach halves. There is no other way to say this. He took one of them in his hands, shook it in our faces, dropped it into a water glass. It came alive there. I am tired of fooling around he said. As for the rights of anyone, tell your people they can go fuck themselves. He swept the ears to the floor with his arm and held the last of his wine in the air. Something for your poetry, no? he said. Some of the ears on the floor caught this scrap of his voice. Some of the ears on the floor were pressed to the ground.

May 1978

—CAROLYN FORCHÉ (B. 1950)

QUESTIONS

1. Who is the narrator of this prose poem? What is her supposed reaction to meeting the Colonel?
2. Discuss the use of irony in the prose poem—e.g., the contrast between the way the Colonel lives at home and what he does in his military function.
3. The last third of the prose poem focuses on a sack full of human ears. What does the narrator suggest when she writes, "Some of the ears on the floor were pressed to the ground"?
4. How would you describe the prose style in the prose poem? Is it restrained or highly dramatic? How does the style contribute to the overall effect?

The Lamb

Little Lamb, who made thee?
Dost thou know who made thee?
Gave thee life and bid thee feed
By the stream and o'er the mead;
Gave thee clothing of delight,   5
Softest clothing wooly bright;
Gave thee such a tender voice,
Making all the vales rejoice!
Little Lamb, who made thee?
Dost thou know who made thee?   10

Little Lamb, I'll tell thee,
Little Lamb, I'll tell thee!
He is callèd by thy name,
For he calls himself a Lamb;
He is meek and he is mild,   15
He became a little child;
I a child and thou a lamb,
We are callèd by his name.
Little Lamb, God bless thee.
Little Lamb, God bless thee.   20

—WILLIAM BLAKE (1757–1827)

QUESTIONS

1. Why does the speaker address the "Little Lamb" (1) directly? What effects does the poem gain from this use of apostrophe?
2. What is the relationship between the two stanzas? Why is the poem constructed in this way?
3. What is the significance of the "lamb" imagery? What connotations does it have?

The Tiger

Tiger! Tiger! burning bright
In the forests of the night,
What immortal hand or eye
Could frame thy fearful symmetry?

In what distant deeps or skies   5
Burnt the fire of thine eyes?

On what wings dare he aspire?
What the hand dare seize the fire?

And what shoulder, and what art,
Could twist the sinews of thy heart?   10
And when thy heart began to beat,
What dread hand forged thy dread feet?

What the hammer? what the chain?
In what furnace was thy brain?
What the anvil? what dread grasp   15
Dare its deadly terrors clasp?

When the stars threw down their spears,
And watered heaven with their tears,
Did he smile his work to see?
Did he who made the Lamb make thee?   20

Tiger! Tiger! burning bright
In the forests of the night,
What immortal hand or eye
Dare frame thy fearful symmetry?

—WILLIAM BLAKE (1757–1827)

QUESTIONS

1. Discuss the relationship of this poem to Blake's "The Lamb." How do the poems make a distinctive and meaningful pairing?
2. What is the meaning of the various questions the speaker asks of the tiger? What are the implications of these questions?
3. What is the symbolic meaning of the tiger? What connotations are associated with this symbol?

SUGGESTIONS FOR WRITING

Explore the contrasting ideas in the following pairs of poems:
1. Brooks, "The Bean Eaters" (page 14) and Clifton, "good times" (page 362).
2. Hayden, "Those Winter Sundays" (page 66) and Roethke, "My Papa's Waltz" (page 128).
3. Hopkins, "Spring" (page 60) and Housman, "Loveliest of Trees" (page 152).
4. Plath, "Black Rook in Rainy Weather" (page 11) and Mathis, "Survival: A Guide" (page 395).
5. John Keats's "Ode to a Nightingale" (page 390) and Percy Bysshe Shelley's "Ode to the West Wind" (page 283).

PRACTICE AP® WRITING PROMPTS

A. E. Housman, "Loveliest of Trees" (pp. 152–153) and Robert Frost, "Stopping by Woods on a Snowy Evening" (p. 153)

"Loveliest of Trees" by A. E. Housman and "Stopping by Woods on a Snowy Evening" by Robert Frost are both set amidst the beauty of the woods. Write an essay in which you compare and contrast the speakers' moods, indicating how each employs a season to frame his particular response to beauty. In your essay, refer to such poetic techniques as metaphor, imagery, and understatement.

....

Natasha Trethewey, "Southern History" (p. 160)

Read "Southern History" by Natasha Trethewey carefully. In a well-written essay, analyze how the author's use of such literary elements as diction, tone, and irony serves to convey the significance of a moment when the speaker is made sharply aware of her racial identity.

....

John Keats "On the Sonnet" (pp. 158–159) and Billy Collins "Sonnet" (pp. 159–160)

Carefully read both "On the Sonnet" by John Keats and "Sonnet" by Billy Collins. Compare the two poems in a well-organized essay, paying particular attention to the ways in which each author makes use of the sonnet's structure to comment upon its suitability for poetic expression.

....

CHAPTER TEN

Tone

Tone, in literature, may be defined as the writer's or speaker's attitude toward the subject, the reader, or herself or himself. It is the emotional coloring, or the emotional meaning, of the work and is an extremely important part of the full meaning. In spoken language, tone is indicated by the inflections of the speaker's voice. If, for instance, a friend tells you, "I'm going to get married today," the facts of the statement are entirely clear. But the emotional meaning of the statement may vary widely according to the tone of voice with which it is uttered. The tone may be ecstatic ("Hooray! I'm going to get married today!"); it may be incredulous ("I can't believe it! I'm going to get married today"); it may be despairing ("Horrors! I'm going to get married today"); it may be resigned ("Might as well face it. I'm going to get married today"). Obviously, a correct interpretation of the tone will be an important part of understanding the full meaning. It may even have rather important consequences. If someone calls you a fool, your interpretation of the tone may determine whether you take it as an insult or as playful banter. If a person says "No" to your proposal of marriage, your interpretation of the tone may determine whether you ask again or start dating someone else.

In poetry, tone is likewise important. We have not really understood a poem unless we have accurately sensed whether the attitude it manifests is playful or solemn, mocking or reverent, calm or excited. But the correct determination of tone in literature is a much more delicate matter than it is in spoken language, for we do not have the speaker's voice to guide us. We must learn to recognize tone by other means. Almost all of the elements of poetry help to indicate its tone: connotation, imagery, and metaphor; irony and understatement; rhythm, sentence construction, and formal pattern. There is therefore no simple formula for recognizing tone. It is an end product of all the elements in a poem. The best we can do is illustrate.

Robert Frost's "Stopping by Woods on a Snowy Evening" (page 153) seems a simple poem, but it has always afforded trouble to beginning readers. A very good student, asked to interpret it, once wrote this: "The poem means that we are forever passing up pleasures to go onward to what we wrongly consider our obligations. We would like to watch the snow fall on the peaceful countryside, but we always have to rush home to supper and other engagements. Frost feels that the average person considers life too short to stop and take time to appreciate true pleasures." This student did a good job in recognizing the central conflict of the poem but went astray in recognizing its tone. Let's examine why.

In the first place, the fact that the speaker in the poem *does* stop to watch the snow fall in the woods immediately establishes him as a human being with more sensitivity and feeling for beauty than most. He is not one of the people of Wordsworth's sonnet (page 48) who, "Getting and spending," have laid waste their imaginative powers and lost the capacity to be stirred by nature. Frost's speaker is contrasted with his horse, who, as a creature of habit and an animal without esthetic perception, cannot understand the speaker's reason for stopping. There is also a suggestion of contrast with the "owner" of the woods, who, if he saw the speaker stopping, might be as puzzled as the horse. (Who most truly "profits" from the woods—its absentee owner or the person who can enjoy its beauty?) The speaker goes on because he has "promises to keep." But the word "promises," though it may here have a wry ironic undertone of regret, has a favorable connotation: people almost universally agree that promises ought to be kept. If the poet had used a different term, say, "things to do," or "business to attend to," or "financial affairs to take care of," or "money to make," the connotations would have been quite different. As it is, the tone of the poem tells us that the poet is sympathetic to the speaker; Frost is endorsing rather than censuring the speaker's action.

Perhaps we may go even further. In the concluding two lines, because of their climactic position, because they are repeated, and because "sleep" in poetry often figuratively refers to death, there is a suggestion of symbolic interpretation: "and many years to live before I die." If we accept this interpretation, it poses a parallel between giving oneself up to contemplation of the woods and dying. The poet's total implication would seem to be that beauty is a distinctively human value that deserves its place in a full life, but to devote one's life to its pursuit, at the expense of other obligations and duties, is tantamount to one's death as a responsible being. The poet therefore accepts the choice the speaker makes, though not without a touch of regret.

Differences in tone, and their importance, are most apparent in poems with similar content. Consider, for instance, the following pair.

To the Snake

Green Snake, when I hung you round my neck
and stroked your cold, pulsing throat
    as you hissed to me, glinting
arrowy gold scales, and I felt
    the weight of you on my shoulders,   5
and the whispering silver of your dryness
    sounded close at my ears—

Green Snake—I swore to my companions that certainly
    you were harmless! But truly
I had no certainty, and no hope, only desiring   10
    to hold you, for that joy,
               which left
a long wake of pleasure, as the leaves moved
and you faded into the pattern
of grass and shadows, and I returned   15
smiling and haunted, to a dark morning.

—DENISE LEVERTOV (1923–1997)

QUESTIONS

1. What figure of speech dominates in the poem? How does that reinforce the closeness the speaker is reporting?
2. Comment on these word pairs: "cold, pulsing" (2), "arrowy gold" (4), "smiling and haunted" (16), and "dark morning" (16). How do they contribute to the emotional meaning?
3. Is the experience of the speaker positive, or negative, or a combination?

A narrow Fellow in the Grass

A narrow Fellow in the Grass
Occasionally rides—
You may have met him? Did you not
His notice sudden is—

The Grass divides as with a Comb—   5
A spotted shaft is seen—
And then it closes at your feet
And opens further on—

He likes a Boggy Acre
A Floor too cool for Corn—   10
Yet when a Boy, and Barefoot—
I more than once at Noon

Have passed, I thought, a Whip lash—
Unbraiding in the Sun
When stooping to secure it   15
It wrinkled, and was gone—

Several of Nature's People
I know, and they know me—
I feel for them a transport
Of cordiality—   20

But never met this Fellow
Attended, or alone
Without a tighter breathing
And Zero at the Bone.

—EMILY DICKINSON (1830–1886)

QUESTIONS

1. Vocabulary: *Whip lash* (whiplash) (13), *transport* (19), *cordiality* (20).
2. Explain the simile in line 5.
3. Characterize the speaker.

Both poems exhibit a fascination with snakes, both relate a personal experience with them, and both focus on the emotional aftermath of that experience. But in tone the two poems are sharply different. The first is ecstatically engaged from the outset, not only emotional but even physical in its presentation of the experience. The second is detached, descriptive, and analytical, revealing its emotional response only in the last stanza. Let us examine the difference.

The first begins with an apostrophe, addressing the snake directly and thus bringing the reader into a close relationship with it as the speaker handles it, hangs it about her neck, strokes it, listens to its hissing, feels its weight, and stares at its beauty. At line 8 she turns to her "companions" to witness her closeness, but dismisses them to focus again on the snake itself. The intense moment of "joy" passes, leaving an intense memory of pleasure and the double response of "smiling" to her companions while being "haunted" by the whole encounter.

The second poem begins descriptively (and in typical Dickinson fashion, mysteriously, because the subject is not named). The snake is a familiar "fellow" who rides through the grass, startling the observer by his sudden appearance and disappearance. At line 11 the speaker reveals himself as a mature man recalling his boyhood experience and his acquired knowledge of the snake's preferred environment. The action then is focused on one particular encounter when the boy mistook the snake for a leather whip lying in the sun and—as boys will—attempted to pick up this exciting implement. The snake disappeared as suddenly as it can appear. The consequence of that moment is then generalized: the adult man has found throughout his life a "cordiality" for natural creatures, but not for snakes. They terrify him, and by implication he would much rather avoid them altogether. That momentary deceptiveness in his young life, when the snake seemed an attractive object, has resulted in continuing animosity.

In understanding the tone of these two poems we might explore the implicit allusion to the story of Eve in the garden of Eden, enticed by the serpent into disobeying God and thus to the punishments that resulted (Genesis 2:5–25). There we are told that Eve and the serpent will be eternal enemies, and that Adam will share in the miseries that ensued. Levertov's poem invites the reader to equate her story of seduction, pleasure, and loss with Eve's experience, focusing chiefly on the seduction in language that implies physical sexuality. Dickinson's poem, by deliberately choosing a male speaker and appealing to the stereotype that makes little boys more curious and aggressive, plays against the feminine stereotype of squeamishness about bugs, worms, snakes, and the like. The boy is attracted to the snake because it resembles an object of boyish self-expression, a weapon to be wielded.

Both poems conclude with a sense of separation from the snake, but with opposite effect: for Dickinson's speaker, a lifelong terror; for Levertov's, a lifelong loss.

We have been discussing tone as if every poem could be distinguished by a single tone. But varying or shifting tones in a single poem are often a valuable means for achieving the poet's purpose, and indeed may create the dramatic structure of a poem. Consider the following:

Since there's no help

Since there's no help, come let us kiss and part;
Nay, I have done, you get no more of me,
And I am glad, yea, glad with all my heart
That thus so cleanly I myself can free;
Shake hands forever, cancel all our vows,   5

And when we meet at any time again,
Be it not seen in either of our brows
That we one jot of former love retain.
Now, at the last gasp of Love's latest breath,
When, his pulse failing, Passion speechless lies,   10
When Faith is kneeling by his bed of death,
And Innocence is closing up his eyes,
Now, if thou wouldst, when all have given him over,
From death to life thou mightst him yet recover.

—MICHAEL DRAYTON (1563–1631)

QUESTIONS

1. What difference in tone do you find between the first eight lines and the last six? In which part is the speaker more sincere? What differences in rhythm and language help to establish the difference in tone?
2. How many figures are there in the allegorical scene in lines 9–12? What do the pronouns "his" and "him" in lines 10–14 refer to? What is dying? Why? How might the person addressed still restore it from death to life?
3. Define the dramatic situation as precisely as possible, taking into consideration both the man's attitude and the woman's.

Accurately determining tone, whether it be the tone of a rejected marriage proposal or of an insulting remark, is extremely important when interpreting language in poetry as well as in everyday conversations. For the experienced reader it will be instinctive and automatic. For the inexperienced reader it will require study. But beyond the general suggestions for reading that we already have made, there are no specific instructions we can give. Recognition of tone requires an increasing familiarity with the meanings and connotations of words, alertness to the presence of irony and other figures, and, above all, careful reading.

Lost Love

My sister spent a whole life in the earth.
She was born, she died.
In between,
not one alert look, not one sentence.

She did what babies do,   5
she cried. But she didn't want to be fed.

Still, my mother held her, trying to change
first fate, then history.

Something did change: when my sister died,
my mother's heart became   10
very cold, very rigid,
like a tiny pendant of iron.

Then it seemed to me my sister's body
was a magnet. I could feel it draw
my mother's heart into the earth,   15
so it would grow.

—LOUISE GLÜCK (B. 1943)

QUESTIONS

1. Usually the theme of "lost love" deals with a romantic relationship, but here it deals with a bond between a mother and daughter. Is the title appropriate?
2. How would you describe the tone of this poem? What is the speaker's attitude toward the mother? Toward her deceased sister?
3. Discuss the images of "iron" (12) and "magnet" (14) in the last two stanzas. Why are they appropriate? How do they contribute to the tone of the poem?

REVIEWING CHAPTER TEN

1. Consider the ways in which tone is part of the total meaning of a poem (you might think of the total meaning as a compound of the intellectual and the emotional).
2. The second paragraph of this chapter lists many of the elements of poetry that contribute to tone; as you examine the first two poems presented in the chapter, try to identify which of the elements are particularly significant in each of them.
3. Tone is customarily identified by an adjective (*wistful, pessimistic, horrified* in the discussion of the first two poems). Choose adjectives to identify the two contrasting tones in "Since there's no help." (Do not settle for the first adjective that pops into mind—this is a good opportunity to exercise your vocabulary and strive for precision.)

My mistress' eyes

My mistress' eyes are nothing like the sun;
Coral is far more red than her lips' red; —
If snow be white, why then her breasts are dun;
If hairs be wires, black wires grow on her head.
I have seen roses damasked,° red and white,   of different colors
But no such roses see I in her cheeks;   6
And in some perfumes is there more delight —
Than in the breath that from my mistress reeks.°   exhales
I love to hear her speak, yet well I know
That music hath a far more pleasing sound;   10
I grant I never saw a goddess go,—
My mistress, when she walks, treads on the ground.
And yet, by heaven, I think my love as rare —
As any she belied with false compare. —

—WILLIAM SHAKESPEARE (1564–1616)

QUESTIONS

1. The speaker draws a contrast between the qualities often praised in exaggerated love poetry and the reality of his mistress's physical attributes. Construct the series of "false compar[isons]" that this poem implies that other poets have used (eyes as bright as the sun, hair like spun gold, etc.).
2. What is the speaker's tone in lines 1–12? Is there anything about those lines that his mistress might find pleasing? (In Shakespeare's time the word "reeks" did not have its modern denotation of "stinks.")
3. The tone clearly shifts with line 13—signaled by the simple phrase "And yet." What is the tone of the last two lines? The last line might be paraphrased "as any woman who has been lied to with false comparisons." How important are truth and lies as subjects in the poem?

Crossing the Bar

Sunset and evening star,
    And one clear call for me!
And may there be no moaning of the bar
    When I put out to sea,

But such a tide as moving seems asleep,   5
    Too full for sound and foam,

When that which drew from out the boundless deep
    Turns again home.

Twilight and evening bell,
    And after that the dark!   10
And may there be no sadness of farewell
    When I embark;

For though from out our bourne of Time and Place
    The flood may bear me far,
I hope to see my Pilot face to face   15
    When I have crossed the bar.

—ALFRED, LORD TENNYSON (1809–1892)

QUESTIONS

1. Vocabulary: *bourne* (13).
2. What two sets of figures does Tennyson use for approaching death? What is the precise moment of death in each set?
3. In troubled weather the wind and waves above the sandbar across a harbor's mouth make a moaning sound. What metaphorical meaning has the "moaning of the bar" (3) here? For what kind of death is the speaker wishing? Why does he want "no sadness of farewell" (11)?
4. What is "that which drew from out the boundless deep" (7)? What is "the boundless deep"? To what is it opposed in the poem? Why is "Pilot" (15) capitalized?

The Oxen

Christmas Eve, and twelve of the clock.
    "Now they are all on their knees,"
An elder said as we sat in a flock
    By the embers in hearthside ease.

We pictured the meek mild creatures where   5
    They dwelt in their strawy pen,
Nor did it occur to one of us there
    To doubt they were kneeling then.

So fair a fancy few would weave
    In these years! Yet, I feel,   10
If someone said on Christmas Eve,
    "Come; see the oxen kneel

"In the lonely barton° by yonder coomb°   farm; valley
    Our childhood used to know,"
I should go with him in the gloom,   15
    Hoping it might be so.

                               —THOMAS HARDY (1840–1928)

QUESTIONS

1. Is the simple superstition referred to in this poem opposed to, or identified with, religious faith? With what implications for the meaning of the poem?
2. What are "these years" (10), and how do they contrast with the years of the poet's boyhood? What event in intellectual history between 1840 and 1915 (the date Hardy composed this poem) was most responsible for the change?
3. Both "Crossing the Bar" and "The Oxen" in their last lines use a form of the verb *hope*. By fully discussing tone, establish the precise meaning of hope in each poem. What degree of expectation does it imply? How should the word be handled in reading Tennyson's poem aloud?

The Flea

Mark but this flea, and mark in this
How little that which thou deny'st me is;
It sucked me first, and now sucks thee,
And in this flea our two bloods mingled be;
Thou know'st that this cannot be said   5
A sin, nor shame, nor loss of maidenhead;
    Yet this enjoys before it woo,
    And pampered swells with one blood made of two,
    And this, alas, is more than we would do.

Oh stay, three lives in one flea spare,   10
Where we almost, yea more than married are.
This flea is you and I, and this
Our marriage bed and marriage temple is;
Though parents grudge, and you, we are met
And cloistered in these living walls of jet.   15
    Though use° make you apt to kill me,   habit
    Let not to that, self-murder added be,
    And sacrilege, three sins in killing three.

Cruel and sudden, hast thou since
Purpled° thy nail in blood of innocence?   crimsoned   20

Wherein could this flea guilty be,
Except in that drop which it sucked from thee?
Yet thou triumph'st and say'st that thou
Find'st not thyself, nor me, the weaker now.
    'Tis true. Then learn how false fears be: 25
    Just so much honor, when thou yield'st to me,
    Will waste, as this flea's death took life from thee.

—JOHN DONNE (1572–1631)

QUESTIONS

1. In many respects this poem is like a miniature play: it has two characters, dramatic conflict, dialogue (though we hear only one speaker), and stage action. The action is indicated by stage directions embodied in the dialogue. What has happened just *preceding* the first line of the poem? What happens *between* the first and second stanzas? What happens *between* the second and third? How does the female character behave and what does she say *during* the third stanza?
2. What has been the past relationship of the speaker and the woman? What has she denied him (2)? How has she habitually "kill[ed]" him (16)? Why has she done so? How does it happen that he is still alive? What is his objective in the poem?
3. According to a traditional Renaissance belief, the blood of lovers "mingled" during sexual intercourse. What is the speaker's argument in stanza 1? Reduce it to paraphrase. How logical is it?
4. What do "parents grudge, and you" in stanza 2? What are the "living walls of jet" (15)? What three things will the woman kill by crushing the flea? What three sins will she commit (18)?
5. Why and how does the woman "triumph" in stanza 3? What is the speaker's response? How logical is his concluding argument?

Bop After Hip Op

For years, I wrote as if without stop—
like lines of spore in a dish, the letters of the
alphabet would come out of me,
like tiny antlers out of my head,
like branches, twigs, stems of a tree,   5
it seemed to be who I was, the thorny
singing. But when the elkhorn
joint of my upper femur was removed
from inside me song went quiet in me,
as if my hair stopped growing—no more   10
tendrils of thought out into the air,
down onto the page. Who had I thought

I was, that I could write what I wanted
about my family? Now I feel
as if I have lost my court case   15
against my mother and father, and the great
forked tongue of my thighbone
has been taken in forfeit. I always wanted
my life to be a comedy,
now I feel in the grip of something   20
inexorable. But I remember a seed,
a dandelion sphere, which I blew on once, and its
silvery runes poured forward. It's as if—
until now—I thought that I would never
fade, or fail, or fall silent, or die.   25
I trusted that I had it coming to me,
without cease, the firework of language.
Futhorc! Let me cry out, again!
Or even just hum, without meaning,
maybe to the tune of "Motherless Child,"   30
mm *mm, mm mm*, mm mm *mm mm mm mm*,
and so she comes in, self-pity—self-compassion,
my darling, my constant one, the scarf dancer.

—SHARON OLDS (B. 1942)

QUESTIONS

1. Vocabulary: *spore* (2), *femur* (8), *inexorable* (21), *runes* (23), *Futhorc* (28).
2. What is this poem about? How would you describe the tone of the poem?
3. Analyze the humor in the poem, and explain why it is appropriate for this subject matter.

Among School Children

I

I walk through the long schoolroom questioning;
A kind old nun in a white hood replies;
The children learn to cipher and to sing,
To study reading-books and history,
To cut and sew, be neat in everything   5
In the best modern way—the children's eyes
In momentary wonder stare upon
A sixty-year-old smiling public man.

II

I dream of a Ledaean body, bent
Above a sinking fire, a tale that she   10
Told of a harsh reproof, or trivial event
That changed some childish day to tragedy—
Told, and it seemed that our two natures blent
Into a sphere from youthful sympathy,
Or else, to alter Plato's parable,   15
Into the yolk and white of the one shell.

III

And thinking of that fit of grief or rage
I look upon one child or t'other there
And wonder if she stood so at that age—
For even daughters of the swan can share   20
Something of every paddler's heritage—
And had that colour upon cheek or hair,
And thereupon my heart is driven wild:
She stands before me as a living child.

IV

Her present image floats into the mind—   25
Did Quattrocento finger fashion it
Hollow of cheek as though it drank the wind
And took a mess of shadows for its meat?
And I though never of Ledaean kind
Had pretty plumage once—enough of that,   30
Better to smile on all that smile, and show
There is a comfortable kind of old scarecrow.

V

What youthful mother, a shape upon her lap
Honey of generation had betrayed,
And that must sleep, shriek, struggle to escape   35
As recollection or the drug decide,
Would think her son, did she but see that shape
With sixty or more winters on its head,
A compensation for the pang of his birth,
Or the uncertainty of his setting forth?   40

VI

Plato thought nature but a spume that plays
Upon a ghostly paradigm of things;
Solider Aristotle played the taws
Upon the bottom of a king of kings;
World-famous golden-thighed Pythagoras   45
Fingered upon a fiddle-stick or strings
What a star sang and careless Muses heard:
Old clothes upon old sticks to scare a bird.

VII

Both nuns and mothers worship images,
But those the candles light are not as those   50
That animate a mother's reveries,
But keep a marble or a bronze repose.
And yet they too break hearts—O Presences
That passion, piety or affection knows,
And that all heavenly glory symbolise—   55
O self-born mockers of man's enterprise;

VIII

Labour is blossoming or dancing where
The body is not bruised to pleasure soul,
Nor beauty born out of its own despair,
Nor blear-eyed wisdom out of midnight oil.   60
O chestnut-tree, great-rooted blossomer,
Are you the leaf, the blossom or the bole?
O body swayed to music, O brightening glance,
How can we know the dancer from the dance?

—WILLIAM BUTLER YEATS (1865–1939)

QUESTIONS

1. Vocabulary: *Ledaean* (9), *Plato* (15), *Quattrocento* (26), *spume* (41), *paradigm* (42), *Aristotle* (43), *Pythagoras* (45).
2. Who is the presumed speaker in this poem?
3. Research and define the allusions to ancient literature found in the poem.
4. Is the final line a rhetorical question? Does it have an answer?

History Lesson

I am four in this photograph, standing
on a wide strip of Mississippi beach,
my hands on the flowered hips

of a bright bikini. My toes dig in,
curl around wet sand. The sun cuts   5
the rippling Gulf in flashes with each

tidal rush. Minnows dart at my feet
glinting like switchblades. I am alone
except for my grandmother, other side

of the camera, telling me how to pose.   10
It is 1970, two years after they opened
the rest of this beach to us,

forty years since the photograph
where she stood on a narrow plot
of sand marked *colored*, smiling,   15

her hands on the flowered hips
of a cotton meal-sack dress.

— NATASHA TRETHEWEY (B. 1966)

QUESTIONS

1. Analyze the tone of this poem. Is it nostalgic? Angry? Bitter? Point to specific passages and images that support your argument.
2. Discuss the significance of the following images: "wide strip" (2) and "narrow plot" (14); "flowered hips / of a bright bikini" (3–4) and "flowered hips / of a cotton meal-sack dress" (16–17); "glinting like switchblades" (8).
3. In what sense does this photograph represent a "History Lesson" (title)?

Dover Beach

The sea is calm tonight,
The tide is full, the moon lies fair
Upon the straits;—on the French coast the light

Gleams and is gone; the cliffs of England stand,
Glimmering and vast, out in the tranquil bay.   5
Come to the window, sweet is the night-air!
Only, from the long line of spray
Where the sea meets the moon-blanched land,
Listen! you hear the grating roar
Of pebbles which the waves draw back, and fling,   10
At their return, up the high strand,
Begin, and cease, and then again begin,
With tremulous cadence slow, and bring
The eternal note of sadness in.

Sophocles long ago   15
Heard it on the Aegean, and it brought
Into his mind the turbid ebb and flow
Of human misery; we
Find also in the sound a thought,
Hearing it by this distant northern sea.   20

The Sea of Faith
Was once, too, at the full, and round earth's shore
Lay like the folds of a bright girdle furled.
But now I only hear
Its melancholy, long, withdrawing roar,   25
Retreating, to the breath
Of the night-wind, down the vast edges drear
And naked shingles° of the world.   pebbled beaches

Ah, love, let us be true
To one another! for the world, which seems   30
To lie before us like a land of dreams,
So various, so beautiful, so new,
Hath really neither joy, nor love, nor light,
Nor certitude, nor peace, nor help for pain;
And we are here as on a darkling plain   35
Swept with confused alarms of struggle and flight,
Where ignorant armies clash by night.

—MATTHEW ARNOLD (1822–1888)

QUESTIONS

1. Vocabulary: *strand* (11), *girdle* (23), *darkling* (35). Identify the physical locale of the cliffs
   of Dover and their relation to the French coast; identify Sophocles and the Aegean.

2. As precisely as possible, define the implied scene: What is the speaker's physical location? Whom is he addressing? What is the time of day and the state of the weather?
3. Discuss the visual and auditory images of the poem and their relation to illusion and reality.
4. The speaker is lamenting the decline of religious faith in his time. Is he himself a believer? Does he see any medicine for the world's maladies?
5. Discuss in detail the imagery in the last three lines. Are the "armies" figurative or literal? What makes these lines so effective?
6. What term or terms would you choose to describe the overall tone of the poem?

MindTap® Read, highlight, and take notes online.

Church Going

Once I am sure there's nothing going on
I step inside, letting the door thud shut.
Another church: matting, seats, and stone,
And little books; sprawlings of flowers, cut
For Sunday, brownish now; some brass and stuff   5
Up at the holy end; the small neat organ;
And a tense, musty, unignorable silence,
Brewed God knows how long. Hatless, I take off
My cycle-clips in awkward reverence,

Move forward, run my hand around the font.   10
From where I stand, the roof looks almost new—
Cleaned, or restored? Someone would know: I don't.
Mounting the lectern, I peruse a few
Hectoring large-scale verses, and pronounce
"Here endeth" much more loudly than I'd meant.   15
The echoes snigger briefly. Back at the door
I sign the book, donate an Irish sixpence,
Reflect the place was not worth stopping for.

Yet stop I did: in fact I often do,
And always end much at a loss like this,   20
Wondering what to look for, wondering, too,
When churches fall completely out of use
What we shall turn them into, if we shall keep
A few cathedrals chronically on show,
Their parchment, plate and pyx in locked cases,   25
And let the rest rent-free to rain and sheep.

Shall we avoid them as unlucky places?
Or, after dark, will dubious women come
To make their children touch a particular stone;
Pick simples for a cancer; or on some   30
Advised night see walking a dead one?
Power of some sort or other will go on
In games, in riddles, seemingly at random;
But superstition, like belief, must die,
And what remains when disbelief has gone?   35
Grass, weedy pavement, brambles, buttress, sky,

A shape less recognizable each week,
A purpose more obscure. I wonder who
Will be the last, the very last, to seek
This place for what it was; one of the crew   40
That tap and jot and know what rood-lofts were?
Some ruin-bibber, randy for antique,
Or Christmas-addict, counting on a whiff
Of gown-and-bands and organ-pipes and myrrh?
Or will he be my representative,   45

Bored, uninformed, knowing the ghostly silt
Dispersed, yet tending to this cross of ground
Through suburb scrub because it held unspilt
So long and equably what since is found
Only in separation—marriage, and birth,   50
And death, and thoughts of these—for whom was built
This special shell? For though I've no idea
What this accoutered frowsty barn is worth,
It pleases me to stand in silence here;

A serious house on serious earth it is,   55
In whose blent air all our compulsions meet,
Are recognized, and robed as destinies.
And that much never can be obsolete,
Since someone will forever be surprising
A hunger in himself to be more serious,   60
And gravitating with it to this ground,
Which, he once heard, was proper to grow wise in,
If only that so many dead lie round.

—PHILIP LARKIN (1922–1985)

QUESTIONS

1. Vocabulary: *Hectoring* (14), *pyx* (25), *dubious* (28), *simples* (30), *accoutered* (53), *frow-sty* (53), *blent* (56). *Large-scale* (14) indicates a print size suited to oral reading; an *Irish sixpence* (17) was a small coin not legal tender in England, the scene of the poem; *rood-lofts* (41) are architectural features found in many early Christian churches; *bibber* and *randy* (42) are figurative, literally meaning "drunkard" and "lustful"; *gown-and-bands* (44) are ornate robes worn by church officials in religious ceremonies.
2. Like "Dover Beach" (first published in 1867), "Church Going" (1954) is concerned with belief and disbelief. In modern England the landscape is dotted with small churches, often charming in their combination of stone (outside) and intricately carved wood (inside). Some are in ruins, some are badly in need of repair, and some are well tended by parishioners who keep them dusted and provide fresh flowers for the diminishing attendance at Sunday services. These churches often have by the entrance a book that visitors can sign as a record of their having been there and a collection box with a sign urging them to drop in a few coins for upkeep, repair, or restoration. In small towns and villages the church is often the chief or only building of architectural or historical interest, and tourist visitors may outnumber parishioners. To which of the three categories of churches mentioned here does Larkin's poem refer?
3. What different denotations does the title contain?
4. In what activity has the speaker been engaging when he stops to see the church? How is it revealed? Why does he stop? Is he a believer? How involved is he in inspecting this church building?
5. Compare the language used by the speakers in "Dover Beach" and "Church Going." Which speaker is more eloquent? Which is more informal and conversational? Without looking back at the texts, try to assign the following words to one poem or the other: *moon-blanched, cycle-clips, darkling, hath, snigger, whiff, drear, brownish, tremulous, glimmering, frowsty, stuff.* Then go back and check your success.
6. Define the tone of "Church Going" as precisely as possible. Compare this tone with that of "Dover Beach."

Engraved on the Collar of a Dog Which I Gave to His Royal Highness

I am his Highness' dog at Kew;
Pray tell me, sir, whose dog are you?

—ALEXANDER POPE (1688–1744)

QUESTIONS

1. Vocabulary: *Kew* (1).
2. What adjective—or noun—best fits the attitude expressed on the dog's collar? Read the two lines aloud, emphasizing the tone in which the lines are written.
3. Is the dog in any way symbolic? Explain.

SUGGESTIONS FOR WRITING

1. Marvell's "To His Coy Mistress" (page 88), Herrick's "To the Virgins, to Make Much of Time" (page 99), and Housman's "Loveliest of Trees" (page 152) all treat a traditional poetic theme known as *carpe diem* ("seize the day"). They differ sharply in tone. Pointing out the differences in poetic technique among them, characterize the tone of each.
2. Describe and account for the differences in tone between the following pairs:
   a. Hopkins, "Spring" (page 60) and Williams, "The Widow's Lament in Springtime" (page 61).
   b. Tennyson, "The Eagle" (page 4) and Mathis, "Survival: A Guide" (page 395).
   c. Owen, "Dulce et Decorum Est" (page 6) and Whitman, "A sight in camp in the daybreak gray and dim" (page 412).
   d. Drayton, "Since there's no help" (page 169) and Addonizio, "Sonnenizio on a Line from Drayton" (page 356).
   e. Blake, "The Lamb" (page 162) and Blake, "The Tiger" (page 162).
   f. Shakespeare, "Winter" (page 5) and Stevens, "The Snow Man" (page 68).

PRACTICE AP® WRITING PROMPTS

Emily Dickinson, "A narrow Fellow in the Grass" (pp. 167–168)

Read "A narrow Fellow in the Grass" by Emily Dickinson with care, paying particular attention to the author's use of sound as well as the sentence structure in the poem. In a well-written essay, analyze how the author employs the resources of language to reveal the speaker's complex attitude toward the poem's subject.

William Shakespeare, "My mistress' eyes are nothing like the sun" (p. 172)

Carefully examine the sonnet "My mistress' eyes are nothing like the sun." Focusing on such elements as diction, imagery, tone, and allusion, analyze the strategy that the speaker uses to achieve his poetic and emotional purposes.

Alfred, Lord Tennyson, "Crossing the Bar" (pp. 172–173)

Read "Crossing the Bar" carefully. Then, in a well-organized essay, analyze how structure, diction, and the poem's two complementary metaphors convey the speaker's attitude toward his own death.

....

Philip Larkin, "Church Going" (pp. 181–183)

Read "Church Going" by Philip Larkin, paying careful attention to the shifts in the speaker's tone. In a thoughtfully organized essay, analyze the author's use of such elements as diction and syntax to control tone and convey the speaker's complex attitude toward the church building and the things that it signifies.

....

CHAPTER ELEVEN

Musical Devices

Poetry obviously makes a greater use of the "music" of language than does language that is not poetry. The poet, unlike the person who uses language to convey only information, chooses words for sound as well as for meaning, and uses the sound as a means of reinforcing meaning. So prominent is this musical quality of poetry that some writers have made it the distinguishing term in their definitions of poetry. Edgar Allan Poe, for instance, describes poetry as "music . . . combined with a pleasurable idea." Whether or not it deserves this much importance, verbal music, like connotation, imagery, and figurative language, is one of the important resources that enable the poet to do more than communicate mere information. The poet may indeed sometimes pursue verbal music for its own sake; more often, at least in first-rate poetry, it is an adjunct to the total meaning or communication of the poem.

The poet achieves musical quality in two broad ways: by the choice and arrangement of sounds and by the arrangement of accents. In this chapter we will consider the first of these.

An essential element in all music is repetition. In fact, we might say that all art consists of giving structure to two elements: repetition and variation. All things we enjoy greatly and lastingly have these two elements. We enjoy the sea endlessly because it is always the same yet always different. We enjoy a baseball game because it contains the same complex combination of pattern and variation. Our love of art, then, is rooted in human psychology. We like the familiar, we like variety, but we like them combined. If we get too much sameness, the result is monotony and tedium; if we get too much variety, the result is bewilderment and confusion. The composer of music, therefore, repeats certain musical tones: repeats them in certain combinations, or chords, and repeats them in certain patterns, or melodies. The poet likewise repeats certain sounds in certain combinations and arrangements, and thus adds musical meaning to verse.

Poets may repeat any unit of sound from the smallest to the largest. They may repeat individual vowel and consonant sounds, whole syllables, words, phrases, lines, or groups of lines. In each instance, in a good poem, the repetition will serve several purposes: it will please the ear, it will emphasize the words in which the repetition occurs, and it will give structure to the poem. The popularity and initial impressiveness of such repetitions are evidenced by their becoming in many instances embedded in the language as clichés like "wild and woolly," "first and foremost," "footloose and fancy-free," "penny-wise, pound-foolish," "dead as a doornail," "might and main," "sink or swim," "do or die," "pell-mell," "helter-skelter," "harum-scarum," "hocus-pocus." Some of these kinds of repetition have names, as we will see.

A syllable consists of a vowel sound that may be preceded or followed by consonant sounds. Any of these sounds may be repeated. The repetition of initial consonant sounds, as in "tried and true," "safe and sound," "fish or fowl," "rhyme or reason," is **alliteration**. The repetition of vowel sounds, as in "mad as a hatter," "time out of mind," "free and easy," or "slapdash," is **assonance**. The repetition of final consonant sounds, as in "first and last," "odds and ends," "short and sweet," "a stroke of luck," or Shakespeare's "struts and frets" (page 137) is **consonance**.*

Repetitions may be used alone or in combination. Alliteration and assonance are combined in such phrases as "time and tide," "thick and thin," "kith and kin," "alas and alack," "fit as a fiddle," and Edgar Allan Poe's famous line, "The viol, the violet, and the vine." Alliteration and consonance are combined in such phrases as "crisscross," "last but not least," "lone and lorn," "good as gold," and Housman's "malt does more than Milton can" (page 383).

Rhyme is the repetition of the accented vowel sound and any succeeding consonant sounds. It is called **masculine** when the rhyme sounds involve only one syllable, as in *bells* and *foretells* or *support* and *retort*. It is **feminine**

---

*Different writers have defined these repetitions in various ways. *Alliteration* is used by some writers to mean any repetition of consonant sounds. *Assonance* has been used to mean the similarity as well as the identity of vowel sounds, or even the similarity of any sounds whatever. *Consonance* has often been reserved for words in which both the initial *and* final consonant sounds correspond, as in *green* and *groan*, *moon* and *mine*. *Rhyme* has been used to mean any sound repetition, including alliteration, assonance, and consonance. In the absence of clear agreement on the meanings of these terms, the terminology chosen here has appeared most useful, with support in usage. Labels are useful in analysis. However, the student should learn to recognize the devices and, more important, should learn to see their function, without worrying too much over nomenclature.

when the rhyme sounds involve two or more syllables, as in *rhyming* and *chiming* or *spitefully* and *delightfully*. It is referred to as **internal rhyme** when one or more rhyming words are *within* the line and as **end rhyme** when the rhyming words are at the *ends* of lines. End rhyme is probably the most frequently used and most consciously sought sound repetition in English poetry. Because it comes at the end of the line, it receives emphasis as a musical effect and perhaps contributes more than any other musical resource except rhythm to give poetry its musical effect as well as its structure.

There exists, however, a large body of poetry that does not employ rhyme and for which rhyme would not be appropriate. Also, there has always been a tendency, especially noticeable in modern poetry, to substitute approximate rhymes for perfect rhymes at the ends of lines. **Approximate rhymes** (also called *slant rhymes*) include words with any kind of sound similarity, from close to fairly remote. Under approximate rhyme we include alliteration, assonance, and consonance or their combinations when used at the end of the line; **half-rhyme** (feminine rhymes in which only half of the word rhymes— the accented half, as in *lightly* and *frightful*, or the unaccented half, as in *yellow* and *willow*); and other similarities too elusive to name. "Because I could not stop for Death" (page 106), "Toads" (page 83), and "Mid-Term Break" (page 125), to different degrees, all employ various kinds of approximate end rhyme. Many contemporary song lyrics, especially in rap music, depend almost entirely on approximate rhyme or assonance for their rhyme schemes.

That night when joy began

That night when joy began
Our narrowest veins to flush,
We waited for the flash
Of morning's leveled gun.

But morning let us pass,   5
And day by day relief
Outgrows his nervous laugh,
Grown credulous of peace,

As mile by mile is seen
No trespasser's reproach,   10
And love's best glasses reach
No fields but are his own.

—W. H. AUDEN (1907–1973)

QUESTIONS

1. What has been the past experience with love of the two people in the poem? What is their present experience? What precisely is the tone of the poem?
2. What basic metaphor underlies the poem? Work it out stanza by stanza. What is "the flash / Of morning's leveled gun" (3–4)? Does line 10 mean that no trespasser reproaches the lovers or that no one reproaches the lovers for being trespassers? Does "glasses" (11) refer to spectacles, drinking glasses, mirrors, or field glasses? Point out three personifications.
3. The rhyme pattern in the poem is intricate and exact. Work it out, considering alliteration, assonance, and consonance.

In addition to the repetition of individual sounds and syllables, the poet may repeat whole words, phrases, lines, or groups of lines. When such repetition is done according to some fixed pattern, it is called a **refrain**. The refrain is especially common in songlike poetry. Shakespeare's "Winter" (page 5) furnishes an example of a refrain.

The Waking

I wake to sleep, and take my waking slow.
I feel my fate in what I cannot fear.
I learn by going where I have to go.

We think by feeling. What is there to know?
I hear my being dance from ear to ear.   5
I wake to sleep, and take my waking slow.

Of those so close beside me, which are you?
God bless the Ground! I shall walk softly there,
And learn by going where I have to go.

Light takes the Tree; but who can tell us how?   10
The lowly worm climbs up a winding stair;
I wake to sleep, and take my waking slow.

Great Nature has another thing to do
To you and me; so take the lively air,
And, lovely, learn by going where to go.   15

This shaking keeps me steady. I should know.
What falls away is always. And is near.

I wake to sleep, and take my waking slow.
I learn by going where I have to go.

—THEODORE ROETHKE (1908–1963)

QUESTIONS

1. The refrains in lines 1 and 3 occur at patterned intervals in this example of the form called *villanelle* (see page 255 for a definition of the form). Even without the definition, you can work out the repetitive pattern—but the key question is, what do these two lines *mean*, as statements both within the first stanza and in each subsequent repetition? Starting with line 1, for what is "sleep" a common metaphor? What would be the meaning if the first phrase were "I was born to die"?
2. Paraphrase the third line, in light of the idea that the first line presents an attitude toward the fact that all living things must die. Where does the speaker "have to go" ultimately? What is the process of his present "going"?
3. Explain the clear-cut attitude toward emotive experience versus intellectual knowledge expressed in line 4. How is that attitude a basis for the ideas in the refrain lines? How does it support line 10?
4. What is it that "Great Nature has . . . to do" (13) to people? How should they live their lives, according to the speaker?
5. Explain the paradox that "shaking keeps [the speaker] steady" (16). Consider the possibility that the speaker is personifying "the Tree" (10) as himself—what then is "fall[ing] away," and how near is it (17)?
6. Is the tone of this poem melancholy? Resigned? Joyous? Explain.

We have not nearly exhausted the possibilities of sound repetition by giving names to a few of the more prominent kinds. The complete study of possible kinds of sound repetition in poetry would be so complex, however, that it would exceed the scope of this introductory text.

Some of the subtlest and loveliest effects escape our net of names. In as short a phrase as this from the prose of John Ruskin—"ivy as light and lovely as the vine"—we notice alliteration in *light* and *lovely*; assonance in *ivy, light*, and *vine*; and consonance in *ivy* and *lovely*. But we have no name to connect the *v* in *vine* with the *v*'s in *ivy* and *lovely*, or the second *l* in *lovely* with the first *l*, or the final syllables of *ivy* and *lovely* with each other; yet these are all an effective part of the music of the line. Also contributing to the music of poetry is the linking of related rather than identical sounds, such as *m* and *n*, or *p* and *b*, or the vowel sounds in *boat, boot*, and *book*.

These various musical repetitions, for trained readers, will ordinarily make an almost subconscious contribution to their reading of the poem: readers will feel their effect without necessarily being aware of what has caused it. There is value, however, in occasionally analyzing a poem for these devices in order to increase awareness of them. A few words of caution are necessary. First, the repetitions are entirely a matter of sound; spelling is irrelevant.

Bear and *pair* are rhymes, but *through* and *rough* are not. *Cell* and *sin, folly* and *philosophy* alliterate, but *sin* and *sugar, gun* and *gem* do not. Second, alliteration, assonance, consonance, and masculine rhyme are matters that ordinarily involve only stressed or accented syllables; for only such syllables ordinarily make enough impression on the ear to be significant in the sound pattern of the poem. For instance, we should hardly consider *as* and *is* in the ninth line of "That night when joy began" (page 188) an example of assonance, for neither word is stressed enough in the reading to make it significant as a sound. Third, the words involved in these repetitions must be close enough together that the ear retains the sound, consciously or subconsciously, from its first occurrence to its second. This distance varies according to circumstances, but for alliteration, assonance, and consonance, the words ordinarily have to be in the same line or adjacent lines. End rhyme bridges a longer gap.

God's Grandeur

The world is charged with the grandeur of God.
   It will flame out, like shining from shook foil;
   It gathers to a greatness, like the ooze of oil
Crushed. Why do men then now not reck his rod?
Generations have trod, have trod, have trod;   5
   And all is seared with trade; bleared, smeared with toil;
   And wears man's smudge and shares man's smell: the soil
Is bare now, nor can foot feel, being shod.

And for all this, nature is never spent;
   There lives the dearest freshness deep down things;   10
And though the last lights off the black West went
   Oh, morning, at the brown brink eastward, springs—
Because the Holy Ghost over the bent
   World broods with warm breast and with ah! bright wings.

—GERARD MANLEY HOPKINS (1844–1889)

QUESTIONS

1. What is the theme of this sonnet?
2. The image in lines 3–4 possibly refers to olive oil being collected in great vats from crushed olives, but the image is much disputed. Explain the simile in line 2 and the symbols in lines 7–8 and 11–12.
3. Explain "reck his rod" (4), "spent" (9), "bent" (13).
4. Using different-colored pencils, encircle and connect examples of alliteration, assonance, consonance, and internal rhyme. Do these help to carry the meaning?

MindTap® Read, highlight, and take notes online.

We should not leave the impression that the use of these musical devices is necessarily or always valuable. Like the other resources of poetry, they can be judged only in the light of the poem's total intention. Many of the greatest works of English poetry—for instance, *Hamlet* and *King Lear* and *Paradise Lost*—do not employ end rhyme. Both alliteration and rhyme, especially feminine rhyme, become humorous or silly if used excessively or unskillfully. If the intention is humorous, the result is delightful; if not, it is fatal. Shakespeare, who knew how to use all these devices to the utmost advantage, parodied their unskillful use in lines like "The preyful princess pierced and pricked a pretty pleasing prickett" in *Love's Labor's Lost* and

> Whereat with blade, with bloody, blameful blade,
> He bravely broached his boiling bloody breast

in *A Midsummer Night's Dream.* Swinburne parodied his own highly alliterative style in "Nephelidia" with lines like "Life is the lust of a lamp for the light that is dark till the dawn of the day when we die." Used skillfully and judiciously, however, musical devices provide a palpable and delicate pleasure to the ear and, even more important, add dimension to meaning.

EXERCISE

Discuss the various ways in which the following poems make use of refrain.
1. Shakespeare, "Winter" (page 5).
2. Shakespeare, "Blow, blow, thou winter wind" (page 193).
3. cummings, "in Just—" (page 141).
4. Blake, "The Lamb" (page 162).
5. Crane, "War Is Kind" (page 365).
6. Dunbar, "Sympathy" (page 370).
7. Clifton, "good times" (page 362).

REVIEWING CHAPTER ELEVEN

1. Review the terms printed in boldface, and as you read on in this chapter take note of the examples that you find (that is, make a conscious search for the materials that normally would not rise above the subconscious in their effects).

2. Musical devices do not convey meaning but reinforce meanings that are established by the other aspects of language; as you explore these musical devices, identify the ways in which emotional and intellectual meanings are conveyed so as to make it clear what the music is reinforcing and supporting.

Blow, blow, thou winter wind

Blow, blow, thou winter wind.
Thou art not so unkind
   As man's ingratitude.
Thy tooth is not so keen,
Because thou art not seen,   5
   Although thy breath be rude.°   rough
Heigh-ho, sing heigh-ho, unto the green holly.
Most friendship is feigning, most loving mere folly.
      Then heigh-ho, the holly!
         This life is most jolly.   10

Freeze, freeze, thou bitter sky,
That dost not bite so nigh°   near the heart
   As benefits forgot.
Though thou the waters warp,
Thy sting is not so sharp   15
   As friend remembered not.
Heigh-ho, sing heigh-ho, unto the green holly.
Most friendship is feigning, most loving mere folly.
      Then heigh-ho, the holly!
         This life is most jolly.   20

—WILLIAM SHAKESPEARE (1564–1616)

QUESTIONS

1. Vocabulary: *Heigh-ho* (7) is an expression of melancholy or disappointment; *holly* (7) is an emblem of cheerfulness (as at Christmas); *warp* (14) implies freezing into ridges.
2. This song from *As You Like It* (Act 2, scene 7), contrasts the social and natural worlds and is sung to celebrate living freely in the forest. What essential qualities does it ascribe to the two environments displayed in the behavior of people and the actions of nature? What paradox does the poem create by presenting the expression "heigh-ho" linked with "the holly"? Are we to take "heigh-ho" at its literal meaning?
3. What musical devices help create the songlike quality of this poem?

We Real Cool

The Pool Players.
Seven At The Golden Shovel.

We real cool. We
Left school. We

Lurk late. We
Strike straight. We

Sing sin. We   5
Thin gin. We

Jazz June. We
Die soon.

—GWENDOLYN BROOKS (1917–2000)

QUESTIONS

1. In addition to end rhyme, what other musical devices does this poem employ?
2. Try reading this poem with the pronouns at the beginning of the lines instead of at the end. What is lost?
3. English teachers in a certain urban school were once criticized for having their students read this poem: it was said to be immoral. What essential poetic device did the critics misunderstand?

Counting-Out Rhyme

Silver bark of beech, and sallow
Bark of yellow birch and yellow
    Twig of willow.

Stripe of green in moosewood maple,
Color seen in leaf of apple,   5
    Bark of popple.

Wood of popple pale as moonbeam,
Wood of oak for yoke and barn-beam,
    Wood of hornbeam.

Silver bark of beech, and hollow   10
Stem of elder, tall and yellow
    Twig of willow.

—EDNA ST. VINCENT MILLAY (1892–1950)

QUESTIONS

1. List all instances of alliteration, assonance, consonance, half-rhyme, internal rhyme, and word repetition.
2. How serious is the purpose of this poem?
3. What is a "counting-out rhyme"? Can you remember any from your childhood? What is being counted here?

The Bells

I

Hear the sledges with the bells—
    Silver bells!
What a world of merriment their melody foretells!
How they tinkle, tinkle, tinkle,
    In the icy air of night!   5
While the stars that oversprinkle
All the heavens, seem to twinkle
    With a crystalline delight;
      Keeping time, time, time,
      In a sort of Runic rhyme,   10
To the tintinnabulation that so musically wells
    From the bells, bells, bells, bells,
      Bells, bells, bells—
From the jingling and the tinkling of the bells.

II

Hear the mellow wedding bells—   15
    Golden bells!
What a world of happiness their harmony foretells!
    Through the balmy air of night
    How they ring out their delight!—
      From the molten-golden notes,   20
      And all in tune,
    What a liquid ditty floats
To the turtle-dove that listens, while she gloats
      On the moon!
      Oh, from out the sounding cells,   25
What a gush of euphony voluminously wells!
      How is swells!
      How it dwells
      On the Future!—how it tells

Of the rapture that impels   30
  To the swinging and the ringing
    Of the bells, bells, bells—
Of the bells, bells, bells, bells,
        Bells, bells, bells—
To the rhyming and the chiming of the bells!   35

              III
  Hear the loud alarum bells—
        Brazen bells!
What a tale of terror, now, their turbulency tells!
    In the startled ear of night
    How they scream out their affright!   40
      Too much horrified to speak,
      They can only shriek, shriek,
          Out of tune,
In a clamorous appealing to the mercy of the fire,
In a mad expostulation with the deaf and frantic fire,   45
        Leaping higher, higher, higher,
      With a desperate desire,
    And a resolute endeavor
    Now—now to sit, or never,
  By the side of the pale-faced moon,   50
      Oh, the bells, bells, bells!
      What a tale their terror tells
          Of Despair!
      How they clang, and clash, and roar!
      What a horror they outpour   55
On the bosom of the palpitating air!
    Yet the ear, it fully knows,
        By the twanging
        And the clanging,
      How the danger ebbs and flows;   60
    Yet the ear distinctly tells,
        In the jangling
        And the wrangling,
      How the danger sinks and swells,
By the sinking or the swelling in the anger of the bells— 65
        Of the bells,—
    Of the bells, bells, bells, bells,
        Bells, bells, bells—
In the clamor and the clangor of the bells!

IV

Hear the tolling of the bells—   70
    Iron bells!
What a world of solemn thought their monody compels!
    In the silence of the night,
    How we shiver with affright
At the melancholy menace of their tone!   75
    For every sound that floats
    From the rust within their throats
      Is a groan.
     And the people—ah, the people—
     They that dwell up in the steeple,   80
      All alone,
  And who tolling, tolling, tolling,
   In that muffled monotone,
  Feel a glory in so rolling
    On the human heart a stone—   85
They are neither man nor woman—
They are neither brute nor human—
    They are Ghouls:—
   And their king it is who tolls:—
   And he rolls, rolls, rolls,   90
   Rolls
    A paean from the bells!
And his merry bosom swells
    With the paean of the bells!
And he dances, and he yells;   95
Keeping time, time, time,
In a sort of Runic rhyme,
    To the paean of the bells—
    Of the bells:
Keeping time, time, time,   100
In a sort of Runic rhyme,
    To the throbbing of the bells—
  Of the bells, bells, bells—
    To the sobbing of the bells;
Keeping time, time, time,   105
   As he knells, knells, knells,
In a happy Runic rhyme,
    To the rolling of the bells—
Of the bells, bells, bells:—

To the tolling of the bells—   110
Of the bells, bells, bells, bells,
Bells, bells, bells—
To the moaning and the groaning of the bells.

—EDGAR ALLAN POE (1809–1849)

QUESTIONS

1. Vocabulary: *sledges* (1); *tintinnabulation* (11); *euphony* (26); *expostulation* (45); *paean* (92); *Runic* (101).
2. What different kinds of bells are described in the poem? How does the sound of the various stanzas comport with the type of bells being described?
3. How would you describe the tone of the poem? Besides his attitude toward the bells, what can we infer about the speaker?
4. What effects do the rhyme scheme and the punctuation have on the way you experience the poem?

Morning Song

Love set you going like a fat gold watch.
The midwife slapped your footsoles, and your bald cry
Took its place among the elements.

Our voices echo, magnifying your arrival. New statue.
In a drafty museum, your nakedness   5
Shadows our safety. We stand round blankly as walls.

I'm no more your mother
Than the cloud that distills a mirror to reflect its own slow
Effacement at the wind's hand.

All night your moth-breath   10
Flickers among the flat pink roses. I wake to listen:
A far sea moves in my ear.

One cry, and I stumble from bed, cow-heavy and floral
In my Victorian nightgown.
Your mouth opens clean as a cat's. The window square   15

Whitens and swallows its dull stars. And now you try
Your handful of notes;
The clear vowels rise like balloons.

—SYLVIA PLATH (1932–1963)

QUESTIONS

1. Discuss the metaphor in the third stanza. How does it help to elucidate the mother's feelings?
2. What is the tone of this poem? Does the speaker feel tenderness toward her baby?
3. Focus on the similes "like a fat gold watch" (1), "clean as a cat's" (15), and "like balloons" (18). What do these similes add to the descriptive power of the poem?
4. Discuss the use of imagery related to sound.

Rite of Passage

As the guests arrive at my son's party
they gather in the living room—
short men, men in first grade
with smooth jaws and chins.
Hands in pockets, they stand around   5
jostling, jockeying for place, small fights
breaking out and calming. One says to another
How old are you? Six. I'm seven. So?
They eye each other, seeing themselves
tiny in the other's pupils. They clear their   10
throats a lot, a room of small bankers,
they fold their arms and frown. *I could beat you
up*, a seven says to a six,
the dark cake, round and heavy as a
turret, behind them on the table. My son,   15
freckles like specks of nutmeg on his cheeks,
chest narrow as the balsa keel of a
model boat, long hands
cool and thin as the day they guided him
out of me, speaks up as a host   20
for the sake of the group.
We could easily kill a two-year-old,
he says in his clear voice. The other
men agree, they clear their throats

like Generals, they relax and get down to 25
playing war, celebrating my son's life.

—SHARON OLDS (B. 1942)

QUESTIONS

1. Vocabulary: *Rite of Passage* (title).
2. What is the implication of the metaphor comparing the boys to "bankers" (11) clearing their throats? Of that comparing them to "Generals" (25) doing the same thing? Is there a "rite of passage" implied in the shift from one comparison to the other?
3. What tones of voice would be appropriate for the phrase *"I'm seven"* and the reply *"So?"* (8)? Explain the image in the next sentence.
4. How are the similes in lines 14–15 and 16–17 linked? How do they function in the progress from bankers to Generals?
5. What is the speaker's tone as she describes the children's violent impulses?
6. The poem displays a considerable amount of musicality—alliteration, assonance, and consonance—through line 21. Identify these devices, and discuss the implication of their absence in the remainder of the poem.

Music Lessons

Sometimes, in the middle of the lesson,
we exchanged places. She would gaze a moment at her hands
spread over the keys; then the small house with its knickknacks,
its shut windows,

its photographs of her sons and the serious husband, 5
vanished as new shapes formed. Sound
became music, and music a white
scarp for the listener to climb

alone. I leaped rock over rock to the top
and found myself waiting, transformed, 10
and still she played, her eyes luminous and willful,
her pinned hair falling down—

forgetting me, the house, the neat green yard,
she fled in that lick of flame all tedious bonds:
supper, the duties of flesh and home, 15
the knife at the throat, the death in the metronome.

—MARY OLIVER (B. 1935)

QUESTIONS

1. Vocabulary: *scarp* (8), *metronome* (16).
2. What musical qualities do you see in the poem? How are they appropriate?
3. Discuss the characterization of the piano teacher. What kind of woman is she? What does the speaker, now a mature adult, see in her that she didn't see when she actually knew the teacher?
4. Why does the speaker use imagery of violence and death in the final line? What poetic effect does this imagery have on the reader?

Traveling through the dark

Traveling through the dark I found a deer
dead on the edge of the Wilson River road.
It is usually best to roll them into the canyon:
that road is narrow; to swerve might make more dead.

By glow of the tail-light I stumbled back of the car   5
and stood by the heap, a doe, a recent killing;
she had stiffened already, almost cold.
I dragged her off; she was large in the belly.

My fingers touching her side brought me the reason—
her side was warm; her fawn lay there waiting,   10
alive, still, never to be born.
Beside that mountain road I hesitated.

The car aimed ahead its lowered parking lights;
under the hood purred the steady engine.
I stood in the glare of the warm exhaust turning red;   15
around our group I could hear the wilderness listen.

I thought hard for us all — my only swerving —,
then pushed her over the edge into the river.

—WILLIAM STAFFORD (1914–1993)

QUESTIONS

1. State precisely the speaker's dilemma. What kind of person is he? Does he make the right decision? Why does he call his hesitation "my only swerving" (17), and how does this connect with the word "swerve" in line 4?
2. What different kinds of imagery and of image contrasts give life to the poem? Do any of the images have symbolic overtones?

3. At first glance this poem may appear to be without end rhyme. Looking closer, do you find any correspondences between lines 2 and 4 in each four-line stanza? Between lines 1 and 3 of stanzas 2 and 3? Between the final words of the concluding couplet? What one line end in the poem has no connection in sound to another line end in its stanza?

Nothing Gold Can Stay

Nature's first green is gold,
Her hardest hue to hold.
Her early leaf's a flower;
But only so an hour.
Then leaf subsides to leaf.   5
So Eden sank to grief,
So dawn goes down to day.
Nothing gold can stay.

—ROBERT FROST (1874–1963)

QUESTIONS

1. Explain the paradoxes in lines 1 and 3.
2. Discuss the poem as a series of symbols. What are the symbolic meanings of "gold" in the final line of the poem?
3. Discuss the contributions of alliteration, assonance, consonance, rhyme, and other repetitions to the effectiveness of the poem.

SUGGESTIONS FOR WRITING

1. Write an essay analyzing the use and effectiveness of alliteration and/or assonance in one of the following:
   a. Shakespeare, "Shall I compare thee to a summer's day?" (page 11).
   b. Dickinson, "There's a certain Slant of light" (page 290).
   c. Donne, "The Good-Morrow" (page 369).
   d. Hopkins, "God's Grandeur" (page 191).
   e. Robinson, "Richard Cory" (page 17).
2. Discuss the rhymes in one of the following. Does the poem employ exact rhymes or approximate rhymes? How do the kind and pattern of rhyme contribute to the poem's effect?
   a. MacLeish, "Ars Poetica" (page 393).
   b. Browning, "My Last Duchess" (page 288).
   c. Dickinson, "A narrow Fellow in the Grass" (page 167).
   d. Plath, "Lady Lazarus" (page 309).
   e. Heaney, "Follower" (page 380).

PRACTICE AP® WRITING PROMPTS

Theodore Roethke, "The Waking" (pp. 189–190)

Read "The Waking," carefully considering the sound of the poem's language and the patterns created by its form. In a well-written essay, analyze the ways in which the author uses sound to develop complexity in the poem's central idea.

....

Mary Oliver, "Music Lessons" (pp. 200–201)

Carefully read Mary Oliver's poem "Music Lessons," paying attention to the musical qualities of the poem's language and structure. In a well-written essay, analyze the speaker's complex reflections on the piano teacher. You may wish to consider figurative language as well as sound devices in your analysis.

....

CHAPTER TWELVE

Rhythm and Meter

Our love of rhythm is rooted even more deeply in us than our love of musical repetition. It is related to the beat of our hearts, the pulse of our blood, the intake and outflow of air from our lungs. Everything that we do naturally and gracefully we do rhythmically. There is rhythm in the way we walk, the way we swim, the way we ride a horse, the way we swing a golf club or a baseball bat. So native is rhythm to us that we read it, when we can, into the mechanical world around us. Our clocks go tick-tick-tick, but we hear tick-tock, tick-tock. The click of railway wheels beneath us patterns itself into a tune in our heads. There is a strong appeal for us in language that is rhythmic.

The term **rhythm** refers to any wavelike recurrence of motion or sound. In speech it is the natural rise and fall of language. All language is to some degree rhythmic, for all language involves alternations between accented and unaccented syllables. Language varies considerably, however, in the degree to which it exhibits rhythm. Sometimes in speech the rhythm is so unobtrusive or so unpatterned that we are scarcely aware of it. Sometimes, as in rap or in oratory, the rhythm is so pronounced that we may be tempted to tap our feet to it.

In every word of more than one syllable, one or more syllables are **accented** or **stressed**; that is, given more prominence in pronunciation than the rest.* We say toDAY, toMORrow, YESterday, interVENE. These accents within individual words are indicated by stress marks in

---

*Although the words *accent* and *stress* generally are used interchangeably, as here, a distinction is sometimes made between them in technical discussions. **Accent**, the relative prominence given a syllable in relation to its neighbors, is then said to result from one or more of four causes: *stress*, or force of utterance, producing loudness; *duration; pitch*; and *juncture*, the manner of transition between successive sounds. Of these, *stress*, in verse written in English, is the most important.

dictionaries, and with many words of more than two syllables primary and secondary stresses are shown (in′-ter-vene″). When words are arranged into a sentence, we give certain words or syllables more prominence in pronunciation than the rest. We say: "He WENT to the STORE" or "ANN is DRIVing her CAR." There is nothing mysterious about this; it is the normal process of language. The major difference between prose and verse is that in prose, these accents occur more or less haphazardly; in verse, the poet may arrange them to occur at regular intervals.

In poetry, as in prose, the rhythmic effects depend almost entirely on what a statement means, and different intended meanings will produce different rhythms even in identical statements. If I say "I don't believe YOU," I mean something different from "*I* don't believe you" or from "I don't beLIEVE you." In speech, these are **rhetorical stresses**, which we use to make our intentions clear. Stressing "I" separates me from others who *do* believe you; stressing "you" separates you from others whom I believe; stressing "believe" intensifies my statement of disbelief. Such rhetorical stressing comes as naturally to us as language itself, and is at least as important in poetry as it is in expressive speaking. It is also basic to understanding the rhythm of poetry, for poetic rhythm depends on the plain, rhetorical stresses to communicate its meaning. We must be able to recognize the meaning of a line of poetry before we can determine its rhythm.

In addition to accent or stress, rhythm is based on pauses. In poetry, as in prose or speech, pauses are the result of natural speech rhythms and the structure of sentences. Periods and commas create pauses, but so does the normal flow of phrases and clauses. Poetry, however, adds another kind of pause arising from the fact that poetry is written in lines. The poetic line is a unit that creates pauses in the flow of speech, sometimes slight and sometimes large. Poets have at their disposal a variety of possibilities when ending a line. An **end-stopped line** is one in which the end of the line corresponds with a natural speech pause; a **run-on line** is one in which the sense of the line moves on without pause into the next line. (There are of course all degrees of end-stops and run-ons. A line ending with a period or semicolon is heavily end-stopped. A line without punctuation at the end is normally considered a run-on line, but it is less forcibly run-on if it ends at a natural speech pause—as between subject and predicate—than if it ends, say, between an article and its noun, between an auxiliary and its verb, or between a preposition and its object.) In addition there are pauses that occur within lines, either grammatical or rhetorical. These are called **caesuras**, and they are another resource for varying the rhythm of lines.

The poetic line is the basic rhythmic unit in **free verse**, the predominating type of poetry now being written. Except for its line arrangement there are no necessary differences between the rhythms of free verse and the rhythms of prose, so our awareness of the line as a rhythmic unit is essential. Consider the rhythmic contrast between end-stopped lines and run-on lines in these two excerpts from poems presented earlier, and notice how the caesuras (marked ||) help to vary the rhythms:

> A noiseless patient spider,
> I marked where on a little promontory it stood isolated,
> Marked how to explore the vacant vast surrounding,
> It launched forth filament, || filament, || filament, || out of
>   itself,
> Ever unreeling them, || ever tirelessly speeding them.
>
> (page 93)

> Sorrow is my own yard
> where the new grass
> flames || as it has flamed
> often before || but not
> with the cold fire
> that closes round me this year.
>
> (page 61)

There is another sort of poetry that depends entirely on ordinary prose rhythms—the **prose poem**, exemplified by Joyce Carol Oates's "Playlet for Voices" (page 400) and Carolyn Forché's "The Colonel" (page 161). Having dispensed even with the line as a unit of rhythm, the prose poem lays its claim to being poetry by its attention to many of the poetic elements presented earlier in this book: connotation, imagery, figurative language, and the concentration of meaning in evocative language.

But most often, when people think of poetry they think of the two broad branches, free verse and metrical verse, which are distinguished mainly by the absence or presence of meter. **Meter** is the identifying characteristic of rhythmic language that elicits foot-tapping. When verse is metrical, the accents of language are so arranged as to occur at apparently equal intervals of time, and it is this interval we mark off with the tap of a foot.

The study of meter is fascinating but highly complex. It is by no means an absolute prerequisite to an enjoyment, even a rich enjoyment, of poetry, any more than is the ability to identify by name the multiplicity of figures of speech. But a knowledge of the fundamentals of meter does have value. It can make the beginning reader more aware of the rhythmic effects of poetry and of how poetry should be read. It can enable the more advanced reader to analyze how certain effects are achieved, to see how rhythm interacts with meaning, and to explain what makes one poem (in this respect) better than another. The beginning student ought to have at least an elementary knowledge of the subject. And it is not so difficult as its traditional terminology might suggest.

Even for the beginner, one essential distinction must be understood: although the terms *rhythm* and *meter* are sometimes used interchangeably, they mean different things. *Rhythm* designates the flow of actual, pronounced sound (or sound heard in the mind's ear), whereas *meter* refers to the patterns that sounds follow when a poet has arranged them into metrical verse. This may be illustrated by an analogy of a well-designed building and the architect's blueprint for its construction. The building, like rhythmic sound, is actual and real; the blueprint for it is an abstract, idealized pattern, like metrical form. When we look at a building, we see the actuality, but we also recognize that it is based on a pattern. The actuality of the building goes beyond the idealized blueprint in a number of ways—it presents us with texture, with color, with varying effects depending on light and shade, with contrasts of building materials. In poetry, the actuality is language arranged in sentences, with a progression through time, with varying emotions, dramatic contrasts of meaning and tone, the revelation of the speaker's situation, and so forth. All these are expressed through the sounds of language, which are constantly shifting to create meanings and implications.

The word *meter* comes from a word meaning "measure" (the word *rhythm* from a word meaning "flow," as in waves). To measure something we must have a unit of measurement. For measuring length we use the inch, foot, yard; for measuring time we use the second, minute, hour. For measuring verse we use the foot, line, and (sometimes) stanza.

One basic unit of meter, the **foot,** consists normally of one accented syllable plus one or two unaccented syllables, though occasionally there may be no unaccented syllables. To determine which syllable in a foot is accented, we compare its sound with that of the other syllables *within the foot,* not with the sounds of syllables in other feet within a line. In fact, because of the varying stresses on syllables in a spoken sentence, it is very unusual for all of the stressed syllables in a line to be equally stressed.

For diagramming the metrical form of verse, various systems of visual symbols have been devised. In this book we shall use a breve (ˇ) to indicate an unstressed syllable, an ictus (′) to indicate a stressed syllable, and a vertical bar (|) to indicate the division between feet. The basic kinds of feet are as follows:

Examples	Name of Foot	Adjectival Form	
˘ ´ ˘ ´ to-day, the sun	Iamb	Iambic	⎤ ⎥ Duple meters
´ ˘ ´ ˘ dai-ly, went to	Trochee	Trochaic	⎦
˘ ˘ ´ ˘ ˘ ´ in-ter-vene, in the dark	Anapest	Anapestic	⎤ ⎥ Triple meters
´ ˘ ˘ ´ ˘ ˘ mul-ti-ple, col-or of	Dactyl	Dactylic	⎦
´ ´ true-blue	Spondee*	Spondaic	

Two kinds of examples are given here, whole words and phrases, to indicate the fact that one must not assume that every individual word will be a foot, nor that divisions between feet necessarily fall between words. In actual lines, one might for example find the word *intervene* constituting parts of two different feet:

˘ ´ | ˘ ´ | ˘ ´
I want to in- ter-vene.

As this example demonstrates, in diagramming meters we must sometimes acknowledge the primary and secondary stresses provided by dictionaries: the word *intervene* provides the stresses for two consecutive feet.

The other basic unit of measurement in metrical verse is the line, which has the same properties as in free verse—it may be end-stopped or run-on, and its phrasing and punctuation will create caesuras. The difference between metrical and free-verse lines is that metrical lines are

---

*In the spondee the accent is thought of as being distributed equally or almost equally over the two syllables and is sometimes referred to as a hovering accent. No whole poems are written in spondees. Hence, there are only four basic meters: iambic, trochaic, anapestic, and dactylic. Iambic and trochaic are called *duple* because they employ two-syllable feet, anapestic and dactylic are called *triple* because they employ three-syllable feet. Of the four standard meters, iambic is by far the most common, followed by anapestic. Trochaic occurs relatively infrequently as the meter of poems, and dactylic is so rare as to be almost a museum specimen.

measured by naming the number of feet in them. The following names indicate number:

Monometer	one foot	Tetrameter	four feet
Dimeter	two feet	Pentameter	five feet
Trimeter	three feet	Hexameter	six feet

The third unit of measurement, the **stanza**, consists of a group of lines whose metrical pattern is repeated throughout the poem. Since much verse is not written in stanzas, we shall save our discussion of this unit till a later chapter.

Although metrical form is potentially uniform in its regularity, the poet may introduce **metrical variations**, which call attention to some of the sounds because they depart from what is regular. Three means for varying meter are **substitution** (replacing the regular foot with another one), **extra-metrical syllables** added at the beginnings or endings of lines, and **truncation** (the omission of an unaccented syllable at either end of a line). Because these represent clear changes in the pattern, they are usually obvious and striking. But even metrical regularity rarely creates a monotonous rhythm because rhythm is the actuality in sound, not the pattern or blueprint of meter. The rhythm of a line of poetry, like the actuality of a building, depends on the components of sound mentioned previously—stress, duration, pitch, and juncture—as these are presented in rhetorically stressed sentences. We may diagram the metrical form of a line, but because no two sentences in English are identical in sound, there can be no formulas or mechanical systems for indicating rhythm. Rhythm must be described rather than formulated.

The process of defining the metrical form of a poem is called **scansion**. To *scan* any specimen of verse, we do three things: (1) we identify the prevailing foot; (2) we name the number of feet in a line—if this length follows any regular pattern; and (3) we describe the stanzaic pattern—if there is one. Try out this skill on the following poem:

Virtue

Sweet day, so cool, so calm, so bright,
    The bridal of the earth and sky;
The dew shall weep thy fall to night,
    For thou must die.

Sweet rose, whose hue, angry and brave,   5
    Bids the rash gazer wipe his eye;

Thy root is ever in its grave,
　　And thou must die.

Sweet spring, full of sweet days and roses,
　　A box where sweets compacted lie;　　　　　　　　10
My music shows ye have your closes,
　　And all must die.

Only a sweet and virtuous soul,
　　Like seasoned timber, never gives;
But though the whole world turn to coal,　　　　　　15
　　Then chiefly lives.

　　　　　　　　　　　　—GEORGE HERBERT (1593–1633)

QUESTIONS

1. Vocabulary: *bridal* (2), *brave* (5), *closes* (11), *coal* (15).
2. How are the four stanzas interconnected? How do they build to a climax? How does the fourth contrast with the first three?

　　The first step in scanning a poem is to read it normally, according to its prose meaning, listening to where the accents fall naturally, and perhaps beating time with the hand. If we have any doubt about how a line should be marked, we should skip it temporarily and go on to lines where we feel greater confidence; that is, to those lines that seem most regular, with accents that fall unmistakably at regular intervals—for we are seeking the poem's pattern, which will be revealed by what is regular in it. In "Virtue" lines 3, 10, and 14 clearly fall into this category, as do the short lines 4, 8, and 12. Lines 3, 10, and 14 may be marked as follows:

The dew | shall weep | thy fall | to night,　　　　　　3

A box | where sweets | com-pact- | ed lie;　　　　　　10

Like sea- | soned tim- | ber, nev- | er gives　　　　　14

Lines 4, 8, and 12 are so nearly identical that we may use line 4 to represent all three.

For thou | must die.　　　　　　4

Surveying what we have done so far, we may with some confidence say that the prevailing metrical foot of the poem is iambic; and we may reasonably hypothesize that the second and third lines of each stanza are tetrameter (four-foot) lines and the fourth line dimeter. What about the first lines? Line 1 contains eight syllables, and since the poem is iambic, we may mark them into four feet. The last six syllables clearly constitute three iambic feet (as a general rule, the last few feet in a line tend to reflect the prevailing meter of a poem).

Sweet day, ˘ so cool, ˘ so calm, ˘ so bright ˘   1

This too, then, is a tetrameter line, and the only question is whether to mark the first foot as another iamb or as a spondee—that is, whether it conforms to the norm established by the iambic meter, or is a substituted foot. The adjective "Sweet" is certainly more important in the line than the repeated adverb "so," and ought to receive more stress than the adverbs on the principle of **rhetorical stress**, by which the plain prose sense governs the pronunciation. But we must remember that in marking metrical stresses, we are only comparing the syllables *within a foot,* so the comparison with the repeated "so" is irrelevant. The real question is whether "Sweet" receives as much emphasis as "day."

As another general rule (but by no means an absolute one), a noun usually receives more stress than an adjective that modifies it, a verb more than its adverbs, and an adjective more than an adverb that modifies it—except when the modifying word points to an unusual or unexpected condition. If the phrase were "fat day" or "red day," we would probably feel that those adjectives were odd enough to warrant stressing them. "Sweet day" does not strike us as particularly unusual, so the noun ought to receive stress. Further, as we notice that each of the first three stanzas begins with "Sweet" modifying different nouns, we recognize that the statement of the poem is drawing attention to the similarities (and differences) of three things that can be called *sweet*—"day," "rose," and "spring." By its repetition before those three nouns, the word *sweet* may come to seem formulaic, and the nouns become the object of attention. On the other hand, the repetition of "Sweet" may seem emphatic, and lead us to give approximately equal stress to both the noun and its adjective. As our purpose is to detect the *pattern* of sounds in the poem, the most likely result of this study will be to mark it iambic. However, judging it to be spondaic would not be incorrect, for ultimately we are reporting what we *hear,* and there is room for subjective differences.

The first feet of lines 5 and 9 raise the same problem as line 1 and should be marked in the same way. Choices of a similar sort occur in other lines (15 and 16). Many readers will quite legitimately perceive line 16 as parallel to lines 4, 8, and 12. Others, however, may argue that the word "Then"—emphasizing what happens to the virtuous soul when everything else has perished—has an importance that should be reflected in both the reading and the scansion, and will therefore mark the first foot of this line as a spondee:

$$\text{Then chief-} \mid \text{ly lives.} \mid \qquad \qquad \text{16}$$

These readers also will hear the third foot in line 15 as a spondee:

$$\text{15}$$
$$\text{But though} \mid \text{the whole} \mid \text{world turn} \mid \text{to coal} \mid$$

Lines 2 and 7 introduce a different problem. Most readers, if they encountered these lines in a paragraph of prose, would read them thus:

The BRIdal of the EARTH and SKY   2
Thy ROOT is EVer in its GRAVE   7

But this reading leaves us with an anomalous situation. First, we have only three stresses where our pattern calls for four. Second, we have three unaccented syllables occurring together, which is almost never found in verse of duple meter. From this situation we may learn an important principle. Although normal reading of the sentences in a poem establishes its metrical pattern, the metrical pattern so established in turn influences the reading. An interactive process is at work. In this poem the pressure of the pattern will cause most practiced readers to stress the second of the three unaccented syllables in both lines slightly more than those on either side of it. In scansion, comparing the syllables within the individual foot, we acknowledge that slight increase of stress by marking those syllables as stressed. (Remember, the marking of the accent does not indicate a *degree* of stress in comparison with other accents in the line.) We mark them thus:

$$\text{The bri-} \mid \text{dal of} \mid \text{the earth} \mid \text{and sky} \mid \qquad \qquad \text{2}$$

$$\text{Thy root} \mid \text{is ev-} \mid \text{er in} \mid \text{its grave} \mid \qquad \qquad \text{7}$$

Line 5 presents a situation about which there can be no dispute. The word "angry," although it occurs in a position where we would expect an iamb, by virtue of its normal pronunciation *must* be accented on the first syllable, and thus must be marked a trochee:

Sweet rose, | whose hue, | an-gry | and brave | 5

There is little question also that the following line begins with a trochee, but the second foot ("rash gaz-") must be examined, for we may wonder whether the adjective *rash* presents an unexpected modification for the noun *gazer*. Since the possibilities seem about equal, we prefer to let the pattern again take precedence, although a spondee would be acceptable:

Bids the | rash gaz- | er wipe | his eye | 6

Similarly, the word "Only," beginning line 13, must be accented on the first syllable, thus introducing a trochaic substitution in the first foot of the line. Line 13 also presents another problem. A modern reader perceives the word "virtuous" as a three-syllable word, but the poet writing in the seventeenth century, when metrical requirements were stricter than they are today, would probably have meant the word to be pronounced as two syllables: *ver*-tyus. Following the tastes of this century, we mark it as three syllables, so introducing an anapest instead of the expected iamb in the last foot:

On-ly | a sweet | and vir- | tu-ous soul | 13

In doing this, however, we are consciously modernizing—altering the probable practice of the poet for the sake of a contemporary audience.

One problem of scansion remains: in the third stanza, lines 9 and 11 differ from the other lines of the poem in two respects. First, they contain an uneven number of syllables (nine rather than the expected eight) and second, they end on unaccented syllables:

Sweet spring, | full of | sweet days | and ros- | es,   9

My mu- | sic shows | ye have | your clos- | es   11

Such leftover unaccented syllables at line ends are examples of extra-metrical syllables and are not counted in identifying and naming the meter. These lines are both tetrameter, and if we tap our feet when reading them, we shall tap four times. Metrical verse will often have one and sometimes two leftover unaccented syllables. In iambic and anapestic verse they will come at the end of the lines; in trochaic and dactylic, at the beginning. They never occur in the middle of a line.

Our metrical analysis of "Virtue" is completed. Although (mainly for ease of discussion) we have skipped about, we have indicated a scansion for all its lines. "Virtue" is written in iambic meter (meaning that most of its feet are iambs), and is composed of four-line stanzas, the first three lines tetrameter, the final line dimeter. We are now ready to make a few generalizations about scansion.

1. Most readers will not ordinarily stop to scan a poem they are reading, and they certainly will not read a poem aloud with the exaggerated emphasis on accented syllables that we sometimes give them in order to make the metrical pattern more apparent. However, occasional scansion of a poem has value, as will be indicated in the next chapter, which discusses the relation of sound and meter to sense. Let's give just one example here. The structure of meaning of "Virtue" is unmistakable; three parallel stanzas concerning things that die are followed by a contrasting fourth stanza concerning the one thing that does not die. The first three stanzas all begin with the word "Sweet" preceding a noun, and the first metrical foot in these stanzas is either an iamb or a spondee. The contrasting fourth stanza, however, begins with a trochee, thus departing both from the previous pattern and from the basic meter of the poem. This departure is significant, for the word "Only" is the hinge upon which the structure of the poem turns, and the metrical reversal gives it emphasis. Thus meter serves meaning.

2. Scansion only begins to reveal the rhythmic quality of a poem. It simply involves classifying all syllables as either accented or unaccented and ignores the sometimes considerable differences between degrees of accent. Whether we call a syllable accented or unaccented depends only on its degree of accent relative to the other syllable(s) in its foot. In lines 2 and 7 of "Virtue," the accents on "of" and "in" are obviously much lighter than on the other accented syllables in the line. Further, unaccented syllables also vary in weight. In line 5 "whose" is clearly heavier than "-gry" or "and," and is arguably even heavier than the accented "of" and "in" of lines 2 and 7. It is not unusual, either, to find the unaccented syllable of a foot receiving more stress than the accented syllable immediately preceding it in another foot, as in this line by Gerard Manley Hopkins (page 191):

It will |flame out |like shin- |ing from |shook foil|

The last four syllables of the line, two perfectly regular iambs, are actually spoken as a sequence of four increasingly stressed accents. A similar sequence of increasing accents occurs in lines 4, 8, and 12 of "Virtue,"

For thou must die   4

since the necessity expressed in the word "must" makes it more heavily stressed than the pronoun "thou." The point is that metrical scansion is incapable of describing subtle rhythmic effects in poetry. It is nevertheless a useful and serviceable tool, for by showing us the metrical *pattern,* it draws attention to the way in which the actuality of sound follows the pattern even while departing from it; that is, recognizing the meter, we can more clearly hear rhythms. The *idea* of regularity helps us be aware of the *actuality* of sounds.

3. Notice that the divisions between feet have no meaning except to help us identify the meter. They do not correspond to the speech rhythms in the line. In the third foot of line 14 of "Virtue," a syntactical pause occurs *within* the foot; and, indeed, feet divisions often fall in the middle of a word. It is sometimes a mistake of beginners to expect the word and the foot to be identical units. We mark the feet divisions only to reveal regularity or pattern, not to indicate rhythm. But in "Virtue," if we examine all the two-syllable words, we find that all eleven of them as isolated words removed from their lines would be called *trochaic.* Yet only two of them— "angry" (5) and "Only" (13)—actually occur as trochaic feet. All the rest are divided in the middle between two iambic feet. This calls for two observations: (a) the rhythm of the poem, the *heard* sound, often runs counter to the meter—iambic feet have what is called a "rising" pattern, yet these words individually and as they are spoken have a "falling" rhythm; and (b) the trochaic hinge word "Only" thus has rhythmic echoes throughout the poem, those preceding it yielding a kind of predictive power, and those following it reinforcing the fact that the sense of the poem turns at that word. This rhythmic effect is especially pronounced in the simile of line 14:

Like sea-|soned tim-|ber, nev-|er gives| 14

Echoing the key word "Only," this line contains three disyllabic words, each of them having a falling rhythm running counter to the iambic meter.

4. Finally—and this is the most important generalization of all— perfect regularity of meter is no criterion of merit. Inexperienced readers

sometimes get the notion that it is. If the meter is regular and the rhythm mirrors that regularity in sound, they may feel that the poet has handled the meter successfully and deserves all credit for it. Actually there is nothing easier for any moderately talented versifier than to make language go ta-DUM ta-DUM ta-DUM. But there are two reasons why this is not generally desirable. The first is that, as we have said, all art consists essentially of repetition and variation. If a rhythm alternates too regularly between light and heavy beats, the result is to banish variation; the rhythm mechanically follows the meter and becomes monotonous. But used occasionally or emphatically, a monotonous rhythm can be very effective, as in the triumphant last line of Tennyson's "Ulysses" (page 111):

To strive, |to seek, |to find, |and not |to yield. |

The second reason is that once a basic meter has been established, deviations from it become highly significant and are a means by which the poet can reinforce meaning. If a meter is too regular and the rhythm shows little deviation from it, the probability is that the poet, instead of adapting rhythm to meaning, has simply forced the meaning into a metrical straitjacket.

Actually what gives the skillful use of meter its greatest effectiveness is to be found in the distinction between meter and rhythm. Once we have determined the basic meter of a poem, say iambic tetrameter, we have an expectation that the rhythm will coincide with it—that the pattern will be identical to the actual sound. Thus, a silent drumbeat is set up in our minds, and this drumbeat constitutes an **expected rhythm.** But the actual rhythm of the words—the **heard rhythm**—will sometimes confirm this expected rhythm and sometimes not. Thus, the two—meter and rhythm—are counterpointed, and the appeal of the verse is magnified, just as when two melodies are counterpointed in music, or when we see two swallows flying together and around each other, following the same general course but with individual variations and so making a more eye-catching pattern than one swallow flying alone. If the heard rhythm conforms too closely to the expected rhythm (meter), the poem becomes dull and uninteresting rhythmically. If it departs too far from the meter, there ceases to be an expected rhythm and the result is likely to be a muddle.

There are several ways by which variation can be introduced into a poem's rhythm. The most obvious way, as we have said, is by the substitution of other kinds of feet for the basic foot. Such metrical variation will always be reflected as a rhythmic variation. In our scansion of line 13 of "Virtue," for instance, we found a trochee and an anapest substituted for the expected iambs in the first and last feet. A less obvious but equally important means of variation is through varying degrees of accent arising from the prose meaning of phrases—from the rhetorical stressing. Although we began our scansion of "Virtue" by marking lines 3, 10, and 14 as perfectly regular metrically, there is actually a considerable rhythmic difference among them. Line 3 is quite regular because the rhythmic phrasing corresponds to the metrical pattern, and the line can be read: ta DUM ta DUM ta DUM ta DUM (The DEW shall WEEP thy FALL to NIGHT). Line 10 is less regular, for the three-syllable word "compacted" cuts across the division between two feet. This should be read: ta DUM ta DUM ta-DUM-ta DUM (a BOX where SWEETS comPACTed LIE). Line 14 is the least regular of these three because here there is no correspondence between rhythmic phrasing and metrical division. This should be read: ta DUM-ta DUM-ta DUM-ta DUM (Like SEAsoned TIMber, NEVer GIVES). Finally, variation can be introduced by **grammatical** and **rhetorical pauses**, whether or not signaled by punctuation (punctuated pauses are usually of longer duration than those occasioned only by syntax and rhetoric, and pauses for periods are longer than those for commas). The comma in line 14, by introducing a grammatical pause (in the middle of a foot), provides an additional variation from its perfect regularity. Probably the most violently irregular line in the poem is line 5,

Sweet rose, whose hue, an-gry and brave,   5

for here the unusual trochaic substitution in the second from last foot of an iambic line (a rare occurrence) is set off and emphasized by the grammatical pause; and also, as we have noted, the unaccented "whose" is considerably heavier than the other unaccented syllables in the line. This trochee "angry" is the first unquestionable metrical substitution in the poem. It occurs in a line which, because it opens a stanza, is subconsciously compared to the first line of the first stanza—an example of regularity with its grammatical pauses separating all four of its feet. Once we have noticed that the first line of the second stanza contains a metrical variation, our attention is called to the fact that after the first, each stanza opens with a line containing a trochee—and that these trochees are moved forward one foot in each of the successive stanzas, from the third position in stanza two, to the second in four, and finally to the first in the concluding stanza. This pattern itself tends to add even more emphasis to the climactic change signaled by the final trochee, "Only." Again, meter and rhythm serve meaning.

The effects of rhythm and meter are several. Like the musical repetitions of sound, the musical repetitions of accent can be pleasing for their own sake. In addition, rhythm works as an emotional stimulus and heightens our awareness of what is going on in a poem. Finally, a poet can adapt the sound of the verse to its content and thus make meter a powerful reinforcement of meaning. We should avoid, however, the notion that there is any mystical correspondence between certain meters or rhythms and certain emotions. There are no "happy" meters and no "melancholy" meters. The "falling" rhythm of line 14 of "Virtue," counterpointed against its "rising" meter, does not indicate a depression of mood or feeling—the line has quite the opposite emotional tone. Poets' choice of meter is probably less important than how they handle it after they have chosen it. In most great poetry, meter and rhythm work intimately with the other elements of the poem to produce the total effect.

And because of the importance of free verse today, we must not forget that poetry need not be metrical at all. Like alliteration and rhyme, like metaphor and irony, even like imagery, meter is simply *one* resource poets may or may not use. Their job is to employ their resources to the best advantage for the object they have in mind—the kind of experience they wish to express. And on no other basis should they be judged.

EXERCISES

1. A term that every student of poetry should know (and should be careful not to confuse with *free verse*) is blank verse. **Blank verse** has a very specific meter: it is *iambic pentameter, unrhymed.* It has a special name because it is the principal English meter; that is, the meter that has been used for a large proportion of the greatest English poetry, including the plays of Shakespeare and the epics of Milton. Iambic pentameter in English seems especially suitable for the serious treatment of serious themes. The natural movement of the English language tends to be iambic. Lines shorter than pentameter tend to be songlike, or at least less suited to sustained treatment of serious material. Lines longer than pentameter tend to break up into shorter units, the hexameter line being read as two three-foot units. Rhyme, although highly appropriate to many short poems, often proves a handicap for a long and lofty work. (The word *blank* indicates that the end of the line is bare of rhyme.)

    Of the following poems, four are in blank verse, two are in other meters, and four are in free verse. Determine in which category each belongs.
    a. Frost, "Birches" (page 371).
    b. Donne, "Break of Day" (page 31).
    c. Stafford, "Traveling through the dark" (page 201).
    d. Plath, "Mirror" (page 36).
    e. Tennyson, "Ulysses" (page 110).
    f. Arnold, "Dover Beach" (page 179).

   g. Auden, "The Unknown Citizen" (page 126).

   h. Yeats, "The Second Coming" (page 417).

   i. Frost, "'Out, Out—'" (page 136).

   j. Pastan, "To a Daughter Leaving Home" (page 223).

2. Examine Browning, "My Last Duchess" (page 288) and Pope, "Sound and Sense" (page 233). Both are in the same meter, iambic pentameter rhymed in couplets, but their general rhythmic effect is markedly different. What accounts for the difference? How does the contrast support our statement that the way poets handle meter is more important than their choice of a meter?

3. Examine Williams, "The Widow's Lament in Springtime" (page 61) and Williams, "The Dance" (page 248). Which is the most forcibly run-on in the majority of its lines? Describe the differences in effect.

REVIEWING CHAPTER TWELVE

1. Review the terms printed in boldface, and as you read on in this chapter take note of the examples that you find; identify the poems as free verse or metrical, and write out scansions of the metrical verse.

2. Using examples from the poems that follow in this chapter, draw clear distinctions between rhythm and meter; and using appropriate adjectives, describe the rhythmic effects (jolly, somber, playful, etc.).

3. When possible, explain how the rhythms of a poem reinforce emotional or intellectual meanings.

"Introduction" to *Songs of Innocence*

Piping down the valleys wild,
Piping songs of pleasant glee,
On a cloud I saw a child,
And he laughing said to me:

"Pipe a song about a Lamb."   5
So I piped with merry cheer.
"Piper, pipe that song again."
So I piped; he wept to hear.

"Drop thy pipe, thy happy pipe;
Sing thy songs of happy cheer."   10

So I sung the same again
While he wept with joy to hear.

"Piper, sit thee down and write
In a book that all may read."
So he vanished from my sight,   15
And I plucked a hollow reed,

And I made a rural pen,
And I stained the water clear,
And I wrote my happy songs
Every child may joy to hear.   20

—WILLIAM BLAKE (1757–1827)

QUESTIONS

1. Poets have traditionally been thought of as inspired by one of the Muses (Greek female divinities whose duties were to nurture the arts). Blake's *Songs of Innocence,* a book of poems about childhood and the state of innocence, includes "The Chimney Sweeper" (page 120) and "The Lamb" (page 162). In this introductory poem to the book, what function is performed by the child on a cloud?
2. What is symbolized by "a Lamb" (5)?
3. What three stages of poetic composition are suggested in stanzas 1–2, 3, and 4–5, respectively?
4. What features of the poems in his book does Blake hint at in this "Introduction"? Name at least four.
5. Mark the stressed and unstressed syllables in lines 1–2 and 9–10. Do they establish the basic meter of the poem? If so, is that meter iambic or trochaic? Or could it be either? Some metrists have discarded the distinction between iambic and trochaic, and between anapestic and dactylic, as being artificial. The important distinction, they feel, is between duple and triple meters. Does this poem support their claim?

Had I the Choice

Had I the choice to tally greatest bards,
To limn their portraits, stately, beautiful, and emulate at will,
Homer with all his wars and warriors—Hector, Achilles, Ajax,
Or Shakespeare's woe-entangled Hamlet, Lear, Othello—Tennyson's
   fair ladies,
Meter or wit the best, or choice conceit to wield in perfect rhyme,
   delight of singers;   5

These, these, O sea, all these I'd gladly barter,
   Would you the undulation of one wave, its trick to me transfer,
   Or breathe one breath of yours upon my verse,
   And leave its odor there.

—WALT WHITMAN (1819–1892)

QUESTIONS

1. Vocabulary: *tally* (1), *limn* (2), *conceit* (5).
2. What poetic qualities does the speaker propose to barter in exchange for what? What qualities do the sea and its waves symbolize?
3. Is this free verse, or metrical verse in duple meter? In what way might this be taken as an imitation of the rhythms of the sea?

Stanzas

When a man hath no freedom to fight for at home,
   Let him combat for that of his neighbors;
Let him think of the glories of Greece and of Rome,
   And get knocked on his head for his labors.

To do good to mankind is the chivalrous plan,   5
   And is always as nobly requited:
Then battle for freedom wherever you can,
   And, if not shot or hanged, you'll get knighted.

—GEORGE GORDON, LORD BYRON (1788–1824)

QUESTIONS

1. Vocabulary: *chivalrous* (5), *requited* (6).
2. Scan the poem. How would you describe its rhythmical effects? How do these effects relate to the poem's tone and general meaning?
3. This poem makes use of feminine rhyme. Does this particular kind of rhyme affect the way you read and understand the poem?
4. How is irony effectively used in this poem, particularly in the final line?

| MindTap® | Read, highlight, and take notes online. |

Insomnia

The moon in the bureau mirror
looks out a million miles
(and perhaps with pride, at herself,

but she never, never smiles)
far and away beyond sleep, or   5
perhaps she's a daytime sleeper.

By the Universe deserted,
she'd tell it to go to hell,
and she'd find a body of water,
or a mirror, on which to dwell.   10
So wrap up care in a cobweb
and drop it down the well

into that world inverted
where left is always right,
where the shadows are really the body,   15
where we stay awake all night,
where the heavens are shallow as the sea
is now deep, and you love me.

—ELIZABETH BISHOP (1911–1979)

QUESTIONS

1. Discuss the symbolism of the moon. What are its connotations? What is the situation in which the moon is being observed in the bureau mirror?
2. Explain the title and how it relates to the poem. Can we infer from the poem the reason for the speaker's insomnia?
3. Can this be called a love poem? Why or why not?

Old Ladies' Home

Sharded in black, like beetles,
Frail as antique earthenware
One breath might shiver to bits,
The old women creep out here
To sun on the rocks or prop   5
Themselves up against the wall
Whose stones keep a little heat.

Needles knit in a bird-beaked
Counterpoint to their voices:
Sons, daughters, daughters and sons,   10
Distant and cold as photos,

Grandchildren nobody knows.
Age wears the best black fabric
Rust-red or green as lichens.

At owl-call the old ghosts flock   15
To hustle them off the lawn.
From beds boxed-in like coffins
The bonneted ladies grin.
And Death, that bald-head buzzard,
Stalls in halls where the lamp wick   20
Shortens with each breath drawn.

—SYLVIA PLATH (1932–1963)

QUESTIONS

1. Vocabulary: *Sharded* (1), *Stalls* (20).
2. Discuss the significance of these natural images: "beetles" (1), "bird-beaked / Counterpoint" (8–9), "Rust-red or green as lichens" (14), "owl-call" (15), "bald-head buzzard" (19). These are all metaphors or similes; in each case, what is being compared to what?
3. What is the speaker's tone?
4. This poem is an example of **syllabic verse,** which counts only the number of syllables per line, regardless of accents. (Plath's "Metaphors" [page 81] is another example.) In this case, the poem is constructed of seven-syllable lines in seven-line stanzas—but there is one line that contains only six syllables. What is the significance of the shortening of that line?
5. The poem contains some rhyme (particularly slant rhyme), and some of the lines contain duple metrical feet. Are these musical effects regular enough to call this a metrical poem?

To a Daughter Leaving Home

When I taught you
at eight to ride
a bicycle, loping along
beside you
as you wobbled away   5
on two round wheels,
my own mouth rounding
in surprise when you pulled
ahead down the curved
path of the park,   10

I kept waiting
for the thud
of your crash as I
sprinted to catch up,
while you grew   15
smaller, more breakable
with distance,
pumping, pumping
for your life, screaming
with laughter,   20
the hair flapping
behind you like a
handkerchief waving
goodbye.

—LINDA PASTAN (B. 1932)

QUESTIONS

1. How does the discrepancy between the title and the event create meaning? Which details of the poem take on symbolic meaning?
2. Write out this poem as prose, ignoring line ends. What poetic effect has been lost? Which of the original line ends are particularly important to meaning and feeling?

Porphyria's Lover

The rain set early in tonight,
    The sullen wind was soon awake,
It tore the elm-tops down for spite,
    And did its worst to vex the lake:
    I listened with heart fit to break.   5
When glided in Porphyria; straight
    She shut the cold out and the storm,
And kneeled and made the cheerless grate
    Blaze up, and all the cottage warm;
    Which done, she rose, and from her form   10
Withdrew the dripping cloak and shawl,
    And laid her soiled gloves by, untied
Her hat and let the damp hair fall,
    And, last, she sat down by my side
    And called me. When no voice replied,   15
She put my arm about her waist,

And made her smooth white shoulder bare,
And all her yellow hair displaced,
    And, stooping, made my cheek lie there,
    And spread, o'er all, her yellow hair,   20
Murmuring how she loved me—she
    Too weak, for all her heart's endeavor,
To set its struggling passion free
    From pride, and vainer ties dissever,
    And give herself to me forever.   25
But passion sometimes would prevail,
    Nor could tonight's gay feast restrain
A sudden thought of one so pale
    For love of her, and all in vain:
    So, she was come through wind and rain.   30
Be sure I looked up at her eyes
    Happy and proud; at last I knew
Porphyria worshipped me: surprise
    Made my heart swell, and still it grew
    While I debated what to do.   35
That moment she was mine, mine, fair,
    Perfectly pure and good: I found
A thing to do, and all her hair
    In one long yellow string I wound
    Three times her little throat around,   40
And strangled her. No pain felt she;
    I am quite sure she felt no pain.
As a shut bud that holds a bee,
    I warily oped her lids: again
    Laughed the blue eyes without a stain.   45
And I untightened next the tress
    About her neck; her cheek once more
Blushed bright beneath my burning kiss:
    I propped her head up as before,
    Only, this time my shoulder bore   50
Her head, which droops upon it still:
    The smiling rosy little head,
So glad it has its utmost will,
    That all it scorned at once is fled,
    And I, its love, am gained instead!   55
Porphyria's love: she guessed not how
    Her darling one wish would be heard.
And thus we sit together now,

And all night long we have not stirred
And yet God has not said a word!   60

—ROBERT BROWNING (1812–1889)

QUESTIONS

1. Why can Porphyria and the speaker not be together in a normal romantic relationship? What has kept them apart?
2. What is the "gay feast" mentioned in line 27?
3. The poem deals, in part, with abnormal human psychology. What kind of a person is the speaker? What does he reveal about himself as the poem proceeds? Why does he take such drastic action?
4. The final line has been read in a variety of ways. Why has God "not said a word"? Does this mean that God has countenanced the murder?
5. How would you describe the metrical pattern in this poem? How does the pattern help reinforce the poem's meaning?

Break, break, break

Break, break, break,
    On thy cold gray stones, O sea!
And I would that my tongue could utter
    The thoughts that arise in me.

O, well for the fisherman's boy,   5
    That he shouts with his sister at play!
O, well for the sailor lad,
    That he sings in his boat on the bay!

And the stately ships go on
    To their haven under the hill;   10
But O for the touch of a vanished hand,
    And the sound of a voice that is still!

Break, break, break,
    At the foot of thy crags, O sea!
But the tender grace of a day that is dead   15
    Will never come back to me.

—ALFRED, LORD TENNYSON (1809–1892)

QUESTIONS

1. In lines 3–4 the speaker wishes he could put his thoughts into words. Does he make those thoughts explicit in the course of the poem?
2. What aspects of life are symbolized by the two images in stanza 2? By the image in lines 9–10? How do lines 11–12 contrast with those images?
3. The basic meter of this poem is anapestic, and all but two lines are trimeter. Which two? What other variations from a strict anapestic trimeter do you find? How many lines (and which ones) display a strict anapestic pattern? With this much variation, would you be justified in calling the poem free verse? Do the departures from a strict metrical norm contribute to the meaning?

Annabel Lee

It was many and many a year ago,
   In a kingdom by the sea,
That a maiden there lived whom you may know
   By the name of Annabel Lee;—
And this maiden she lived with no other thought   5
   Than to love and be loved by me.

She was a child and *I* was a child,
   In this kingdom by the sea,
But we loved with a love that was more than love—
   I and my Annabel Lee—   10
With a love that the wingéd seraphs of Heaven
   Coveted her and me.

And this was the reason that, long ago,
   In this kingdom by the sea,
A wind blew out of a cloud by night   15
   Chilling my Annabel Lee;
So that her high-born kinsmen came
   And bore her away from me,
To shut her up in a sepulchre
   In this kingdom by the sea.   20

The angels, not half so happy in Heaven,
   Went envying her and me;
Yes! that was the reason (as all men know,
   In this kingdom by the sea)

That the wind came out of the cloud, chilling 25
    And killing my Annabel Lee.

But our love it was stronger by far than the love
    Of those who were older than we—
    Of many far wiser than we—
And neither the angels in Heaven above 30
    Nor the demons down under the sea
Can ever dissever my soul from the soul
    Of the beautiful Annabel Lee:—

For the moon never beams without bringing me dreams
    Of the beautiful Annabel Lee; 35
And the stars never rise but I see the bright eyes
    Of the beautiful Annabel Lee;
And so, all the night-tide, I lie down by the side
Of my darling, my darling, my life and my bride
    In her sepulchre there by the sea— 40
    In her tomb by the side of the sea.

—EDGAR ALLAN POE (1809–1849)

QUESTIONS

1. Edgar Allan Poe once said that "the death of a beautiful young woman" was the most poetic of subjects. Look up Poe's biography online and try to account for this opinion.
2. The speaker in "Annabel Lee" feels, of course, both grief and intense love for the lost Annabel. How do the rhythm and meter of the poem help to convey these emotions?
3. Discuss the use of repetition in the poem. Why is this effective?

SUGGESTIONS FOR WRITING

The following suggestions are for brief writing exercises, not for full critical essays. The suggestions here could constitute a part of a full essay that includes some discussion of the contribution of rhythm and meter to the total meaning of a poem.

1. Scan one of the following metrical poems, and indicate how the rhythmic effects (including substitutions and variations from the metrical norm) contribute to meaning:
   a. Dickinson, "Because I could not stop for Death" (page 106).
   b. Shelley, "Ozymandias" (page 122); consider regular and irregular meters in lines 10–14.

   c. Blake, "Introduction" to *Songs of Innocence* (page 219; see question 5).

   d. Tennyson, "Break, break, break" (page 226; see question 3).

2. In the following free-verse poems, discuss how the line forms a rhythmic unit, paying particular attention to run-on and end-stopped lines:

   a. Williams, "The Widow's Lament in Springtime" (page 61; particularly examine lines 20–24).

   b. Pastan, "To a Daughter Leaving Home" (page 223; see question 2, and particularly examine lines 12–14, 15–16, 19–20, 21–24).

   c. Hughes, "Theme for English B" (page 386).

   d. Whitman, "When I Heard the Learn'd Astronomer" (page 158).

PRACTICE AP® WRITING PROMPTS

Walt Whitman, "Had I the Choice" (pp. 220–221)

In Whitman's brief free-verse statement "Had I the Choice," the speaker wishes he could create the sort of sensual delight with words that nature makes using its ability to appeal to all our senses. Read "Had I the Choice" several times. Then write an essay in which you discuss Whitman's attempts to use words as musical instruments.

. . . .

Linda Pastan, "To a Daughter Leaving Home" (pp. 223–224)

Read "To a Daughter Leaving Home" carefully. Then, taking into consideration the poem's title, explain how the rite of passage described in the poem reflects the speaker's feelings as she learns to let her child go. In your essay, consider such elements as simile, sound devices, and rhythm.

. . . .

Robert Browning, "Porphyria's Lover" (pp. 224–226)

Read Browning's dramatic monologue "Porphyria's Lover" carefully, listening with the mind's inner ear to the poem's regular iambic tetrameter and its regular pattern of rhyme. In a well-written essay, analyze the tension between the poem's rhythm and the natural sentence sense of the speaker's language, showing how each contributes to the poem's overall effect.

. . . .

CHAPTER THIRTEEN

Sound and Meaning

Rhythm and sound cooperate to produce what we call the music of poetry. This music, as we have pointed out, may serve two general functions: it may be enjoyable in itself, or it may reinforce meaning and intensify the communication.

Pure pleasure in sound and rhythm exists from a very early age in the human being—probably from the age the baby first starts cooing in his or her cradle, certainly from the age that children begin chanting nursery rhymes and skipping rope. The appeal of the following verse, for instance, depends almost entirely on its "music":

> Pease porridge hot,
> Pease porridge cold,
> Pease porridge in the pot
> Nine days old.

—ANONYMOUS

There is very little sense here; the attraction comes from the emphatic rhythm, the emphatic rhymes (with a strong contrast between the short vowel and short final consonant of *hot–pot* and the long vowel and long final consonant combination of *cold–old*), and the heavy alliteration (exactly half the words begin with *p*). From nonsense rhymes such as this, many of us graduate to a love of more meaningful poems whose appeal resides largely in the sounds they make. Much of the pleasure that we find in a poem like Edgar Allan Poe's "The Bells" (page 195) derives from its musical qualities.

The peculiar function of poetry as distinguished from music, however, is to convey not sounds but meaning or experience *through* sounds. In first-rate poetry, sound exists neither for its own sake nor for mere decoration, but to enhance the meaning. Its function is to support the leading player, not to steal the scene.

The poet may reinforce meaning through sound in numerous ways. Without claiming to exhaust them, we can include most of the chief means under four general headings: (1) choose words that sound like their meanings, (2) choose sounds and group them, (3) control the speed and movement of the lines, and (4) control both the sound and meter.

First, the poet can choose words whose sound in some degree suggests their meaning. In its narrowest sense this is called **onomatopoeia.** Strictly defined, it means the use of words that, at least supposedly, sound like what they mean, such as *hiss*, *snap*, and *bang*. Animal noises offer many examples—*bow-wow, cock-a-doodle-do, oink*—and sometimes poets may even invent words to represent them, as Shakespeare does in "Winter" (page 5) when the owl sings "Tu-whit, tu-who!" Poetry, of course, does not usually present the vocalized sounds made by animals, but onomatopoeia often expresses the sounds of movements or actions, as in the following examples: "The harness *jingles*" in Housman's "Is my team plowing" (page 29); "Neighbors *rustle* in and out" in Dickinson's "There's been a Death, in the Opposite House" (page 32); the mourners *"creak* across" in Dickinson's "I felt a Funeral, in my Brain" (page 62); and in Heaney's "The Forge" (page 64) we hear *ring*, *hiss*, *clatter*, *grunts*, and *slam*. Generally, we can detect the presence of onomatopoetic words simply by sounding them, but you can also use your dictionary to verify your discovery: most have the term "imitative" as part of the information about word origins.

The usefulness of onomatopoeia, of course, is strictly limited, because it occurs only where the poet is describing sound, and most poems do not describe sound. But by combining onomatopoeia with other devices that help convey meaning, the poet can achieve subtle or bold emotional effects.

In addition to onomatopoetic words there is another group of words, sometimes called **phonetic intensives,** whose sound, by a process as yet obscure, to some degree connects with their meaning. An initial *fl* sound, for instance, is often associated with the idea of moving light, as in *flame*, *flare, flash, flicker, flimmer.* An initial *gl* also frequently accompanies the idea of light, usually unmoving, as in *glare, gleam, glint, glow, glisten.* An initial *sl* often introduces words meaning "smoothly wet," as in *slippery, slick, slide, slime, slop, slosh, slobber, slushy.* An initial *st* often suggests strength, as in *staunch, stalwart, stout, sturdy, stable, steady, stocky, stern, strong, stubborn, steel.* Short *i* often goes with the idea of smallness, as in *inch, imp, thin, slim, little, bit, chip, sliver, chink, slit, sip, whit, tittle, snip, wink, glint, glimmer, flicker, pigmy, midge, chick, kid, kitten, minikin, miniature.* Long *o* or *oo* may suggest melancholy or sorrow, as in *moan, groan, woe, mourn, forlorn, toll, doom, gloom, moody.* Final *are* sometimes goes with the idea of a big light or noise, as *flare, glare, stare, blare.* Medial *att* suggests some kind of particled movement as in *spatter, scatter,* *shatter, chatter, rattle, prattle, clatter, batter.* Final *er* and *le* indicate repetition, as in *glitter, flutter, shimmer, whisper, jabber, chatter, clatter, sputter, flicker, twitter, mutter,* and *ripple, bubble, twinkle, sparkle, rattle, rumble, jingle.*

None of these various sounds is invariably associated with the idea that it seems to suggest and, in fact, a short *i* is found in *thick* as well as *thin,* in *big* as well as *little.* Language is a complex phenomenon. But there is enough association between these sounds and ideas to suggest some sort of intrinsic if obscure relationship. A word like *flicker,* although not onomatopoetic (because it does not refer to sound) would seem somehow to suggest its sense, with the *fl* suggesting moving light, the *i* suggesting smallness, the *ck* suggesting sudden cessation of movement (as in *crack, peck, pick, hack,* and *flick*), and the *er* suggesting repetition. The preceding list of sound-idea correspondences is only a very partial one. A complete list, though it would involve only a small proportion of words in the language, would probably be longer than that of the more strictly onomatopoetic words, to which they are related.

Eight O'Clock

He stood, and heard the steeple
    Sprinkle the quarters on the morning town.
One, two, three, four, to market-place and people
    It tossed them down.

Strapped, noosed, nighing his hour,   5
    He stood and counted them and cursed his luck;
And then the clock collected in the tower
    Its strength, and struck.

—A. E. HOUSMAN (1859–1936)

QUESTIONS

1. Vocabulary: *quarters* (2).
2. Eight A.M. was the traditional hour in England for putting condemned criminals to death. Discuss the force of "morning" (2) and "struck" (8). Discuss the appropriateness of the image of the clock collecting its strength. Can you suggest any reason for the use of "nighing" (5) rather than *nearing?*
3. Consider the contribution to meaning of the following phonetic intensives: "steeple" and "Sprinkle" (1, 2), "stood" (1, 6), "Strapped" (5), "strength" and "struck" (8). Comment on the frequent *k* sounds leading up to "struck" in the second stanza.

A second and far more important way that the poet can reinforce meaning through sound is to choose sounds and group them so that the effect is smooth and pleasant sounding (*euphonious*) or rough and harsh sounding (*cacophonous*). Generally, vowels are more pleasing than consonants because vowels are musical tones, whereas consonants are merely noises. A line with a high percentage of vowel sounds in proportion to consonant sounds will therefore tend to be more melodious than one in which the proportion is low. The vowels and consonants themselves differ considerably in quality. The "long" vowels, such as those in *fate*, *reed*, *rhyme*, *coat*, *food*, and *dune,* are fuller and more resonant than the "short" vowels, as in *fat*, *red*, *rim*, *cot*, *foot*, and *dun*. Of the consonants, some are fairly mellifluous, such as the "liquids," *l*, *m*, *n*, and *r*; the soft *v* and *f* sounds; the semivowels *w* and *y*; and such combinations as *th* and *wh*. Others, such as the "plosives," *b, d, g, k, p,* and *t,* are harsher and sharper in their effect. These differences in sound are the poet's materials. Good poets, however, will not necessarily seek out the sounds that are pleasing and attempt to combine them in melodious combinations. Rather, they will use **euphony** and **cacophony** as they are appropriate to content. Consider, for instance, the following lines.

Sound and Sense

True ease in writing comes from art, not chance,
As those move easiest who have learned to dance.
'Tis not enough no harshness gives offense,
The sound must seem an echo to the sense:
Soft is the strain when Zephyr gently blows,   5
And the smooth stream in smoother numbers flows;
But when loud surges lash the sounding shore,
The hoarse, rough verse should like the torrent roar;
When Ajax strives some rock's vast weight to throw,
The line too labors, and the words move slow;   10
Not so, when swift Camilla scours the plain,
Flies o'er the unbending corn, and skims along the main.
Hear how Timotheus' varied lays surprise,
And bid alternate passions fall and rise!

—ALEXANDER POPE (1688–1744)

QUESTIONS

1. Vocabulary: *numbers* (6), *lays* (13).
2. This excerpt is from a long poem (called *An Essay on Criticism*) on the arts of writing and judging poetry. Which line states the thesis of the passage?
3. There are four classical allusions: Zephyr (5) was god of the west wind; Ajax (9), a Greek warrior noted for his strength; Camilla (11), a legendary queen reputedly so fleet of foot that she could run over a field of grain without bending the blades

or over the sea without wetting her feet; and Timotheus (13), a famous Greek rhapsodic poet. How do these allusions enable Pope to achieve greater economy?

4. Copy the passage and scan it. Then, considering both meter and sounds, show how Pope practices what he preaches. (Incidentally, on which syllable should "alternate" in line 14 be accented? Does the meter help you to know the pronunciation of "Timotheus" in line 13?)

MindTap® Read, highlight, and take notes online.

There are no strictly onomatopoetic words in this passage, and yet the sound seems marvelously adapted to the sense. When the poem is about soft, smooth effects (lines 5–6), there is an abundance of alliteration (*s* in *soft, strain, smooth stream, smoother*) and consonance (the voiced *s* or *z* sound in *Zephyr, blows, numbers flows*; the voiced *th* of *smooth* and *smoother*). When harshness and loudness are the subject, the lines become cacophonous and even the pleasant smoothness of *s*-alliteration when coupled with *sh* evokes angry hissing: "*s*urges la*sh* the *s*ounding *sh*ore, / The hoar*s*e, rough ver*s*e *sh*ould. . . ." Heavy labor is expressed in cacophony ("Ajax strives some rock's vast weight to throw"), while lightness and speed are expressed with euphonious short *i* sounds ("sw*i*ft Cam*i*lla . . . sk*i*ms"). Throughout the passage there is a remarkable correspondence between the pleasant-sounding and the pleasant in idea, the unpleasant-sounding and the unpleasant in idea.

As the excerpt from Alexander Pope also demonstrates, a third way in which a poet can reinforce meaning through sound is by controlling the speed and movement of the lines by the choice and use of meter, by the choice and arrangement of vowel and consonant sounds, and by the disposition of pauses. In meter, the unaccented syllables usually go faster than the accented syllables; hence, the triple meters are swifter than the duple. But the poet can vary the tempo of any meter by the use of substitute feet. Generally, whenever two or more unaccented syllables come together, the effect will be to speed up the pace of the line; when two or more accented syllables come together, the effect will be to slow it down. This pace will also be affected by the vowel lengths and by whether the sounds are easily run together. The long vowels take longer to pronounce than the short ones. Some words are easily run together, while others demand that the position of the mouth be re-formed before the next word is uttered. It takes much longer, for instance, to say "Watch dogs catch much meat" than to say "My aunt is away," yet the number of syllables is the same. And finally, the poet can slow down the speed of a line through the introduction of grammatical and rhetorical pauses. Consider lines 54–56 from Tennyson's "Ulysses" (page 111):

The lights|be-gín|to twin-|kle from|the rocks;|

Thĕ lóng|dáy wanés;|thĕ slów|moón clímbs;|thĕ deép| 55

Moáns roúnd|wĭth mán-|ў̆ voí-|cĕs. . . .

In these lines Tennyson wished the movement to be slow, in accordance with the slow waning of the long day and the slow climbing of the moon. His meter is iambic pentameter. This is not a swift meter, but in lines 55–56 he slows it down further, by (a) introducing three spondaic feet, thus bringing three accented syllables together in two separate places; (b) choosing for his accented syllables words that have long vowel sounds or diphthongs that the voice hangs onto: "long," "day," "wanes," "slow," "moon," "climbs," "deep," "Moans," "round"; (c) choosing words that are not easily run together (except for "day" and "slow," each of these words begins and ends with consonant sounds that require varying degrees of readjustment of the mouth before pronunciation can continue); and (d) introducing two grammatical pauses, after "wanes" and "climbs," and a rhetorical pause after "deep." The result is an extremely effective use of the movement of the verse to accord with the movement suggested by the words.

A fourth way for a poet to fit sound to sense is to control both sound and meter in such a way as to emphasize words that are important in meaning. This can be done by highlighting such words through alliteration, assonance, consonance, or rhyme; by placing them before a pause; or by skillfully placing or displacing them in the metrical scheme. We have already seen how George Herbert pivots the structure of meaning in "Virtue" (page 209) on a trochaic substitution in the initial foot of his final stanza. For an additional example, let us look again at Drayton's "Since there's no help" (page 169). This poem is a sonnet—fourteen lines of iambic pentameter—in which a lover threatens to abandon his courtship if the woman he desires will not go to bed with him. In the first eight lines he pretends to be *glad* that they are parting so cleanly. In the last six lines, however, he paints a vivid picture of the death of his personified Love/Passion for her but intimates that even at this last moment ("Now") she could restore it to life—by satisfying his sexual desires:

Nów, ăt|thĕ lást|gásp ŏf|Lóve's lá-|tĕst breáth,|

When, his pulse failing, Passion speechless lies,   10

When Faith is kneeling by his bed of death,

Ănd Ín-|nŏ-cénce|ĭs clós-|ĭng úp|hĭs eýes,|

Now, if thou wouldst, when all have given him o-ver,*

From death to life thou mightst him yet re-cov-er.

The emphasis is on *Now*. In a matter of seconds, the speaker indicates, it will be too late: his Love/Passion will be dead, and he himself will be gone. The word "Now" begins line 9. It also begins a new sentence and a new direction in the poem. It is separated from what has gone before by a period at the end of the preceding line. Metrically it initiates a tro-chee, thus breaking away from the poem's basic iambic meter (line 8 is perfectly regular). In all these ways—its initial position in line, sentence, and thought, and its metrical irregularity—the word "Now" is given extraordinary emphasis appropriate to its importance in the context. Its repetition in line 13 reaffirms this importance, and there again it is given emphasis by its positional and metrical situation. It begins both a line and the final rhyming couplet, is separated by punctuation from the line before, and participates in a metrical inversion. (The lines before and after are metrically regular.)

While Herbert and Drayton use metrical deviation to give emphasis to important words, Tennyson, in the concluding line of "Ulysses," uses marked regularity, plus skillful use of grammatical pauses, to achieve the same effect.

We are not now that strength which in old days

Moved earth and heav-en, that which we are, we are:

One e-qual tem-per of he-ro-ic hearts,

Made weak by time and fate, but strong in will

To strive, to seek, to find, and not to yield.   70

The blank-verse rhythm throughout "Ulysses" is remarkably subtle and varied, but the last line is not only regular in its scansion but heavily regu-lar, for a number of reasons. First, all the words are monosyllables. Second,

---

*Drayton probably intended "given" to be pronounced as one syllable (*giv'n*), and most sixteenth-century readers would have pronounced it thus in this poem.

the unaccented syllables are all very small and unimportant words—four *to*s and one *and*—whereas the accented syllables consist of four important verbs and a very important *not*. Third, each of the verbs is followed by a grammatical pause pointed off by a mark of punctuation. The result is to cause a pronounced alternation between light and heavy syllables that brings the accent down on the four verbs and the *not* with sledgehammer blows. The line rings out like a challenge, which it is.

I heard a Fly buzz—when I died

I heard a Fly buzz—when I died—
The Stillness in the Room
Was like the Stillness in the Air—
Between the Heaves of Storm—

The Eyes around—had wrung them dry—   5
And Breaths were gathering firm
For that last Onset—when the King
Be witnessed—in the Room—

I willed my Keepsakes—Signed away
What portion of me be   10
Assignable—and then it was
There interposed a Fly—

With Blue—uncertain stumbling Buzz—
Between the light—and me—
And then the Windows failed—and then   15
I could not see to see—

—EMILY DICKINSON (1830–1886)

QUESTIONS

1. It is important to understand the sequence of events in this deathbed scene. Arrange the following events in correct chronological order: (a) the willing of keepsakes, (b) the weeping of mourners, (c) the appearance of the fly, (d) the preternatural stillness in the room.
2. What or who are the "Eyes" and the "Breaths" in lines 5–6? What figures of speech are involved in these lines? Is the speaker making out her will in lines 9–11? What *is* she doing?

3. What sort of expectation is set up by phrases like "last Onset" (7), "the King" (7), and "Be witnessed" (8)?
4. Explain "the Windows failed" (15) and "I could not see to see" (16).

We may well conclude our discussion of the adaptation of sound to sense by analyzing this poem. It consists of four four-line stanzas of alternating iambic tetrameter (first and third lines) and iambic trimeter (second and fourth); the first and third lines are unrhymed, the second and fourth display approximate rhymes in the first three stanzas (*Room/Storm, firm/Room, be/Fly*). The fourth stanza uses an exact rhyme that echoes the last word in line 3 of the preceding stanza (*was* and *Buzz*) and comes to an emphatic conclusion of both the stanza and the poem with an exact rhyme (*me/see*). The poem depicts a speaker's recollection of her own deathbed scene, focusing on the suspenseful interval during which she and her loved ones await the arrival of death—ironically symbolized in the closing lines as a common housefly. But the poem does not move chronologically. Surprisingly, it begins with its conclusion, the apparently trivial fact that the last conscious perception was hearing the buzzing fly; then it proceeds to summarize the events leading up to that moment.

How is the poem's sound fitted to its sense? In the opening stanzas, the pace is slow and even solemn, the rhythm perfectly matching the meter, as befits this apparently momentous occasion with its "Stillness," its quiet, breathless awaiting of "the King"—death itself. The approximate rhymes provide a formal unity even as they convey an atmosphere of unease, an uncertainty and fear in the face of imminent death; and the dashes contribute to the poem's measured, stately rhythm. Then the poem returns to the insignificant topic of its opening line and invests it with enormous meaning.

The one onomatopoetic word in the poem is *Buzz*, introduced abruptly in line 1 without capitalization and then reintroduced with intensity in line 13. In line 11, the final word, *was*, though unrhymed in its own stanza and unrhymed in the formal rhyme scheme, nevertheless is an exact rhyme for *Buzz* in the first line of the final stanza. In line 12, the word *interposed* continues the buzzing into the final stanza. In line 13 the vowel sound of *Buzz* is preceded by the identical vowel sounds in "*u*ncertain" and "st*u*mbling," making three short *u* sounds in close succession. Finally, the *b* sound in *Buzz* is preceded in line 13 by the *b*s in "*B*lue" and "stum-*b*ling." Thus, *all* the sounds in *Buzz*—its initial and final consonants and its vowel—are heard at least three times in lines 11–13. This outburst of onomatopoetic effect consummates the aural imagery promised in the opening line, "I *heard* a Fly buzz."

But line 13 combines images of color and motion as well as sound. Though the sound imagery is the most important, the poem concludes with a reference to the speaker's dimming eyesight, and we may infer that she *saw* a blur of the bluebottle's deep metallic blue as well as hearing its buzz. This image is an example of **synesthesia**, the stimulation of two or more senses simultaneously, especially as here, where one sense perception is described in terms of another (as in a "Blue . . . Buzz"). The images of motion between "Blue" and "Buzz" also belong to both the visual and aural modes of sensing. The speaker hears and imperfectly sees the "uncertain" flight of the fly as it bumbles from one pane of glass to another, its buzzing now louder, now softer. Furthermore, the exact rhymes in the last stanza that pick up on "was" in the preceding one underscore the abrupt finality of the speaker's confrontation with death, and thus the sudden end of her human perception.

In analyzing verse for correspondence between sound and sense, we need to be very cautious not to make exaggerated claims. A great deal of nonsense has been written about the moods of certain meters and the effects of certain sounds, and it is easy to suggest correspondences that exist only in our imaginations. Nevertheless, the first-rate poet has nearly always an instinctive tact about handling sound so that it in some degree supports meaning. One of the few absolute rules that applies to the judgment of poetry is that the form should be adequate to the content. This rule does not mean that there must always be a close and easily demonstrable correspondence. It does mean that there will be no glaring discrepancies.

The selection that introduces this chapter ("Pease porridge hot") illustrates the use of sound in verse almost purely for its own sake, and it is, as significant poetry, among the most trivial passages in the whole book. But beyond this there is an abundant range of poetic possibilities where sound is pleasurable for itself without violating meaning and where sound to varying degrees corresponds with and corroborates meaning; and in this rich middle range lie many of the great pleasures of reading poetry.

EXERCISES

In each of the following paired quotations, the named poet wrote the version that more successfully adapts sound to sense. As specifically as possible, account for the superiority of the better version.

1. a. Go forth—and Virtue, ever in your sight,
        Shall be your guide by day, your guard by night.
    b. Go forth—and Virtue, ever in your sight,
        Shall point your way by day, and keep you safe at night. —**CHARLES CHURCHILL**

2. a. How charming is divine philosophy!
      Not harsh and rough as foolish men suppose
      But musical as is the lute of Phoebus.
   b. How charming is divine philosophy!
      Not harsh and crabbed as dull fools suppose
      But musical as is Apollo's lute. —JOHN MILTON
3. a. All day the fleeing crows croak hoarsely over the snow.
   b. All day the out-cast crows croak hoarsely across the whiteness.
      —ELIZABETH COATSWORTH
4. a. Your talk attests how bells of singing gold
      Would sound at evening over silent water.
   b. Your low voice tells how bells of singing gold
      Would sound at twilight over silent water. —EDWIN ARLINGTON ROBINSON
5. a. A thousand streamlets flowing through the lawn,
      The moan of doves in gnarled ancient oaks,
      And quiet murmuring of countless bees.
   b. Myriads of rivulets hurrying through the lawn,
      The moan of doves in immemorial elms,
      And murmuring of innumerable bees. —ALFRED, LORD TENNYSON
6. a. It is the lark that sings so out of tune,
      Straining harsh discords and unpleasing sharps.
   b. It is the lark that warbles out of tune
      In harsh discordant tones with doleful flats. —WILLIAM SHAKESPEARE
7. a. "Artillery" and "armaments" and "implements of war"
      Are phrases too severe to please the gentle Muse.
   b. Bombs, drums, guns, bastions, batteries, bayonets, bullets,—
      Hard words, which stick in the soft Muses' gullets. —LORD BYRON
8. a. The hands of the sisters Death and Night incessantly softly
      wash again, and ever again, this soiled world.
   b. The hands of the soft twins Death and Night repeatedly
      wash again, and ever again, this dirty world. —WALT WHITMAN
9. a. The curfew sounds the knell of parting day,
      The lowing cattle slowly cross the lea,
      The plowman goes wearily plodding his homeward way,
      Leaving the world to the darkening night and me.
   b. The curfew tolls the knell of parting day,
      The lowing herd wind slowly o'er the lea,
      The plowman homeward plods his weary way,
      And leaves the world to darkness and to me. —THOMAS GRAY
10. a. Let me chastise this odious, gilded bug,
       This painted son of dirt, that smells and bites.
    b. Yet let me flap this bug with gilded wings,
       This painted child of dirt, that stinks and stings. —ALEXANDER POPE

REVIEWING CHAPTER THIRTEEN

....

1. Review the terms in the chapter presented in boldface.
2. The chapter presents four important means by which sound reinforces meaning; in reviewing them, decide whether the meaning being reinforced is intellectual or emotional, or both.
3. In the following poems, identify any of the devices by which sound reinforces meaning, being sure to define the meaning that is being reinforced—and identifying any elements of poetry that are employed in creating that meaning.

Anthem for Doomed Youth

What passing-bells for these who die as cattle?
Only the monstrous anger of the guns.
Only the stuttering rifles' rapid rattle
Can patter out their hasty orisons.
No mockeries now for them; no prayers nor bells,   5
Nor any voice of mourning save the choirs—
The shrill, demented choirs of wailing shells;
And bugles calling for them from sad shires.

What candles may be held to speed them all?
Not in the hands of boys, but in their eyes   10
Shall shine the holy glimmers of good-byes.
The pallor of girls' brows shall be their pall;
Their flowers the tenderness of patient minds,
And each slow dusk a drawing-down of blinds.

—WILFRED OWEN (1893–1918)

QUESTIONS

1. Vocabulary: *passing-bells* (1), *orisons* (4), *shires* (8), *pall* (12). It was the custom during World War I to draw down the blinds in homes where a son had been lost (14).
2. How do lines 1–8 and 9–14 of this sonnet differ in (a) geographical setting, (b) subject matter, (c) kind of imagery used, and (d) tone? Who are the "boys" (10) and "girls" (12) referred to in the sestet?

3. What central metaphorical image runs throughout the poem? What secondary metaphors build up the central one?
4. Why are the "doomed youth" said to die "as cattle" (1)? Why would prayers, bells, and so on, be "mockeries" for them (5)?
5. Show how sound is adapted to sense throughout the poem.

Suicide off Egg Rock

Behind him the hotdogs split and drizzled
On the public grills, and the ochreous salt flats,
Gas tanks, factory stacks — that landscape
Of imperfections his bowels were part of —
Rippled and pulsed in the glassy updraught.   5
Sun struck the water like a damnation.
No pit of shadow to crawl into,
And his blood beating the old tattoo
I am, I am, I am. Children
Were squealing where combers broke and the spindrift   10
Raveled wind-ripped from the crest of the wave.
A mongrel working his legs to a gallop
Hustled a gull flock to flap off the sandspit.

He smoldered, as if stone-deaf, blindfold,
His body beached with the sea's garbage,   15
A machine to breathe and beat forever.
Flies filing in through a dead skate's eyehole
Buzzed and assailed the vaulted brainchamber.
The words in his book wormed off the pages.
Everything glittered like blank paper.   20

Everything shrank in the sun's corrosive
Ray but Egg Rock on the blue wastage.
He heard when he walked into the water

The forgetful surf creaming on those ledges.

—SYLVIA PLATH (1932–1963)

QUESTIONS

1. Vocabulary: *ochreous* (2), *updraught* (5), *spindrift* (10).
2. Describe the setting of the poem. Does it contribute to the subject matter of suicide?

3. Isolate the major images and relate them to the theme of the poem.
4. In the final line, the surf is "forgetful" in what sense?

Night and the Creation of Geography

The screeching cries
of the killdeer in the night create
their own narrow channels through the blades
of broken grasses and sharp-edged
dunes lining the shore.
           Likewise,   5
the nightjar's whistle cuts a passage,
like a stream, across the open desert.
Only the nightjar knows the stars
of that passage, just as the limpkin's
wail is a direction only the limpkin forges   10
through the marshlands.
           The furrows
of the field cricket's triplet chirps and shrill
courtship trills transform the sorrels
and doveweeds in the ditch, fashioning
needle ways and grids of space by the run   15
of their own notes.
          And the thin cough-bark
of the bobcat establishes another sparse and arid
stalk among the rocks and brushy land where
it roots and withers.
          No one can fully explore
the corridor made through the dark by the coyote's   20
jagged shrieks and clacking yaps, those yelping
howls like sheer descending cliffs, a noise
jumbled like rock-filled gulches and gulleys.
None but the coyote.
          On icy plains, the snowy
owl occupies the cavern of its own silence,   25
a cavern formed by its quest for sweet blood
of lemming or hare. Within the polished,
black-and-white crystals of the freezing
night air, the owl watches from the warm
hollow of its stillness.   30

—PATTIANN ROGERS (B. 1940)

QUESTIONS

1. Vocabulary: *killdeer* (2), *nightjar's* (6), *limpkin's* (9), *sorrels* (13), *lemming* (27).
2. Through many examples of birds and other animals that are said to create geography with their sounds, the poem fashions a myth. What figure of speech is chiefly used? What is the meaning of that myth? Which animal creates its world with silence?
3. Find examples of onomatopoeia and phonetic intensives. Does the poem tend to be cacaphonous or euphonious? What do these sound effects contribute to meaning?

Aunt Jennifer's Tigers

Aunt Jennifer's tigers prance across a screen,
Bright topaz denizens of a world of green.
They do not fear the men beneath the tree;
They pace in sleek chivalric certainty.

Aunt Jennifer's fingers fluttering through her wool   5
Find even the ivory needle hard to pull.
The massive weight of Uncle's wedding band
Sits heavily upon Aunt Jennifer's hand.

When Aunt is dead, her terrified hands will lie
Still ringed with ordeals she was mastered by.   10
The tigers in the panel that she made
Will go on prancing, proud and unafraid.

—ADRIENNE RICH (1929–2012)

Blackberry Eating

I love to go out in late September
among fat, overripe, icy, black blackberries
to eat blackberries for breakfast,
the stalks very prickly, a penalty
they earn for knowing the black art   5
of blackberry-making; and as I stand among them
lifting the stalks to my mouth, the ripest berries
fall almost unbidden to my tongue,
as words sometimes do, certain peculiar words
like *strengths* or *squinched*,   10
many-lettered, one-syllabled lumps,
which I squeeze, squinch open, and splurge well

in the silent, startled, icy, black language
of blackberry-eating in late September.

—GALWAY KINNELL (1927–2014)

QUESTIONS

1. Vocabulary: *black art* (5), *squinched* (10).
2. What comparison does the poet find between "certain peculiar words" (9) and blackberries? How appropriate is it?
3. Is the poem free verse or metrical? How do various musical devices reinforce its meaning?

The Skunk

Up, black, striped and damasked like the chasuble
At a funeral Mass, the skunk's tail
Paraded the skunk. Night after night
I expected her like a visitor.

The refrigerator whinnied into silence.　　　　　　　　5
My desk light softened beyond the verandah.
Small oranges loomed in the orange tree.
I began to be tense as a voyeur.

After eleven years I was composing
Love-letters again, broaching the word 'wife'　　　　10
Like a stored cask, as if its slender vowel
Had mutated into the night earth and air

Of California. The beautiful, useless
Tang of eucalyptus spelt your absence.
The aftermath of a mouthful of wine　　　　　　　15
Was like inhaling you off a cold pillow.

And there she was, the intent and glamorous,
Ordinary, mysterious skunk,
Mythologized, demythologized,
Snuffing the boards five feet beyond me.　　　　　20

It all came back to me last night, stirred
By the sootfall of your things at bedtime,
Your, head-down, tail-up hunt in a bottom drawer
For the black plunge-line nightdress.

—SEAMUS HEANEY (1939–2013)

QUESTIONS

1. Vocabulary: *damasked, chasuble* (1), *eucalyptus* (14).
2. Why does the speaker stress the skunk's tail? Focus on this statement: "the skunk's tail / Paraded the skunk" (2–3).
3. Explore the contrast between pleasant smells ("the orange tree" [7], "eucalyptus" [14]) and the smell of the skunk.
4. In the final stanza, why does the speaker compare the skunk to his wife? Is this intended as an insult? Or is it a loving comparison?

Fern Hill

Now as I was young and easy under the apple boughs
About the lilting house and happy as the grass was green,
    The night above the dingle starry,
      Time let me hail and climb
    Golden in the heydays of his eyes,   5
And honored among wagons I was prince of the apple towns
And once below a time I lordly had the trees and leaves
      Trail with daisies and barley
    Down the rivers of the windfall light.

And as I was green and carefree, famous among the barns   10
About the happy yard and singing as the farm was home,
    In the sun that is young once only,
      Time let me play and be
    Golden in the mercy of his means,
And green and golden I was huntsman and herdsman,
    the calves   15
Sang to my horn, the foxes on the hills barked clear and cold,
      And the sabbath rang slowly
    In the pebbles of the holy streams.

All the sun long it was running, it was lovely, the hay
Fields high as the house, the tunes from the chimneys,
    it was air   20
      And playing, lovely and watery
        And fire green as grass.
    And nightly under the simple stars
As I rode to sleep the owls were bearing the farm away,
All the moon long I heard, blessed among stables,
    the nightjars   25
      Flying with the ricks, and the horses
        Flashing into the dark.

And then to awake, and the farm, like a wanderer white
With the dew, come back, the cock on his shoulder: it was all
   Shining, it was Adam and maiden,   30
      The sky gathered again
   And the sun grew round that very day.
So it must have been after the birth of the simple light
In the first, spinning place, the spellbound horses
   walking warm
      Out of the whinnying green stable   35
        On to the fields of praise.

And honored among foxes and pheasants by the gay house
Under the new made clouds and happy as the heart was long,
   In the sun born over and over,
      I ran my heedless ways,   40
   My wishes raced through the house high hay
And nothing I cared, at my sky blue trades, that time allows
In all his tuneful turning so few and such morning songs
   Before the children green and golden
      Follow him out of grace,   45

Nothing I cared, in the lamb white days, that time would
   take me
Up to the swallow thronged loft by the shadow of my hand,
   In the moon that is always rising,
      Nor that riding to sleep
   I should hear him fly with the high fields   50
And wake to the farm forever fled from the childless land.
Oh as I was young and easy in the mercy of his means,
      Time held me green and dying
   Though I sang in my chains like the sea.

                  —DYLAN THOMAS (1914–1953)

QUESTIONS

1. Vocabulary: *dingle* (3), *nightjars* (25), *ricks* (26).
2. The opening stanzas of this poem describe the speaker's early years. What sort of youth did he have? Which images help convey his memories?
3. Analyze the allusion to "Adam" in line 30. Why is the allusion appropriate?
4. When do you notice a change in the poem's tone? For the speaker, what kind of experience is the transition from youth to maturity?

The Dance

In Breughel's great picture, The Kermess,
the dancers go round, they go round and
around, the squeal and the blare and the
tweedle of bagpipes, a bugle and fiddles
tipping their bellies (round as the thick-   5
sided glasses whose wash they impound)
their hips and their bellies off balance
to turn them. Kicking and rolling about
the Fair Grounds, swinging their butts, those
shanks must be sound to bear up under such   10
rollicking measures, prance as they dance
in Breughel's great picture, The Kermess.

—WILLIAM CARLOS WILLIAMS (1883–1963)

QUESTIONS

1. Peter Breughel the Elder was a sixteenth-century Flemish painter of peasant life. A *kermess* is an annual outdoor festival or fair. How would you characterize the mood of the people depicted in this poem?
2. Examine the poem for alliteration, consonance, assonance, and onomatopoeia. When you pronounce the syllable *ound* (lines 2, 3, 5, 6, 9, 10), how does the shape your mouth makes seem to intensify the effect?
3. Scan the poem. (Notice that the initial syllable in lines 2, 3, and 8 has the effect of completing the rhythm of the preceding line.) What one word in the poem echoes the prevailing metrical foot, describes the rhythm of the poem, and defines the mood of the picture?
4. How does sound reinforce content in this poem? What is the attitude of the speaker to the activities shown in the picture?

SUGGESTIONS FOR WRITING

Write a short essay discussing the relationship of the poem's sound to its meaning in one of the following.

1. Dickinson, "I felt a Funeral, in my Brain" (page 62).
2. Rogers, "Night and the Creation of Geography" (page 243).
3. Hopkins, "Spring" (page 60).
4. Keats, "Ode on a Grecian Urn" (page 286).
5. Hardy, "The Ruined Maid" (page 379).
6. Owen, "Dulce et Decorum Est" (page 6).
7. Stevens, "The Snow Man" (page 68).
8. Yeats, "Sailing to Byzantium" (page 300).

PRACTICE AP® WRITING PROMPTS

Emily Dickinson, "I heard a Fly buzz—when I died" (pp. 237–238)

Emily Dickinson's poem "I heard a Fly buzz—when I died" imagines a recollection of the actual moment of death. Read the poem carefully, and write a well-organized essay in which you analyze the speaker's complex perceptions of death—as anticipated and as experienced. Show how the author employs point of view and the resources of poetic language to shape the overall meaning of the poem.

CHAPTER FOURTEEN

Pattern

Art, ultimately, is organization. It is a searching for order and significance. Most artists seek to transform the chaotic nature of experience into a meaningful and coherent pattern, largely by means of selection and arrangement. For this reason we evaluate a poem partially by the same criteria that an English instructor uses to evaluate a student's essay—by its unity, its coherence, and its proper placing of emphasis. A well-constructed poem contains neither too little nor too much; every part of the poem belongs where it is and could be placed nowhere else; any interchanging of two stanzas, two lines, or even two words, would to some extent damage the poem and make it less effective. We come to feel, with a truly first-rate poem, that the choice and placement of every word are inevitable, that they could not be otherwise.

In addition to the internal ordering of the materials—the arrangement of ideas, images, thoughts, sentences, which we refer to as the poem's **structure**—the poet may impose some external pattern on a poem, may give it not only its internal order of materials but an external shape or **form**. Such formality appeals to the human instinct for design, the instinct that has prompted people, at various times, to tattoo and paint their bodies, to decorate their swords and armor with beautiful and complex tracery, and to choose patterned fabrics for their clothing, carpets, and curtains. The poet appeals to our love of the shapely.

In general, a poem may be cast in one of the three broad kinds of form: continuous form, stanzaic form, and fixed form. In **continuous form**, as illustrated by "The Widow's Lament in Springtime" (page 61), "After Apple-Picking" (page 65), "Ulysses" (page 110), and "My Last Duchess" (page 288), the element of design is slight. The lines follow each other without formal grouping, the only breaks being dictated by units of meaning, as paragraphs are in prose. But even here there are degrees of pattern. "The

Widow's Lament in Springtime" has neither regular meter nor rhyme. "After Apple-Picking," on the other hand, is metrical; it has no regularity of length of line, but the meter is predominantly iambic; in addition, every line rhymes with another, though not according to any fixed pattern. "Ulysses" is regular in both meter and length of line: it is unrhymed iambic pentameter, or blank verse. And to these regularities "My Last Duchess" adds regularity of rhyme, for it is written in rhyming pentameter couplets. Thus, in increasing degrees, the authors of "After Apple-Picking," "Ulysses," and "My Last Duchess" have chosen a predetermined pattern in which to cast their work.

In **stanzaic form,** the poet writes in a series of **stanzas**; that is, repeated units having the same number of lines, usually the same metrical pattern, and often the same **rhyme scheme.** The poet may choose some traditional stanza pattern or invent an original one. The traditional stanza patterns (for example, terza rima, ballad meter, rhyme royal, Spenserian stanza) are many, and the student specializing in literature will wish to become familiar with some of them; the general student should know that they exist. Often the use of one of these traditional stanza forms constitutes a kind of literary allusion. When we are aware of the traditional use of a stanza form, or of its previous use by a great poet for a particular subject or experience, we may find additional subtleties of meaning in its later use. Robert Frost employs the same verse form for his poem about a moral quest as Dante uses for his great poem about moral truth, *The Divine Comedy,* with meaningful results (see "Acquainted with the Night," page 264).

Stanzaic form, like continuous form, exhibits degrees of formal pattern. The poem "in Just—" (page 141) is divided into alternating stanzas of four lines and one line, but the four-line stanzas have no formal resemblance to each other except for the number of lines, and the one-line stanzas are similarly disparate. In "Winter" (page 5) and "Blow, blow, thou winter wind" (page 193) Shakespeare employs a refrain in addition to the patterns of meter and rhyme. The following poem illustrates additional elements of design.

The Pulley

When God at first made man,
Having a glass of blessings standing by,
"Let us," said he, "pour on him all we can:
Let the world's riches, which dispersèd lie,
Contract into a span."   5

So Strength first made a way;
Then Beauty flowed; then Wisdom, Honor, Pleasure.
When almost all was out, God made a stay,
Perceiving that alone of all his treasure
    Rest in the bottom lay.   10

"For if I should," said he,
"Bestow this jewel also on my creature,
    He would adore my gifts instead of me,
And rest in Nature, not the God of Nature;
    So both should losers be.   15

"Yet let him keep the rest,
But keep them with repining restlessness:
    Let him be rich and weary, that at least,
If goodness lead him not, yet weariness
    May toss him to my breast."   20

—GEORGE HERBERT (1593–1633)

QUESTIONS

1. Vocabulary: *span* (5, archaic meaning).
2. The words "riches" (4), "treasure" (9), "jewel" (12), and "gifts" (13) create an extended metaphor. What is being compared to things of material value? Does the word "rich" in line 18 refer to the same thing as "riches" in line 4?
3. The title "The Pulley" refers to a simple mechanical device for lifting weights. How does a pulley work? How does it metaphorically express the meaning of the last stanza?
4. To what does "both" (15) refer? What are God's final intentions?

A stanza form may be described by designating four things: the rhyme scheme (if there is one), the position of the refrain (if there is one), the prevailing metrical foot, and the number of feet in each line. Rhyme scheme is traditionally designated by using letters of the alphabet to indicate the rhyming lines, and *x* for unrhymed lines. Refrain lines may be indicated by a capital letter, and the number of feet in the line by a numerical exponent after the letter. Thus, the stanza pattern of Browning's "Meeting at Night" (page 58) is iambic tetrameter *abccba* (or iambic *abccba*^{4}); that of "The Pulley" is iambic $a^3bab^5a^3$.

A **fixed form** is a traditional pattern that applies to a whole poem. In French poetry many fixed forms have been widely used: rondeaus, rondels, villanelles, triolets, sestinas, ballades, double ballades, and others. In English poetry, although most of the fixed forms have been experimented with, perhaps only two—the sonnet and the villanelle—have really taken hold.

Although it is classified as a fixed form, through centuries of practice the **sonnet** has attained a degree of flexibility. It must be fourteen lines in length, and it almost always is iambic pentameter, but in structure and rhyme scheme there may be considerable leeway. Most sonnets, however, conform more or less closely to one of two general models or types: the Italian and the English.

The **Italian,** or *Petrarchan,* **sonnet** (so-called because the Italian poet Petrarch practiced it so extensively) is divided usually between eight lines called the **octave,** using two rhymes arranged *abbaabba,* and six lines called the **sestet,** using any arrangement of either two or three rhymes: *cdcdcd* and *cdecde* are common patterns. The division between octave and sestet in the Italian sonnet (indicated by the rhyme scheme and sometimes marked off in printing by a space) usually corresponds to a division of thought. The octave may, for instance, present a situation and the sestet a comment, or the octave an idea and the sestet an example, or the octave a question and the sestet an answer. Thus, the form reflects the structure.

On First Looking into Chapman's Homer

Much have I traveled in the realms of gold,
    And many goodly states and kingdoms seen;
    Round many western islands have I been
Which bards in fealty to Apollo hold.
Oft of one wide expanse had I been told   5
    That deep-browed Homer ruled as his demesne;
    Yet did I never breathe its pure serene
Till I heard Chapman speak out loud and bold:
Then felt I like some watcher of the skies
    When a new planet swims into his ken;   10
Or like stout Cortez when with eagle eyes
    He stared at the Pacific—and all his men
Looked at each other with a wild surmise—
    Silent, upon a peak in Darien.

—JOHN KEATS (1795–1821)

QUESTIONS

1. Vocabulary: *fealty* (4), *Apollo* (4), *demesne* (6), *ken* (10). *Darien* (14) is an ancient name for the Isthmus of Panama.
2. John Keats, at age twenty-one, could not read Greek and was probably acquainted with Homer's *Iliad* and *Odyssey* only through the translations of Alexander Pope, which to him very likely seemed prosy and stilted. Then one day he and a friend found a vigorous poetic translation by the Elizabethan poet George Chapman.

Keats and his friend, enthralled, sat up late at night excitedly reading aloud to each other from Chapman's book. Toward morning Keats walked home and, before going to bed, wrote the previous sonnet and sent it to his friend. What common ideas underlie the three major figures of speech in the poem?

3. What is the rhyme scheme? What division of thought corresponds to the division between octave and sestet?

4. Balboa, not Cortez, discovered the Pacific. How seriously does this mistake detract from the value of the poem?

The **English,** or *Shakespearean,* **sonnet** (invented by the English poet Surrey and made famous by Shakespeare) consists of three **quatrains** and a concluding **couplet,** rhyming *abab cdcd efef gg.* Again, the units marked off by the rhymes and the development of the thought often correspond. The three quatrains, for instance, may present three examples and the couplet a conclusion, or (as in the following example) the quatrains three metaphorical statements of one idea and the couplet an application.

That time of year

That time of year thou mayst in me behold
When yellow leaves, or none, or few, do hang
Upon those boughs which shake against the cold,
Bare ruined choirs where late the sweet birds sang.
In me thou see'st the twilight of such day   5
As after sunset fadeth in the west,
Which by and by black night doth take away,
Death's second self, that seals up all in rest.
In me thou see'st the glowing of such fire,
That on the ashes of his youth doth lie   10
As the deathbed whereon it must expire,
Consumed with that which it was nourished by.
This thou perceivest, which makes thy love more strong,
To love that well which thou must leave ere long.

—WILLIAM SHAKESPEARE (1564–1616)

QUESTIONS

1. Vocabulary: *choirs* (4).

2. What are the three major images introduced by the three quatrains? What do they have in common? Can you see any reason for presenting them in this particular order, or might they be rearranged without loss?

3. Each of the images is to some degree complicated rather than simple. For instance, what additional image is introduced by "Bare ruined choirs" (4)? Explain its appropriateness.

4. What additional comparisons are introduced in the second and third quatrains? Explain line 12.
5. Whom does the speaker address? What assertion does he make in the concluding couplet, and with what degree of confidence? Paraphrase these lines so as to state their meaning as clearly as possible.

The tradition of the sonnet has proved useful because it seems effective or appropriate for certain types of subject matter and treatment. By its history as the vehicle for love poetry in the sixteenth century, the sonnet is particularly effective when used for the serious treatment of love. But it has also been used for the discussion of death, religion, political situations, and various other serious subjects. There is, of course, no magical or mysterious identity between certain forms and certain types of content, but there may be more or less correspondence. A form may seem appropriate or inappropriate. Excellent sonnets have been written outside the traditional areas.

The **villanelle**, with its complex pattern of repetition and rhyme, has become a significant form in English only in the past hundred years or so, but of the fixed forms it probably now ranks second to the sonnet. The form requires only two rhyme sounds, and its nineteen lines are divided into five three-line stanzas (**tercets**) and a four-line concluding quatrain. The first and third lines of the first stanza serve as rhyming refrain lines— the first line repeated at the ends of the second and fourth stanzas, and the third repeated at the ends of the third and fifth stanzas. In the concluding stanza, the refrains are repeated as lines 18 and 19. We can express the pattern thus: $A^1bA^2 \ abA^1 \ abA^2 \ abA^1 \ abA^2 \ abA^1A^2$ (in this case, the numerical exponent identifies which of the two rhyming refrain lines is being used).

Poets have been attracted to villanelles partly because they are notoriously difficult to compose effectively, thus posing a challenge to a poet's technical skill, and partly because the varying emphases given to repeated lines, along with the repetition itself, can achieve haunting, unforgettable effects. The original French models were usually lighthearted and witty, exploiting the potential for cleverness and humor inherent in the form, but modern poets often have employed the villanelle for serious subject matter. The following example, composed when the poet's father was near death, is perhaps the most famous villanelle in English.

Do Not Go Gentle into That Good Night

Do not go gentle into that good night,
Old age should burn and rave at close of day;
Rage, rage against the dying of the light.

Though wise men at their end know dark is right,
Because their words had forked no lightning they   5
Do not go gentle into that good night.

Good men, the last wave by, crying how bright
Their frail deeds might have danced in a green bay,
Rage, rage against the dying of the light.

Wild men who caught and sang the sun in flight,   10
And learn, too late, they grieved it on its way,
Do not go gentle into that good night.

Grave men, near death, who see with blinding sight
Blind eyes could blaze like meteors and be gay,
Rage, rage against the dying of the light.   15

And you, my father, there on the sad height,
Curse, bless, me now with your fierce tears, I pray.
Do not go gentle into that good night.
Rage, rage against the dying of the light.

—DYLAN THOMAS (1914–1953)

QUESTIONS

1. Discuss the various meanings in this poem of the common phrase "good night."
2. Apart from the fixed form, the poem creates another structural principle in stanzas two through six by describing in turn "wise men" (4), "Good men" (7), "Wild men" (10), and "Grave men" (13). How does the speaker view these various types of men in their differing stances toward both life and death?
3. There are several oxymorons (paradoxical expressions) in the poem: "dark is right" (4), "blinding sight" (13), "the sad height" (16), and "Curse, bless, me now" (17). How do these contribute to the poem's meaning?

A good villanelle avoids the potentially monotonous effects of repetition by varying the stress patterns and the meaning of the repeated lines. In Thomas's poem, for example, the third line is a direct address by the speaker to his father, whereas the repetition in line 9 describes the rage "Good men" feel just before their deaths. Similarly, the poem deftly alternates lines containing grammatical pauses, such as line 7, with lines having no pauses, such as line 8; the blend of run-on and end-stopped lines likewise helps to vary the rhythm. The fixed form also serves the poem's meaning, since the repetition and the circular quality of the villanelle, its continued reiteration of the same two lines, emphasizes the speaker's emotional treadmill, his desperate and perhaps hopeless prayer that his father might rage against death. As in all good poetry, a fixed form like the villanelle does not merely display the poet's technical ability but appropriately supports the tone and meaning of the poem.

Initially, it may seem absurd that poets should choose to confine themselves in an arbitrary formal mold with prescribed meter and rhyme scheme. They do so partly from the desire to carry on a tradition, as all of us carry out certain traditions for their own sake, else why should we bring a tree indoors at Christmas time? Traditional forms are also useful because they have provided a challenge to the poet, and good poets are inspired by the challenge: it will call forth ideas and images that might not otherwise have come. They will subdue the form rather than be subdued by it; they will make it do what they require. There is no doubt that the presence of a net makes good tennis players more precise in their shots than they otherwise might be. And finally, for the poet and for the reader, there is the pleasure of form itself.

EXERCISES

The typographical shape of a poem on the page (whether, for example, printed with a straight left-hand margin or with a system of indentations) is determined sometimes by the poet, sometimes by the printer, sometimes by an editor. Examine each of the following poems and try to deduce what *principle* (if any) determined its typographical design:

1. Shakespeare, "Winter" (page 5).
2. Marvell, "To His Coy Mistress" (page 88).
3. Hughes, "Harlem" (page 73).
4. Plath, " Lady Lazarus" (page 309).
5. cummings, "in Just—" (page 141).
6. Poe, "The Bells" (page 195).
7. Yeats, "Leda and the Swan" (page 148).
8. Donne, "The Flea" (page 174).
9. Blake, "The Lamb" (page 162).

REVIEWING CHAPTER FOURTEEN

1. Distinguish between structure and form, and review the definitions of the three broad types of form in poetry; using examples from the following poems in the chapter, define both the form and the structure of the poem.

2. Examine the definitions of the two types of sonnet, and explore the way in which the form of each seems to promote the structure of materials in the poem.

3. The villanelle also suggests the structure of the poem's materials; using examples from the following poems, define that implied structure.
4. Poetic forms may rely on the reader's familiarity with the subjects customarily presented in such forms—and poets may employ a form either
to fulfill a reader's expectations or ironically to play against them. Find
examples of both uses of the forms of the sonnet and the villanelle.

One Art

The art of losing isn't hard to master;
so many things seem filled with the intent
to be lost that their loss is no disaster.

Lose something every day. Accept the fluster
of lost door keys, the hour badly spent.   5
The art of losing isn't hard to master.

Then practice losing farther, losing faster:
places, and names, and where it was you meant
to travel. None of these will bring disaster.

I lost my mother's watch. And look! my last, or   10
next-to-last, of three loved houses went.
The art of losing isn't hard to master.

I lost two cities, lovely ones. And, vaster,
some realms I owned, two rivers, a continent.
I miss them, but it wasn't a disaster.   15

—Even losing you (the joking voice, a gesture
I love) I shan't have lied. It's evident
the art of losing's not too hard to master
though it may look like (*Write* it!) like disaster.

—ELIZABETH BISHOP (1911–1979)

QUESTIONS

1. What various denotations of "lose" and its derivative forms are relevant to the
context? What connotations are attached to the separate denotative meanings?

2. Explain how "owned" (14) and "lost" (13) shift the meanings of possessing and losing.
3. What seems to be the purpose of the speaker in the first three tercets (three-line units)? How is the advice given there supported by the personal experiences related in the next two tercets?
4. The concluding quatrain (four-line unit) contains direct address to a person, as well as a command the speaker addresses to herself. How do these details reveal the real purpose of the poem? *Can* all kinds of losses be mastered with one "art of losing"?

Mad Girl's Love Song

I shut my eyes and all the world drops dead;
I lift my lids and all is born again.
(I think I made you up inside my head.)

The stars go waltzing out in blue and red,
And arbitrary blackness gallops in: 5
I shut my eyes and all the world drops dead.

I dreamed that you bewitched me into bed
And sung me moon-struck, kissed me quite insane.
(I think I made you up inside my head.)

God topples from the sky, hell's fires fade: 10
Exit seraphim and Satan's men:
I shut my eyes and all the world drops dead.

I fancied you'd return the way you said,
But I grow old and I forget your name.
(I think I made you up inside my head.)   15

I should have loved a thunderbird instead;
At least when spring comes they roar back again.
I shut my eyes and all the world drops dead.
(I think I made you up inside my head.)

—SYLVIA PLATH (1932–1963)

QUESTIONS

1. Discuss the relationship of form to content in the poem. Why is it appropriate that this particular poem is written in the villanelle form?

2. The spaker calls herself "Mad" (title) and "insane" (8). Compare the use of these terms with that in Dickinson's "Much Madness is divinest Sense" (page 115). What different forms of "madness" are being discussed?
3. Discuss the rhythmic effects of the poem. How do they reinforce the meaning?

From *Romeo and Juliet*

ROMEO   If I profane with my unworthiest hand
           This holy shrine, the gentle sin is this:
           My lips, two blushing pilgrims, ready stand
           To smooth that rough touch with a tender kiss.

JULIET   Good pilgrim, you do wrong your hand too much,   5
           Which mannerly devotion shows in this;
           For saints have hands that pilgrims' hands do touch,
           And palm to palm is holy palmers' kiss.

ROMEO   Have not saints lips, and holy palmers too?

JULIET   Ay, pilgrim, lips that they must use in prayer.   10

ROMEO   O! then, dear saint, let lips do what hands do;
           They pray, "Grant thou, lest faith turn to despair."

JULIET   Saints do not move,° though grant for prayer's
           sake.   propose, instigate

ROMEO   Then move not, while my prayer's effect I take.

—WILLIAM SHAKESPEARE (1564–1616)

QUESTIONS

1. These fourteen lines occur in Act 1, scene 5, of Shakespeare's play. They are the first words exchanged between Romeo and Juliet, who are meeting, for the first time, at a masquerade ball given by her father. Struck by Juliet's beauty, Romeo has come up to greet her. What stage action accompanies this passage?
2. What is the basic metaphor created by such religious terms as "profane" (1), "shrine" (2), "pilgrims" (3), and "holy palmers" (8)? How does this metaphor affect the tone of the relationship between Romeo and Juliet?
3. What play on words do you find in lines 8 and 13–14? What two meanings has line 11?
4. By meter and rhyme scheme, these lines form a sonnet. Do you think this was coincidental or intentional on Shakespeare's part? Discuss.

Death, be not proud

Death, be not proud, though some have callèd thee
Mighty and dreadful, for thou art not so;
For those whom thou think'st thou dost overthrow

Die not, poor death, nor yet canst thou kill me.
From rest and sleep, which but thy pictures be,   5
Much pleasure—then, from thee much more must flow;
And soonest° our best men with thee do go,   readiest
Rest of their bones and soul's delivery.
Thou art slave to fate, chance, kings, and desperate men,
And dost with poison, war, and sickness dwell;   10
And poppy or charms can make us sleep as well,
And better than thy stroke. Why swell'st thou then?
One short sleep passed, we wake eternally,
And death shall be no more; death, thou shalt die.

—JOHN DONNE (1572–1631)

QUESTIONS

1. What two figures of speech dominate the poem?
2. Why should death not be proud? List the speaker's major reasons. Are they consistent? Logical? Persuasive?
3. Discuss the tone of the poem. Is the speaker (a) a man of assured faith with a firm conviction that death is not to be feared or (b) a man desperately trying to convince himself that there is nothing to fear in death?
4. In form, this sonnet blends the English and Italian models. Explain. Is its organization of thought closer to the Italian or the English sonnet?

The Folly of Being Comforted

One that is ever kind said yesterday:
'Your well-belovèd's hair has threads of grey,
And little shadows come about her eyes;
Time can but make it easier to be wise
Though now it seem impossible, and so   5
All that you need is patience.'
                    Heart cries, 'No,
I have not a crumb of comfort, not a grain.
Time can but make her beauty over again:
Because of that great nobleness of hers
The fire that stirs about her, when she stirs,   10
Burns but more clearly. O she had not these ways
When all the wild summer was in her gaze.'

O heart! O heart! if she'd but turn her head,
You'd know the folly of being comforted.

—WILLIAM BUTLER YEATS (1865–1939)

QUESTIONS

1. How can the friend's pointing out that the woman shows signs of aging be considered an attempt to "comfort" the speaker? What does that imply about the relationship between the speaker and his "well-belovèd" (2)?
2. The personification of "Heart" (6, 13) is contrasted to the friend's attempt to make the speaker "wise." Explain what the outburst from "Heart" means, and how it is an answer to the friend's reasonable advice.
3. The poem is 14 lines of iambic pentameter. Is it a sonnet?

The White City

I will not toy with it nor bend an inch.
Deep in the secret chambers of my heart
I muse my life-long hate, and without flinch
I bear it nobly as I live my part.
My being would be a skeleton, a shell,   5
If this dark Passion that fills my every mood,
And makes my heaven in the white world's hell,
Did not forever feed me vital blood.
I see the mighty city through a mist—
The strident trains that speed the goaded mass,   10
The poles and spires and towers vapor-kissed,
The fortressed port through which the great ships pass,
The tides, the wharves, the dens I contemplate,
Are sweet like wanton loves because I hate.

—CLAUDE MCKAY (1890–1948)

QUESTIONS

1. Claude McKay was a native black Jamaican who as an adult lived in New York. Why does the speaker "hate" (3) the city?
2. Traditionally, sonnets originated as love poems. Why might McKay have cast this poem in sonnet form?
3. How does the city feed the speaker with "vital blood" (8)?
4. Why are the elements of the New York landscape described in the last line as "sweet like wanton loves" (14)?

Villanelle

The first line will not go away
though the middle ones will disappear,
and the third, like the first, is bound to get more play.

Examples of this type are written every day,
and whether uplifting or drear,   5
that first line will just not go away.

It seems some lines have the right of way.
It's their job to reappear,
for example, the third, designed to get more play.

Whether you squawk like an African Grey   10
or sing sweetly to the inner ear,
the line you wrote first will just not go away.

You may compose all night and day
under a bare lightbulb or a crystal chandelier,
but line number three must get more play.   15

How can a poet hope to go wildly astray
or sing out like a romantic gondolier
when the first line will not go away
and the third always has the final say?

—BILLY COLLINS (B. 1941)

QUESTIONS

1. Discuss this adaptation of the villanelle form. In what ways does it adhere strictly to the prescribed form? In what ways does it not?
2. What is the speaker's attitude toward the form? Does he seem to admire or feel contemptuous toward villanelles?
3. The speaker's ambivalence is perhaps best conveyed in lines 16–17. How do these lines sum up his feelings toward the villanelle form?

We Wear the Mask

We wear the mask that grins and lies,
It hides our cheeks and shades our eyes,—
This debt we pay to human guile;
With torn and bleeding hearts we smile,
And mouth with myriad subtleties.   5
Why should the world be over-wise,
In counting all our tears and sighs?

> Nay, let them only see us, while
>> We wear the mask.
>
> We smile, but, O great Christ, our cries   10
> To thee from tortured souls arise.
> We sing, but oh the clay is vile
> Beneath our feet, and long the mile;
> But let the world dream otherwise,
>> We wear the mask!   15

—PAUL LAURENCE DUNBAR (1872–1906)

QUESTIONS

1. The poet was African American. What racial theme is implied in the poem? What kind of "mask" is the speaker describing?
2. How would you define the tone of this poem? Is the speaker angry? Who are the "tortured souls" (11)?
3. How do the departures from the strict sonnet form contribute to the effect of the poem?

> MindTap® Read, highlight, and take notes online.

Acquainted with the Night

> I have been one acquainted with the night.
> I have walked out in rain—and back in rain.
> I have outwalked the furthest city light.
>
> I have looked down the saddest city lane.
> I have passed by the watchman on his beat   5
> And dropped my eyes, unwilling to explain.
>
> I have stood still and stopped the sound of feet
> When far away an interrupted cry
> Came over houses from another street,
>
> But not to call me back or say good-by;   10
> And further still at an unearthly height,
> One luminary clock against the sky
>
> Proclaimed the time was neither wrong nor right.
> I have been one acquainted with the night.

—ROBERT FROST (1874–1963)

QUESTIONS

1. How does the speaker reveal the strength of his purpose in his night-walking? Can you specify what that purpose is? What symbolic meanings does the night hold?
2. How is the poem structured into sentences? What is the effect of repeating the phrase "I have"? of repeating line 1 at the conclusion? How do these repetitions affect the tone of the poem?
3. Some critics have interpreted the "luminary clock" (12) literally—as the illuminated dial of a tower clock; others have interpreted it figuratively as the full moon. Of what, in either case, is it a symbol? Does the clock tell accurate chronometric time? What kind of "time" is it proclaiming in line 13? Is knowing *that* kind of time the speaker's quest?
4. The poem contains fourteen lines—like a sonnet. But its rhyme scheme is **terza rima**, an interlocking scheme with the pattern *aba bcb cdc,* etc., a formal arrangement that implies continual progression. How does Frost bring the progression to an end? Terza rima was the form memorably employed by Dante for his *Divine Comedy,* of which the *Inferno* is the best-known section. In what ways does Frost's poem allude to the subject and framework of that poem?

Villanelle for an Anniversary

A spirit moved, John Harvard walked the yard,
The atom lay unsplit, the west unwon,
The books stood open and the gates unbarred.

The maps dreamt on like moondust. Nothing stirred.
The future was a verb in hibernation.   5
A spirit moved, John Harvard walked the yard.

Before the classic style, before the clapboard,
All through the small hours on an origin,
The books stood open and the gates unbarred.

Night passage of a migratory bird.   10
Wingflap. Gownflap. Like a homing pigeon
A spirit moved, John Harvard walked the yard.

Was that his soul (look) sped to its reward
By grace or works? A shooting star? An omen?
The books stood open and the gates unbarred.   15

Begin again where frosts and tests were hard.
Find yourself or founder. Here, imagine

A spirit moved, John Harvard walked the yard,
The books stand open and the gates unbarred.

—SEAMUS HEANEY (1939–2013)

QUESTIONS

1. John Harvard (1607–1638), an English clergyman who arrived in Massachusetts in 1637, bequeathed his library and a sum of money to the new college at Cambridge, which was then named in his honor.
2. How do the refrain lines of this villanelle help to reinforce its meaning?
3. How do you interpret line 3, "The book stood open and the gates unbarred"? In line 14, what is the meaning of the phrase "grace or works"? How is this an important distinction?
4. What is the impact of the final stanza? What additional meanings have the refrain lines gathered by the end of the poem?

Delight in Disorder

A sweet disorder in the dress
Kindles in clothes a wantonness.
A lawn° about the shoulders thrown   linen scarf
Into a fine distractïon;
An erring lace, which here and there   5
Enthralls the crimson stomacher;
A cuff neglected, and thereby
Ribbons to flow confusedly;
A winning wave, deserving note,
In the tempestuous petticoat;   10
A careless shoestring, in whose tie
I see a wild civility;
Do more bewitch me than when art
Is too precise in every part.

—ROBERT HERRICK (1591–1674)

QUESTIONS

1. Vocabulary: *wantonness* (2), *stomacher* (6).
2. The phrase "wild civility" (12) is another example of oxymoron. Discuss the effectiveness of this device in this phrase and examine the poem for other examples.
3. Consider the relationship of form to structure in this poem. How does this contribute to the meaning?

SUGGESTIONS FOR WRITING

Following are two lists: one of sonnets and the other of villanelles. Using one or two examples of either form, explore the effectiveness of the relationship of structure to form. In particular, be alert for variations or departures from the form and what these contribute to meaning and emotional effect.

Sonnets
Wordsworth, "The world is too much with us" (page 48).
Shelley, "Ozymandias" (page 122).
Donne, "Batter my heart, three-personed God" (page 124).
Yeats, "Leda and the Swan" (page 148).
Frost, "Design" (page 156).
Drayton, "Since there's no help" (page 169).
Shakespeare, "My mistress' eyes" (page 172).
Owen, "Anthem for Doomed Youth" (page 241).

Villanelles
Bishop, "One Art" (page 258).
Roethke, "The Waking" (page 189).
Plath, "Mad Girl's Love Song" (page 259).

PRACTICE AP® WRITING PROMPTS

Paul Laurence Dunbar, "We Wear the Mask" (pp. 263–264)

African American poet Paul Laurence Dunbar was the son of slaves. Read Dunbar's "We Wear the Mask" carefully. Then write an essay in which you show how the speaker's language effectively demonstrates the contradiction between the façade he presents to the world and the emotions he truly feels.

....

Elizabeth Bishop, "One Art" (pp. 258–259)

Read Elizabeth Bishop's "One Art" carefully, paying attention to the ways in which the author stretches the boundaries of the traditional villanelle form. In a well-organized essay, analyze how the author harnesses the pattern of the villanelle to convey the complexity of the speaker's reflection on the perception of loss. You may wish to look with particular care at the poem's final line.

....

CHAPTER FIFTEEN

Evaluating Poetry I

Sentimental, Rhetorical, Didactic Verse

The attempt to evaluate a poem should never be made before the poem is understood; and, unless one has developed the capacity to experience poetry intellectually and emotionally, any judgments one makes will be of little worth. A person who likes no wines can hardly be a judge of them. But the ability to make judgments, to discriminate between good and bad, great and good, good and half-good, is surely a primary object of all liberal education. One's appreciation of poetry is incomplete unless it includes discrimination.

In judging a poem, as in judging any work of art, we need to ask three basic questions: (1) *What is its central purpose?* (2) *How fully has this purpose been accomplished?* (3) *How important is this purpose?* We must answer the first question in order to understand the poem. Questions 2 and 3 are those by which we evaluate it. Question 2 judges the poem on a scale of perfection. Question 3 judges it on a scale of significance.

For answering the first of our evaluative questions, *How fully has the poem's purpose been accomplished?,* there are no easy yardsticks that we can apply. We cannot ask: Is the poem melodious? Does it have smooth rhythm? Does it use good grammar? Does it contain figures of speech? Are the rhymes perfect? Excellent poems exist without any of these attributes. We can judge any element in a poem only as it contributes or fails to contribute to the achievement of the central purpose; and we can judge the total poem only as these elements work together to form an integrated whole. But we can at least attempt a few generalizations. A wholly successful poem contains no excess words, no words that do not bear their full weight in contributing to the total experience, and no words that are used just to fill out the meter. Each word is the best word for expressing the total meaning: there are no inexact words forced by the rhyme scheme or the metrical pattern. The word order is the best order for expressing the author's total meaning; distortions or departures from normal order are for emphasis or some other meaningful purpose. The diction, the images, and the figures of speech are fresh, not trite (except, of course, when the poet uses trite language deliberately for purposes of irony). The sound of the poem does not clash with its sense, or the form with its content; and in general both sound and pattern are used to support meaning. The organization of the poem is the best possible organization: images and ideas are so effectively arranged that any rearrangement would be harmful to the poem. Always remember, however, that a good poem may have flaws. We should never damn a poem for its flaws if these flaws are amply compensated for by positive excellence.

What constitutes excellence in poetry? One criterion is that its combination of thought, emotion, language, and sound must be fresh and original. As the poet and critic Ezra Pound insisted, good writing must "make it new." An excellent poem will neither be merely imitative of previous literature nor appeal to stock, preestablished ways of thinking and feeling. The following discussion highlights three particular ways in which a poem can fail to achieve excellence—if a poem is sentimental, excessively rhetorical, or purely didactic—in which case we would probably call it "verse" rather than true poetry.

Sentimentality is indulgence in emotion for its own sake, or expression of more emotion than an occasion warrants. Sentimentalists are gushy, stirred to tears by trivial or inappropriate causes; they weep at all weddings and all funerals; they are made ecstatic by manifestations of young love; they clip locks of hair, gild baby shoes, and talk baby talk. Sentimental *literature* is "tear-jerking" literature. It aims primarily at stimulating the emotions directly rather than at communicating experience truly and freshly; it depends on trite and well-tried formulas for exciting emotion; it revels in old oaken buckets, rocking chairs, mother love, and the pitter-patter of little feet; it oversimplifies; it is unfaithful to the full complexity of human experience.

Rhetorical poetry uses a language more glittering and high-flown than its substance warrants. It offers a spurious vehemence of language—language without a corresponding reality of emotion or thought underneath. It is oratorical, overelegant, artificially eloquent. It is superficial and, again, often basically trite. It loves rolling phrases like "from the rocky coast of Maine to the sun-washed shores of California" and "our heroic dead" and "Old Glory." It deals in generalities. At its worst it is bombast. In this book an example is offered by the two lines quoted from the play within a play in the fifth act of Shakespeare's *A Midsummer Night's Dream:*

Whereat with blade, with bloody, blameful blade,
He bravely broached his boiling bloody breast.

Another example may be found in the player's recitation in *Hamlet* (in Act 2, scene 2):

Out, out, thou strumpet Fortune! All you gods,
In general synod take away her power,
Break all the spokes and fellies from her wheel,
And bowl the round nave down the hill of heaven
As low as to the fiends!

Didactic poetry has as a primary purpose to teach or preach. It is probable that all the very greatest poetry teaches in subtle ways, without being expressly didactic; and much expressly didactic poetry ranks high in poetic excellence: that is, it accomplishes its teaching without ceasing to be poetry. But when the didactic purpose supersedes the poetic purpose, when the poem communicates information or moral instruction only, then it ceases to be didactic poetry and becomes didactic verse. Such verse appeals to people who read poetry primarily for noble thoughts or inspiring lessons and, like them prettily expressed. It is recognizable often by its lack of any specific situation, the flatness of its diction, the poverty of its imagery and figurative language, its emphasis on moral platitudes, its lack of poetic freshness. It is either very trite or has little to distinguish it from informational prose except rhyme or meter. Donne's "Hymn to God My God, in My Sickness" (page 107) is an example of didactic *poetry.* The familiar couplet

Early to bed and early to rise,
Makes a man healthy, wealthy, and wise

is aptly characterized as didactic *verse.*

Undoubtedly, so far in this chapter, we have spoken too categorically, have made our distinctions too sharp and definite. All poetic excellence is a matter of degree. There are no absolute lines between sentimentality and true emotion, artificial and genuine eloquence, didactic verse and didactic poetry. Although the difference between extreme examples is easy to recognize, subtler discriminations are harder to make.

A final caution to students: when making judgments on literature, always be honest. Do not pretend to like what you do not like. Do not be afraid to admit a liking for what you do like. A genuine enthusiasm for the second-rate piece is much better than false enthusiasm or no enthusiasm at all. Be neither hasty nor timorous in making your judgments. When you have attentively read a poem and thoroughly considered it, decide what you think. Do not hedge, equivocate, or try to find out others' opinions before forming your own. But, having formed an opinion and expressed it, do not allow it to harden into a narrow-minded bias. Compare your opinion with the opinions of others and allow yourself to change yours when convinced of its error: in this way you learn.

In the pairs of poems for comparison that follow in this chapter, the distinction to be made is not always between bad and good; it may be between varying degrees of poetic merit.

REVIEWING CHAPTER FIFTEEN

1. Review the three basic questions to be answered in evaluating a poem.
2. Explore the three weaknesses that may lead us to judge a poem less than excellent, finding examples of each in the poems that follow in this chapter.

God's Will for You and Me

Just to be tender, just to be true,
Just to be glad the whole day through,
Just to be merciful, just to be mild,
Just to be trustful as a child,
Just to be gentle and kind and sweet,   5
Just to be helpful with willing feet,
Just to be cheery when things go wrong,
Just to drive sadness away with a song,
Whether the hour is dark or bright,
Just to be loyal to God and right,   10
Just to believe that God knows best,
Just in his promises ever to rest—

Just to let love be our daily key,
That is God's will for you and me.

Pied Beauty

Glory be to God for dappled things—
    For skies of couple-color as a brinded cow;
        For rose-moles all in stipple upon trout that swim;
Fresh-firecoal chestnut-falls; finches' wings;
        Landscape plotted and pieced—fold, fallow and plow;   5
        And all trades, their gear and tackle and trim.
All things counter, original, spare, strange;
    Whatever is fickle, freckled (who knows how?)
        With swift, slow; sweet, sour; adazzle, dim;
He fathers-forth whose beauty is past change: 10
        Praise him.

QUESTION

Which is the superior poem? Explain in full.

MindTap° Read, highlight, and take notes online.

Pitcher

His art is eccentricity, his aim
How not to hit the mark he seems to aim at,

His passion how to avoid the obvious,
His technique how to vary the avoidance.

The others throw to be comprehended. He   5
Throws to be a moment misunderstood.
Yet not too much. Not errant, arrant, wild,
But every seeming aberration willed.

Not to, yet still, still to communicate
Making the batter understand too late.   10

The Old-Fashioned Pitcher

How dear to my heart was the old-fashioned hurler
    Who labored all day on the old village green.

He did not resemble the up-to-date twirler
    Who pitches four innings and ducks from the scene.
The up-to-date twirler I'm not very strong for;   5
    He has a queer habit of pulling up lame.
And that is the reason I hanker and long for
    The pitcher who started and finished the game.

      The old-fashioned pitcher,
        The iron-armed pitcher,   10
      The stout-hearted pitcher
        Who finished the game.

QUESTION

Which poem is the more interesting and more meaningful? Why?

A Poison Tree

I was angry with my friend:
I told my wrath, my wrath did end.
I was angry with my foe:
I told it not, my wrath did grow.

And I watered it in fears,   5
Night and morning with my tears;
And I sunnèd it with smiles,
And with soft deceitful wiles.

And it grew both day and night
Till it bore an apple bright;   10
And my foe beheld it shine,
And he knew that it was mine,

And into my garden stole
When the night had veiled the pole:°   sky
In the morning glad I see   15
My foe outstretched beneath the tree.

The Most Vital Thing in Life

When you feel like saying something
    That you know you will regret,

Or keenly feel an insult
    Not quite easy to forget,
That's the time to curb resentment   5
    And maintain a mental peace,
For when your mind is tranquil
    All your ill-thoughts simply cease.

It is easy to be angry
    When defrauded or defied,   10
To be peeved and disappointed
    If your wishes are denied;
But to win a worthwhile battle
    Over selfishness and spite,
You must learn to keep strict silence   15
    Though you know you're in the right.

So keep your mental balance
    When confronted by a foe,
Be it enemy in ambush
    Or some danger that you know.   20
If you are poised and tranquil
    When all around is strife,
Be assured that you have mastered
    The most vital thing in life.

QUESTION

Which poem has more poetic merit? Explain.

Lower New York: At Dawn

Here is the dawn a hopeless thing to see:
    Sordid and pale as is the face of one
    Who sinks exhausted in oblivion
    After a night of deep debauchery.
Here, as the light reveals relentlessly   5
    All that the soul has lost and greed has won,
    Scarce we believe that somewhere now the sun
    Dawns overseas in stainless majesty.
Yet the day comes!—ghastly and harsh and thin
    Down the cold street; and now, from far away,   10
    We hear a vast and sullen rumor run,

As of the tides of ocean turning in . . .
And know, for yet another human day,
The world's dull, dreadful labor is begun!

Composed upon Westminster Bridge, September 3, 1802

Earth has not anything to show more fair:
Dull would he be of soul who could pass by
A sight so touching in its majesty:
This City now doth, like a garment, wear
The beauty of the morning; silent, bare,   5
Ships, towers, domes, theaters, and temples lie
Open unto the fields, and to the sky,
All bright and glittering in the smokeless air.
Never did sun more beautifully steep
In his first splendor, valley, rock, or hill;   10
Ne'er saw I, never felt, a calm so deep!
The river glideth at his own sweet will:
Dear God! the very houses seem asleep,
And all that mighty heart is lying still!

QUESTION

Which poem has more freshness of language?

Piano

Softly, in the dusk, a woman is singing to me;
Taking me back down the vista of years, till I see
A child sitting under the piano, in the boom of the tingling
    strings
And pressing the small, poised feet of a mother who smiles as
    she sings.

In spite of myself, the insidious mastery of song   5
Betrays me back, till the heart of me weeps to belong
To the old Sunday evenings at home, with winter outside
And hymns in the cozy parlor, the tinkling piano our guide.

So now it is vain for the singer to burst into clamor
With the great black piano appassionato. The glamour   10
Of childish days is upon me, my manhood is cast
Down in the flood of remembrance, I weep like a child for
    the past.

The Days Gone By

O the days gone by! O the days gone by!
The apples in the orchard, and the pathway through the rye;
The chirrup of the robin, and the whistle of the quail
As he piped across the meadows sweet as any nightingale;
When the bloom was on the clover, and the blue was in
    the sky,   5
And my happy heart brimmed over in the days gone by.

In the days gone by, when my naked feet were tripped
By the honey-suckle's tangles where the water-lilies dipped,
And the ripples of the river lipped the moss along the brink
Where the placid-eyed and lazy-footed cattle came to
    drink,   10
And the tilting snipe stood fearless of the truant's wayward
    cry
And the splashing of the swimmer, in the days gone by.

O the days gone by! O the days gone by!
The music of the laughing lip, the luster of the eye;
The childish faith in fairies, and Aladdin's magic ring—   15
The simple, soul-reposing, glad belief in everything,—
When life was like a story, holding neither sob nor sigh,
In the golden olden glory of the days gone by.

QUESTION

Which poem is more rhetorical in treating the subject?

I would not paint—a picture

I would not paint—a picture—
I'd rather be the One

Its bright impossibility
To dwell—delicious—on
And wonder how the fingers feel   5
Whose rare—celestial—stir—
Evokes so sweet a torment—
Such sumptuous—Despair—

I would not talk, like Cornets—
I'd rather be the One   10
Raised softly to the Ceilings—
And out, and easy on—
Through Villages of Ether—
Myself endued Balloon
By but a lip of Metal—   15
The pier to my Pontoon—

Nor would I be a Poet—
It's finer—Own the Ear—
Enamored—impotent—content—
The License to revere,   20
A privilege so awful
What would the Dower be,
Had I the Art to stun myself
With Bolts—of Melody!

If I can stop one Heart from breaking

If I can stop one Heart from breaking
I shall not live in vain
If I can ease one Life the Aching
Or cool one Pain

Or help one fainting Robin   5
Unto his Nest again
I shall not live in Vain.

QUESTION

These two poems by Emily Dickinson both deal with the art of writing poetry, but
they deal with the topic in very different ways. Which of the two poems is the more
fresh and original?

When I have fears that I may cease to be

When I have fears that I may cease to be
    Before my pen has gleaned my teeming brain,
Before high-pilèd books, in charactery,°   written symbols
    Hold like rich garners the full-ripened grain;
When I behold, upon the night's starred face,   5
    Huge cloudy symbols of a high romance,
And think that I may never live to trace
    Their shadows, with the magic hand of chance;
And when I feel, fair creature of an hour,
    That I shall never look upon thee more,   10
Never have relish in the faery power
    Of unreflecting love—then on the shore
Of the wide world I stand alone, and think
    Till love and fame to nothingness do sink.

O Solitude!

O Solitude! if I must with thee dwell,
    Let it not be among the jumbled heap
    Of murky buildings; climb with me the steep—
Nature's observatory—whence the dell,
Its flowery slopes, its river's crystal swell,   5
    May seem a span; let me thy vigils keep
    'Mongst boughs pavilioned, where the deer's swift leap
Startles the wild bee from the fox-glove bell.
But though I'll gladly trace these scenes with thee,
    Yet the sweet converse of an innocent mind,   10
    Whose words are images of thoughts refined,
Is my soul's pleasure; and it sure must be
    Almost the highest bliss of human-kind,
When to thy haunts two kindred spirits flee.

QUESTION

Both poems are by John Keats (1795–1821). Which of them displays true excellence?
Explain.

SUGGESTIONS FOR WRITING

In each of the following pairs, both poems have literary merit, but one is clearly a more ambitious and more successful poem. Choose one pair and write a short essay in which you argue which is the better of the two poems, and why.

1. Owen, "Dulce et Decorum Est" (page 6) and Crane, "War Is Kind" (page 365).
2. Dickinson, "I felt a Funeral, in my Brain" (page 62) and Plath, "Mad Girl's Love Song" (page 259).
3. Clifton, "good times" (page 362) and Hughes, "Theme for English B" (page 386).
4. Yeats, "The Folly of Being Comforted" (page 261) and Bishop, "Insomnia" (page 221).

PRACTICE AP® WRITING PROMPTS

Gerard Manley Hopkins, "Pied Beauty" (p. 272) and William Wordsworth, "Composed upon Westminster Bridge, September 3, 1802" (p. 275)

In "Pied Beauty" and "Composed upon Westminster Bridge, September 3, 1802," the speakers express strikingly different ideas about the world's beauty. Write an essay in which you compare and contrast these conceptions of beauty. Include in your analysis how poetic elements such as rhythm, form, diction, and figurative language convey the poets' concepts.

....

Robert Francis, "Pitcher" (p. 272)

Carefully read "Pitcher" by Robert Francis, considering its literal truth: a baseball pitcher often succeeds by tricking a batter into swinging at a ball that cannot be hit well, if it can be hit at all, or into failing to recognize a hittable pitch. In a well-written essay, analyze the poem's extended central metaphor, showing how it illuminates the poem's figurative meaning.

....

CHAPTER SIXTEEN

Evaluating Poetry 2

Poetic Excellence

If a poem has successfully met the test of the question, *How fully has it accomplished its purpose?* we are ready to subject it to our second evaluative question: *How important is its purpose?*

Great poetry must, of course, be good poetry. Noble intent alone cannot redeem a work that does not measure high on the scale of accomplishment; otherwise the sentimental and purely didactic verse of much of the preceding chapter would stand with the world's masterpieces. But once a work has been judged as successful on the scale of execution, its final standing will depend on its significance of purpose.

Suppose, for instance, we consider three examples in our text: the anonymous verse "Pease Porridge Hot" (page 230); the poem "It sifts from Leaden Sieves" by Emily Dickinson (page 74); and Shakespeare's sonnet "That time of year" (page 254). Each of these would probably be judged by critics as successful in what it sets out to do. "Pease Porridge Hot" is a charming nursery rhyme that makes clever use of rhyme and alliteration. But what is this verse *about?* Virtually nothing. Dickinson's poem, in contrast, *is* poetry, and very good poetry. It appeals richly to our senses and to our imaginations, and it succeeds excellently in its purpose: to convey the appearance and the quality of falling and newly fallen snow as well as a sense of the magic and the mystery of nature. Yet when we compare this excellent poem with Shakespeare's, we again see important differences. Although Dickinson's poem engages the senses and the imagination and may affect us with wonder and cause us to meditate on nature, it does not deeply engage the emotions or the intellect. It does not come as close to the core of human living and suffering as does Shakespeare's sonnet. In fact, it is concerned primarily with that staple of small talk: the weather. On the other hand, Shakespeare's sonnet evokes the universal human concerns of growing old, approaching death, and love. Of these three selections, then, Shakespeare's is the greatest. It "says" more than Dickinson's poem or the nursery rhyme, it communicates a richer experience, and it successfully accomplishes a more significant purpose. The reader will get from it a deeper enjoyment because it is nourishing as well as delightful.

Great poetry engages the whole person—senses, imagination, emotion, intellect; it does not touch us merely on one or two sides of our nature. Great poetry seeks not merely to entertain us but also to give us pleasure as well as bring us into the nature of human experience with fresh or renewed insights. Great poetry, we might say, gives us a broader and deeper understanding of life, of other people, and of ourselves, always with the qualification, of course, that the kind of insight literature gives is not necessarily the kind that can be summed up in a simple "lesson" or "moral." It is *knowledge*—*felt* knowledge, *new* knowledge—of the complexities of human nature and of the tragedies and sufferings, the excitements and joys, that characterize human experience.

Yet, after all, we have provided no easy yardsticks or rule-of-thumb measures for literary judgment. There are no mechanical tests. The final measuring rod can be only the responsiveness, the taste, and the discernment of the reader. Such taste and discernment are partly a native endowment, partly the product of experience, and partly the achievement of conscious study, training, and intellectual effort. Taste and discernment cannot be achieved suddenly or quickly; they can never be achieved in perfection. The pull is a long and a hard one. But success, even relative success, brings enormous personal and aesthetic rewards.

The Canonization

For God's sake, hold your tongue, and let me love!
 Or chide my palsy or my gout,
My five gray hairs or ruined fortune flout;
With wealth your state, your mind with arts improve,
  Take you a course,° get you a place,   career 5
   Observe his honor° or his grace,°   judge; bishop
Or the king's real or his stamped face°   on a coin
  Contemplate; what you will, approve,°   try out
   So you will let me love.

Alas, alas, who's injured by my love?   10
 What merchant ships have my sighs drowned?

Who says my tears have overflowed his ground?
When did my colds a forward° spring remove?   early
   When did the heats which my veins fill
   Add one more to the plaguy bill?   15
Soldiers find wars, and lawyers find out still
   Litigious men which quarrels move,
     Though she and I do love.

Call us what you will, we are made such by love.
   Call her one, me another fly;°   moth 20
We are tapers too, and at our own cost die;
And we in us find the eagle and the dove;
   The phoenix riddle hath more wit°   meaning
   By us; we two, being one, are it.
So to one neutral thing both sexes fit.   25
   We die and rise the same, and prove
     Mysterious by this love.

We can die by it, if not live by love,
   And if unfit for tombs and hearse
Our legend be, it will be fit for verse;   30
And if no piece of chronicle° we prove,   history
   We'll build in sonnets pretty rooms:
   As well a well-wrought urn becomes
The greatest ashes as half-acre tombs,
   And by these hymns all shall approve°   confirm 35
     Us canonized for love,

And thus invoke us: "You whom reverend love
   Made one another's hermitage,
You to whom love was peace, that now is rage,
Who did the whole world's soul contract, and drove   40
   Into the glasses of your eyes
   (So made such mirrors and such spies
That they did all to you epitomize)
   Countries, towns, courts: beg from above
     A pattern of your love!"   45

—JOHN DONNE (1572–1631)

QUESTIONS

1. Vocabulary: *Canonization* (title), *tapers* (21), *phoenix* (23), *invoke* (37), *epitomize*
(43). "[R]eal" (7), pronounced as two syllables, puns on *royal*. The "plaguy bill" (15)
is a list of plague victims. The word "die" (21, 26, 28) in seventeenth-century slang

meant to experience the sexual climax. To understand lines 21 and 28, one also needs to be familiar with the Renaissance superstition that every act of sexual intercourse shortened one's life by one day. The "eagle" and the "dove" (22) are symbols for strength and mildness. "[P]attern" (45) is a model that one can copy.

2. Who is the speaker and what is his condition? How old is he? To whom is he speaking? What has his auditor been saying to him before the opening of the poem? What sort of values can we ascribe to the auditor by inference from the first stanza? What value does the speaker oppose to these? How does the stanzaic pattern of the poem emphasize this value?

3. The sighs, tears, fevers, and chills in the second stanza were commonplace in the love poetry of Donne's time. How does Donne make them fresh? What is the speaker's argument in this stanza? How does it begin to turn from pure defense to offense in the last three lines of the stanza?

4. How are the things to which the lovers are compared in the third stanza *arranged*? Does their ordering reflect in any way the arrangement of the whole poem? Elucidate line 21. Interpret or paraphrase lines 23–27.

5. Explain the first line of the fourth stanza. What status does the speaker claim for himself and his beloved in the last line of this stanza?

6. In what sense is the last stanza an invocation? Who speaks in it? To whom? What powers are ascribed to the lovers in it?

7. What do the following words from the poem have in common: "Mysterious" (27), "hymns" (35), "canonized" (36), "reverend" (37), "hermitage" (38)? What judgment about love does the speaker make by the use of these words?

Ode to the West Wind

I

O wild West Wind, thou breath of Autumn's being,
Thou, from whose unseen presence the leaves dead
Are driven, like ghosts from an enchanter fleeing,

Yellow, and black, and pale, and hectic red,
Pestilence-stricken multitudes: O thou,   5
Who chariotest to their dark wintry bed

The winged seeds, where they lie cold and low,
Each like a corpse within its grave, until
Thine azure sister of the Spring shall blow

Her clarion o'er the dreaming earth, and fill   10
(Driving sweet buds like flocks to feed in air)
With living hues and odours plain and hill:

Wild Spirit, which art moving everywhere;
Destroyer and preserver; hear, oh hear!

II
Thou on whose stream, mid the steep sky's commotion, 15
Loose clouds like earth's decaying leaves are shed,
Shook from the tangled boughs of Heaven and Ocean,

Angels of rain and lightning: there are spread
On the blue surface of thine aëry surge,
Like the bright hair uplifted from the head 20

Of some fierce Maenad, even from the dim verge
Of the horizon to the zenith's height,
The locks of the approaching storm. Thou dirge

Of the dying year, to which this closing night
Will be the dome of a vast sepulchre, 25
Vaulted with all thy congregated might

Of vapours, from whose solid atmosphere
Black rain, and fire, and hail will burst: oh hear!

III
Thou who didst waken from his summer dreams
The blue Mediterranean, where he lay, 30
Lull'd by the coil of his crystalline streams,

Beside a pumice isle in Baiae's bay,
And saw in sleep old palaces and towers
Quivering within the wave's intenser day,

All overgrown with azure moss and flowers 35
So sweet, the sense faints picturing them! Thou
For whose path the Atlantic's level powers

Cleave themselves into chasms, while far below
The sea-blooms and the oozy woods which wear
The sapless foliage of the ocean, know 40

Thy voice, and suddenly grow gray with fear,
And tremble and despoil themselves: oh hear!

IV
If I were a dead leaf thou mightest bear;
If I were a swift cloud to fly with thee;
A wave to pant beneath thy power, and share   45

The impulse of thy strength, only less free
Than thou, O uncontrollable! If even
I were as in my boyhood, and could be

The comrade of thy wanderings over Heaven,
As then, when to outstrip thy skiey speed   50
Scarce seem'd a vision; I would ne'er have striven

As thus with thee in prayer in my sore need.
Oh, lift me as a wave, a leaf, a cloud!
I fall upon the thorns of life! I bleed!

A heavy weight of hours has chain'd and bow'd   55
One too like thee: tameless, and swift, and proud.

V
Make me thy lyre, even as the forest is:
What if my leaves are falling like its own!
The tumult of thy mighty harmonies

Will take from both a deep, autumnal tone,   60
Sweet though in sadness. Be thou, Spirit fierce,
My spirit! Be thou me, impetuous one!

Drive my dead thoughts over the universe
Like wither'd leaves to quicken a new birth!
And, by the incantation of this verse,   65

Scatter, as from an unextinguish'd hearth
Ashes and sparks, my words among mankind!
Be through my lips to unawaken'd earth

The trumpet of a prophecy! O Wind,
If Winter comes, can Spring be far behind?   70

—PERCY BYSSHE SHELLEY (1792–1822)

QUESTIONS

1. A Maenad (21) is a crazed dancer, worshipper of the god of wine; Baiae's bay is close to Naples, Italy.
2. Vocabulary: *hectic* (4); *azure* (9); *clarion* (10); *zenith's* (22); *dirge* (23); *sepulcher* (25); *pumice* (32); *lyre* (57); *tumult* (59).
3. The poem's rhyme scheme is called *terza rima*; look up this form, find other famous examples, and describe the way in which the form is appropriate in Shelley's poem.
4. What emotions does the west wind call up in the speaker? Are they positive or negative, or a mixture of the two?
5. Line 54, "I fall upon the thorns of life! I bleed!" has caused much controversy, some critics considering it a valid cry of anguish and others condemning it as mere self-pity. What is your own reaction when reading the line?
6. Discuss the final, rhetorical question in lines 69–70. How would you answer it?

Ode on a Grecian Urn

Thou still unravished bride of quietness,
    Thou foster-child of silence and slow time,
Sylvan historian, who canst thus express
    A flowery tale more sweetly than our rhyme:
What leaf-fringed legend haunts about thy shape   5
    Of deities or mortals, or of both,
        In Tempe or the dales of Arcady?
    What men or gods are these? What maidens loth?
What mad pursuit? What struggle to escape?
    What pipes and timbrels? What wild ecstasy?   10

Heard melodies are sweet, but those unheard
    Are sweeter; therefore, ye soft pipes, play on;
Not to the sensual ear, but, more endeared,
    Pipe to the spirit ditties of no tone:
Fair youth, beneath the trees, thou canst not leave   15
    Thy song, nor ever can those trees be bare;
        Bold lover, never, never canst thou kiss,
Though winning near the goal—yet, do not grieve;
    She cannot fade, though thou hast not thy bliss,
For ever wilt thou love, and she be fair!   20

Ah, happy, happy boughs! that cannot shed
    Your leaves, nor ever bid the spring adieu;
And, happy melodist, unwearièd,
    For ever piping songs for ever new;

More happy love! more happy, happy love!   25
    For ever warm and still to be enjoyed,
        For ever panting and for ever young;
All breathing human passion far above,
    That leaves a heart high-sorrowful and cloyed,
        A burning forehead, and a parching tongue.   30

Who are these coming to the sacrifice?
    To what green altar, O mysterious priest,
Lead'st thou that heifer lowing at the skies,
    And all her silken flanks with garlands drest?
What little town by river or sea shore,   35
    Or mountain-built with peaceful citadel,
        Is emptied of its folk, this pious morn?
And, little town, thy streets for evermore
    Will silent be; and not a soul to tell
        Why thou are desolate, can e'er return.   40

O Attic shape! Fair attitude! with brede
    Of marble men and maidens overwrought,
With forest branches and the trodden weed;
    Thou, silent form, dost tease us out of thought
As doth eternity: Cold Pastoral!   45
    When old age shall this generation waste,
        Thou shalt remain, in midst of other woe
    Than ours, a friend to man, to whom thou say'st,
Beauty is truth, truth beauty,—that is all
    Ye know on earth, and all ye need to know.*   50

—JOHN KEATS (1795–1821)

QUESTIONS

1. The poem is an extended apostrophe addressed to a painted vase from ancient Greece. There are two separate scenes on the urn; the speaker summarizes their subjects in lines 5–10, and then specifically addresses them in 11–30 and 31–40. As completely as you can, describe what each of the scenes depicts.

2. What three denotations of "still" (1) are appropriate to the metaphorical identities ascribed to the urn in lines 1–4? What modes of sensory experience and of knowledge are evoked in those lines?

*(49–50) In the 1820 edition of Keats's poems the words "Beauty is truth, truth beauty" were enclosed in quotation marks, and the poem is often reprinted that way. It is now generally agreed, however, on the basis of contemporary transcripts of Keats's poem, that Keats intended the entire last two lines to be spoken by the urn.

3. The structure of the poem includes the speaker's shifting motivations in the spaces *between* the stanzas. For example, lines 5–10 request information about the actions depicted on the urn, but lines 11–14 dismiss the need for answers. What do you suppose motivates that change?

4. Lines 15–28 celebrate the scene because it has captured in a still moment the intensity of pursuit and desire. Explain. How is that permanence contrasted to the reality of "breathing human passion" (28)?

5. In the fourth stanza the speaker turns to the second scene, again with a series of questions requesting specific information. How do the concluding lines of the third stanza motivate this shift of subject? Lines 31–34 are questions about what the speaker *sees* on the urn; lines 35–40 refer to something he cannot see—and are expressed in a tone of desolation. What is it that leads the speaker to that tone? What has *he* done to cause it?

6. In the final stanza, the speaker does not engage himself with the subjects of the scenes but with "shape" (41), "form" (44), and "attitude" (41—in its older meaning, the posture of a painted figure). What at the end of the preceding stanza might cause the speaker to withdraw his imagination from the scenes and to comment in general on the "form" of the urn? Explain lines 44–45 and the culminating oxymoron "Cold Pastoral."

7. The footnote bases its deduction—that the last two lines in their entirety are claimed by the speaker to be the urn's advice to "man" (48)—on external evidence. Can you find internal support for this in the obsolete grammatical usage in line 50? How is the urn's message suited to the experience that the speaker has undergone?

My Last Duchess

Ferrara

That's my last duchess painted on the wall,
Looking as if she were alive. I call
That piece a wonder, now; Fra Pandolf's hands
Worked busily a day, and there she stands.
Will 't please you sit and look at her? I said   5
"Fra Pandolf" by design, for never read
Strangers like you that pictured countenance,
The depth and passion of its earnest glance,
But to myself they turned (since none puts by
The curtain I have drawn for you, but I)   10
And seemed as they would ask me, if they durst,
How such a glance came there; so, not the first
Are you to turn and ask thus. Sir, 'twas not
Her husband's presence only, called that spot
Of joy into the Duchess' cheek; perhaps   15

Fra Pandolf chanced to say, "Her mantle laps
Over my lady's wrist too much," or, "Paint
Must never hope to reproduce the faint
Half-flush that dies along her throat." Such stuff
Was courtesy, she thought, and cause enough   20
For calling up that spot of joy. She had
A heart—how shall I say?—too soon made glad,
Too easily impressed; she liked whate'er
She looked on, and her looks went everywhere.
Sir, 'twas all one! My favor at her breast,   25
The dropping of the daylight in the West,
The bough of cherries some officious fool
Broke in the orchard for her, the white mule
She rode with round the terrace—all and each
Would draw from her alike the approving speech,   30
Or blush, at least. She thanked men—good! but thanked
Somehow—I know not how—as if she ranked
My gift of a nine-hundred-years-old name
With anybody's gift. Who'd stoop to blame
This sort of trifling? Even had you skill   35
In speech—which I have not—to make your will
Quite clear to such an one, and say, "Just this
Or that in you disgusts me; here you miss,
Or there exceed the mark"—and if she let
Herself be lessoned so, nor plainly set   40
Her wits to yours, forsooth, and made excuse,
—E'en then would be some stooping; and I choose
Never to stoop. Oh, sir, she smiled, no doubt,
Whene'er I passed her; but who passed without
Much the same smile? This grew; I gave commands;   45
Then all smiles stopped together. There she stands
As if alive. Will 't please you rise? We'll meet
The company below, then. I repeat,
The Count your master's known munificence
Is ample warrant that no just pretense   50
Of mine for dowry will be disallowed;
Though his fair daughter's self, as I avowed
At starting, is my object. Nay, we'll go
Together down, sir. Notice Neptune, though,
Taming a sea-horse, thought a rarity,   55
Which Claus of Innsbruck cast in bronze for me!

—ROBERT BROWNING (1812–1889)

QUESTIONS

1. Vocabulary: *favor* (25), *officious* (27), *munificence* (49).
2. Ferrara is in Italy. The time is during the Renaissance, probably the sixteenth century. To whom is the Duke speaking? What is the occasion? Are the Duke's remarks about his last Duchess a digression, or do they have some relation to the business at hand?
3. Characterize the Duke as fully as you can. How does your characterization differ from the Duke's opinion of himself? What kind of irony is this?
4. Why was the Duke dissatisfied with his last Duchess? Was it sexual jealousy? What opinion do you get of the Duchess's personality, and how does it differ from the Duke's opinion?
5. What characteristics of the Italian Renaissance appear in the poem (marriage customs, social classes, art)? What is the Duke's attitude toward art? Is it insincere?
6. What happened to the Duchess? Should Browning have told us?

There's a certain Slant of light

There's a certain Slant of light,
Winter Afternoons—
That oppresses, like the Heft
Of Cathedral Tunes—

Heavenly Hurt, it gives us—   5
We can find no scar,
But internal difference,
Where the Meanings, are—

None may teach it—Any—
'Tis the Seal Despair—   10
An imperial affliction
Sent us of the Air—

When it comes, the Landscape listens—
Shadows—hold their breath—
When it goes, 'tis like the Distance   15
On the look of Death—

—EMILY DICKINSON (1830–1886)

QUESTIONS

1. This is one of Dickinson's most famous poems dealing with human psychological states. Here the speaker calls her state of mind "Despair" (10), but many today would consider it "clinical depression." What particular images help convey the speaker's depressed state of mind?

2. The scene is carefully set: a winter afternoon, a speaker attempting to describe what she feels. How does the poem relate a possibly fleeting psychological state to such issues as religious faith, self-examination, and death?

3. Could it be argued that this experience, however painful, is ultimately a positive one for the speaker? What is the significance of the oxymorons "Heavenly Hurt" (5) and "imperial affliction" (11)?

4. Discuss the use of abstractions in this poem: "Hurt" (5), "Meanings" (8), "Despair" (10), "Death" (16). How do these abstractions work to enlarge the poem's meaning beyond a mere depiction of a specific person's temporary mood?

5. The final stanza describes the moment of great tension when the "Seal" (10) of despair falls upon the speaker. Why does she imagine that the entire landscape participates in this personal crisis? Does this suggest a self-absorbed projection onto the landscape or an honest attempt to understand and describe her mental state?

6. Discuss the concluding simile, "like the Distance / On the look of Death—". Do any specific visual images come to mind as you ponder this abstract phrase? Could "Death" here be interpreted as meaning "a dead person"?

MindTap®   Read, highlight, and take notes online.

Home Burial

He saw her from the bottom of the stairs
Before she saw him. She was starting down,
Looking back over her shoulder at some fear.
She took a doubtful step and then undid it
To raise herself and look again. He spoke   5
Advancing toward her: "What is it you see
From up there always—for I want to know."
She turned and sank upon her skirts at that,
And her face changed from terrified to dull.
He said to gain time: "What is it you see,"   10
Mounting until she cowered under him.
"I will find out now—you must tell me, dear."
She, in her place, refused him any help
With the least stiffening of her neck and silence.
She let him look, sure that he wouldn't see,   15
Blind creature; and awhile he didn't see.
But at last he murmured, "Oh," and again, "Oh."

"What is it—what?" she said.

                            "Just that I see."

"You don't," she challenged. "Tell me what it is."

"The wonder is I didn't see at once.   20
I never noticed it from here before.
I must be wonted to it—that's the reason.
The little graveyard where my people are!
So small the window frames the whole of it.
Not so much larger than a bedroom, is it?   25
There are three stones of slate and one of marble,
Broad-shouldered little slabs there in the sunlight
On the sidehill. We haven't to mind *those*.
But I understand: it is not the stones,
But the child's mound—"

                  "Don't, don't, don't, don't,"
she cried.   30

She withdrew, shrinking from beneath his arm
That rested on the banister, and slid downstairs;
And turned on him with such a daunting look,
He said twice over before he knew himself:
"Can't a man speak of his own child he's lost?"   35

"Not you! Oh, where's my hat? Oh, I don't need it!
I must get out of here. I must get air.
I don't know rightly whether any man can."

"Amy! Don't go to someone else this time.
Listen to me. I won't come down the stairs."   40
He sat and fixed his chin between his fists.
"There's something I should like to ask you, dear."

"You don't know how to ask it."

                  "Help me, then."

Her fingers moved the latch for all reply.

"My words are nearly always an offense.   45
I don't know how to speak of anything
So as to please you. But I might be taught,
I should suppose. I can't say I see how.
A man must partly give up being a man
With women-folk. We could have some arrangement   50

By which I'd bind myself to keep hands off
Anything special you're a-mind to name.
Though I don't like such things 'twixt those that love.
Two that don't love can't live together without them.
But two that do can't live together with them."   55
She moved the latch a little. "Don't—don't go.
Don't carry it to someone else this time.
Tell me about it if it's something human.
Let me into your grief. I'm not so much
Unlike other folks as your standing there   60
Apart would make me out. Give me my chance.
I do think, though, you overdo it a little.
What was it brought you up to think it the thing
To take your mother-loss of a first child
So inconsolably—in the face of love.   65
You'd think his memory might be satisfied—"

"There you go sneering now!"

                                    "I'm not, I'm not!
You make me angry. I'll come down to you.
God, what a woman! And it's come to this,
A man can't speak of his own child that's dead."   70

"You can't because you don't know how to speak.
If you had any feelings, you that dug
With your own hand—how could you?—his little grave;
I saw you from that very window there,
Making the gravel leap and leap in air,   75
Leap up, like that, like that, and land so lightly
And roll back down the mound beside the hole.
I thought, Who is that man? I didn't know you.
And I crept down the stairs and up the stairs
To look again, and still your spade kept lifting.   80
Then you came in. I heard your rumbling voice
Out in the kitchen, and I don't know why,
But I went near to see with my own eyes.
You could sit there with the stains on your shoes
Of the fresh earth from your own baby's grave   85
And talk about your everyday concerns.
You had stood the spade up against the wall
Outside there in the entry, for I saw it."

"I shall laugh the worst laugh I ever laughed.
I'm cursed. God, if I don't believe I'm cursed."   90
"I can repeat the very words you were saying:
'Three foggy mornings and one rainy day
Will rot the best birch fence a man can build.'
Think of it, talk like that at such a time!
What had how long it takes a birch to rot   95
To do with what was in the darkened parlor?
You *couldn't* care! The nearest friends can go
With anyone to death, comes so far short
They might as well not try to go at all.
No, from the time when one is sick to death,   100
One is alone, and he dies more alone.
Friends make pretense of following to the grave,
But before one is in it, their minds are turned
And making the best of their way back to life
And living people, and things they understand.   105
But the world's evil. I won't have grief so
If I can change it. Oh, I won't, I won't!"

"There, you have said it all and you feel better.
You won't go now. You're crying. Close the door.
The heart's gone out of it: why keep it up?   110
Amy! There's someone coming down the road!"

"*You*—oh, you think the talk is all. I must go—
Somewhere out of this house. How can I make you—"

"If—you—do!" She was opening the door wider.
"Where do you mean to go? First tell me that.   115
I'll follow and bring you back by force. I *will!*—"

—ROBERT FROST (1874–1963)

QUESTIONS

1. Vocabulary: *wonted* (22).
2. The poem centers on a conflict between husband and wife. What causes the conflict? Why does Amy resent her husband? What is *his* dissatisfaction with Amy?
3. Characterize the husband and wife respectively. What is the chief difference between them? Does the poem take sides? Is either presented more sympathetically than the other?
4. The poem does not say how long the couple have been married or how long the child has been buried. Does it contain suggestions from which we may make rough inferences?

5. The husband and wife both generalize on the other's faults during the course of the poem, attributing them to all men or to all women or to people in general. Point out these generalizations. Are they valid?
6. Finish the unfinished sentences in lines 30, 66, 112, 113, 116.
7. Comment on the function of lines 25, 39, 92–93.
8. Following are three paraphrased and abbreviated versions of statements made in published discussions of the poem. Which would you support? Why?
   a. The young wife is gradually persuaded by her husband's kind yet firm reasonableness to express her feelings in words and to recognize that human nature is limited and cannot sacrifice everything to sorrow. Though she still suffers from excess grief, the crisis is past, and she will eventually be brought back to life.
   b. At the end, the whole poem is epitomized by the door that is neither open nor shut. The wife cannot really leave; the husband cannot really make her stay. Neither husband nor wife is capable of decisive action, of either self-liberation or liberation of the other.
   c. Her husband's attempt to talk, since it is the wrong kind of talk, only leads to her departure at the poem's end.

The Love Song of J. Alfred Prufrock

S'io credesse che mia risposta fosse
A persona che mai tornasse al mondo,
Questa fiamma staria senza piu scosse.
Ma perciocche giammai di questo fondo
Non torno vivo alcun, s'i'odo il vero,
Senza tema d'infamia ti rispondo.

Let us go then, you and I,
When the evening is spread out against the sky
Like a patient etherized upon a table;
Let us go, through certain half-deserted streets,
The muttering retreats   5
Of restless nights in one-night cheap hotels
And sawdust restaurants with oyster-shells:
Streets that follow like a tedious argument
Of insidious intent
To lead you to an overwhelming question. . . .   10
Oh, do not ask, "What is it?"
Let us go and make our visit.

In the room the women come and go
Talking of Michelangelo.

The yellow fog that rubs its back upon the window-panes,   15
The yellow smoke that rubs its muzzle on the window-panes
Licked its tongue into the corners of the evening,
Lingered upon the pools that stand in drains,
Let fall upon its back the soot that falls from chimneys,
Slipped by the terrace, made a sudden leap,   20
And seeing that it was a soft October night,
Curled once about the house, and fell asleep.

And indeed there will be time
For the yellow smoke that slides along the street,
Rubbing its back upon the window-panes;   25
There will be time, there will be time
To prepare a face to meet the faces that you meet;
There will be time to murder and create,
And time for all the works and days of hands
That lift and drop a question on your plate;   30
Time for you and time for me,
And time yet for a hundred indecisions,
And for a hundred visions and revisions,
Before the taking of a toast and tea.

In the room the women come and go   35
Talking of Michelangelo.

And indeed there will be time
To wonder, "Do I dare?" and "Do I dare?"
Time to turn back and descend the stair,
With a bald spot in the middle of my hair—   40
(They will say: "How his hair is growing thin!")
My morning coat, my collar mounting firmly to the chin,
My necktie rich and modest, but asserted by a simple pin—
(They will say: "But how his arms and legs are thin!")
Do I dare   45
Disturb the universe?
In a minute there is time
For decisions and revisions which a minute will reverse.

For I have known them all already, known them all—
Have known the evenings, mornings, afternoons,   50
I have measured out my life with coffee spoons;

I know the voices dying with a dying fall
Beneath the music from a farther room.
     So how should I presume?

And I have known the eyes already, known them all—   55
The eyes that fix you in a formulated phrase,
And when I am formulated, sprawling on a pin,
When I am pinned and wriggling on the wall,
Then how should I begin
To spit out all the butt-ends of my days and ways?   60
     And how should I presume?

And I have known the arms already, known them all—
Arms that are braceleted and white and bare
(But in the lamplight, downed with light brown hair!)
Is it perfume from a dress   65
That makes me so digress?
Arms that lie along a table, or wrap about a shawl.
     And should I then presume?
     And how should I begin?

             *   *   *

Shall I say, I have gone at dusk through narrow streets   70
And watched the smoke that rises from the pipes
Of lonely men in shirt-sleeves, leaning out of windows? . . .

I should have been a pair of ragged claws
Scuttling across the floors of silent seas.

             *   *   *

And the afternoon, the evening, sleeps so peacefully!   75
Smoothed by long fingers,
Asleep . . . tired . . . or it malingers,
Stretched on the floor, here beside you and me.
Should I, after tea and cakes and ices,
Have the strength to force the moment to its crisis?   80
But though I have wept and fasted, wept and prayed,
Though I have seen my head (grown slightly bald)
     brought in upon a platter,
I am no prophet—and here's no great matter;
I have seen the moment of my greatness flicker,
And I have seen the eternal Footman hold my coat, and
     snicker,   85
And in short, I was afraid.

And would it have been worth it, after all,
After the cups, the marmalade, the tea,
Among the porcelain, among some talk of you and me,
Would it have been worth while,   90
To have bitten off the matter with a smile,
To have squeezed the universe into a ball
To roll it toward some overwhelming question,
To say: "I am Lazarus, come from the dead,
Come back to tell you all, I shall tell you all"—   95
If one, settling a pillow by her head,
    Should say: "That is not what I meant at all.
    That is not it, at all."

And would it have been worth it, after all,
Would it have been worth while,   100
After the sunsets and the dooryards and the sprinkled streets,
After the novels, after the teacups, after the skirts that trail
    along the floor—
And this, and so much more?—
It is impossible to say just what I mean!
But as if a magic lantern threw the nerves in patterns   105
    on a screen:
Would it have been worth while
If one, settling a pillow or throwing off a shawl,
And turning toward the window, should say:
    "That is not it at all,
    That is not what I meant, at all."   110

*   *   *

No! I am not Prince Hamlet, nor was meant to be;
Am an attendant lord, one that will do
To swell a progress, start a scene or two,
Advise the prince; no doubt, an easy tool,
Deferential, glad to be of use,   115
Politic, cautious, and meticulous;
Full of high sentence, but a bit obtuse;
At times, indeed, almost ridiculous—
Almost, at times, the Fool.

I grow old . . . I grow old . . .   120
I shall wear the bottoms of my trousers rolled.°   cuffed

Shall I part my hair behind? Do I dare to eat a peach?
I shall wear white flannel trousers, and walk upon the beach.
I have heard the mermaids singing, each to each.

I do not think that they will sing to me.   125

I have seen them riding seaward on the waves
Combing the white hair of the waves blown back
When the wind blows the water white and black.

We have lingered in the chambers of the sea
By sea-girls wreathed with seaweed red and brown   130
Till human voices wake us, and we drown.

—T. S. ELIOT (1888–1965)

QUESTIONS

1. Vocabulary: *insidious* (9), *Michelangelo* (14, 36), *muzzle* (16), *malingers* (77), *progress* (113), *Deferential* (115), *Politic* (116), *meticulous* (116), *sentence* (117).

2. This poem may be for some readers the most difficult in the book because it uses a "stream of consciousness" technique (that is, it presents the apparently random thoughts going through a person's head within a certain time interval), in which the transitional links are psychological rather than logical, and also because it uses allusions that may be unfamiliar to you. Even if you do not at first understand the poem in detail, you should be able to get from it a quite accurate picture of Pru-frock's character and personality. What kind of person is he? (Answer this as fully as possible.) From what class of society does he come? What one line especially well sums up the nature of his past life? A brief initial orientation may be helpful: Prufrock is apparently on his way, at the beginning of the poem, to a late afternoon tea, at which he wishes (or does he?) to make a declaration of love to some lady who will be present. The "you and I" of the first line are divided parts of Prufrock's own nature, for he is experiencing internal conflict. Does he or does he not make the declaration? Where does the climax of the poem come? If the portion leading up to the climax is devoted to Prufrock's effort to prepare himself psychologically to make the declaration (or to postpone such effort), what is the portion after the climax devoted to?

3. The poem contains a number of striking or unusual figures of speech. Most of them in some way reflect Prufrock's own nature or his desires or fears. From this point of view discuss lines 2–3; 15–22 and 75–78; 57–58; 73–74; and 124–131. What figure of speech is lines 73–74? In what respect is the title ironic?

4. The poem makes extensive use of literary allusion. The Italian epigraph is a passage from Dante's *Inferno* in which a man in Hell tells a visitor that he would never tell his story if there were a chance that it would get back to living ears. In line 29 the phrase "works and days" is the title of a long poem—a

description of agricultural life and a call to toil—by the early Greek poet Hesiod. Line 52 echoes the opening speech of Shakespeare's *Twelfth Night.* The prophet of lines 81–83 is John the Baptist, whose head was delivered to Salome by Herod as a reward for her dancing (Matthew 14:1–11, and Oscar Wilde's play *Salome*). Line 92 echoes the closing six lines of Marvell's "To His Coy Mistress" (page 88). Lazarus (94–95) may be either the beggar Lazarus (of Luke 16) who was not permitted to return from the dead to warn a rich man's brothers about Hell, the Lazarus (of John 11) whom Christ raised from death, or both. Lines 111–119 allude to a number of characters from Shakespeare's *Hamlet:* Hamlet himself, the chamberlain Polonius, and various minor characters including probably Rosencrantz, Guildenstern, and Osric. "Full of high sentence" (117) echoes Chaucer's description of the Clerk of Oxford in the Prologue to *The Canterbury Tales.* Relate as many of these allusions as you can to the character of Prufrock. How is Prufrock particularly like Hamlet, and how is he unlike him? Contrast Prufrock with the speaker in "To His Coy Mistress."

Sailing to Byzantium

That is no country for old men. The young
In one another's arms, birds in the trees
—Those dying generations—at their song,
The salmon-falls, the mackerel-crowded seas,
Fish, flesh, or fowl, commend all summer long   5
Whatever is begotten, born, and dies.
Caught in that sensual music all neglect
Monuments of unaging intellect.

An aged man is but a paltry thing,
A tattered coat upon a stick, unless   10
Soul clap its hands and sing, and louder sing
For every tatter in its mortal dress,
Nor is there singing school but studying
Monuments of its own magnificence;
And therefore I have sailed the seas and come   15
To the holy city of Byzantium.

O sages standing in God's holy fire
As in the gold mosaic of a wall,
Come from the holy fire, perne° in a gyre,   spin
And be the singing-masters of my soul.   20
Consume my heart away; sick with desire
And fastened to a dying animal

It knows not what it is; and gather me
Into the artifice of eternity.

Once out of nature I shall never take   25
My bodily form from any natural thing,
But such a form as Grecian goldsmiths make
Of hammered gold and gold enameling
To keep a drowsy Emperor awake;
Or set upon a golden bough to sing   30
To lords and ladies of Byzantium
Of what is past, or passing, or to come.

—WILLIAM BUTLER YEATS (1865–1939)

(Title) *Byzantium:* Ancient eastern capital of the Roman Empire; in this poem symbolically a holy
city of the imagination. (1) *That:* Ireland, or the ordinary sensual world. (27–31) *such . . . Byzantium:* The Byzantine emperor Theophilus had made for himself mechanical golden birds that sang
upon the branches of a golden tree.

QUESTIONS

1. Vocabulary: *gyre* (19).
2. What kind of "country" is being described in the first line? Why does a learned old
   man not belong in that country?
3. Contrast the speaker's native country, Ireland, with Byzantium. What are the characteristics of each? Which does the speaker prefer, and why?
4. Why does the speaker want his heart to be consumed so that he can be gathered
   "Into the artifice of eternity" (24)? Is he longing simply for death, or for something
   else?
5. Normally we think of "artificial" as a pejorative term, and "natural" as a positive
   attribute. But in the last stanza, especially, the speaker reverses the usual connotations of these concepts. Explain why, and describe the kind of world in which the
   speaker wishes to dwell.

Sunday Morning

1

Complacencies of the peignoir, and late
Coffee and oranges in a sunny chair,
And the green freedom of a cockatoo
Upon a rug mingle to dissipate
The holy hush of ancient sacrifice.   5

She dreams a little, and she feels the dark
Encroachment of that old catastrophe,
As a calm darkens among water-lights.
The pungent oranges and bright, green wings
Seem things in some procession of the dead,   10
Winding across wide water, without sound.
The day is like wide water, without sound,
Stilled for the passing of her dreaming feet
Over the seas, to silent Palestine,
Dominion of the blood and sepulchre.   15

2

Why should she give her bounty to the dead?
What is divinity if it can come
Only in silent shadows and in dreams?
Shall she not find in comforts of the sun,
In pungent fruit and bright, green wings, or else   20
In any balm or beauty of the earth,
Things to be cherished like the thought of heaven?
Divinity must live within herself:
Passions of rain, or moods in falling snow;
Grievings in loneliness, or unsubdued   25
Elations when the forest blooms; gusty
Emotions on wet roads on autumn nights;
All pleasures and all pains, remembering
The bough of summer and the winter branch.
These are the measures destined for her soul.   30

3

Jove in the clouds had his inhuman birth.
No mother suckled him, no sweet land gave
Large-mannered motions to his mythy mind.
He moved among us, as a muttering king,
Magnificent, would move among his hinds,   35
Until our blood, commingling, virginal,
With heaven, brought such requital to desire
The very hinds discerned it, in a star.
Shall our blood fail? Or shall it come to be
The blood of paradise? And shall the earth   40
Seem all of paradise that we shall know?
The sky will be much friendlier then than now,
A part of labor and a part of pain,

And next in glory to enduring love,
Not this dividing and indifferent blue.   45

4

She says, "I am content when wakened birds,
Before they fly, test the reality
Of misty fields, by their sweet questionings;
But when the birds are gone, and their warm fields
Return no more, where, then, is paradise?"   50
There is not any haunt of prophecy,
Nor any old chimera of the grave,
Neither the golden underground, nor isle
Melodious, where spirits gat them home,
Nor visionary south, nor cloudy palm   55
Remote on heaven's hill, that has endured
As April's green endures; or will endure
Like her remembrance of awakened birds,
Or her desire for June and evening, tipped
By the consummation of the swallow's wings.   60

5

She says, "But in contentment I still feel
The need of some imperishable bliss."
Death is the mother of beauty; hence from her,
Alone, shall come fulfillment to our dreams
And our desires. Although she strews the leaves   65
Of sure obliteration on our paths,
The path sick sorrow took, the many paths
Where triumph rang its brassy phrase, or love
Whispered a little out of tenderness,
She makes the willow shiver in the sun   70
For maidens who were wont to sit and gaze
Upon the grass, relinquished to their feet.
She causes boys to pile new plums and pears
On disregarded plate. The maidens taste
And stray impassioned in the littering leaves.   75

6

Is there no change of death in paradise?
Does ripe fruit never fall? Or do the boughs
Hang always heavy in that perfect sky,
Unchanging, yet so like our perishing earth,

With rivers like our own that seek for seas   80
They never find, the same receding shores
That never touch with inarticulate pang?
Why set the pear upon those river-banks
Or spice the shores with odors of the plum?
Alas, that they should wear our colors there,   85
The silken weavings of our afternoons,
And pick the strings of our insipid lutes!
Death is the mother of beauty, mystical,
Within whose burning bosom we devise
Our earthly mothers waiting, sleeplessly.   90

                                7
Supple and turbulent, a ring of men
Shall chant in orgy on a summer morn
Their boisterous devotion to the sun,
Not as a god, but as a god might be,
Naked among them, like a savage source.   95
Their chant shall be a chant of paradise,
Out of their blood, returning to the sky;
And in their chant shall enter, voice by voice,
The windy lake wherein their lord delights,
The trees, like serafin, and echoing hills,   100
That choir among themselves long afterward.
They shall know well the heavenly fellowship
Of men that perish and of summer morn.
And whence they came and whither they shall go
The dew upon their feet shall manifest.   105

                                8
She hears, upon that water without sound,
A voice that cries, "The tomb in Palestine
Is not the porch of spirits lingering.
It is the grave of Jesus, where he lay."
We live in an old chaos of the sun,   110
Or old dependency of day and night,
Or island solitude, unsponsored, free,
Of that wide water, inescapable.
Deer walk upon our mountains, and the quail
Whistle about us their spontaneous cries;   115
Sweet berries ripen in the wilderness;
And, in the isolation of the sky,

At evening, casual flocks of pigeons make
Ambiguous undulations as they sink,
Downward to darkness, on extended wings.   120

—WALLACE STEVENS (1879–1955)

QUESTIONS

1. Vocabulary: *peignoir* (1), *hinds* (35, 38), *requital* (37), *chimera* (52), *consummation* (60), *obliteration* (66), *serafin* (seraphim) (100). "[G]at" (54) is an obsolete past tense of "get."
2. The poem presents a woman meditating on questions of death, mutability, and permanence, beginning with a stanza that sets the stage and shows her being drawn to these questions beyond her conscious will. The meditation proper is structured as a series of questions and answers stated in direct or indirect quotations, with the answer to a preceding question suggesting a further question, and so forth. In reading through the poem, paraphrase the sequence of implied or stated questions, and the answers to them.
3. The opening scene (stanza 1), in a collection of images and details, indicates the means the woman has chosen to avoid thinking of the typical "Sunday morning" topic, the Christian religion. Define the means she employs. Trace the further references to fruits and birds throughout the poem, and explain the ordering principle that ties them together (for example, what development of idea or attitude is implied in the sequence oranges/plums and pears/wild berries?).
4. What symbolic meanings are implied by the images of (a) water, (b) the sun, and (c) birds and other animals?
5. Why does the woman give up her desire for unchanging permanence? With what does she replace it? What is her final attitude toward a world that includes change and death? What is meant by "Death is the mother of beauty" (63, 88)?
6. The poet wrote, "This is not essentially a woman's meditation on religion and the meaning of life. It is anybody's meditation" (*Letters of Wallace Stevens,* ed. Holly Stevens [New York: Knopf, 1966], 250). Can you justify that claim?

The Weary Blues

Droning a drowsy syncopated tune,
Rocking back and forth to a mellow croon,
  I heard a Negro play.
Down on Lenox Avenue the other night
By the pale dull pallor of an old gas light   5
  He did a lazy sway. . . .
  He did a lazy sway. . . .
To the tune o' those Weary Blues.
With his ebony hands on each ivory key

He made that poor piano moan with melody.   10
   O Blues!
Swaying to and fro on his rickety stool
He played that sad raggy tune like a musical fool.
   Sweet Blues!
Coming from a black man's soul.   15
   O Blues!
In a deep song voice with a melancholy tone
I heard that Negro sing, that old piano moan—
   "Ain't got nobody in all this world,
   Ain't got nobody but ma self.   20
   I's gwine to quit ma frownin'
   And put ma troubles on the shelf."
Thump, thump, thump, went his foot on the floor.
He played a few chords then he sang some more—
   "I got the Weary Blues   25
   And I can't be satisfied.
   Got the Weary Blues
   And can't be satisfied—
   I ain't happy no mo'
   And I wish that I had died."   30
And far into the night he crooned that tune.
The stars went out and so did the moon.
The singer stopped playing and went to bed
While the Weary Blues echoed through his head.
He slept like a rock or a man that's dead.   35

—LANGSTON HUGHES (1902–1967)

QUESTIONS

1. Vocabulary: *syncopated* (1), *raggy* (13).
2. What kind of music is the blues? Why is the form of "The Weary Blues" appropriate to a poem about this music?
3. The poem makes frequent use of repetition. What effect does this have on the reader?
4. Who is the speaker, and why does he respond so intensely to the piano player's "sad raggy tune" (13)?
5. The two quoted lyrics from the piano player's song (19–22 and 25–30) convey quite different messages and emotions. Describe these contrasting lyrics. What is the effect of this contrast on the reader's understanding of the song?
6. The piano player sings and plays "far into the night" (31). How is the music beneficial to him? Does the speaker derive a similar benefit?
7. Analyze the final line. How does the simile form an appropriate closure to the poem?

The Fish

I caught a tremendous fish
and held him beside the boat
half out of water, with my hook
fast in a corner of his mouth.
He didn't fight.   5
He hadn't fought at all.
He hung a grunting weight,
battered and venerable
and homely. Here and there
his brown skin hung in strips   10
like ancient wallpaper,
and its pattern of darker brown
was like wallpaper:
shapes like full-blown roses
stained and lost through age.   15
He was speckled with barnacles,
fine rosettes of lime,
and infested
with tiny white sea-lice,
and underneath two or three   20
rags of green weed hung down.
While his gills were breathing in
the terrible oxygen
—the frightening gills,
fresh and crisp with blood,   25
that can cut so badly—
I thought of the coarse white flesh
packed in like feathers,
the big bones and the little bones,
the dramatic reds and blacks   30
of his shiny entrails,
and the pink swim-bladder
like a big peony.
I looked into his eyes
which were far larger than mine   35
but shallower, and yellowed,
the irises backed and packed
with tarnished tinfoil

seen through the lenses
of old scratched isinglass. 40
They shifted a little, but not
to return my stare.
—It was more like the tipping
of an object toward the light.
I admired his sullen face, 45
the mechanism of his jaw,
and then I saw
that from his lower lip
—if you could call it a lip—
grim, wet, and weaponlike, 50
hung five old pieces of fish-line,
or four and a wire leader
with the swivel still attached,
with all their five big hooks
grown firmly in his mouth. 55
A green line, frayed at the end
where he broke it, two heavier lines,
and a fine black thread
still crimped from the strain and snap
when it broke and he got away. 60
Like medals with their ribbons
frayed and wavering,
a five-haired beard of wisdom
trailing from his aching jaw.
I stared and stared 65
and victory filled up
the little rented boat,
from the pool of bilge
where oil had spread a rainbow
around the rusted engine 70
to the bailer rusted orange,
the sun-cracked thwarts,
the oarlocks on their strings,
the gunnels—until everything
was rainbow, rainbow, rainbow! 75
And I let the fish go.

—ELIZABETH BISHOP (1911–1979)

QUESTIONS

1. Explore the multiple denotations of "tremendous" (1) and the connotations attached to them. How does the richness of that word prepare you for the complexity of the poem?
2. In what ways are many of the images paradoxical in their emotional evocations? Where does the poem create imagery out of the speaker's imagination rather than her present observation?
3. Much of the imagery is elucidated by figurative comparisons or is itself figurative. Find examples of both uses of figures, and trace what they convey in the way of ideas and/or emotions.
4. Whose "victory" fills the boat (66–67)? What is the nature of that victory? Might the term apply to more than one kind of victory?
5. What literally is the "rainbow" (69)? To what is it transformed in lines 74–75? What accounts for the transformation?
6. Explain how the tone of the poem shifts and develops. What is happening to the speaker as she observes and comments upon the physical aspects of the fish?
7. Why does the speaker "let the fish go" (76)? Is the fish symbolic?

Lady Lazarus

I have done it again.
One year in every ten
I manage it—

A sort of walking miracle, my skin
Bright as a Nazi lampshade,   5
My right foot

A paperweight,
My face a featureless, fine
Jew linen.

Peel off the napkin   10
O my enemy.
Do I terrify?—

The nose, the eye pits, the full set of teeth?
The sour breath
Will vanish in a day.   15

Soon, soon the flesh
The grave cave ate will be
At home on me

And I a smiling woman.
I am only thirty.   20
And like the cat I have nine times to die.

This is Number Three.
What a trash
To annihilate each decade.

What a million filaments.   25
The peanut-crunching crowd
Shoves in to see

Them unwrap me hand and foot—
The big strip tease.
Gentlemen, ladies   30

These are my hands
My knees.
I may be skin and bone,

Nevertheless, I am the same, identical woman.
The first time it happened I was ten.   35
It was an accident.

The second time I meant
To last it out and not come back at all.
I rocked shut

As a seashell.   40
They had to call and call
And pick the worms off me like sticky pearls.

Dying
Is an art, like everything else.
I do it exceptionally well.   45

I do it so it feels like hell.
I do it so it feels real.
I guess you could say I've a call.

It's easy enough to do it in a cell.
It's easy enough to do it and stay put.   50
It's the theatrical

Comeback in broad day
To the same place, the same face, the same brute
Amused shout:

'A miracle!'   55
That knocks me out.
There is a charge

For the eyeing of my scars, there is a charge
For the hearing of my heart—
It really goes.   60

And there is a charge, a very large charge
For a word or a touch
Or a bit of blood

Or a piece of my hair or my clothes.
So, so, Herr Doktor.   65
So, Herr Enemy.

I am your opus,
I am your valuable,
The pure gold baby

That melts to a shriek.   70
I turn and burn.
Do not think I underestimate your great concern.

Ash, ash—
You poke and stir.
Flesh, bone, there is nothing there—   75

A cake of soap,
A wedding ring,
A gold filling.

Herr God, Herr Lucifer
Beware   80
Beware.

Out of the ash
I rise with my red hair
And I eat men like air.

—SYLVIA PLATH (1932–1963)

QUESTIONS

1. Explore the Biblical reference to Lazarus (title) as a symbol for one who survives a suicide attempt. Sylvia Plath attempted suicide at least twice during her short life; this poem was written four months before she finally succeeded in 1963 at the age of thirty.
2. In the speaker's allegory, she identifies herself with the Jews during the Holocaust and with a striptease artist. Compare these references to the psychodrama of a suicidal poet. Who is "the peanut-crunching crowd" (26)? How can dying be said to constitute "an art" (44)?
3. Find a biographical essay on Plath either in the library or on the Internet. Can this poem be understood without knowing details of Plath's relationship to her father and her estranged husband, Ted Hughes?

PRACTICE AP® WRITING PROMPTS

Robert Browning, "My Last Duchess" (pp. 288–290)

Robert Browning's poem "My Last Duchess" is a dramatic monologue in which the Duke of Ferrara speaks to the representative of a count whose daughter the duke wishes to marry. In the poem, he is speaking about his previous wife, his "last duchess." Read the poem with care, and then write an essay in which you show how Browning uses word choice, conversational rhythms, and implied tone of voice to create a discrepancy between what the speaker believes he is communicating and what he is actually revealing about himself.

Elizabeth Bishop, "The Fish" (pp. 307–309)

Read "The Fish" carefully, paying close attention to the speaker's conflicted attitude toward the fish. Then write a well-organized essay in which you describe the speaker's shifting perspective. Show how such elements as imagery, paradox, diction, and tone support the poem's meaning.

PART TWO

Writing about Poetry

Writing about Poetry

I. Why Write about Literature?   p. 315

II. For Whom Do You Write?   p. 315

III. Two Basic Approaches   p. 317
  1. Explication   p. 317
  2. Analysis   p. 318

IV. Choosing a Topic   p. 318
  1. Essays That Focus on a Single Poem   p. 319
  2. Essays of Comparison and Contrast   p. 319
  3. Essays on a Number of Poems by a Single Author   p. 320
  4. Essays on a Number of Poems with Some Feature Other Than Authorship in Common   p. 322

V. Proving Your Point   p. 322

VI. Writing the Essay   p. 324

VII. Introducing Quotations (Q1–Q11)   p. 326

VIII. Documentation   p. 332
  1. Textual Documentation (TD1–TD5)   p. 333
  2. Parenthetical Documentation (PD1–PD5)   p. 335
  3. Documentation by Works Cited   p. 336
  4. Documentation of Electronic Sources   p. 339

IX. Stance and Style (S1–S6)   p. 341

X. Grammar, Punctuation, and Usage: Common Problems   p. 344
  1. Grammar (G1–G2)   p. 344
  2. Punctuation (P1–P5)   p. 344
  3. Usage (U1–U2)   p. 346

XI. Writing Samples   p. 349
  1. Explication: "A Study of Reading Habits"   p. 349
  2. Analysis: Diction in "Spring in the Classroom"   p. 351

I. Why Write about Literature?

Written assignments in a literature class have two purposes: (1) to give you additional practice in writing clearly and persuasively, and (2) to deepen your understanding of literary works by leading you to read and think about a few works more searchingly than you might otherwise do. But these two purposes are private. To be successful, your essay must have a public purpose as well: it should be written to enlighten others besides yourself. Even if no one else ever reads your essay, you should never treat it as a private note to your instructor. You should write every essay as if it were intended for publication.

II. For Whom Do You Write?

The audience for whom you write will govern both the content and expression of your essay. You need to know something about your readers' backgrounds—national, racial, social, religious—and be able to make intelligent guesses about their knowledge, interests, and previous reading. In writing about George Herbert's "Redemption" (page 100) for a Hindu audience, you might need to include explanations of Christian belief and biblical stories that would be unnecessary for a western European or American audience. But this is the most crucial question about an audience: *Has the audience read the work you are writing about?* The book reviewer in your Sunday newspaper generally writes about a newly published book that the audience has not read. A reviewer's purpose is to let readers know something of what the book is about and to give them some notion of whether they will enjoy or profit from reading it. At an opposite extreme, the scholar writing in a specialized scholarly journal can generally assume an audience *has* read the work, has a knowledge of previous interpretations of the work, and is familiar with other works in its period or genre. The scholar's purpose, not infrequently, is to persuade this audience that some new information or some new way of looking at the work appreciably deepens or alters its meaning or significance.

Clearly, essays written for such dissimilar audiences and with such unique purposes differ considerably in content, organization, and style. Book reviewers reviewing a new novel will include a general idea of its plot while being careful not to reveal the outcome. Scholars will assume that readers already know the plot and will have no compunction about discussing its outcome. Reviewers will try to write interestingly and engagingly about the novel and to persuade readers that they have valid grounds for their opinions of its worth, but their manner will generally be informal. Scholars are more interested in presenting a cogent argument, logically arranged and solidly based on evidence. They will be more formal, and may use critical terms and refer to related works that would be unfamiliar to nonspecialized readers. In documentation, the two types of essays will be quite different. Reviewers' only documentation is normally the identification of the novel's title, author, publisher, and price, at the top of the review. For other information and opinions they hope that a reader will rely on their intelligence, knowledge, and judgment. Scholars, on the other hand, may furnish an elaborate array of citations of other sources of information, allowing the reader to verify the accuracy or basis of any important part of their argument. Scholars expect to be challenged, and they see to it that all parts of their arguments are buttressed.

For whom, then, should *you* write? Unless your instructor stipulates (or you request) a different audience, the best plan is to assume that you are writing for the other members of your class. Pretend that your class publishes a journal of which it also constitutes the readership. Your instructor is the editor and determines editorial policy. If you write about a poem that has been assigned for class reading, you assume that your audience might be familiar with it. (This kind of writing is generally of the greatest educational value, for it is most open to challenge and class discussion, and places on you a heavier burden of proof.) If you compare an assigned poem with one that has not been assigned, you must gauge what portion of your audience might be familiar with the unassigned poem, and proceed accordingly. If the unassigned poem is a later sonnet in the Shakespearean form, which you are comparing to one by Shakespeare, you will not need to provide a definition of the rhyme scheme of the form, for you can assume that *this* audience is familiar with the form of a sonnet; but you cannot assume familiarity with all of the sonnets of Shakespeare. You know that, as members of the same class, your readers have certain backgrounds and interests in common and are at comparable levels of education. Anything you know about your audience may be important for how you write your essay and what you put in it.

Assuming members of your class as your audience carries another advantage: you can also assume that they are familiar with the definitions and examples given in this book, and therefore you can avoid wasting space by quoting or paraphrasing the book. There will be no need to tell them that blank verse is unrhymed iambic pentameter, or that Emily Dickinson's poems are untitled, or that Tennyson is a nineteenth-century poet.

III. Two Basic Approaches

In a beginning study of poetry, most writing will focus on a careful reading of details of the assigned work as the basis for any further exploration. Traditionally, the approach will be structured as an *explication* or an *analysis.*

1. Explication

An *explication* (literally, an "unfolding") is a detailed elucidation of a work, sometimes line by line or word by word, which includes not only *what* that work means but *how* it means what it means. It thus considers all relevant aspects of a work—speaker, connotative words and double meanings, images, figurative language, allusions, form, structure, sound, rhythm—and discusses, if not all of these, at least the most important. (There is no such thing as exhausting the meanings and the ways to those meanings in a complex piece of literature, and the explicator must settle for something less than completeness.) Explication follows from what we sometimes call "close reading"—looking at a piece of writing, as it were, through a magnifying glass.

Clearly, the kinds of literature for which an explication is appropriate are limited. First, the work must be rich enough to repay the kind of close attention demanded. One would not think of explicating "Pease Porridge Hot (unless for purposes of parody), for it has no meanings that need elucidation and no "art" worthy of comment. Second, the work must be short enough to be encompassed in a relatively brief discussion. A thorough explication of *Othello* would be longer than the play itself and would tire the patience of the most dogged reader. Explications work best with short poems. (Sonnets like Shakespeare's "That time of year" [page 254] and Frost's "Design" [page 156] almost beg for explication.) Explication sometimes may also be appropriate for passages in long poems, as, for example, the lines spoken by Macbeth after the death of his wife (page 137) or the "sonnet" from *Romeo and Juliet* (page 260). But explication as a critical form should perhaps be separated from explication as a method. Whenever you elucidate even a small part of a literary work by a close examination that relates it to the whole, you are essentially explicating (unfolding). For example, if you elaborate at length on the multiple denotations and connotations of the title of Langston Hughes's "Cross" (page 47) as they relate to that poem's central purpose, you are explicating the title.

For a sample of an explication, see "A Study of Reading Habits" (page 25). The text of this book uses the explicative method frequently, but has no pure examples of explication. The discussions of "A Noiseless Patient Spider" (page 93) and "Digging" (page 96) come close to being explications, and might have been so designated had they included discussions of other relevant aspects of the poems (connotative language, imagery, structure and form, and so forth). Understanding and Evaluating Poetry on page 10 should be helpful to you in writing an explication of a poem. Not all the questions will be applicable to every poem, and you need not answer all those that are applicable, but you should begin by considering all that apply and then work with those that are central and important for your explication.

2. Analysis

An *analysis* (literally a "breaking up" or separation of something into its constituent parts), instead of trying to examine all parts of a work in relation to the whole, selects for examination of *one* aspect or element or part that relates to the whole. Clearly, an analysis is a better approach to longer works and to prose works than is an explication. A literary work may be usefully approached through almost any of its elements, so long as you relate this element to the central meaning or the whole. (An analysis of meter is pointless unless it shows how meter serves the meaning.) As always, it is important to choose a topic appropriate to the space available. "Visual and auditory imagery in 'The Love Song of J. Alfred Prufrock'" (page 295) is too large a topic to be usefully treated in one or two pages, but the irony of the refrain about the women talking of Michelangelo could be suited to such a length. Conversely, it might be too great a challenge to write a ten-page essay on so limited a topic, though the Michelangelo refrain could contribute a valuable page or two of discussion in a longer essay about Eliot's irony, or about the various effects of the refrains in the poem. For a sample of an analysis of one aspect of a poem, see "Diction in 'Spring in the Classroom'" page 351.

IV. Choosing a Topic

As editor of this imaginary publication, your instructor is responsible for the nature of its contents. Instructors may be very specific in their assignments, or they may be very general, inviting you to submit an essay on any subject within a broadly defined area of interest. They will also have editorial policies concerning length of essays, preparation of manuscripts, and deadlines for submission (all of which should be meticulously heeded). Instructors may further specify whether the essay should be entirely the work of your own critical thinking, or whether it is to be an investigative assignment—that is, one involving research into what other writers have written concerning your subject and the use of their findings, where relevant, to help you support your own conclusions.

Let us consider four kinds of essays you might write: (1) essays that focus on a single poem; (2) essays of comparison and contrast; (3) essays on a number of poems by a single author; and (4) essays on a number of poems having some feature other than authorship in common.

1. Essays That Focus on a Single Poem

If your assignment is a specific one (How does the question–answer structure of "Is my team plowing" [page 29] reveal the speaker's psychological state? What does personification add to Tennyson's "The Eagle" [page 4]? How is structure fitted to form in Shakespeare's "That time of year" [page 254]?), your task is clear-cut. You have only to read the selection carefully (obviously more than once), formulate your answer, and support it with corroborating evidence from within the text as cogently and convincingly as possible. In order to convince your readers that your answer is the best one, you will need to examine and account for apparently contrary evidence as well as clearly supportive evidence; otherwise, skeptical readers, reluctant to change their minds, might simply refer to "important points" that you have "overlooked."

Specific questions like these, when they are central to the poem and may be a matter of dispute, make excellent topics for essays. You may discover them for yourself when you disagree with a classmate about the interpretation of a poem. The study questions following many of the selections in this anthology frequently suggest topics of this kind.

If your assignment is more general and if you are given some choice about which poem you wish to write on, it is usually best to choose one you enjoyed, regardless of whether you entirely understood it. (You are more likely to write a good essay on a selection you liked than on one you disliked, and you should arrive at a fuller understanding of it while thinking through your essay.) You must then decide what kind of essay you will write, taking into account the length and kind of selection you have chosen and the amount of space at your disposal.

2. Essays of Comparison and Contrast

The comparison and contrast of two poems having one or more features in common may be an illuminating exercise because the similarities highlight the differences, or vice versa, and thus lead to a better understanding not only of both pieces but of literary processes in general. The works selected may be similar in subject but different in tone, similar in meaning but different in literary value, similar in means but different in the ends they achieve or, conversely, similar in tone but different in subject, similar in literary value but different in meaning, and so on. In writing such an essay, it is usually best to decide first whether the similarities or the differences are more significant, begin with a brief summary of the less significant, and then concentrate on the more significant.

A number of selections in this book have been "paired" to encourage just this kind of study: "Spring" and "The Widow's Lament in Springtime" in Chapter 4; "On the Sonnet" and "Sonnet," "Southern History" and "The Colonel," "The Lamb" and "The Tiger" in Chapter 9; "To the Snake" and "A narrow Fellow in the Grass," "Dover Beach" and "Church Going" in Chapter 10; and all six pairs of poems in Chapter 15. In addition, many of the suggestions for writing at the ends of chapters group together comparable poems.

3. Essays on a Number of Poems by a Single Author

Most readers, when they discover a poem they particularly like, look for other works by the same author. The essay that focuses on a single author rather than a single work is the natural corollary of such an interest. The most common concern in an essay of this type is to identify the characteristics that make this author different from other authors and therefore of particular interest to you. What are the poet's characteristic subjects, attitudes, or themes? With what kinds of life does the poet characteristically deal? What are the poet's preferred literary forms? What tones does the poet favor? Is the poet ironic, witty, serious, comic, tragic? Is the poet's vision directed principally inward or outward? In short, what configuration of patterns makes the poet's fingerprints unique? Your essay may consider one or more of these questions. The five "Featured Poets," Emily Dickinson, John Donne, Robert Frost, John Keats, and Sylvia Plath, are represented in this book by a sufficient number of poems to support such an essay without turning to outside sources. Any of the five poets listed in the Table of Contents as a "Contemporary Collection"—Billy Collins, Louise Glück, Seamus Heaney, Sharon Olds, and Natasha Trethewey—might also serve that purpose. In addition, consulting the Index reveals that the book contains three or more poems by each of the following: W. H. Auden, William Blake, Gwendolyn Brooks, Robert Browning, e.e. cummings, Thomas Hardy, George Herbert, Gerard Manley Hopkins, A. E. Housman, Langston Hughes, Philip Larkin, Mary Oliver, Adrienne Rich, William Shakespeare, Wallace Stevens, Alfred, Lord Tennyson, Walt Whitman, William Carlos Williams, William Wordsworth, and William Butler Yeats.

A more ambitious type of essay on a single poet examines the poems for signs of development. The attitudes that any person, especially a poet, takes toward the world may change with the passing from adolescence to adulthood to old age. So also may a poet's means of expressing attitudes and judgments. Although some authors are remarkably consistent in outlook and expression throughout their careers, others manifest surprising changes. What are the differences between early Yeats, middle Yeats, and late Yeats? To write such an essay, you must have accurate information about the dates when works were written, and the works must be read in chronological order. When you have mastered the differences, you may be able to illustrate them through close examination of two or three poems— one for each stage.

When readers become especially interested in the works of a particular poet, they may develop a curiosity about the poet's life as well. This is a legitimate interest and, if there is sufficient space and your editor/ instructor permits it, you may want to incorporate biographical information into your essay. If so, however, you should heed three caveats. First, your main interest should be in the literature itself; the biographical material should be subordinated to and used in service of your examination of the work. In general, discuss only those aspects of the poet's life that bear directly on the work: biography should not be used as "filler." Second, you should be extremely cautious about identifying an event in a work with an event in the life of the author. Almost never are poems exact transcriptions of the writers' personal experiences. Authors fictionalize themselves when they put themselves into imaginative works. Even in their autobiographies, where they intend to give accurate accounts of their lives, writers must select incidents from the vast complexity of their experiences. Even the sharpest of memories might be defective in some ways, and, at best, writers work from their own points of view. In short, when you realize that even autobiography cannot be an absolutely reliable transcription of historical fact, you should be more fully prepared not to expect a perfect equation of events in a work of imaginative fiction with events in the life of the author. Third, you must document the sources of your information about the author's life (see pages 332–333, 336–341).

4. Essays on a Number of Poems with Some Feature Other Than Authorship in Common

You might also write a successful essay on poems by various poets that have some feature in common, such as subject matter, form, poetic devices, and the like. Discovering the ways in which different works employ a particular feature can be illuminating. Probably the most familiar essay of this type is the one that treats works having a similar thematic concern (love, war, religious belief or doubt, art, adolescence, initiation, maturity, old age, death, parents and children, racial conflict, social injustice). But an essay may also examine particular forms of literature such as the Italian sonnet, the dramatic monologue, or the descriptive lyric. Topics of this kind may be further limited by time or place or number—Elizabethan love lyrics, four attitudes toward death, satires of bureaucracy.

V. Proving Your Point

In writing about literature, your object generally is to convince your readers that your understanding of a work is valid and important and to lead them to share that understanding. When writing about other subjects, it may be appropriate to persuade your readers through various rhetorical means—through eloquent diction, structural devices that create suspense, analogies, personal anecdotes, and the like. But readers of essays about literature usually look for "proof." They want you to show them *how* the work, or the element you are discussing, does what you claim it does. Like scientists who require proof of the sort that they can duplicate in their own laboratories, readers of criticism want access to the process of inference, analysis, and deduction that has led to your conclusions, so that they may respond as you have done.

To provide this proof is no easy task, for it requires the development of your own reading and writing skills. In addition, you must have developed a responsible interpretation of the poem and of the way it achieves its effects; you should be able to point out precisely how it communicates its meanings; and you should be able to present your experience of it clearly and directly.

When you have spent considerable time in coming to understand and respond to a work of literature, it may become so familiar that it seems self-evident to you, and you will need to "back off" sufficiently to be able to put yourself in your readers' position—they may have vague feelings about the poem ("I like it" or "It moves me deeply"), without knowing what it is that produced those feelings. It is your job to refine the feelings and define away the vagueness.

Some forms of "proof" rarely do the job. Precision does not result from explaining a metaphor metaphorically ("When Shakespeare's Juliet calls parting from Romeo a 'sweet sorrow,' the reader is reminded of taking bitter-tasting medicine"). Nor can you prove anything about a work by hypothesizing about what it might have been if it did not contain what it does ("If Dickinson had concluded 'A narrow Fellow in the Grass' by writing 'Without gasping for breath / And feeling chilled,' the poem would be much less effective"—this is equivalent to saying "If the poem were not what it is, it would not be what it is"). Your own personal experiences will rarely help your readers ("My anxiety, excitement, and awkwardness at my first skiing lesson were like the mixed feelings Prufrock imagines for himself at the tea party"—*your* reader hasn't shared your experience of that lesson). Even your personal history of coming to understand a literary work will seldom help ("At a first reading, Williams's 'The Red Wheelbarrow' seems empty and pointless, until one realizes its meaning"—most literature does not yield up its richness on a first reading, so this approach has nothing to add to your reader's understanding). Just as in formal logic, argument by analogy is not regarded as valid, so in critical discourse analogies are usually unconvincing ("The rhythm of this sonnet is like the trot of a three-legged racehorse"). These strategies all have in common the looseness and vagueness of trying to define something by saying what it is not, or what it is like, rather than dealing with what it *is*.

"Proof" in writing about literature is primarily an exercise in strict definition. Juliet's phrase "sweet sorrow" (quoted in the preceding paragraph) derives its feeling from the paradoxical linking of sweetness and grief as a representation of the conflicting emotions of love. To provide an appropriate definition of the effect of the phrase, you would need to identify the figure of speech as paradox, and to investigate the way in which love can simultaneously inflict pain and give pleasure, and you might find it useful to point to the alliteration that ties these opposites together. Obviously, comparing this kind of proof to that required by science is inexact, since what you are doing is reminding your readers, or perhaps informing them, of feelings that are associated with language, not of the properties of chemical compounds. Furthermore, a scientific proof is incomplete if it does not present every step in a process. If that requirement were placed on literary analysis, a critical essay would be interminable, since more can always be said about any interpretive point. So, rather than attempting to prove every point that you make, you should aim to demonstrate that your *method* of analysis is valid by providing persuasive proof of your major point or points. If you have shown that your handling of a major point is sound, your readers will tend to trust your judgment on lesser matters.

VI. Writing the Essay

The general procedures for writing a good essay on literature are much the same as the procedures for writing a good essay on any subject.

1. As soon as possible after receiving the assignment, read carefully and thoughtfully the literary materials on which it is based, mulling over the problem to be solved or—if the assignment is general—a good choice of subject, jotting down notes, and sidelining or underlining important passages if the book is your own. (If you use a library book, use sticky notes to indicate of such passages so that you can readily find them again.) Be sure to read the assigned material more than once.

2. Then, rather than proceeding directly to the writing of the essay, put the materials aside for several days and let them steep in your mind. The advantage of this is that your subconscious mind, if you have truly placed the problem in it, will continue to work on the problem while you are engaged in other activities, indeed even while you are asleep. Repeated investigations into the psychology of creativity have shown that great solutions to scientific and artistic problems frequently occur while the scientist or artist is thinking of something else; the answer pops into consciousness as if out of nowhere but really out of the hidden recesses of the mind where it has been quietly incubating. Whether this apparent "miracle" happens to you or not, it is probable that you will have more ideas if you sit down to write after some time has passed than if you try to write your essay immediately after reading the material.

3. When you are ready to write (allow yourself as long an incubation period as possible, but also allow ample time for writing, looking things up, revising, and correcting your final copy), type on your computer screen a list of the ideas you have, select connecting ideas relevant to your problem or to a single acceptable subject, and formulate a thesis statement that will clearly express in one sentence what you wish to say about that subject. Make a rough outline, rearranging your ideas in the order that will best support your thesis. Do they make a coherent case? Have you left out anything necessary to demonstrate your thesis? If so, add it in the appropriate place. Then begin to write, using your rough outline as a guide. Write this first draft as swiftly as possible, not yet focusing on sentence structure, grammar, diction, spelling, or verification of sources. Concentrate on putting on the screen what is in your head and on your outline without interrupting the flow of thought for any other purpose. If alternative ways of expressing a thought occur to you, put them all down for a later decision. Nothing is more unprofitable than staring at a blank monitor and wondering, with Eliot's Prufrock, "How shall I begin?" Just begin.

Get something down onto your computer screen. It may look awful, but you can shape and polish it later.

4. After you have something written, it is much easier to see what should be done with it. The next step is to revise. Does your essay proceed from an introductory paragraph that either defines the problem to be solved or states your thesis, through a series of logically arranged paragraphs that advance toward a solution of the problem or demonstrate your thesis, to a final paragraph that either solves the problem or sums up and restates your thesis but in somewhat different words? If not, analyze the difficulty. Do the paragraphs need reorganization or amplification? Are more examples needed? Does the thesis itself need modification? Make whatever adjustments are necessary for a logical and convincing demonstration. This may require a rewriting of the essay, or it may call only for a few deletions or insertions, or a shifting of one sentence or paragraph from one place to another.

Notice that you are expected to organize your essay according to your purpose or thesis. This frequently will mean that you will not be moving line by line and stanza by stanza through a poem, following the structure that the poet created, but rather ordering your essay in the most effective way to make your point. If you do discuss the poem in the order in which its materials are presented, your reader will naturally expect your thesis to include some comment on the poem's structure. The exception to this is an essay devoted entirely to explication, since in that case you will be expected to follow the structure of the poem.

5. In your revision (if not earlier), be sure that the stance expressed in your statements and judgments is firm and forthright, not weak and wishy-washy. Don't allow your essay to become a sump of phrases like "it seems to me that," "I think [or feel] that," "this word might connote," "this line could mean," and "in my opinion." Your readers know that the content of your essay expresses your thoughts; you need to warn them only when it expresses someone else's. And don't be weak-kneed in expressing your opinion. Even if you are not 100 percent sure of your rightness, write as if you are presenting a truth. Realizing beforehand that you will need to state your interpretations and conclusions confidently should also help you to strive for a greater degree of certainty as you read and interpret.

6. Having revised your essay for the logic, coherence, confidence, and completeness of its argument, your next step is to revise it for effectiveness of expression. Do this slowly and carefully. How many words can you cut out without loss of meaning? Are your sentences constructed for maximum force and economy? Are they correctly punctuated? Do the pronouns have clear antecedents? Do the verbs agree with their subjects? Are the

tenses consistent? Have you chosen the most exact words and spelled them correctly? Now is the time to use the dictionary, to verify quotations and other references, and to supply whatever documentation is needed. A conscientious writer will put an essay through several revisions.

7. After all is in order, write or type your final copy, being sure to follow the editorial policies of your instructor for the submission of manuscripts.

8. Read over your final copy slowly and carefully, and correct any mistakes (omissions, repetitions, typographical errors) you may have made in copying from your draft. This final step—too often omitted due to haste or fatigue—is extremely important and may make the difference between an A or a C essay, or between a C essay and an F. It is easy to make careless mistakes in copying, but your reader should not be counted on to recognize the difference between a copying error and one of ignorance. Moreover, the smallest error may utterly destroy the sense of what you have written. For example, omission of a "not" may make your essay say the exact opposite of what you meant it to say. Few instructors require or want you to recopy or retype a whole page of your essay at this stage. It is enough to make neat corrections in ink on the paper itself.

VII. Introducing Quotations

When writing about literature, it is often desirable, sometimes imperative, to quote from the work under discussion. Quoted material is needed (a) to provide essential evidence in support of your argument and (b) to set before your reader any passage that you are going to examine in detail. It will also keep your reader in contact with the text and allow you to use felicitous phrasing from the text to enhance your own presentation. You must, however, be careful not to overquote. If an essay consists of more than 20 percent quotation, it loses the appearance of a closely knit argument and seems instead merely a collection of quotations strung together like birds perched along a power line. Avoid, especially, unnecessary use of long quotations. Readers tend to skip them. Consider carefully whether the quoted material may not be more economically presented by paraphrase or effectively shortened by ellipsis points (see Q9 on page 331). Readers faced with a long quotation may reasonably expect you to examine it in some detail; that is, the longer your quotation, the more you should do with it.

As a general rule in analytical writing, quotations should be included for the purpose of supporting or proving a point, not for the purpose of recreating the experience of the poem for your reader. You may assume that your reader has already read the poem and does not need to have it summarized—

but on the other hand, you should not send your reader back to the book to reread in order to understand your references to it. Analysis is the process of demonstrating how the parts work together to create the whole; it must examine these parts in detail and show how they work together. Quoting presents details, and analysis shows how the details do what you claim they do. If a quotation seems entirely self-evident to you so that you have nothing to explain about it, then it is not really worth quoting. If it is self-evident, your reader has already understood all there is to know about it.

As with every other aspect of good writing, the use of quotation is a matter of intelligence and tact. There are no hard-and-fast rules, since the amount of material you quote and the way you explain the significance of your quotations will vary, depending on the poem you are writing about and the kind of essay you are writing. In general, however, you should limit direct quotation to words, phrases, or short passages that are so well written and illuminating that to paraphrase them would dilute the force of your argument. Such quotation strengthens your own writing by showing that you have mastered the material and can offer the crucial evidence directly from the text. On the other hand, if the *content* of a passage (especially a long passage) is more significant than the specific language the author uses, then a paraphrase is probably adequate. Either way, be sure that you quote or paraphrase selectively, keeping your own ideas about the poem in the foreground; and also be sure that your quotation or paraphrase directly supports your argument.

Principles and Guidelines

There is no legislative body that establishes laws governing the formal aspects of quoting, documenting, or any other aspect of writing. The only "rules" are the editorial policies of the publisher to whom you submit your work. (In the case of essays being written as class assignments, your "publisher" is your instructor.) There is, however, a national organization—the Modern Language Association of America—that is so influential that its policies for its own publications and its recommendations for others are adopted by most journals of literary criticism and scholarship. The instructions that follow are in general accord with those stated in the *MLA Handbook for Writers of Research Essays,* 8th edition (New York: MLA, 2015). In your course, your instructor will inform you of any editorial policies in effect that differ from those given here or in the *MLA Handbook.* The examples used in this section are all drawn from Housman's "Terence, this is stupid stuff" (page 383).

Q1. If the quotation is short (normally not more than two or three lines of verse), put it in quotation marks and introduce it directly into the text of your essay.

> Terence, in a rejoinder to his friend's complaint about
> the melancholy sobriety of his poetry, reminds him,
>
> a   "There's brisker pipes than poetry," and the English
>
> b   gentry "brews / Livelier liquor than the Muse"
>   (16, 19–20).

Q2. If the quotation is long (normally more than three lines of verse), begin it on a new line (and resume the text of your essay on a new line following the quotation); double-space it (like the rest of your essay); and indent it twice as far from the left margin (ten spaces or one inch) as you do for a new paragraph (five spaces or one-half inch). If a ten-space indentation is unsuitable because the verse lines are either too long or too short, center the quotation between the margins. *Do not enclose it in quotation marks.* Since the indentation and the line arrangement both signal a quotation, the use of quotation marks would be redundant.

> In the final verse paragraph, Terence describes the terror
> of Mithridates's would-be assassins:
>> They poured strychnine in his cup
>> And shook to see him drink it up:
>> They shook, they stared as white's their shirt:
>> Them it was their poison hurt. (71–74)

The two boxed examples illustrate the *run-in* quotation (Q1), where the quotation is "run in" with the writer's own text, and the *set-off* or *block* quotation (Q2), which is separated from the writer's text.

Q3. In quoting verse, it is extremely important to preserve the line arrangement of the original because the verse line is a rhythmic unit and thus affects meaning. When more than one line of verse is run in, the lines are separated by a virgule (or diagonal slash with one letter-space on each side), and capitalization follows that of the original (see Q1.b).

Q4. In general, sentences containing a quotation are punctuated as they would be if there were no quotation. In Q1.a earlier, a comma precedes the quoted sentence as it would if there were no quotation marks. In Q2, a colon precedes the quoted sentence because it is long and complex. In Q1.b, there is no punctuation at all before the quotation. Do not put punctuation before a quotation unless it is otherwise called for.

Q5. Your quotation must combine with its introduction to make a grammatically correct sentence. The normal processes of grammar and syntax, like the normal processes of punctuation, are unaffected by quoting. Subjects must agree with their verbs, verbs must be consistent in tense, pronouns must have their normal relation with antecedents.

WRONG	Terence says, "And I myself a sterling lad" (34).
	(Incomplete sentence)
RIGHT	Terence calls himself "a sterling lad" (34).

WRONG	Terence confesses that he has "been to Ludlow fair / And left my necktie God knows where" (29–30).
	(The pronoun "my" does not agree in person with its antecedent "he.")
RIGHT	Terence confesses, "I have been to Ludlow fair / And left my necktie God knows where" (29–30).

WRONG	Terence says that "The world, it was the old world yet" (39).
	(Incorrect mixture of direct and indirect quotation)
RIGHT	Terence says, "The world, it was the old world yet" (39).

WRONG	Terence says that he "have been to Ludlow fair" (29).
	(Subject and verb of subordinate clause lack agreement.)
RIGHT	Terence says that he has "been to Ludlow fair" (29).

Q6. Your introduction must supply enough context to make the quotation meaningful. Be careful that all pronouns in the quotation have clearly identifiable antecedents.

WRONG	Terence begins his narration by saying, "Why, if 'tis dancing you would be, / There's brisker pipes than poetry" (15–16). *(Who wants to dance?)*
RIGHT	Terence begins his reply to his friend by saying, "Why, if 'tis dancing you would be, / There's brisker pipes than poetry" (15–16)

Q7. The words within your quotation marks must be quoted *exactly* from the original.

WRONG	Terence confesses that "in lovely muck he's lain," where he slept "happily till he woke again" (35–36).

Q8. It is permissible to insert or supply words in a quotation *if* you enclose them within brackets. Brackets (parentheses with square corners) are used to indicate *your* changes or additions. If parentheses were used, the reader might interpret the enclosed material as the *author's* (as part of the quotation). Avoid excessive use of brackets: they make quotations more difficult to read and comprehend. Often paraphrase will serve as well as quotation, particularly if you are not explicitly analyzing the language of a passage.

CORRECT	Terence confesses that "in lovely muck [he's] lain," where he slept "Happ[ily] till [he] woke again" (35–36).
BETTER	Terence confesses that when drunk he's slept in muck—and happily, until he woke up.

Notice that a word or letters within brackets can either replace a word in the original (as in the substitution of *he's* for the original "I've") or be added to explain or complete the original (as with *-ily*). Since a reader understands that brackets signal either substitution or addition, it is super-fluous to include the words for which the substitutions are made.

WRONG	Terence confesses that "in lovely muck I've [he's] lain" (35).

Your sentences, including bracketed words, must read as if there were no brackets:

RIGHT	Terence summarizes his philosophy when he advises his friend that

> since the world has still
> Much good, but much less good than ill,
> And . . . / Luck's a chance, but trouble's sure,
> [He should] face it as a wise man would,
> And train for ill and not for good. (43–48)

Q9. It is permissible to omit words from quoted material, but *only* if the omission is indicated. Three *spaced* periods are used to indicate the omission (technically they are called "ellipsis points"). The third line in the preceding quotation is an example. If there are four periods, one is the normal period at the end of a sentence; the other three indicate the ellipsis.

The statement just concluded, if quoted, might be shortened in the following way: "It is permissible to omit words . . . if the omission is indicated. Three *spaced* periods are used to indicate the omission. . . . If there are four periods, one is the normal period at the end of a sentence."

It is usually not necessary to indicate ellipsis at the beginning or ending of a quotation (the very act of quoting implies that something precedes and follows)—unless what you quote is in some way contradicted by its original context, as for example by a "not" preceding the material you quote.

Q10. Single quotation marks are used for quotations within quotations. Thus, if double quotes occur *within* a run-in quotation, they should be reduced to single quotes. (In a block quotation, the quotation marks would remain unchanged.)

> Terence (who speaks the whole poem) begins by quoting a complaining friend. To the demand for "'a tune to dance to,'" Terence instead offers a defense of sober poetry that will "do good to heart and head" (14, 55).

Single quotation marks are not used for any other purposes and should not be substituted for double quotes.

Q11. At the conclusion of a run-in quotation, commas and periods are conventionally placed *within* quotation marks; semicolons and colons are placed outside. (The convention is based on appearance, not on logic.) Question marks and exclamation points are placed inside if they belong to the quoted sentence, outside if they belong to your sentence. (This *is* based on logic.) Special rules apply when the quotation is followed by parenthetical documentation (see PD4, page 336). The following examples are all correct:

> "Mithridates, he died old," Terence concludes (76).
> Terence concludes, "Mithridates, he died old" (76).
> "[W]hy was Burton built on Trent?" Terence asks (18).
> Does Housman endorse the friend's preference for "a tune to dance to" (14)?

VIII. Documentation

Documentation is the process of identifying the sources of materials used in your essay. The sources are of two kinds: primary and secondary. *Primary* sources are materials written *by* the author being studied, and may be confined to the single work being discussed. *Secondary* sources are materials by other writers *about* the author or work being discussed, or materials having some bearing on that work. Documentation serves two purposes: (1) it enables your readers to check any material they may think you have misinterpreted and (2) it enables you to make proper acknowledgment of information, ideas, opinions, or phraseology that are not your own.

It is difficult to overemphasize the second of these purposes. The use of someone else's ideas or insights in your own words, since it does not require quotation marks, makes an even heavier demand for acknowledgment than does quoted material. Although you need not document matters of common knowledge, your use without acknowledgment of material that is uniquely someone else's is not only dishonest but illegal (plagiarism), and could result in penalties ranging from an F on the essay through expulsion from school to a term in jail, depending on the magnitude of the offense.

Documentation may be given in (1) the text of your essay; (2) a parenthesis placed within the text of your essay; or (3) a list of Works Cited placed at the end of your essay but keyed to parenthetical references within the essay. The three methods are progressively more formal.

In any case, the type of documentation required in your class will be chosen by your instructor, who may wish to have you practice several methods so that you will learn their use.

1. Textual Documentation

Every literary essay contains textual documentation. A title like "Dramatic Irony in 'My Last Duchess'" identifies the poem that will furnish the main materials in an essay. A paragraph beginning "In the second verse paragraph . . ." locates more specifically the source of what follows. An informally documented essay is one that relies on textual documentation exclusively. Perhaps the majority of articles published in newspapers and periodicals with wide circulation are of this kind. Informal documentation works best for essays written on a single short work, without use of secondary sources, for readers without great scholarly expectations. A first-rate essay could be written on Wallace Stevens's "Sunday Morning" using only textual documentation. The poet's name and the title of the poem mentioned somewhere near the beginning of the essay, plus a few phrases such as "In the opening stanza" or "In the vision of the orgiastic future" or "The final image of the pigeons" might provide all the documentation needed for this audience. The poem is short enough that the reader can easily locate any detail within it. If the essay is intended for the hypothetical journal published by your literature class (all of whose members are using the same text), its readers can readily locate the poem. But the informal method, although less appropriate, can also be used for more complex subjects, and can even accommodate secondary sources with phrases such as "As Helen Vendler points out in her study of Stevens's longer poems. . . ."

Principles and Guidelines

TD1. Enclose titles of short stories, articles, and poems (unless they are book-length) in quotation marks; italicize titles of plays, magazines, newspapers, and books. Do not italicize or put the title of your own essay in quotation marks. The general principle is that titles of separate publications are italicized; titles of selections or parts of books are put within quotation marks. Full-length plays, such as *Othello* and *Oedipus Rex,* although often reprinted as part of an anthology, are elsewhere published as separate books and should be italicized.

TD2. Capitalize the first word and all important words in titles. Do not capitalize articles, prepositions, and conjunctions except when they begin the title ("The Unknown Citizen," "To the Virgins, to Make Much of Time," "A Study of Reading Habits").

TD3. When the title above a poem is identical with its first line or a major part of its first line, there is a strong presumption that the poet left the poem untitled and the editor or anthologist has used the first line or part of it to serve as a title. In such a case you may *use* the first line as a title, but should not *refer* to it as a title. For example, you might write that "Dickinson's 'There's a certain Slant of light' is a powerful poem about a depressed psychological state." But you should not write, "Dickinson repeats her title in the first line of 'There's a certain Slant of light' because she wants to emphasize her main point." In using it as a title, capitalize only those words that are capitalized in the first line.

TD4. Never use page numbers in the body of your discussion because a page is not a structural part of a poem. You may refer in your discussion to verse paragraphs, sections, stanzas, and lines, as appropriate, but use page numbers *only* in parenthetical documentation where a specific edition of the work has been named.

TD5. Spell out numerical references when they precede the unit they refer to; use numbers when they follow the unit (the second paragraph, or paragraph 2; the fourth line, or line 4; the tenth stanza, or stanza 10). Use the first of these alternative forms sparingly, and only with small numbers. Never write "In the thirty-fourth and thirty-fifth lines . . . ," for to do so is to waste good space and irritate your reader; write "In lines 34–35. . . ."

2. Parenthetical Documentation

Parenthetical documentation allows brief citations of sources for the quotations, paraphrases, or other uses of ideas that you incorporate into your writing assignments in an introductory literature course, and in other essays that you might have occasion to undertake as well. The brief information given in parenthetical documentation directs your reader to the full bibliographic information for your source that is listed in the Works Cited section at the end of your essay. The parenthetical information might be as simple as giving the surnames of one or more authors or editors of a given source, with a page number, or a range of page numbers, as appropriate. For the readers of our hypothetical journal, the reference to a poem might look like this:

> In Robert Frost's "Home Burial" (Johnson and Arp 291), the poet examines . . .

In subsequent references, only inclusive line numbers need be given:

> Amy's silent gesture underscores her sense that her husband cannot understand her feelings: "Her fingers moved the latch for all reply" (44).

If more than one source is used, each must be identified, if referred to subsequently, by an abbreviated version of the Works Cited entry, normally the author's last name, or if several works by a single author are cited, by the author's last name and a shortened title. In any case, use the shortest identification that will differentiate the source from all the others.

Principles and Guidelines

PD1. After its first reference, your principal primary source requires only a page reference. For long poems, however, it may be more useful to give line or stanza numbers, if these are easily available, rather than page numbers. For a short poem, line numbers are unnecessary and should be omitted; nor is there any need to cite a page number. For plays in verse, citation by line number (preceded by act and scene number) will usually be more useful than citation by page—for example, *Othello* (5.2.133).

PD2. Documentation for run-in quotations always follows the quotation marks. If the quotation ends with a period, move it to the end of the documentation. If it ends with an exclamation point or question mark, leave it, but put a period after the documentation as well. The following examples are from "Home Burial":

> "She moved the latch a little. 'Don't—don't go.'" (56).
> "'There you go sneering now!'" (67).

PD3. With block quotations, parenthetical documentation follows the last mark of punctuation without further punctuation after the parentheses.

> He saw her from the bottom of the stairs
> Before she saw him. She was starting down,
> Looking back over her shoulder at some fear. (1–3)

PD4. Avoid cluttering your essay with excessive documentation. When possible, use one note to cover a series of short quotations. (See example, Q1.) Remember that short poems need no parenthetical documentation at all after the first reference. Do not document well-known sayings or proverbs that you use for stylistic purposes and that form no part of the substance of your investigation (and of course be wary of including hackneyed commonplaces in your formal writing).

PD5. It is customary in a formal essay to document all quoted materials. Do not, however, assume that *only* quotations need documentation. The first purpose of documentation (see page 332) is to allow the reader to check the primary text concerning any major or possibly controversial interpretation. If you declare, for example, that the climax of a long poem occurs in a passage that you choose not to quote for full analysis, it may be more important for the reader to have line numbers for that passage than quotations from the poem. Judgment must be exercised.

> The vividness with which Amy recalls her husband's remark
> the morning of the burial is evidence that the words have been
> preying on her mind (92–93).

3. Documentation by Works Cited

When your assignment requires you to use secondary sources, your instructor may require you to create a list of "Works Cited" to be located at the end of your essay. Any book, article, website, or other source you use or quote from must be referenced parenthetically in the body of your essay so that the reader can easily locate the complete source in your Works Cited list.

Your first step should be to create the Works Cited list (no longer called a "Bibliography," for it commonly cites not just books but other sources of information as well). Use the new Works Cited format first detailed in the eighth edition of the *MLA Handbook*. Then you should locate each instance in your essay where you have quoted from or paraphrased a source. In order to identify the source, you should normally give the author's last name and the page number from which the quotation or paraphrase is taken.

For example, let's say you are writing a research essay on Emily Dickinson and one of your sources is David Porter's book *The Art of Emily Dickinson's Early Poetry*. Typically you would cite a quotation from the book in this manner: (Porter 141). There are instances, however, in which more information might be needed. For example, David Porter also wrote another book on Dickinson, called *Dickinson: The Modern Idiom*. If both of Porter's books are in your Works Cited list, then, in each instance of quotation or paraphrase, you need to identify the source parenthetically by using a shortened form of the title of the particular book you are citing. These citations might follow the form as follows: (Porter, *Early Poetry,* 141) or (Porter, *Modern Idiom*, 252). The key principle to remember is that you should keep the parenthetical citations as brief and clear as possible so that your reader will have no trouble finding the particular source you are citing.

Here is another example of when you must provide more information than just the author's last name and the relevant page number or numbers: you might have, for example, two authors in your Works Cited list with the last name of Smith. In this case, you need to be specific about which of the two authors you are quoting. Thus, the parenthetical citations might read (M. Smith 88) or (J. Smith 138). Note that the initial is required only when there are two sources on the Works Cited list whose primary authors share the same last name.

Always keep the *MLA Handbook* nearby when preparing the parenthetical documentation and the Works Cited list. The new MLA format for Works Cited entries emphasizes nine core elements and formats them consistently regardless of whether a given source is a book, journal article, online database, blog, podcast, or any of a number of other sources of information. The nine core elements, in order, are

1. author
2. title of source
3. title of the larger source (or "container"), such as the journal (container) in which an article (source) is published, or the volume (container), assembled by an editor, that contains chapters (sources) contributed by different authors.
4. other contributors
5. version (such as a revised or updated edition)
6. number (such as volume and issue numbers for periodicals, or season and episode numbers for television shows)

7. publisher (note that "Harvard UP," for example, is to be used rather than "Harvard University Press"). Note that the city where the publisher is located is *not* listed.
8. publication date
9. location, meaning the specific place (such as the page number or DOI—digital object identifier) in the source where the quoted or paraphrased material can be found.

The *MLA Handbook* provides many illustrative examples of cited entries. Here are some additional examples:

Single-Authored Book

Buckingham, Willis J. *Emily Dickinson: An Annotated Bibliography.* Indiana UP, 1970.

Dual-Authored Book

Gilbert, Sandra M., and Susan Gubar. *The Madwoman in the Attic: The Woman Writer and the Nineteenth-Century Literary Imagination.* Reprint. Yale UP, 2000.

Two Works by the Same Author

Porter, David. *The Art of Emily Dickinson's Early Poetry.* Harvard UP, 1966.
-------. *Dickinson: The Modern Idiom.* Harvard UP, 1981.

Book with an Author and an Editor

Dickinson, Emily. *Selected Letters.* Edited by Thomas H. Johnson, Harvard UP, 1986.

Selection from an Anthology or Textbook

Dickinson, Emily. "Because I could not stop for Death." *Perrine's Sound and Sense: An Introduction to Poetry*, edited by Greg Johnson and Thomas R. Arp, 13th ed., Cengage, 2017, p. 106.

Journal Article

Wilson, Suzanne M. "Structural Patterns in the Poetry of Emily Dickinson." *American Literature*, vol. 35, 1963, pp. 53–59.

Journal Article Online

Winther, Per. "On Editing Emily Dickinson." *American Studies in Scandinavia*, vol. 11, 1979, pp. 25–40, http://ej.lib.cbs.dk/index.php/assc/article/viewFile/1617/1647

Magazine Article

Stamm, Edith Perry. "Emily Dickinson: Poetry and Punctuation." *Saturday Review*, vol. 46, 30 March 1963, pp. 26ff.

Newspaper Article Online

Gordinier, Jeff. Emily Dickinson: Sweet Genius." *Diner's Journal: The New York Times Blog on Dining Out*, 19 Oct. 2011, 5:24 p.m. Dinersjournal. blogs.nytimes.com/2011/10/19/emily-dickinson-sweet-genius/?_r=0

Television Program

"Loaded Gun: Life, Death, and Dickinson." *Independent Lens*, produced, directed, and written by Jim Wolpaw, Independent Television Service (ITVS), 2015.

4. Documentation of Electronic Sources

As with all sources, electronic sources are cited in your essay as brief parenthetical references and then in full in your list of Works Cited. However, unlike textual sources, which usually clearly state author, title, date of publication, and publisher, electronic sources may or may not provide information that enables your reader to access the exact source of your materials.

Your parenthetical citations normally will include the name of the author and a page number. If the source is not paginated, the name of the author may suffice; if it is divided by paragraphs, sections, or screen numbers, after the author's name use abbreviations "par." or "sec.," or the word "screen," followed by the appropriate number.

Here are examples of parenthetical citations from an essay on Robert Frost's "Home Burial." Following the list of examples are the full source citations as they appear in the Works Cited section of the essay.

Scholarly Project or Information Database

Frost believed that the best poems were those that sounded like people talking when read aloud (Pritchard).

Document within a Scholarly Project of Information Database

Some scholars believe that "Home Burial" is an autobiographical poem, given that Frost's eldest child died in 1900 ("Robert Lee Frost" sec. 1).

Article in Scholarly Journal

Scholars note that Frost's goal was to demonstrate the beauty in everyday speech and language by incorporating dialogue into his poems (Evans).

Article in an Encyclopedia

Although he was born in San Francisco, Frost felt more at home in New England, which often served as the setting in his poems ("Frost, Robert" par.1).

Work from an Online Service

Scholars note that "Home Burial" exemplifies Frost's other work, which studies how places and settings change in light of human suffering and tragedy ("Frost, Robert" *Encyclopedia*).

CD-ROM Nonperiodical Publication

According to the *Oxford English Dictionary*, the word *home* can refer not only to the place where one lives but also to the place of final rest after death ("Home").

Works Cited

Evans, William R. "Frost's 'Sound of Sense' and a Popular Audience." *American Literature*, vol. 53, no. 1, 1981, pp. 116–124.

"Frost, Robert." *Encyclopedia Britannica*, 2006. Encyclopedia Britannica Premium Service. 15 Mar. 2006. www.britannica.com/eb/article—9035504.

"Frost, Robert." *Encyclopedia Britannica*, 2006. Infoplease.com. 7 Mar. 2006. Keyword: Robert Frost.

"Home." *The Oxford English Dictioinary*, 2nd ed. CD-ROM. Oxford UP, 2001.

Pritchard, William H. "Frost's Life and Career." *Modern American Poetry,* Feb. 2000. www.english.uiuc.edu/maps/poets/a_f/frost/life.html.

"Robert Lee Frost." Contemporary Literary Criticism, 2003. Gale Group. www.galenet.com/servlet.

University of Texas Library, 8 Mar. 2006. www.lib.utexas.edu/indexes/s-Literaturesinenglish.html.

IX. Stance and Style

In section II, "For Whom Do You Write?", we discussed the assumed audience for your critical writing. Now we must consider the other half of the reader/writer equation. We might ask the parallel question "Who Are You?" except that would imply that we are asking about your own personal identity. Rather, since we defined your audience hypothetically as members of your class, we need to define "you" in terms of the voice that your audience will expect and appreciate. There are certain conventional expectations that are aroused when we read critical analyses of literature, and what follows are a few suggestions that may lead you to adopt the stance that your readers will expect. If these sound prescriptive (or if your instructor suggests others), remember that writing about literature is essentially persuasive writing, its purpose being to persuade your readers to agree with your interpretation; the means of persuasion are many, and the writer's stance is only one of them. What we provide here are a few "hints" that have been valuable to students in the past, and may be helpful to you.

S1. *Avoid first-person pronouns.* This injunction warns you away from unnecessarily intruding yourself into your critical statements, with a consequent loss of power and precision. Consider the relative force of these approaches:

POOR	It seems to me that Owen captures the horror of war by describing a man dying of poison gas.
GOOD	Owen captures the horror of war by describing a man dying of poison gas.
BETTER	The image of a man dying of poison gas evokes the horror of war.

The first example dilutes the statement by making it sound tentative and opinionated. It allows your reader to respond, "Why should I consider that seriously, since the writer confesses that it's only a private opinion rather than a fact?" As a critic, you should adopt the stance of the sensitive person who is confident of the accuracy of her or his insights—even when in your heart you may *feel* tentative or unsure. Say it with an air of confidence.

The third example is "better" because it observes the following suggestion.

S2. *Write about the poem.* When analyzing a poem or some aspect of it, you should be sure that the thesis or topic of a paragraph or essay (and its thesis sentences) focuses on your topic. You will usually not be writing about a *poet* but about a *poem,* so try to avoid using the poet's name as the subject.

POOR	Tennyson uses personification when he refers to the eagle's talons as "hands."
	(This focuses on "Tennyson" [subject] and "uses" [verb].)
GOOD	The word "hands" describing the eagle's talons personifies him.
	(Subject, "word"; verb, "personifies.")

Try also to avoid the verb *uses*, since your focus is not on a poet using a poetic device but on the result of that use—not on an author selecting a device to achieve a purpose but on the result of that selection. The easiest way to get rid of the word *use* or the idea of *using* is simply to delete it:

POOR	The speaker uses the word "green" to suggest freshness.
GOOD	The word "green" suggests freshness.

The revised version cuts the wordiness and is more direct.

S3. *Be cautious about passive constructions.* In analyzing literature, the passive voice presents three potential problems: (1) it may fail to identify its subject and thus (2) may introduce vagueness, and (3) it is often a weak and wordy way to say something that you can say directly and forcefully. It may also be a roundabout way to write about an author rather than a work.

POOR	Soldiers with their packs are used as a comparison to beggars with sacks.
GOOD	Soldiers with their packs resemble beggars with sacks.

S4. *Be cautious about praise.* Praising a poem or a poet with such adverbs as *cleverly, carefully, remarkably, beautifully,* and so forth, is much less effective than presenting and analyzing the details that you find praiseworthy. Your opinion is important, but your reader wants the opportunity to share it—and such labeling doesn't really afford that opportunity.

S5. *Avoid preparatory circumlocution.* Don't write a "table of contents" as an introductory paragraph, and eliminate such phrases as "in order to understand X we must examine Y." Just go ahead and examine Y, and trust your reader to recognize its relevance. Another example: "Z is a significant aspect of the poem" (or, even worse, "It is interesting to note that Z is a significant aspect"). If Z is significant, just go ahead and say what it signifies; if it is interesting, let what is interesting about it be your topic.

Such circumlocution is sometimes called "treading water," since it is generally only a way of keeping afloat on the page until you get a good idea of the direction you really want to swim. You wouldn't walk into a room and announce, "I am now going to tell you that I'm here," or "I will tell you how interested you'll be to notice that I'm here." You'd say, "Here I am!"

It is perfectly all right to use such space-wasters in preliminary drafts—as ways of keeping your pen or keyboard in action while you are figuring out which way you are going to swim. Just be sure to edit them from your finished text.

S6. *Avoid negative hypotheses.* An example of negative hypothesis is introduced with an example on page 322, "Proving Your Point." Here's another: "If Shakespeare had made 'Winter' into a sermon, all of the poem's best features would have been lost." But he *didn't,* so a critical analysis can neither speculate about what he might have done had he done otherwise, or prove that what he did do is better by comparison—there is nothing to compare.

On the other hand, in the process of coming to understand a poem (as distinct from presenting the results of that process in your writing), it can be valuable to entertain such hypotheses. For example, in discussing connotation, we suggest that imagining possible alternative words can sharpen your appreciation of the poet's actual choice (see study questions for Dickinson, "There is no Frigate like a Book" [page 42] or Oliver, "Spring in the Classroom" [page 44]).

X. Grammar, Punctuation, and Usage: Common Problems

1. Grammar

G1. In discussing the action of a literary work, rely primarily on the present tense (even when the work itself uses the past), keeping the past, future, and perfect tenses available for prior or subsequent actions; for example:

> When Amy withdraws from her husband and slides
> downstairs "beneath his arm / That [rests] on the banister"
> (31–32), the references to sliding, a staircase, and a banister
> create an ironic allusion to what will be revealed as their central
> concern, the dead child.

G2. Do not let pronouns refer to nouns in the possessive case. Antecedents of pronouns should always hold a strong grammatical position: a possessive is a mere modifier, like an adjective.

WRONG	In Frost's poem "Home Burial," he writes . . .
	(Antecedent of "he" is in possessive case.)
RIGHT	In his poem "Home Burial," Frost writes . . .
	(Antecedent of "his" is the subject of the sentence.)

2. Punctuation

P1. The insertion of a parenthetical phrase in your sentence structure (as, for example, in parenthetical documentation) does not alter the normal punctuation of the rest of the sentence. Do not, as the preceding sentence doesn't, place a comma after a parenthetical phrase unless it belonged there before the parenthesis was inserted. You wouldn't write, "Owen's poem, is about the horror of war," so don't include that comma when you insert a parenthesis.

WRONG	Owens' poem (Johnson and Arp 6) is about the horror of war.

And it is an inflexible rule of punctuation: never place a comma immediately before a parenthesis.

P2. Do not set off restrictive appositives with commas. A restrictive appositive is one necessary to the meaning of the sentence; a nonrestrictive appositive could be left out without changing the meaning.

WRONG	In his book, *A Boy's Will*, Robert Frost . . .
	(*Without the title we do not know which of Frost's books is referred to. As punctuated, the sentence falsely implies that Frost wrote only one book.*)
RIGHT	In his book *A Boy's Will*, Robert Frost . . .
RIGHT	In his first book, *A Boy's Will*, Robert Frost . . .
	(*The adjective* first *identifies the book. The title simply supplies additional information and could be omitted without changing the meaning.*)

P3. Words used simply as words should be underlined, italicized, or put in quotation marks.

WRONG	The sixth word in "The Road Not Taken" is yellow.
	(*This statement is false; all the words in the poem are black.*)
RIGHT	The sixth word in "The Road Not Taken" is "yellow."

Since the word "yellow" is quoted from the poem, it has here been put in quotation marks. However, if you list a series of words from the poem, you may prefer underlining or italics for the sake of appearance. Whichever system you choose, be consistent throughout your paper.

P4. Observe the conventions of typed manuscripts: (1) put a space after an abbreviating period (p. 7, not p.7; pp. 10–13, not pp.10–13); (2) use two hyphens (--) to represent a dash, and do not put spaces before or after them.

P5. Observe the standard for forming possessives. For a singular noun, add an apostrophe and an *s* (a student's duty, yesterday's mail, the dress's hemline). For a plural noun, add only an apostrophe (the students' duties, seven days' mail). For proper nouns, the same rules apply (Keats's odes, Donne's sonnets, Hopkins's poem).

Do not confuse the contraction *it's* (it is) with the possessive *its* (belonging to it). *Its* is an exception to the general rule requiring apostrophes for possessives.

3. Usage

U1. Although accepted usage changes with time, and the distinctions between the following pairs of words are fading, many instructors will bless you if you try to preserve them.

convince, persuade. Convince pertains to belief (conviction); *persuade* pertains to either action or belief. The following sentences observe the distinction. "In 'To His Coy Mistress' the speaker tries to persuade a young woman to sleep with him." "In 'To His Coy Mistress' the speaker tries to convince a young woman that she has nothing to lose by sleeping with him." "I persuaded him to have another drink although he was convinced he shouldn't."

describe, define. Describe means to delineate the visual appearance of something; *define* means to state the meaning of a word or phrase, or to explain the essential quality of something. Reserve *describe* and *description* for talking about how things look.

disinterested, uninterested. A disinterested judge is one who has no "stake" or personal interest in the outcome of a case and who can therefore judge fairly; an uninterested judge goes to sleep on the bench. A good judge is interested in the case but disinterested in its outcome. An uninterested reader finds reading boring. A disinterested reader? Perhaps one who can enjoy a book whatever its subject matter.

imply, infer. A writer or speaker implies; a reader or listener infers. An implication is a meaning hinted at but not stated outright. An inference is a conclusion drawn from evidence not complete enough for proof. If you imply that I am a snob, I may infer that you do not like me.

lover, beloved. In older literature, the word *lover* usually meant one of two things—a man who was sexually involved, or any person who felt affection or esteem for another person or persons. In the case of the former, *lover* generally designated the male partner and *beloved* his female partner. In the case of the latter usage, no sexual implications are involved.

sensuous, sensual. Sensuous normally pertains to the finer senses, *sensual* to the appetites. Good poetry is sensuous: it appeals through the imagination to the senses. A voluptuous woman, an attractive man, or a rich dessert may have a sensual appeal that stirs a desire for possession.

quote, quotation. The word *quote* was originally only a verb. Today the use of "single quotes" and "double quotes" in reference to quotation marks is almost universally accepted; but, although the use of "quote" for "quotation" is common in informal speech, it is still unacceptable in formal writing.

Note also that quoting is an act performed by the writer about literature, not by the writer of literature.

WRONG	Shakespeare's famous quotation "To be or not to be"...
RIGHT	The famous quotation from Shakespeare, "To be or not to be"...

U2. Some words and phrases to be avoided are the following.

center around. This is a geometrical impossibility. A story may perhaps center *on* a certain feature, but to make it center *around* that feature is to make the hub surround the wheel.

just as. This phrase as a term of comparison is too precise for discussing literature because the adjective *just* means *exactly* or *identical in every possible way,* almost an impossibility in comparing literary works. You should take the trouble to establish the points of similarity and dissimilarity between things that you are comparing.

lifestyle. This overused neologism, especially inappropriate for use with older literature, is too general to mean much. One dictionary defines it as "a person's typical approach to living, including his moral attitudes, preferred entertainment, fads, fashions, etc." If you wish to define someone's moral attitudes, do so; if you try to define a person's "lifestyle," you have a monumental task of all-inclusive definition. It's easier just to avoid it.

348 PART TWO / WRITING ABOUT POETRY

society. The problem with this word is that it is too often used only vaguely as a substitute for some more precise idea. Any poem that does deal with "society" will clearly indicate a *particular* society—the world of servants and workers in sixteenth-century England (Shakespeare's "Winter," page 5) or the world of racial and class distinctions that Langston Hughes evokes in "Cross" (page 47). In those cases, once one has defined the particular society and its characteristics, the term might legitimately be used. But don't use it simply to mean "people in general at that time in that place." And it is important to avoid the glib assumption that *society* makes a person do something. A person's desire to be a member of a social group may lead to actions that appear to be imposed or forced, but what makes a person conform is the desire to be or remain a member, not the fact that there are codes of behavior. See Mary Oliver's "Spring in the Classroom" (page 44).

somewhat (also *rather, more or less, as it were, in a manner*). All of these terms are specifically designed to avoid or evade precision—to create a sense of vagueness. Since clarity and precision are the goals of critical analysis, these terms should be avoided. They also sound wishy-washy, while you should strive to sound firm and convinced.

upset. As an adjective to define an emotional condition, the word is too vague. Your dictionary will tell you that its synonyms are "distressed, disturbed, agitated, perturbed, irritated," and so forth. All of those terms are more precise than *upset,* and the one that most nearly indicates your meaning should be chosen.

what the author is trying to say is. The implication of this expression is that the author *failed* to say it. You don't say "I'm trying to get to Boston" if you are already there; give the author credit for having got where he or she was going.

Others suggested by your instructor:

_____   _____

_____   _____

_____   _____

XI. Writing Samples

1. Explication

"A Study of Reading Habits"

The first noteworthy feature of Philip Larkin's "A Study of Reading Habits" (Johnson and Arp, 25) is the ironic discrepancy between the formal language of its title and the colloquial, slangy, even vulgar language of the poem itself. The title by its tone implies a formal sociological research paper, possibly one that samples a cross section of a population and draws conclusions about people's reading. The poem presents, instead, the confessions of one man whose attitudes toward reading have progressively deteriorated to the point where books seem to him "a load of crap." The poem's real subject, moreover, is not the man's reading habits but the revelation of life and character they provide.

The poem is patterned in three stanzas having an identical rhyme scheme (*abcbac*) and the same basic meter (iambic trimeter). The stanzaic division of the poem corresponds to the internal structure of meaning, for the three stanzas present the speaker at three stages of his life: as schoolboy, adolescent, and adult. Larkin signals the chronological progression in the first lines of the stanzas by the words "When," "Later," and "now." The "now" is the present out of which the adult speaks, recalling the two earlier periods.

The boy he remembers in stanza 1 was unhappy, both in his home and, even more so, at school. Perhaps small and bullied by bigger boys, probably an indifferent student, making poor grades, and scolded by teachers, he found a partial escape from his miseries through reading. The books he read—tales of action and adventure that pitted good guys against bad guys, were full of physical conflict, and ended with victory for the good guys—enabled him to construct a fantasy life in which he identified with the virtuous hero and in his imagination beat up villains twice his size, thus reversing the situations of his real life.

In stanza 2 the speaker recalls his adolescence, when his dreams were of sexual rather than muscular prowess. True to the prediction of "ruining [his] eyes" in stanza 1, he had to wear spectacles, which he describes hyperbolically as "inch-thick"—a further detriment to his social life. To compensate for his lack of success with girls, he envisioned himself as a Dracula figure with cloak and fangs, enjoying a series of sexual triumphs. His reading continued to feed his fantasy life, but, instead of identifying with the virtuous hero, he identified with the glamorous, sexually ruthless villain. The poet puns on the word "ripping" (the speaker "had ripping times in the dark"), implying both the British slang meaning of "splendid" and the violence of the rapist who rips the clothes off his victim.

In stanza 3 the speaker, now a young adult, confesses that he no longer reads much. His accumulated experience of personal failure and his long familiarity with his weaknesses have made it impossible for him to identify, even in fantasy, with the strong, virtuous hero or the viciously potent villain. He can no longer hide from himself the truth that he resembles more closely the weak secondary characters of the escapist tales he picks up. He recognizes himself in the undependable "dude" who fails the heroine, or the cowardly storekeeper who knuckles under to the bad guys. He therefore has turned to a more powerful means of escape, one that protects him from dwelling on what he knows about himself: drunkenness. His final words are memorable— so "unpoetical" in a traditional sense, so poetically effective in characterizing this speaker. "Get stewed," he says, "Books are a load of crap."

It would be a serious mistake to identify the speaker of the poem, or his attitudes or his language, with the poet. Poets, unless they are in a cynical or depressed mood, do not think that "books are a load of crap." Philip Larkin, moreover, an English poet and a graduate of Oxford, was for many years until his death a university librarian (Hamilton, 288). "A Study of Reading Habits" is both dramatic and ironic. It presents a first-person speaker who has been unable to cope with the reality of his life in any of its stages and has, therefore, turned toward various means of escaping it. His confessions reveal a progressive deterioration of values (from good to evil to sodden indifference) and a decline in reading tastes (from adventure stories to prurient sexual novels to none) that reflect his downward slide.

Works Cited

Hamilton, Ian, editor. *The Oxford Companion to Twentieth-Century Poetry*. Oxford UP, 1994.

Johnson, Greg, and Thomas R. Arp. *Perrine's Sound and Sense: An Introduction to Poetry*, 13th ed. Cengage, 2017.

Comments

The title of this essay is enclosed in quotation marks because the writer has used the title of the poem for the title of the essay. The essay uses textual and parenthetical documentation. Line numbers for quotations from the poem are not supplied because the poem is too short to require them: they would serve no useful purpose. Notice that in quoting from stanza 1, the writer has changed the phrase "ruining my eyes" to fit the essay's syntax, but has indicated the alteration by putting the changed word within brackets. The essay is written for an American audience; if it had been written for an English audience the writer would not have needed to explain that "ripping" is British slang or to have made it a point that the poet is English. The essay is documented for an audience using this textbook. If it were directed toward a wider audience, the writer would make reference for the text of the poem not to a textbook or anthology but to the volume of Larkin's poetry containing this poem (*Collected Poems,* ed. Anthony Thwaite [London: Faber, 1988], 131). Also, the writer would probably wish to include the poet's name in his title: Philip Larkin's "A Study of Reading Habits" or An Explication of Larkin's "A Study of Reading Habits." Since Larkin's nationality and his profession as a librarian are not common knowledge, the essay documents a biographical source where that information is found.

2. Analysis

Diction in "Spring in the Classroom"

Mary Oliver's "Spring in the Classroom" (Johnson and Arp 44) surprisingly juxtaposes two contrasted concepts throughout the poem, providing much of its charm as well as its poetic unity. As the poem builds toward its surprise ending, it uses thoughtful and colorful diction to illustrate these concepts.

The poem is divided into two stanzas: in the first, the speaker sets the scene; in the second, she convincingly dramatizes the contrasted concepts through human action. The entire poem employs a first-person plural point of view, suggesting that the particular identity of the speaker is unimportant. She is simply one of a classroom full of like-minded students who while away the school hours by staring out the window and wishing they could escape outside to enjoy the beautiful spring afternoon.

In the first stanza, the two contrasted concepts become clear: one presents the "dry" (1) atmosphere of the classroom, while the other portrays the "greening woodlot" (3) typifying the natural beauty outside, which the students watch with such longing. The classroom has the teacher, "Miss Willow Bangs" (2), the boring lessons, and the barrier-like windows that keep the students inside. The woodlot, however, has "secrets and increases" (4), "hidden nests and kind" (5). Contemplating it, the children feel "warmed" (6), their "old mud blood murmuring" (7), the latter phrase emphasizing its importance through assonance and alliteration. When the students feel too bored, they carve their initials into desk with small knives, in the time-honored schoolroom tradition, and the speaker specifies that their initials are "pulsing" (11) with the "mud blood" mentioned above. The stanza concludes that the children are indignant to be confined "without pity and beyond reason" (12) by their teacher, whose physical description suggests (deceptively, as it turns out) that she is part of the dry schoolroom atmosphere, "her eyes two stones behind glass, / Her legs thick, her heart / In love with pencils and arithmetic" (13–15).

The second stanza pulls back from such close observation to summarize the students' unhappy condition, sitting "like captives" (17) with "one gorgeous day lost after another" (16). They are so angry, the speaker asserts, that they could easily be led to "plot mutiny, even murder" (20). But then the surprise ending arrives:

And then one day, Miss Willow Bangs, we saw you
As we ran wild in our three o'clock escape
Past the abandoned swings; you were leaning
All furry and blooming against the old brick wall
In the Art Teacher's arms. (22–26)

Here the diction once again underscores the meaning, for it turns out that Miss Willow Bangs, far from being a cruel prison warden, also must have been suffering from the dry, unnatural confinement indoors, and longed to be "furry and blooming" in concert with the rest of the natural world outside.

Even the diction found in the poem's title implies the contrasted concepts present throughout the poem. "Spring in the Classroom," in the speaker's eyes, is almost a conflict in terms, since spring, she feels, should

be a time when one is outdoors. The classroom with all its dryness and confinement represents everything against which the speaker's childlike heart
rebels. Only through the careful, selective use of diction is the speaker able
to dramatize this dominant theme.

Comments

The title of this essay is not set off in quotation marks—the writer uses
them only to set off the title of the poem. Line numbers are given for
all direct quotations, except when the quotation is being used a second
time. Note that the writer does not use every possible detail in the poem
to support the essay's thesis, but simply chooses those that underscore
its argument most effectively. The essay includes the general meaning of
the poem as an orientation for the meaningful presentation of the details,
but its main focus is on the quality of language as that contributes to the
general meaning.

PART THREE

Poems for Further
Reading

Sonnenizio on a Line from Drayton

Since there's no help, come let us kiss and part;
or kiss anyway, let's start with that, with the kissing part,
because it's better than the parting part, isn't it—
we're good at kissing, we like how that part goes:
we part our lips, our mouths get near and nearer,   5
then we're close, my breasts, your chest, our bodies partway
to making love, so we might as well, part of me thinks—
the wrong part, I know, the bad part, but still
let's pretend we're at that party where we met
and scandalized everyone, remember that part? Hold me   10
like that again, unbutton my shirt, part of you
wants to I can tell, I'm touching that part and it says
yes, the ardent partisan, let it win you over,
it's hopeless, come, we'll kiss and part forever.

—KIM ADDONIZIO (B. 1954)

Musée des Beaux Arts

About suffering they were never wrong,
The Old Masters: how well they understood
Its human position; how it takes place
While someone else is eating or opening a window or just
    walking dully along;
How, when the aged are reverently, passionately waiting   5
For the miraculous birth, there always must be
Children who did not specially want it to happen, skating
On a pond at the edge of the wood:
They never forgot
That even the dreadful martyrdom must run its course   10
Anyhow in a corner, some untidy spot
Where the dogs go on with their doggy life and the
    torturer's horse
Scratches its innocent behind on a tree.

In Brueghel's *Icarus,* for instance: how everything
    turns away
Quite leisurely from the disaster; the plowman may   15
Have heard the splash, the forsaken cry,

But for him it was not an important failure; the sun shone
As it had to on the white legs disappearing into the green
Water; and the expensive delicate ship that must have seen
Something amazing, a boy falling out of the sky,   20
Had somewhere to get to and sailed calmly on.

—W. H. AUDEN (1907–1973)

On Her Loving Two Equally

I

How strong does my passion flow,
Divided equally twixt two?
Damon had ne'er subdued my heart
Had not Alexis took his part;
Nor could Alexis powerful prove,   5
Without my Damon's aid, to gain my love.

II

When my Alexis present is,
Then I for Damon sigh and mourn;
But when Alexis I do miss,
Damon gains nothing but my scorn.   10
But if it chance they both are by,
For both alike I languish, sigh, and die.

III

Cure then, thou mighty wingéd god,
This restless fever in my blood;
One golden-pointed dart take back: 15
But which, O Cupid, wilt thou take?
If Damon's, all my hopes are crossed;
Or that of my Alexis, I am lost.

—APHRA BEHN (1640–1689)

Manners

for a Child of 1918

My grandfather said to me
as we sat on the wagon seat,

"Be sure to remember to always
speak to everyone you meet."

We met a stranger on foot.   5
My grandfather's whip tapped his hat.
"Good day, sir. Good day. A fine day."
And I said it and bowed where I sat.

Then we overtook a boy we knew
with his big pet crow on his shoulder.   10
"Always offer everyone a ride;
don't forget that when you get older,"

my grandfather said. So Willy
climbed up with us, but the crow
gave a "Caw!" and flew off. I was worried.   15
How would he know where to go?

But he flew a little way at a time
from fence post to fence post, ahead;
and when Willy whistled he answered.
"A fine bird," my grandfather said,   20

"and he's well brought up. See, he answers
nicely when he's spoken to.
Man or beast, that's good manners.
Be sure that you both always do."

When automobiles went by,   25
the dust hid the people's faces,
but we shouted "Good day! Good day!
Fine day!" at the top of our voices.

When we came to Hustler Hill,
he said that the mare was tired,   30
so we all got down and walked,
as our good manners required.

—ELIZABETH BISHOP (1911–1979)

The Garden of Love

I went to the Garden of Love,
And saw what I never had seen:
A Chapel was built in the midst,
Where I used to play on the green.

And the gates of this Chapel were shut,   5
And "Thou shalt not" writ over the door;
So I turned to the Garden of Love
That so many sweet flowers bore;

And I saw it was filled with graves,
And tomb-stones where flowers should be;   10
And Priests in black gowns were walking their rounds,
And binding with briars my joys and desires.

—WILLIAM BLAKE (1757–1827)

a song in the front yard

I've stayed in the front yard all my life.
I want a peek at the back
Where it's rough and untended and hungry weed grows.
A girl gets sick of a rose.

I want to go in the back yard now   5
And maybe down the alley,
To where the charity children play.
I want a good time today.

They do some wonderful things.
They have some wonderful fun.   10

My mother sneers, but I say it's fine
How they don't have to go in at quarter to nine.
My mother, she tells me that Johnnie Mae
Will grow up to be a bad woman.
That George'll be taken to Jail soon or late   15
(On account of last winter he sold our back gate).

But I say it's fine. Honest, I do.
And I'd like to be a bad woman, too,
And wear the brave stockings of night-black lace
And strut down the streets with paint on my face.   20

—GWENDOLYN BROOKS (1917–2000)

Sadie and Maud

Maud went to college.
Sadie stayed at home.
Sadie scraped life
With a fine-tooth comb.

She didn't leave a tangle in.   5
Her comb found every strand.
Sadie was one of the livingest chits
In all the land.

Sadie bore two babies
Under her maiden name.   10
Maud and Ma and Papa
Nearly died of shame.

When Sadie said her last so-long
Her girls struck out from home.
(Sadie had left as heritage   15
Her fine-tooth comb.)

Maud, who went to college,
Is a thin brown mouse.
She is living all alone
In this old house.   20

—GWENDOLYN BROOKS (1917–2000)

She Walks in Beauty

She walks in beauty, like the night
     Of cloudless climes and starry skies,
And all that's best of dark and bright
     Meet in her aspect and her eyes,

Thus mellowed to that tender light   5
    Which heaven to gaudy day denies.

One shade the more, one ray the less,
    Had half impaired the nameless grace
Which waves in every raven tress
    Or softly lightens o'er her face,   10
Where thoughts serenely sweet express
    How pure, how dear their dwelling-place.

And on that cheek and o'er that brow
    So soft, so calm, yet eloquent,
The smiles that win, the tints that glow,   15
    But tell of days in goodness spent,—
A mind at peace with all below,
    A heart whose love is innocent.

                    —GEORGE GORDON, LORD BYRON (1788–1824)

Witness

An ordinary evening in Wisconsin
seen from a Greyhound bus—mute aisles
of merchandise the sole inhabitants
of the half-darkened Five and Ten,

the tables of the single lit café awash   5
with unarticulated pathos, the surface membrane
of the inadvertently transparent instant
when no one is looking: outside town

the barns, their red gone dark with sundown,
withhold the shudder of a warped terrain—   10
the castle rocks above, tree-clogged ravines
already submarine with nightfall, flocks

(like dark sheep) of toehold junipers,
the lucent arms of birches: purity
without a mirror, other than a mind bound   15
elsewhere, to tell it how it looks

                    —AMY CLAMPITT (1920–1994)

good times

My Daddy has paid the rent
and the insurance man is gone
and the lights is back on
and my uncle Brud has hit
for one dollar straight   5
and they is good times
good times
good times

My Mama has made bread
and Grampaw has come   10
and everybody is drunk
and dancing in the kitchen
and singing in the kitchen
oh these is good times
good times   15
good times

oh children think about the
good times

—LUCILLE CLIFTON (1936–2010)

Mask

I tied a paper mask onto my face,
my lips almost inside its small red mouth.
Turning my head to the left, to the right,
I looked like someone I once knew, or was,
with straight white teeth and boyish bangs.   5
My ordinary life had come as far as it would,
like a silver arrow hitting cypress.
Know your place or you'll rue it, I sighed
to the mirror. To succeed, I'd done things
I hated; to be loved, I'd competed promiscuously: 10
my essence seemed to boil down to only this.
Then I saw my own hazel irises float up,
like eggs clinging to a water plant,
seamless and clear, in an empty, pondlike face.

—HENRI COLE (B. 1956)

Kubla Khan

In Xanadu did Kubla Khan
A stately pleasure-dome decree:
Where Alph, the sacred river, ran
Through caverns measureless to man
    Down to a sunless sea.   5
So twice five miles of fertile ground
With walls and towers were girdled round:
And here were gardens bright with sinuous rills,
Where blossomed many an incense-bearing tree;
And here were forests ancient as the hills,   10
Enfolding sunny spots of greenery.

But oh! that deep romantic chasm which slanted
Down the green hill athwart a cedarn cover!
A savage place! as holy and enchanted
As e'er beneath a waning moon was haunted   15
By woman wailing for her demon-lover!
And from this chasm, with ceaseless turmoil seething,
As if this earth in fast thick pants were breathing,
A mighty fountain momently was forced:
Amid whose swift half-intermitted burst   20
Huge fragments vaulted like rebounding hail,
Or chaffy grain beneath the thresher's flail:
And 'mid these dancing rocks at once and ever
It flung up momently the sacred river.
Five miles meandering with a mazy motion   25
Through wood and dale the sacred river ran,
Then reached the caverns measureless to man,
And sank in tumult to a lifeless ocean:
And 'mid this tumult Kubla heard from far
Ancestral voices prophesying war!   30

    The shadow of the dome of pleasure
    Floated midway on the waves;
      Where was heard the mingled measure
    From the fountain and the caves.
It was a miracle of rare device,   35
A sunny pleasure-dome with caves of ice!

    A damsel with a dulcimer
    In a vision once I saw:

It was an Abyssinian maid,
And on her dulcimer she played,   40
Singing of Mount Abora.
Could I revive within me
Her symphony and song,
To such a deep delight, 'twould win me,
That with music loud and long,   45
I would build that dome in air,
That sunny dome! those caves of ice!
And all who heard should see them there,
And all should cry, Beware! Beware!
His flashing eyes, his floating hair!   50
Weave a circle round him thrice,
And close your eyes with holy dread,
For he on honey-dew hath fed,
And drunk the milk of Paradise.

—SAMUEL TAYLOR COLERIDGE (1772–1834)

The Dead

The dead are always looking down on us, they say,
while we are putting on our shoes or making a sandwich,
they are looking down through the glass-bottom boats of heaven
as they row themselves slowly through eternity.

They watch the tops of our heads moving below on earth,   5
and when we lie down in a field or on a couch,
drugged perhaps by the hum of a warm afternoon,
they think we are looking back at them,

which makes them lift their oars and fall silent
and wait, like parents, for us to close our eyes.   10

—BILLY COLLINS (B. 1941)

Weighing the Dog

It is awkward for me and bewildering for him
as I hold him in my arms in the small bathroom,
balancing our weight on the shaky blue scale,

but this is the way to weigh a dog and easier
than training him to sit obediently on one spot   5
with his tongue out, waiting for the cookie.

With pencil and paper I subtract my weight
from our total to find out the remainder that is his,
and I start to wonder if there is an analogy here.

It could not have to do with my leaving you   10
though I never figured out what you amounted to
until I subtracted myself from our combination.

You held me in your arms more than I held you
through all those awkward and bewildering months
and now we are both lost in strange and distant
  neighborhoods.   15

—BILLY COLLINS (B. 1941)

War Is Kind

Do not weep, maiden, for war is kind.
Because your lover threw wild hands toward the sky
And the affrighted steed ran on alone,
Do not weep.
War is kind.   5

  Hoarse, booming drums of the regiment,
  Little souls who thirst for fight,
  These men were born to drill and die.
  The unexplained glory flies above them,
  Great is the battle god, great, and his kingdom   10
  A field where a thousand corpses lie.

Do not weep, babe, for war is kind.
Because your father tumbled in the yellow trenches,
Raged at his breast, gulped and died,
Do not weep.
War is kind.   15

Swift blazing flag of the regiment,
Eagle with crest of red and gold,
These men were born to drill and die.
Point for them the virtue of slaughter,   20
Make plain for them the excellence of killing
And a field where a thousand corpses lie.

Mother whose heart hung humble as a button
On the bright splendid shroud of your son,
Do not weep.   25
War is kind.

—STEPHEN CRANE (1871–1900)

Buffalo Bill's defunct

Buffalo Bill's
defunct
            who used to
            ride a watersmooth-silver
                                    stallion   5
and break onetwothreefourfive pigeonsjustlikethat
                                                          Jesus

he was a handsome man
                              and what i want to know is
how do you like your blueeyed boy
Mister Death   10

—e. e. cummings (1894–1962)

the Cambridge ladies who live in furnished souls

the Cambridge ladies who live in furnished souls
are unbeautiful and have comfortable minds
(also, with the church's protestant blessings
daughters, unscented shapeless spirited)
they believe in Christ and Longfellow, both dead,   5
are invariably interested in so many things—

at the present writing one still finds
delighted fingers knitting for the is it Poles?
perhaps. While permanent faces coyly bandy
scandal of Mrs. N and Professor D   10
. . . .the Cambridge ladies do not care, above
Cambridge if sometimes in its box of
sky lavender and cornerless, the
moon rattles like a fragment of angry candy

—e. e. cummings (1894–1962)

I died for Beauty—but was scarce

I died for Beauty—but was scarce
Adjusted in the Tomb
When One who died for Truth, was lain
In an adjoining Room—

He questioned softly "Why I failed"?   5
"For Beauty", I replied—
"And I—for Truth—Themself are One—
We Brethren, are", He said—

And so, as Kinsmen, met a Night—
We talked between the Rooms—   10
Until the Moss had reached our lips—
And covered up—our names—

—EMILY DICKINSON (1830–1886)

Song: Go and catch a falling star

Go and catch a falling star,
    Get with child a mandrake root,
Tell me where all past years are,
    Or who cleft the devil's foot,
Teach me to hear mermaids singing,   5
    Or to keep off envy's stinging,
        And find
        What wind
Serves to advance an honest mind.

If thou be'st born to strange sights,   10
   Things invisible to see,
Ride ten thousand days and nights,
   Till age snow white hairs on thee;
Thou, when thou return'st, wilt tell me
   All strange wonders that befell thee,   15
     And swear
     No where
Lives a woman true and fair.

If thou find'st one, let me know;
   Such a pilgrimage were sweet.   20
Yet do not; I would not go,
   Though at next door we might meet.
Though she were true when you met her,
   And last till you write your letter,
     Yet she   25
     Will be
False, ere I come, to two or three.

—JOHN DONNE (1572–1631)

(2) *mandrake:* supposed to resemble a human being because of its forked root.

The Apparition

When by thy scorn, O murderess, I am dead,
   And that thou thinkst thee free
From all solicitation from me,
Then shall my ghost come to thy bed,
And thee, feigned vestal, in worse arms shall see;   5
Then thy sick taper° will begin to wink,   candle
And he, whose thou art then, being tired before,
Will, if thou' stir, or pinch to wake him, think
   Thou call'st for more,
And in false sleep will from thee shrink.   10
And then, poor aspen wretch, neglected, thou,
Bathed in a cold quicksilver sweat, wilt lie
   A verier° ghost than I.   truer
What I will say, I will not tell thee now,
Lest that preserve thee; and since my love is spent,   15

I had rather thou shouldst painfully repent,
Than by my threatenings rest still innocent.

—JOHN DONNE (1572–1631)

The Good-Morrow

I wonder, by my troth, what thou and I
Did till we loved? were we not weaned till then,
But sucked on country pleasures childishly?
Or snorted we in the seven sleepers' den?
'Twas so; but this, all pleasures fancies be.   5
If ever any beauty I did see,
Which I desired, and got, 'twas but a dream of thee.

And now good-morrow to our waking souls,
Which watch not one another out of fear;
For love all love of other sights controls,   10
And makes one little room an everywhere.
Let sea-discoverers to new worlds have gone;
Let maps to other,° worlds on worlds have shown; others
Let us possess one world; each hath one, and is one.

My face in thine eye, thine in mine appears,   15
And true plain hearts do in the faces rest;
Where can we find two better hemispheres
Without sharp north, without declining west?
Whatever dies was not mixed equally;
If our two loves be one, or thou and I   20
Love so alike that none can slacken, none can die.

—JOHN DONNE (1572–1631)

(4) *seven sleepers' den:* a cave where, according to Christian legend, seven youths escaped persecution and slept for two centuries.

Pescadero

The little goats like my mouth and fingers,

and one stands up against the wire fence, and taps on the fence board
a hoof made blacker by the dirt of the field,

pushes her mouth forward to my mouth,
so that I can see the smallish squared seeds of her teeth,   5
and the bristle-whiskers,

and then she kisses me, though I know it doesn't mean "kiss,"

then leans her head way back, arcing her spine, goat yoga,
all pleasure and greeting and then good-natured indifference: she loves me,

she likes me a lot, she takes interest in me, she doesn't know me at all   10
or need to, having thus acknowledged me. Though I am all happiness,

since I have been welcomed by the field's small envoy, and the splayed hoof,
fragrant with soil, has rested on the fence board beside my hand.

—MARK DOTY (B. 1953)

Sympathy

   I know what the caged bird feels, alas!
     When the sun is bright on the upland slopes;
When the wind stirs soft through the springing grass,
And the river flows like a stream of glass;
     When the first bird sings and the first bud opes,   5
And the faint perfume from its chalice steals—
I know what the caged bird feels!

I know why the caged bird beats his wing
     Till its blood is red on the cruel bars;
For he must fly back to his perch and cling   10
When he fain would be on the bough a-swing;
     And a pain still throbs in the old, old scars
And they pulse again with a keener sting—
I know why he beats his wing!

I know why the caged bird sings, ah me,   15
     When his wing is bruised and his bosom sore;—
When he beats his bars and he would be free;
It is not a carol of joy or glee,
     But a prayer that he sends from his heart's deep core,

But a plea, that upward to Heaven he flings— 20
I know why the caged bird sings!

—PAUL LAURENCE DUNBAR (1872–1906)

I Sit and Sew

I sit and sew—a useless task it seems,
My hands grown tired, my head weighed down with dreams—
The panoply of war, the martial tred of men,
Grim-faced, stern-eyed, gazing beyond the ken
Of lesser souls, whose eyes have not seen Death, 5
Nor learned to hold their lives but as a breath—
But—I must sit and sew.

I sit and sew—my heart aches with desire—
That pageant terrible, that fiercely pouring fire
On wasted fields, and writhing grotesque things 10
Once men. My soul in pity flings
Appealing cries, yearning only to go
There in that holocaust of hell, those fields of woe—
But—I must sit and sew.

The little useless seam, the idle patch; 15
Why dream I here beneath my homely thatch,
When there they lie in sodden mud and rain,
Pitifully calling me, the quick ones and the slain?
You need me, Christ! It is no roseate dream
That beckons me—this pretty futile seam, 20
It stifles me—God, must I sit and sew?

—ALICE MOORE DUNBAR-NELSON (1875–1935)

Birches

When I see birches bend to left and right
Across the lines of straighter darker trees,
I like to think some boy's been swinging them.
But swinging doesn't bend them down to stay
As ice-storms do. Often you must have seen them 5
Loaded with ice a sunny winter morning

After a rain. They click upon themselves
As the breeze rises, and turn many-colored
As the stir cracks and crazes their enamel.
Soon the sun's warmth makes them shed crystal shells   10
Shattering and avalanching on the snow-crust—
Such heaps of broken glass to sweep away
You'd think the inner dome of heaven had fallen.
They are dragged to the withered bracken by the load,
And they seem not to break; though once they are bowed   15
So low for long, they never right themselves:
You may see their trunks arching in the woods
Years afterwards, trailing their leaves on the ground
Like girls on hands and knees that throw their hair
Before them over their heads to dry in the sun.   20
But I was going to say when Truth broke in
With all her matter-of-fact about the ice-storm
I should prefer to have some boy bend them
As he went out and in to fetch the cows—
Some boy too far from town to learn baseball,   25
Whose only play was what he found himself,
Summer or winter, and could play alone.
One by one he subdued his father's trees
By riding them down over and over again
Until he took the stiffness out of them,   30
And not one but hung limp, not one was left
For him to conquer. He learned all there was
To learn about not launching out too soon
And so not carrying the tree away
Clear to the ground. He always kept his poise   35
To the top branches, climbing carefully
With the same pains you use to fill a cup
Up to the brim, and even above the brim.
Then he flung outward, feet first, with a swish,
Kicking his way down through the air to the ground.   40
So was I once myself a swinger of birches.
And so I dream of going back to be.
It's when I'm weary of considerations,
And life is too much like a pathless wood
Where your face burns and tickles with the cobwebs   45
Broken across it, and one eye is weeping
From a twig's having lashed across it open.
I'd like to get away from earth awhile

And then come back to it and begin over.
May no fate willfully misunderstand me   50
And half grant what I wish and snatch me away
Not to return. Earth's the right place for love:
I don't know where it's likely to go better.
I'd like to go by climbing a birch tree,
And climb black branches up a snow-white trunk   55
Toward heaven, till the tree could bear no more,
But dipped its top and set me down again.
That would be good both going and coming back.
One could do worse than be a swinger of birches.

—ROBERT FROST (1874–1963)

Mending Wall

Something there is that doesn't love a wall,
That sends the frozen-ground-swell under it,
And spills the upper boulders in the sun;
And makes gaps even two can pass abreast.
The work of hunters is another thing: 5
I have come after them and made repair
Where they have left not one stone on a stone,
But they would have the rabbit out of hiding,
To please the yelping dogs. The gaps I mean,
No one has seen them made or heard them made,   10
But at spring mending-time we find them there.
I let my neighbor know beyond the hill;
And on a day we meet to walk the line
And set the wall between us once again.
We keep the wall between us as we go.   15
To each the boulders that have fallen to each.
And some are loaves and some so nearly balls
We have to use a spell to make them balance:
"Stay where you are until our backs are turned!"
We wear our fingers rough with handling them.   20
Oh, just another kind of outdoor game,
One on a side. It comes to little more:
There where it is we do not need the wall:
He is all pine and I am apple orchard.
My apple trees will never get across   25
And eat the cones under his pines, I tell him.

He only says, "Good fences make good neighbors."
Spring is the mischief in me, and I wonder
If I could put a notion in his head:
"*Why* do they make good neighbors? Isn't it   30
Where there are cows? But here there are no cows.
Before I built a wall I'd ask to know
What I was walling in or walling out,
And to whom I was like to give offense.
Something there is that doesn't love a wall,   35
That wants it down." I could say "Elves" to him,
But it's not elves exactly, and I'd rather
He said it for himself. I see him there,
Bringing a stone grasped firmly by the top
In each hand, like an old-stone savage armed.   40
He moves in darkness as it seems to me,
Not of woods only and the shade of trees.
He will not go behind his father's saying,
And he likes having thought of it so well
He says again, "Good fences make good neighbors."   45

—ROBERT FROST (1874–1963)

Cousins

My son's very graceful; he has perfect balance.
He's not competitive, like my sister's daughter.

Day and night, she's always practicing.
Today, it's hitting softballs into the copper beech,
retrieving them, hitting them again.   5
After a while, no one even watches her.
If she were any stronger, the tree would be bald.

My son won't play with her; he won't even ride bicycles with her.
She accepts that; she's used to playing by herself.
The way she sees it, it isn't personal: 10
whoever won't play doesn't like losing.

It's not that my son's inept, that he doesn't do things well.
I've watched him race: he's natural, effortless—
right from the first, he takes the lead.

And then he stops. It's as though he was born rejecting   15
the solitude of the victor.

My sister's daughter doesn't have that problem.
She may as well be first; she's already alone.

—LOUISE GLÜCK (B. 1943)

Primavera

Spring comes quickly: overnight
the plum tree blossoms,
the warm air fills with bird calls.

In the plowed dirt, someone has drawn a picture of the sun
with rays coming out all around   5
but because the background is dirt, the sun is black.
There is no signature.

Alas, very soon everything will disappear:
the bird calls, the delicate blossoms. In the end,
even the earth itself will follow the artist's name into oblivion.   10

Nevertheless, the artist intends
a mood of celebration.

How beautiful the blossoms are—emblems of the resilience of life.
The birds approach eagerly.

—LOUISE GLÜCK (B. 1943)

"Ah, Are You Digging on My Grave?"

"Ah, are you digging on my grave
    My loved one?—planting rue?"
—"No: yesterday he went to wed
One of the brightest wealth has bred.
'It cannot hurt her now,' he said,   5
    'That I should not be true.'"

"Then who is digging on my grave?
    My nearest dearest kin?"

—"Ah, no: they sit and think, 'What use!
'What good will planting flowers produce?   10
No tendance of her mound can loose
   Her spirit from Death's gin.'"°   snare

"But some one digs upon my grave?
   My enemy?—prodding sly?"
—"Nay: when she heard you had passed the Gate   15
That shuts on all flesh soon or late,
She thought you no more worth her hate,
   And cares not where you lie."

"Then, who is digging on my grave?
   Say—since I have not guessed!"   20
—"O it is I, my mistress dear,
Your little dog, who still lives near,
And much I hope my movements here
   Have not disturbed your rest?"

"Ah, yes! *You* dig upon my grave . . .   25
   Why flashed it not on me
That one true heart was left behind!
What feeling do we ever find
To equal among human kind
   A dog's fidelity!"   30

"Mistress, I dug upon your grave
   To bury a bone, in case
I should be hungry near this spot
When passing on my daily trot.
I am sorry, but I quite forgot   35
   It was your resting-place."

—THOMAS HARDY (1840–1928)

Channel Firing

That night your great guns, unawares,
Shook all our coffins as we lay,
And broke the chancel window-squares,
We thought it was the Judgment-day

And sat upright. While drearisome 5
Arose the howl of wakened hounds:
The mouse let fall the altar-crumb,
The worms drew back into the mounds,

The glebe cow drooled. Till God called, "No;
It's gunnery practice out at sea 10
Just as before you went below;
The world is as it used to be:

"All nations striving strong to make
Red war yet redder. Mad as hatters
They do no more for Christès sake 15
Than you who are helpless in such matters.

"That this is not the judgment-hour
For some of them's a blessed thing,
For if it were they'd have to scour
Hell's floor for so much threatening. . . . 20

"Ha, ha. It will be warmer when
I blow the trumpet (if indeed
I ever do; for you are men,
And rest eternal sorely need)."

So down we lay again. "I wonder, 25
Will the world ever saner be,"
Said one, "than when He sent us under
In our indifferent century!"

And many a skeleton shook his head.
"Instead of preaching forty year," 30
My neighbour Parson Thirdly said,
"I wish I had stuck to pipes and beer."

Again the guns disturbed the hour,
Roaring their readiness to avenge,
As far inland as Stourton Tower, 35
And Camelot, and starlit Stonehenge.

—THOMAS HARDY (1840–1928)

(35–36) *Stourton Tower:* memorial at the spot where Alfred the Great resisted the invading Danes in 879; *Camelot:* legendary capital of Arthur's kingdom; *Stonehenge:* mysterious circle of huge stones erected in Wiltshire by very early inhabitants of Britain. The three references move backward in time through the historic, the legendary, and the prehistoric.

Hap

If but some vengeful god would call to me
From up the sky, and laugh: 'Thou suffering thing,
Know that thy sorrow is my ecstasy,
That thy love's loss is my hate's profiting!'

Then would I bear it, clench myself, and die,   5
Steeled by the sense of ire unmerited;
Half-eased in that a Powerfuller than I
Had willed and meted me the tears I shed.

But not so. How arrives it joy lies slain,
And why unblooms the best hope ever sown?   10
—Crass Casualty obstructs the sun and rain,
And dicing Time for gladness casts a moan. . . .
These purblind Doomsters had as readily strown
Blisses about my pilgrimage as pain.

—THOMAS HARDY (1840–1928)

The Darkling Thrush

I leant upon a coppice gate
    When Frost was specter-gray,
And Winter's dregs made desolate
    The weakening eye of day.
The tangled bine-stems scored the sky   5
    Like strings of broken lyres,
And all mankind that haunted nigh
    Had sought their household fires.

The land's sharp features seemed to be
    The Century's corpse outleant,   10
His crypt the cloudy canopy,
    The wind his death-lament.
The ancient pulse of germ and birth
    Was shrunken hard and dry,

And every spirit upon earth   15
   Seemed fervourless as I.

At once a voice arose among
   The bleak twigs overhead
In a full-hearted evensong
   Of joy illimited;   20
An aged thrush, frail, gaunt, and small,
   In blast-beruffled plume,
Had chosen thus to fling his soul
   Upon the growing gloom.

So little cause for carolings   25
   Of such ecstatic sound
Was written on terrestrial things
   Afar or nigh around,
That I could think there trembled through
   His happy good-night air   30
Some blessed Hope, whereof he knew
   And I was unaware.

—THOMAS HARDY (1840–1928)

The Ruined Maid

"O 'Melia, my dear, this does everything crown!
Who could have supposed I should meet you in Town?°   London
And whence such fair garments, such prosperi-ty?"
"O didn't you know I'd been ruined?" said she.

"You left us in tatters, without shoes or socks,   5
Tired of digging potatoes, and spudding up docks;
And now you've gay bracelets and bright feathers three!"
"Yes: that's how we dress when we're ruined," said she.

"At home in the barton you said 'thee' and 'thou,'
And 'thik oon,' and 'theäs oon,' and 't'other'; but now   10
Your talking quite fits 'ee for high compa-ny!"
"Some polish is gained with one's ruin," said she.

"Your hands were like paws then, your face blue and bleak
But now I'm bewitched by your delicate cheek,
And your little gloves fit as on any la-dy!"   15
"We never do work when we're ruined," said she.

"You used to call home-life a hag-ridden dream,
And you'd sigh, and you'd sock; but at present you seem
To know not of megrims or melancho-ly!"
"True. One's pretty lively when ruined," said she.   20

"I wish I had feathers, a fine sweeping gown,
And a delicate face, and could strut about Town!"
"My dear—a raw country girl, such as you be,
Cannot quite expect that. You ain't ruined," said she.

—THOMAS HARDY (1840–1928)

Follower

My father worked with a horse-plow,
His shoulders globed like a full sail strung
Between the shafts and the furrow.
The horses strained at his clicking tongue.

An expert. He would set the wing   5
And fit the bright steel-pointed sock.
The sod rolled over without breaking.
At the headrig, with a single pluck

Of reins, the sweating team turned round
And back into the land. His eye   10
Narrowed and angled at the ground,
Mapping the furrow exactly.

I stumbled in his hobnailed wake,
Fell sometimes on the polished sod;
Sometimes he rode me on his back   15
Dipping and rising to his plod.

I wanted to grow up and plow,
To close one eye, stiffen my arm.
All I ever did was follow
In his broad shadow round the farm.   20

I was a nuisance, tripping, falling,
Yapping always. But today

It is my father who keeps stumbling
Behind me, and will not go away.

—SEAMUS HEANEY (1939–2013)

Love

Love bade me welcome; yet my soul drew back,
    Guilty of dust and sin.
But quick-eyed Love, observing me grow slack
    From my first entrance in,
Drew nearer to me, sweetly questioning   5
    If I lacked anything.

"A guest," I answered, "worthy to be here."
    Love said, "You shall be he."
"I, the unkind, ungrateful? Ah my dear,
    I cannot look on Thee."   10
Love took my hand, and smiling, did reply,
    "Who made the eyes but I?"

"Truth, Lord, but I have marred them; let my shame
    Go where it doth deserve."
"And know you not," says Love, "who bore the blame?"   15
    "My dear, then I will serve."
"You must sit down," says Love, "and taste my meat."
    So I did sit and eat.

—GEORGE HERBERT (1593–1633)

Peace

Sweet Peace, where dost thou dwell? I humbly crave,
    Let me once know.
  I sought thee in a secret cave,
    And asked if Peace were there.
A hollow wind did seem to answer, "No,   5
    Go seek elsewhere."

I did, and going did a rainbow note.
    "Surely," thought I,
  "This is the lace of Peace's coat;

I will search out the matter."   10
But while I looked, the clouds immediately
       Did break and scatter.

Then went I to a garden, and did spy
       A gallant flower,
   The Crown Imperial. "Sure," said I,   15
    "Peace at the root must dwell."
But when I digged, I saw a worm devour
       What showed so well.

At length I met a reverend good old man,
       Whom when for Peace   20
   I did demand, he thus began:
    "There was a prince of old
At Salem dwelt, who lived with good increase
       Of flock and fold.

"He sweetly lived; yet sweetness did not save   25
       His life from foes.
   But after death out of his grave
       There sprang twelve stalks of wheat;
Which many wondering at, got some of those
       To plant and set.   30

"It prospered strangely, and did soon disperse
       Through all the earth,
   For they that taste it do rehearse°   *declare*
    That virtue lies therein,
A secret virtue, bringing peace and mirth   35
       By flight of sin.

"Take of this grain, which in my garden grows,
       And grows for you;
   Make bread of it; and that repose
       And peace, which everywhere   40
With so much earnestness you do pursue,
       Is only there."

—GEORGE HERBERT (1593–1633)

"Terence, this is stupid stuff"

"Terence, this is stupid stuff:
You eat your victuals fast enough;
There can't be much amiss, 'tis clear,
To see the rate you drink your beer.
But oh, good Lord, the verse you make,   5
It gives a chap the belly-ache.
The cow, the old cow, she is dead;
It sleeps well, the horned head:
We poor lads, 'tis our turn now
To hear such tunes as killed the cow.   10
Pretty friendship 'tis to rhyme
Your friends to death before their time
Moping melancholy mad:
Come, pipe a tune to dance to, lad."

Why, if 'tis dancing you would be,   15
There's brisker pipes than poetry.
Say, for what were hop-yards meant,
Or why was Burton built on Trent?
Oh many a peer of England brews
Livelier liquor than the Muse,   20
And malt does more than Milton can
To justify God's ways to man.
Ale, man, ale's the stuff to drink
For fellows whom it hurts to think:
Look into the pewter pot   25
To see the world as the world's not.
And faith, 'tis pleasant till 'tis past:
The mischief is that 'twill not last.
Oh I have been to Ludlow fair
And left my necktie God knows where,   30
And carried half-way home, or near,
Pints and quarts of Ludlow beer:
Then the world seemed none so bad,
And I myself a sterling lad;
And down in lovely muck I've lain,   35
Happy till I woke again.
Then I saw the morning sky:
Heigho, the tale was all a lie;
The world, it was the old world yet,

I was I, my things were wet,   40
And nothing now remained to do
But begin the game anew.

    Therefore, since the world has still
Much good, but much less good than ill,
And while the sun and moon endure   45
Luck's a chance, but trouble's sure,
I'd face it as a wise man would,
And train for ill and not for good.
'Tis true, the stuff I bring for sale
Is not so brisk a brew as ale: 50
Out of a stem that scored the hand
I wrung it in a weary land.
But take it: if the smack is sour,
The better for the embittered hour;
It should do good to heart and head   55
When your soul is in my soul's stead;
And I will friend you, if I may,
In the dark and cloudy day.

    There was a king reigned in the East:
There, when kings will sit to feast,   60
They get their fill before they think
With poisoned meat and poisoned drink.
He gathered all that springs to birth
From the many-venomed earth;
First a little, thence to more,   65
He sampled all her killing store;
And easy, smiling, seasoned sound,
Sate the king when healths went round.
They put arsenic in his meat
And stared aghast to watch him eat;   70
They poured strychnine in his cup
And shook to see him drink it up:
They shook, they stared as white's their shirt:
Them it was their poison hurt.
—I tell the tale that I heard told.   75
Mithridates, he died old.

—A. E. HOUSMAN (1859–1936)

To an Athlete Dying Young

The time you won your town the race
We chaired you through the market-place;
Man and boy stood cheering by,
And home we brought you shoulder-high.

Today, the road all runners come,   5
Shoulder-high, we bring you home,
And set you at your threshold down,
Townsman of a stiller town.

Smart lad, to slip betimes away
From fields where glory does not stay   10
And early though the laurel grows
It withers quicker than the rose.

Eyes the shady night has shut
Cannot see the record cut,
And silence sounds no worse than cheers   15
After earth has stopped the ears:

Now you will not swell the rout
Of lads that wore their honors out,
Runners whom renown outran
And the name died before the man.   20

So set, before its echoes fade,
The fleet foot on the sill of shade,
And hold to the low lintel up
The still-defended challenge-cup.

And round that early-laureled head   25
Will flock to gaze the strengthless dead,
And find unwithered on its curls
The garland briefer than a girl's.

—A. E. HOUSMAN (1859–1936)

Theme for English B

The instructor said,

> *Go home, and write*
> *a page tonight.*
> *And let that page come out of you—*
> *Then, it will be true.*   5

I wonder if it's that simple?
I am twenty-two, colored, born in Winston-Salem.
I went to school there, then Durham, then here
to this college on the hill above Harlem.
I am the only colored student in my class.   10
The steps from the hill lead down into Harlem,
through a park, then I cross St. Nicholas,
Eighth Avenue, Seventh, and I come to the Y,
the Harlem Branch Y, where I take the elevator
up to my room, sit down, and write this page: 15

It's not easy to know what is true for you or me
at twenty-two, my age. But I guess I'm what
I feel and see and hear, Harlem, I hear you:
hear you, hear me—we two—you, me, talk on this page.
(I hear New York, too.) Me—who?   20
Well, I like to eat, sleep, drink, and be in love.
I like to work, read, learn, and understand life.
I like a pipe for a Christmas present,
or records—Bessie, bop, or Bach.
I guess being colored doesn't make me *not* like   25
the same things other folks like who are other races.
So will my page be colored that I write?
Being me, it will not be white.
But it will be
a part of you, instructor.   30
You are white—
yet a part of me, as I am a part of you.
That's American.
Sometimes perhaps you don't want to be a part of me.
Nor do I often want to be a part of you.   35
But we are, that's true!
As I learn from you,

I guess you learn from me—
although you're older—and white—
and somewhat more free.   40

This is my page for English B.

—LANGSTON HUGHES (1902–1967)

(24) Bessie Smith: African American blues singer ((1894–1937)).

The Death of the Ball Turret Gunner

From my mother's sleep I fell into the State,
And I hunched in its belly till my wet fur froze.
Six miles from earth, loosed from its dream of life,
I woke to black flak and the nightmare fighters.
When I died they washed me out of the turret with a hose.   5

—RANDALL JARRELL (1914–1965)

(Title) *Ball Turret:* the poet wrote, "A ball turret was a plexiglass sphere set into the belly of a B-17 or B-24 [bomber during World War II], and inhabited by two .50 caliber machine-guns and one man, a short small man. When this gunner tracked with his machine-guns a fighter [plane] attacking from below, he revolved with the turret; hunched in his little sphere, he looked like the fetus in the womb."

Still to be neat

Still° to be neat, still to be dressed,   always
As you were going to a feast;
Still to be powdered, still perfumed;
Lady, it is to be presumed,
Though art's hid causes are not found,   5
All is not sweet, all is not sound.

Give me a look, give me a face
That makes simplicity a grace;
Robes loosely flowing, hair as free;
Such sweet neglect more taketh me   10
Then all th' adulteries of art.
They strike mine eyes, but not my heart.

—BEN JONSON (1572–1637)

To Celia

Drink to me only with thine eyes,
    And I will pledge with mine;
Or leave a kiss but in the cup,
    And I'll not ask for wine.
The thirst that from the soul doth rise   5
    Doth ask a drink divine;
But might I of Jove's nectar sup,
    I would not change for thine.

I sent thee late a rosy wreath,
    Not so much honoring thee   10
As giving it a hope that there
    It could not withered be.
But thou thereon didst only breathe,
    And sent'st it back to me;
Since when it grows, and smells, I swear,   15
    Not of itself but thee.

—BEN JONSON (1572–1637)

La Belle Dame sans Merci

A Ballad

O, what can ail thee, knight-at-arms,
    Alone and palely loitering?
The sedge has withered from the lake,
    And no birds sing.

O, what can ail thee, knight-at-arms,   5
    So haggard and so woe-begone?
The squirrel's granary is full,
    And the harvest's done.

I see a lily on thy brow,
    With anguish moist and fever dew;   10
And on thy cheeks a fading rose
    Fast withereth too.

I met a lady in the meads,
    Full beautiful—a faery's child,
Her hair was long, her foot was light,   15
    And her eyes were wild.

I made a garland for her head,
    And bracelets too, and fragrant zone;
She looked at me as she did love,
    And made sweet moan.   20

I set her on my pacing steed,
    And nothing else saw all day long;
For sidelong would she bend, and sing
    A faery's song.

She found me roots of relish sweet,   25
    And honey wild, and manna dew,
And sure in language strange she said—
    "I love thee true."

She took me to her elfin grot,
    And there she wept and sighed full sore,   30
And there I shut her wild wild eyes
    With kisses four.

And there she lullèd me asleep
    And there I dreamed—Ah! woe betide!
The latest dream I ever dreamed   35
    On the cold hill side.

I saw pale kings and princes too,
    Pale warriors, death-pale were they all;
They cried—"La Belle Dame sans Merci
    Hath thee in thrall!"   40

I saw their starved lips in the gloam
    With horrid warning gapèd wide,
And I awoke and found me here
    On the cold hill's side.

And this is why I sojourn here   45
    Alone and palely loitering,
Though the sedge has withered from the lake,
    And no birds sing.

—JOHN KEATS (1795–1821)

The title means "The beautiful lady without pity."

Ode to a Nightingale

My heart aches, and a drowsy numbness pains
    My sense, as though of hemlock° I had drunk,   a poison
Or emptied some dull opiate to the drains
    One minute past, and Lethe-wards had sunk:
'Tis not through envy of thy happy lot,   5
    But being too happy in thine happiness,—
        That thou, light-wingèd Dryad° of the trees,   wood nymph
           In some melodious plot
Of beechen green, and shadows numberless,
    Singest of summer in full-throated ease.   10

O for a draught of vintage! that hath been
    Cooled a long age in the deep-delved earth,
Tasting of Flora° and the country green,   goddess of flowers
    Dance, and Provençal song, and sunburnt mirth!
O for a beaker full of the warm South,   15
    Full of the true, the blushful Hippocrene,
        With beaded bubbles winking at the brim,
           And purple-stainèd mouth;
    That I might drink, and leave the world unseen,
    And with thee fade away into the forest dim: 20

Fade far away, dissolve, and quite forget
    What thou among the leaves hast never known,
The weariness, the fever, and the fret
    Here, where men sit and hear each other groan;
Where palsy shakes a few, sad, last gray hairs,   25
    Where youth grows pale, and specter-thin, and dies,
        Where but to think is to be full of sorrow
           And leaden-eyed despairs,
    Where Beauty cannot keep her lustrous eyes,
    Or new Love pine at them beyond tomorrow.   30

Away! away! for I will fly to thee,
    Not charioted by Bacchus and his pards,
But on the viewless° wings of Poesy,   invisible
    Though the dull brain perplexes and retards:
Already with thee! tender is the night,   35
    And haply the Queen-Moon is on her throne,
        Clustered around by all her starry Fays;
           But here there is no light,

Save what from heaven is with the breezes blown
 Through verdurous glooms and winding mossy ways.   40

I cannot see what flowers are at my feet,
 Nor what soft incense hangs upon the boughs,
But, in embalmèd° darkness, guess each sweet   perfumed
 Wherewith the seasonable month endows
The grass, the thicket, and the fruit-tree wild;   45
 White hawthorn, and the pastoral eglantine;
  Fast fading violets covered up in leaves;
   And mid-May's eldest child,
 The coming musk-rose, full of dewy wine,
  The murmurous haunt of flies on summer eves.   50

Darkling° I listen; and, for many a time   in darkness
 I have been half in love with easeful Death,
Called him soft names in many a musèd rhyme,
 To take into the air my quiet breath;
Now more than ever seems it rich to die,   55
 To cease upon the midnight with no pain,
  While thou art pouring forth thy soul abroad
   In such an ecstasy!
 Still wouldst thou sing, and I have ears in vain—
  To thy high requiem become a sod.   60

Thou wast not born for death, immortal Bird!
 No hungry generations tread thee down;
The voice I hear this passing night was heard
 In ancient days by emperor and clown:
Perhaps the self-same song that found a path   65
 Through the sad heart of Ruth, when, sick for home,
  She stood in tears amid the alien corn;
   The same that oft-times hath
 Charmed magic casements, opening on the foam
  Of perilous seas, in faery lands forlorn.   70

Forlorn! the very word is like a bell
 To toll me back from thee to my sole self!
Adieu! the fancy cannot cheat so well
 As she is famed to do, deceiving elf.
Adieu! adieu! thy plaintive anthem fades   75
 Past the near meadows, over the still stream,
  Up the hill-side; and now 'tis buried deep

In the next valley-glades:
Was it a vision, or a waking dream?
Fled is that music:—Do I wake or sleep?   80

—JOHN KEATS (1795–1821)

(4) *Lethe:* river of forgetfulness in the Greek underworld. (14) *Provençal:* Provence, a wine-growing region in southern France famous, in the Middle Ages, for troubadours. (16) *Hippocrene:* fountain of the Muses on Mt. Helicon in Greece. (32) *Bacchus . . . pards:* Bacchus, god of wine, had a chariot drawn by leopards. (66) *Ruth:* see Bible, Ruth 2.

This living hand

This living hand, now warm and capable
Of earnest grasping, would, if it were cold
And in the icy silence of the tomb,
So haunt thy days and chill thy dreaming nights
That thou wouldst wish thine own heart dry of blood   5
So in my veins red life might stream again,
And thou be conscience-calmed—see here it is—
I hold it towards you.

—JOHN KEATS (1795–1821)

To Sleep

O soft embalmer of the still midnight,
    Shutting, with careful fingers and benign,
Our gloom-pleas'd eyes, embower'd from the light,
    Enshaded in forgetfulness divine:
O soothest Sleep! if so it please thee, close   5
    In midst of this thine hymn my willing eyes,
Or wait the amen, ere thy poppy throws
    Around my bed its lulling charities.
Then save me, or the passed day will shine
Upon my pillow, breeding many woes,—   10
    Save me from curious Conscience, that still lords
Its strength for darkness, burrowing like a mole;
    Turn the key deftly in the oiled wards,
And seal the hushed Casket of my Soul.

—JOHN KEATS (1795–1821)

After Making Love We Hear Footsteps

For I can snore like a bullhorn
or play loud music
or sit up talking with any reasonably sober Irishman
and Fergus will only sink deeper
into his dreamless sleep, which goes by all in one flash,   5
but let there be that heavy breathing
or a stifled come-cry anywhere in the house
and he will wrench himself awake
and make for it on the run—as now, we lie together,
after making love, quiet, touching along the length of our bodies,   10
familiar touch of the long-married,
and he appears—in his baseball pajamas, it happens,
the neck opening so small he has to screw them on—
and flops down between us and hugs us and snuggles himself to
     sleep,
his face gleaming with satisfaction at being this very child.   15

In the half darkness we look at each other
and smile
and touch arms across this little, startlingly muscled body—
this one whom habit of memory propels to the ground of his making,
sleeper only the mortal sounds can sing awake,   20
this blessing love gives again into our arms.

—GALWAY KINNELL (1927–2014)

Ars Poetica

A poem should be palpable and mute
As a globed fruit,

Dumb
As old medallions to the thumb,

Silent as the sleeve-worn stone   5
Of casement ledges where the moss has grown—

A poem should be wordless
As the flight of birds.

*

A poem should be motionless in time
As the moon climbs,   10

Leaving, as the moon releases
Twig by twig the night-entangled trees,

Leaving, as the moon behind the winter leaves,
Memory by memory the mind—

A poem should be motionless in time   15
As the moon climbs.

                    *

A poem should be equal to:
Not true.

For all the history of grief
An empty doorway and a maple leaf.   20

For love
The leaning grasses and two lights above the sea—

A poem should not mean
But be.

—ARCHIBALD MACLEISH (1892–1982)

The Passionate Shepherd to His Love

Come live with me and be my Love,
And we will all the pleasures prove
That hills and valleys, dales and fields,
Or woods or steepy mountain yields.

And we will sit upon the rocks,   5
And see the shepherds feed their flocks
By shallow rivers, to whose falls
Melodious birds sing madrigals.

And I will make thee beds of roses
And a thousand fragrant posies;   10
A cap of flowers, and a kirtle
Embroider'd all with leaves of myrtle.

A gown made of the finest wool
Which from our pretty lambs we pull;
Fair-linèd slippers for the cold,   15
With buckles of the purest gold.

A belt of straw and ivy-buds
With coral clasps and amber studs:
And if these pleasures may thee move,
Come live with me and be my Love.   20

The shepherd swains shall dance and sing
For thy delight each May morning:
If these delights thy mind may move,
Then live with me and be my Love.

—CHRISTOPHER MARLOWE (1564–1593)

Survival: A Guide

It's not easy living here, waiting to be charmed
by the first little scribble of green. Even in May
the crows want to own the place, and the heron, old bent thing,
spends hours looking like graying bark,
part of a dead trunk lying over opaque water.   5
She strikes the pose so long I begin to worry
she's determined to be something ordinary.
The small lakes continue their slide into bog and muck—
remember when they ran clear, an invisible spring
renewing the water? But the ducks stay longer, amusing   10
ruffle and chatter. I can be distracted.

If I do catch her move, the heron appears
to have no particular fear or hunger, her gaunt body
hinged haphazardly, a few gears unlocking
one wing, then another. More than a generation here   15
and every year more drab.
Once I called her blue heron, as in Great Blue,
true to a book—part myth, part childhood's color.
Older now, I see her plain: a mere surviving
against a weedy bank with fox dens   20
and the ruthless, overhead patrol.
Some blind clockwork keeps her going.

—CLEOPATRA MATHIS (B. 1947)

Story

What matters most is private and vast and can't be seen
on the brain scan, though it may burn orange or blue

or a toasty gold in the amygdala,
a magnolia-green in the cingulum, the cinnamon

or burnt wine of an old tin roof all through the fornix.   5
For the story only you know, the day is coming

when someone has found out how to read
each synapse, how to extract your past and play it back

like a movie, for anyone to see, but even then—
and this makes me laugh—there will have to be an angle   10

of witness, like a seat in the audience, and all
anyone will see from there, as always, is what they can.

It's once upon a time, still, but the soul of what follows
glows the color of chance, and who knows

how holy it is?   15

—JUDSON MITCHAM (B. 1948)

Stroke

The starry night will still look good in black,
but the arteries will thicken with luck,
the noon sky will darken in the lake,
the crow will drop the nickel from its beak,

the graveyard will crack its hilarious book,   5
the sun will feel cool on the farmer's neck,
the talkers will capsize in the little creek,
the rock star will step on his rake,

and the kitten will rip through the croker sack,
and the crucifix will throw off its yoke,   10

and the hospital will be beautiful with shock,
and the lame joke will work,

and the ghost, at last, will let go of the wreck,
and God will pick up that rock.

—JUDSON MITCHAM (B. 1948)

Apartment Living

So those despotic loves have become known to you,
rubbing cold hands up your thighs, leaving oily trails,
whispering, *Just how you like it, right?*
Upstairs the sorority girls are playing charades
again, smoking cigarettes, wearing shifts, burning   5
pain into their synapses.
Life is a needle. And now it pricks you:
the silver light in which you realize
your attempts at decadence
tire the earth and tire you. The etymology   10
of "flag" as in "to signal to stop"
is unknown. It is time to sit and watch. Don't
call that one again, he's pitiless in his self-certainty.
You used to be so.
You laid your black dress on the bed.   15
You stepped in your heels over sidewalk cracks.
You licked mint and sugar from the cocktail mixer,
singing nonsense songs,
and the strangers, they sang along.

—MEGHAN O'ROURKE (B. 1976)

Bloodline, Elegy: Su Qijian
Family, Beijing

In the mud-colored Hai River a swirl of infant-girl bodies.
In the river-trance the infant girls are propelled with the current.
You stare, you blink—she has vanished.
But—here is another, and
soon, another.   5
How small, how fleeting, of no more consequence than a kitten

an infant girl drowned at birth
before the first breath has been drawn, and expelled—
No crying. We do not shatter the peace of the morning, with crying.
See how good we are!   10

In the mud-river so many, you could not count how many.
Out of the bloody womb the small bodies betray the infant girls
for they are revealed incomplete between the legs, pitiable
the *not-male*, the doomed.

We have not been drowned in the Hai River for we   15
are of the privileged Su Qijian family. And yet
our dreams are filled with drowning amid the swirl
of infant-girl bodies in the Hai River
sweeping past our home.
We do not want to know how the infant girls are our sisters or our   20
aunts.
We do not want to know how they are us for (it is said) they are not us,
that is all we have been told.
And we did not see these infant-girl bodies in the swirl of the mud-river
for we had not yet been born.

We are the largest family in Beijing. We are very proud to be of the 25
Su Qijian family of Beijing. We have been chosen for the honor
of meeting you today because we are a perfect family (it is said) for
we have been born and our baby girls not drowned. *Bloodline* is all, and
in our bloodline it is a marvel, it is a source of great pride, how our
mother, our grandmothers, our great-grandmothers had not been   30
thrown into the mud-river to drown but were allowed to live.

So we know, we are blessed! We are very special amid
so many millions drowned in the Hai River as in the great Yangtze
and how many millions perished in the Revolution of no more
consequence than infant girls extinguished before they can draw breath 35
or cry.

Especially, we do not cry.
We have never cried.
You will not hear us cry—*See how good we are! Even*
in the agony of death, our tiny lungs filled with the mud-river.   40

We of the Su Qijian family have never lamented or mourned
for our privilege is to have been allowed to be born.
We are alive, there are twenty-nine of us alive and not one
of us has been drowned at birth. So we are blessed, we are of the
People's Republic of China. We are alive.   45

For some Chinese couples just one baby was allowed. For some others,
more than one baby was allowed. And for some, girl-babies were
allowed. We do not understand these decrees
and we do not question.

Bloodline is the very god. Bloodline is the nation.   50
Bloodline is property of the Office of China State Council Information.

* * *

And then in a dream it is revealed—
it is the mothers of our family who drowned our sisters!

Long ago it happened, in those years
before we were born. It was a different China then (it is said),   55
it is not the same China now. Our beautiful mother
pleads for understanding. All our mothers weep and tear their hair
in shame! They would tear out their eyes that such ugliness
might spare them.

How is it possible, our mothers are those very mothers   60
who tossed the infant-girls into the river to drown...
Oh but it happened long ago. The world was different then.
Shuxia is saying, Junxia is saying, Lixia is saying
they are not evil. Not one of the women of the Su Qijian family
is evil, they plead with us to understand, and to forgive.   65
Our babies who are your sisters were torn from our arms,
we could not nurse them, we were forbidden. *You see,*
we had no choice. We are but
female, we had no choice but to drown our own.

It is China thrumming with its many millions that is alive   70
that is the marvel. In the distance you see the eye of our god
the China Central Television Tower rising above the suety Beijing
skyline, that is a greater marvel. *Rejoice! Our great nation*
is the future, and your nation is of the past.

What is the meaning of our lives, we never ask. 75
The creatures of the hive do not question the hive.
The creatures of the river that do not drown
in the river do not question the river for the river
has spared them and that is the blessing. This is the meaning
of all of our lives, and not just Chinese lives. 80
That we are is the meaning, and that we have been blessed
is the meaning, and that we are not drowned
in the Hai River with our infant sisters is the meaning.

In parting here is our gift to you, our American visitors: a plastic
bag of photographs of Chinese monuments, Chinese citizens, the mud- 85
colored Hai River at dawn when it glitters with light like the scales of a
great serpent whose head you cannot see thousands of miles upstream,
and whose tail you cannot see thousands of miles downstream, that
abides forever.

—JOYCE CAROL OATES (B. 1938)

Playlet for Voices

May I serve you? This is delicious. Please sit anywhere. Please take off
your coats. You are very generous. You are very sweet. Is it still snowing
out? We're so grateful. Has everyone been introduced? Shall I take your
coats? Just slip your gloves in here. Thank you very much. Please pass
it on. Please come back soon. This *is* delicious. Is the walk icy? Can you 5
find your way? Let's close the door quickly!

Will you have another serving? Why won't you have another serving?
Thank you very much. It doesn't matter, please sit anywhere. We are in
the habit of sitting anywhere. It is a custom to sit anywhere. Thank you
very much, this is delicious, may I have the recipe? Is it cold outside? 10
Can you find your way?

Siblings and parents (it is said) devour every second child in order to
gain "mystical strength." Among the Pitjantjara tribe of Australia. Yes,
thank you. You are so generous. We're so grateful to be invited. Yes,
that is her likeness on the wall. *Thank* you. You are exceptionally kind. 15
Will you have another serving—and pass it on? There is a theory that
they devour their infants partly for reasons of "nourishment" as well but

it's farfetched, isn't it, since an infant only a few days old is a minimal feast indeed. Except if it is named. If they have given it a name. No, I don't suppose baptism—they wouldn't be that advanced. Would they be that advanced? But if it has a name then it can't be eaten. If it has a name then it is safe from its parents and siblings and can't be eaten. Why do you suppose that is? What curious customs! Some people will believe anything they are told! 20

Actually they are artificial flowers. Actually they are primroses and not "roses." Would you like to sit here? Has everyone been introduced? Has everyone had a second helping? It must be freezing outside. It's warmer by the fire. Let's adjourn to the other room. Coffee, brandy. Where are our coats? Whose gloves are these? She died suddenly. One of the physicians commented on morbid obesity. It was a lingering death as many are but, at the end, sudden: That is often the case. How can we be responsible for aboriginal behavior in Australia? 25

30

May I serve you? Is this smoke annoying you? May I take your coat? Why must you leave so early? Yes, but we must leave. But you have just arrived. Thank you *very* much, we are all extremely grateful. 35

Have you all been introduced? It was a merciful death as deaths go these days. Please take another serving, you haven't eaten anything. There is more than enough for everyone. Three days' preparation have gone into this meal. She was secretly disappointed. That is often the case. This is certainly a privilege—where will you sit? *This* is delicious. Why are you shivering? Come sit by the fire. Have you all been introduced? It is ten-thirty. It is so frequently ten-thirty. Death was said to have been caused by heart failure. It is always ten-thirty in this room. Why must you leave so early? Thank you *very* much. Please come back soon. 40

This is exquisite: May I have the recipe? You are very sweet to have invited us. She has been dead now—oh, I'd say more than a year: fifteen months at least. Is it eighteen months? Yes, it is a good likeness. Yes, some traits are misleading. The roses *are* beautiful but they are not ours. Actually they are primroses. Please have another serving and pass it on. Is the bowl too hot? Must you leave so early? Has everyone been introduced? But you have just arrived. But we are very grateful. Yes, these *are* my gloves. 45

50

—JOYCE CAROL OATES (B. 1938)

I Go Back to May 1937

I see them standing at the formal gates of their colleges,
I see my father strolling out
under the ochre sandstone arch, the
red tiles glinting like bent
plates of blood behind his head, I   5
see my mother with a few light books at her hip
standing at the pillar made of tiny bricks with the
wrought-iron gate still open behind her, its
sword-tips black in the May air,
they are about to graduate, they are about to get married,   10
they are kids, they are dumb, all they know is they are
innocent, they would never hurt anybody.
I want to go up to them and say Stop,
don't do it—she's the wrong woman,
he's the wrong man, you are going to do things   15
you cannot imagine you would ever do,
you are going to do bad things to children,
you are going to suffer in ways you never heard of,
you are going to want to die. I want to go
up to them there in the late May sunlight and say it,   20
her hungry pretty blank face turning to me,
her pitiful beautiful untouched body,
his arrogant handsome blind face turning to me,
his pitiful beautiful untouched body,
but I don't do it. I want to live. I   25
take them up like the male and female
paper dolls and bang them together
at the hips like chips of flint as if to
strike sparks from them, I say
Do what you are going to do, and I will tell about it.   30

—Sharon Olds (b. 1942)

The Connoisseuse of Slugs

When I was a connoisseuse of slugs
I would part the ivy leaves, and look for the
naked jelly of those gold bodies,
translucent strangers glistening along the
stones, slowly, their gelatinous bodies   5

at my mercy. Made mostly of water, they would shrivel
to nothing if they were sprinkled with salt,
but I was not interested in that. What I liked
was to draw aside the ivy, breathe the
odor of the wall, and stand there in silence   10
until the slug forgot I was there
and sent its antennae up out of its
head, the glimmering umber horns
rising like telescopes, until finally the
sensitive knobs would pop out the ends,   15
delicate and intimate. Years later,
when I first saw a naked man,
I gasped with pleasure to see that quiet
mystery reenacted, the slow
elegant being coming out of hiding and   20
gleaming in the dark air, eager and so
trusting you could weep.

—Sharon Olds (b. 1942)

Moth

Matthew 6:19

Come bumble-footed ones,
dust squigglers, furry ripplers,

inchers and squirmers
humble in gray and brown,

find out our secret places,   5
devour our hearts,

measure us, geometer, with your curved teeth!
Leaves lick at the window, clouds

stream away,
yet we lie here,   10

perfect,
locked in our dark chambers

when we could rise in you
brief, splendid

twenty-plume, gold   15
spotted ghost, pink scavenger,

luna whose pale-green wings
glow with moons and planets

at one with the burning world
whose one desire is to escape itself.   20

—KATHA POLLITT (B. 1949)

Ode on Solitude

Happy the man, whose wish and care
A few paternal acres bound,
Content to breathe his native air,
                            In his own ground.

Whose herds with milk, whose fields with bread,   5
Whose flocks supply him with attire,
Whose trees in summer yield him shade,
                            In winter fire.

Blest! who can unconcern'dly find
Hours, days, and years slide soft away,   10
In health of body, peace of mind,
                            Quiet by day,

Sound sleep by night; study and ease
Together mix'd; sweet recreation,
And innocence, which most does please,   15
                            With meditation.

Thus let me live, unseen, unknown;
Thus unlamented let me die;
Steal from the world, and not a stone
                            Tell where I lie.   20

—ALEXANDER POPE (1688–1744)

Eros Turannos

She fears him, and will always ask
   What fated her to choose him;
She meets in his engaging mask
   All reasons to refuse him;
But what she meets and what she fears   5
Are less than are the downward years,
Drawn slowly to the foamless weirs
   Of age, were she to lose him.

Between a blurred sagacity
   That once had power to sound him,   10
And Love, that will not let him be
   The Judas that she found him,
Her pride assuages her almost,
As if it were alone the cost.
He sees that he will not be lost,   15
   And waits and looks around him.

A sense of ocean and old trees
   Envelopes and allures him;
Tradition, touching all he sees,
   Beguiles and reassures him;   20
And all her doubts of what he says
Are dimmed with what she knows of days—
Till even prejudice delays
   And fades, and she secures him.

The falling leaf inaugurates   25
   The reign of her confusion;
The pounding wave reverberates
   The dirge of her illusion;
And home, where passion lived and died,
Becomes a place where she can hide,   30
While all the town and harbor side
   Vibrate with her seclusion.

We tell you, tapping on our brows,
   The story as it should be,
As if the story of a house   35
   Were told, or ever could be;

We'll have no kindly veil between
Her visions and those we have seen,
As if we guessed what hers have been,
    Or what they are or would be.   40

Meanwhile we do no harm; for they
    That with a god have striven,
Not hearing much of what we say,
    Take what the god has given;
Though like waves breaking it may be,   45
Or like a changed familiar tree,
Or like a stairway to the sea
    Where down the blind are driven.

—EDWIN ARLINGTON ROBINSON (1869–1935)

(Title) *Eros Turannos:* Tyrannical Love.

Mr. Flood's Party

Old Eben Flood, climbing alone one night
Over the hill between the town below
And the forsaken upland hermitage
That held as much as he should ever know
On earth again of home, paused warily.   5
The road was his with not a native near;
And Eben, having leisure, said aloud,
For no man else in Tilbury Town to hear:

"Well, Mr. Flood, we have the harvest moon
Again, and we may not have many more;   10
The bird is on the wing, the poet says,
And you and I have said it here before.
Drink to the bird." He raised up to the light
The jug that he had gone so far to fill,
And answered huskily: "Well, Mr. Flood,   15
Since you propose it, I believe I will."

Alone, as if enduring to the end
A valiant armor of scarred hopes outworn,
He stood there in the middle of the road
Like Roland's ghost winding a silent horn.   20

Below him, in the town among the trees,
Where friends of other days had honored him,
A phantom salutation of the dead
Rang thinly till old Eben's eyes were dim.

Then, as a mother lays her sleeping child   25
Down tenderly, fearing it may awake,
He set the jug down slowly at his feet
With trembling care, knowing that most things break;
And only when assured that on firm earth
It stood, as the uncertain lives of men   30
Assuredly did not, he paced away,
And with his hand extended, paused again:

"Well, Mr. Flood, we have not met like this
In a long time; and many a change has come
To both of us, I fear, since last it was   35
We had a drop together. Welcome home!"
Convivially returning with himself,
Again he raised the jug up to the light;
And with an acquiescent quaver said:
"Well, Mr. Flood, if you insist, I might.   40

"Only a very little, Mr. Flood—
For auld lang syne. No more, sir; that will do."
So, for the time, apparently it did,
And Eben evidently thought so too;
For soon amid the silver loneliness   45
Of night he lifted up his voice and sang,
Secure, with only two moons listening,
Until the whole harmonious landscape rang—

"For auld lang syne." The weary throat gave out,
The last word wavered, and the song was done.   50
He raised again the jug regretfully
And shook his head, and was again alone.
There was not much that was ahead of him,
And there was nothing in the town below—
Where strangers would have shut the many doors   55
That many friends had opened long ago.

—Edwin Arlington Robinson (1869–1935)

(11) *bird:* Mr. Flood is quoting from *The Rubáiyát of Omar Khayyám*, "The bird of Time . . . is on the wing." (20) *Roland:* hero of the French epic poem *The Song of Roland*. He died fighting a rearguard action for Charlemagne against the Moors in Spain: before his death he sounded a call for help on his famous horn, but the king's army arrived too late.

MindTap® Read, highlight, and take notes online.

Song

When I am dead, my dearest,
    Sing no sad songs for me;
Plant thou no roses at my head,
    Nor shady cypress tree;
Be the green grass above me   5
    With showers and dewdrops wet;
And if thou wilt, remember,
    And if thou wilt, forget.

I shall not see the shadows,
    I shall not feel the rain;   10
I shall not hear the nightingale
    Sing on, as if in pain;
And dreaming through the twilight
    That doth not rise nor set,
Haply I may remember,   15
    And haply may forget.

—CHRISTINA ROSSETTI (1830–1894)

Up-Hill

Does the road wind up-hill all the way?
    Yes, to the very end.
Will the day's journey take the whole long day?
    From morn to night, my friend.

But is there for the night a resting-place?   5
    A roof for when the slow dark hours begin.
May not the darkness hide it from my face?
    You cannot miss that inn.

Shall I meet other wayfarers at night?
    Those who have gone before.   10

Then must I knock, or call when just in sight?
    They will not keep you waiting at that door.

Shall I find comfort, travel-sore and weak?
    Of labor you shall find the sum.
Will there be beds for me and all who seek?   15
    Yea, beds for all who come.

—CHRISTINA ROSSETTI (1830–1894)

Let me not to the marriage of true minds

Let me not to the marriage of true minds
Admit impediments. Love is not love
Which alters when it alteration finds,
Or bends with the remover to remove.
O no! it is an ever-fixèd mark   5
That looks on tempests and is never shaken;
It is the star to every wandering bark,
Whose worth's unknown, although his height be taken.
Love's not Time's fool, though rosy lips and cheeks
Within his bending sickle's compass come;   10
Love alters not with his brief hours and weeks,
But bears it out even to the edge of doom.
If this be error and upon me proved,
I never writ, nor no man ever loved.

—WILLIAM SHAKESPEARE (1564–1616)

One day I wrote her name upon the strand

One day I wrote her name upon the strand,°   beach
But came the waves and washèd it away:
Again I wrote it with a second hand,
But came the tide, and made my pains his prey.
"Vain man," said she, "that dost in vain assay°   attempt 5
A mortal thing so to immortalize.
For I myself shall, like to this, decay,
And eek° my name be wipèd out likewise."   also
"Not so," quoth I, "let baser things devise
To die in dust, but you shall live by fame: 10

My verse your virtues rare shall eternize,
And in the heavens write your glorious name,
Where whenas death shall all the world subdue
Our love shall live, and later life renew."

—EDMUND SPENSER (1552–1599)

Anecdote of the Jar

I placed a jar in Tennessee,
And round it was, upon a hill.
It made the slovenly wilderness
Surround that hill.

The wilderness rose up to it,   5
And sprawled around, no longer wild.
The jar was round upon the ground
And tall and of a port in air.

It took dominion everywhere.
The jar was gray and bare.   10
It did not give of bird or bush,
Like nothing else in Tennessee.

—WALLACE STEVENS (1879–1955)

A Description of the Morning

Now hardly here and there a hackney-coach
Appearing, showed the ruddy morn's approach.
Now Betty from her master's bed had flown,
And softly stole to discompose her own.
The slip-shod 'prentice from his master's door   5
Had pared the dirt, and sprinkled round the floor.
Now Moll had whirled her mop with dextrous airs,
Prepared to scrub the entry and the stairs.
The youth with broomy stumps began to trace
The kennel's edge, where wheels had worn the place.   10
The small-coal man was heard with cadence deep,

Till drowned in shriller notes of chimney-sweep.
Duns at his lordship's gate began to meet;
And Brickdust Moll had screamed through half the street.
The turnkey now his flock returning sees,   15
Duly let out a-nights to steal for fees.
The watchful bailiffs take their silent stands;
And schoolboys lag with satchels in their hands.

—JONATHAN SWIFT (1667–1745)

Blond

Certainly it was possible—somewhere
in my parents' genes the recessive traits
that might have given me a different look:
not attached earlobes or my father's green eyes,
but another hair color—gentleman-preferred,   5
have-more-fun blond. And with my skin color,
like a good tan—an even mix of my parents'—
I could have passed for white.

When on Christmas day I woke to find
a blond wig, a pink sequined tutu,   10
and a blond ballerina doll, nearly tall as me,
I didn't know to ask, nor that it mattered,
if there'd been a brown version. This was years before
my grandmother nestled the dark baby
into our crèche, years before I'd understand it   15
as primer for a Mississippi childhood.

Instead, I pranced around our living room
in a whirl of possibility, my parents looking on
at their suddenly strange child. In the photograph
my mother took, my father—almost   20
out of the frame—looks on as Joseph must have
at the miraculous birth: I'm in the foreground—
my blond wig a shining halo, a newborn likeness
to the child that chance, the long odds,
might have brought.   25

—NATASHA TRETHEWEY (B. 1966)

Miscegenation

In 1965 my parents broke two laws of Mississippi;
they went to Ohio to marry, returned to Mississippi.

They crossed the river into Cincinnati, a city whose name
begins with a sound like *sin,* the sound of wrong—*mis* in Mississippi.

A year later they moved to Canada, followed a route the same   5
as slaves, the train slicing the white glaze of winter, leaving
    Mississippi.

Faulkner's Joe Christmas was born in winter, like Jesus, given his
    name
for the day he was left at the orphanage, his race unknown in
    Mississippi.

My father was reading *War and Peace* when he gave me my name.
I was born near Easter, 1966, in Mississippi.   10

When I turned 33 my father said, *It's your Jesus year—you're the same
age he was when he died.* It was spring, the hills green in Mississippi.

I know more than Joe Christmas did. Natasha is a Russian name—
though I'm not; it means *Christmas child,* even in Mississippi.

—NATASHA TRETHEWEY (B. 1966)

A sight in camp in the daybreak gray and dim

A sight in camp in the daybreak gray and dim,
As from my tent I emerge so early sleepless,
As slow I walk in the cool fresh air the path near by the
    hospital tent,
Three forms I see on stretchers lying, brought out there
    untended lying,
Over each the blanket spread, ample brownish woolen
    blanket,   5
Gray and heavy blanket, folding, covering all.

Curious I halt and silent stand,
Then with light fingers I from the face of the nearest the first
    just lift the blanket;
Who are you elderly man so gaunt and grim, with well-gray'd
    hair, and flesh all sunken about the eyes?
Who are you my dear comrade?   10

Then to the second I step—and who are you my child and
    darling?
Who are you sweet boy with cheeks yet blooming?
Then to the third—a face nor child nor old, very calm, as of
    beautiful yellow-white ivory;
Young man I think I know you—I think this face is the face
    of the Christ himself,
Dead and divine and brother of all, and here again he lies.   15

—WALT WHITMAN (1819–1892)

Hours continuing long, sore and heavy-hearted

Hours continuing long, sore and heavy-hearted
Hours of the dusk, when I withdraw to a lonesome and unfrequented
    spot, seating myself, leaning my face in my hands;
Hours sleepless, deep in the night, when I go forth, speeding
    swiftly the country roads, or through the city streets, or   5
    pacing miles and miles, stifling plaintive cries;
Hours discouraged, distracted—for the one I cannot content
    myself without, soon I saw him content himself without me;
Hours when I am forgotten, (O weeks and months are passing,
    but I believe I am never to forget!)   10
Sullen and suffering hours! (I am ashamed—but it is
    useless—I am what I am;)
Hours of my torment — I wonder if other men ever have the
    like, out of the like feelings?
Is there even one other like me—distracted—his friend,   15
    his lover, lost to him?
Is he too as I am now? Does he still rise in the morning, dejected,
    thinking who is lost to him? and at night, awaking, think who
    is lost?

Does he too harbor his friendship silent and endless? harbor his   20
    anguish and passion?
Does some stray reminder, or the casual mention of a name, bring the
    fit back upon him, taciturn and deprest?
Does he see himself reflected in me? In these hours, does he see the
    face of his hours reflected?

—WALT WHITMAN (1819–1892)

I wandered lonely as a cloud

I wandered lonely as a cloud
That floats on high o'er vales and hills,
When all at once I saw a crowd,
A host, of golden daffodils;
Beside the lake, beneath the trees,   5
Fluttering and dancing in the breeze.

Continuous as the stars that shine
And twinkle on the milky way,
They stretched in never-ending line
Along the margin of a bay: 10
Ten thousand saw I at a glance,
Tossing their heads in sprightly dance.

The waves beside them danced; but they
Outdid the sparkling waves in glee;
A poet could not but be gay,   15
In such a jocund company;
I gazed—and gazed—but little thought
What wealth the show to me had brought:

For oft, when on my couch I lie
In vacant or in pensive mood,   20
They flash upon that inward eye
Which is the bliss of solitude;
And then my heart with pleasure fills,
And dances with the daffodils.

—WILLIAM WORDSWORTH (1770–1850)

My heart leaps up when I behold

My heart leaps up when I behold
    A rainbow in the sky:
So was it when my life began;
So is it now I am a man;
So be it when I shall grow old,   5
    Or let me die!
The Child is father of the Man;
And I could wish my days to be
Bound each to each by natural piety.

—WILLIAM WORDSWORTH (1770–1850)

The Solitary Reaper

Behold her, single in the field,
Yon solitary Highland lass!
Reaping and singing by herself;
Stop here, or gently pass!
Alone she cuts and binds the grain,   5
And sings a melancholy strain;
O listen! for the vale profound
Is overflowing with the sound.

No nightingale did ever chant
More welcome notes to weary bands   10
Of travelers in some shady haunt
Among Arabian sands.
A voice so thrilling ne'er was heard
In springtime from the cuckoo-bird,
Breaking the silence of the seas   15
Among the farthest Hebrides.

Will no one tell me what she sings?—
Perhaps the plaintive numbers° flow   measures
For old, unhappy, far-off things,
And battles long ago.   20
Or is it some more humble lay,°   song
Familiar matter of today?

Some natural sorrow, loss, or pain
That has been, and may be again?

Whate'er the theme, the maiden sang   25
As if her song could have no ending;
I saw her singing at her work,
And o'er the sickle bending—
I listened, motionless and still;
And, as I mounted up the hill,   30
The music in my heart I bore
Long after it was heard no more.

—WILLIAM WORDSWORTH (1770–1850)

My galley chargèd with forgetfulness

My galley chargèd with forgetfulness
   Thorough sharp seas in winter nights doth pass
   'Tween rock and rock; and eke mine enemy, alas,
   That is my lord, steereth with cruelness;
And every oar a thought in readiness,   5
   As though that death were light in such a case.
   An endless wind doth tear the sail apace
   Of forcèd sighs, and trusty fearfulness.
A rain of tears, a cloud of dark disdain,
   Hath done the wearied cords great hinderance;   10
   Wreathèd with error and eke with ignorance,
The stars be hid that led me to this pain;
   Drownèd is reason that should me consort,
   And I remain despairing of the port.

—THOMAS WYATT (1503–1542)

The Lake Isle of Innisfree

I will arise and go now, and go to Innisfree,
And a small cabin build there, of clay and wattles made:
Nine bean-rows will I have there, a hive for the honey-bee,
And live alone in the bee-loud glade.

And I shall have some peace there, for peace comes
   dropping slow,   5

Dropping from the veils of the morning to where the
  cricket sings;
There midnight's all a glimmer, and noon a purple glow,
And evening full of the linnet's wings.

I will arise and go now, for always night and day
I hear lake water lapping with low sounds by the shore;   10
While I stand on the roadway, or on the pavements gray,
I hear it in the deep heart's core.

—WILLIAM BUTLER YEATS (1865–1939)

The Second Coming

Turning and turning in the widening gyre
The falcon cannot hear the falconer;
Things fall apart; the center cannot hold;
Mere anarchy is loosed upon the world,
The blood-dimmed tide is loosed, and everywhere   5
The ceremony of innocence is drowned;
The best lack all conviction, while the worst
Are full of passionate intensity.

Surely some revelation is at hand;
Surely the Second Coming is at hand.   10
The Second Coming! Hardly are those words out
When a vast image out of *Spiritus Mundi*
Troubles my sight: somewhere in sands of the desert
A shape with lion body and the head of a man,
A gaze blank and pitiless as the sun,   15
Is moving its slow thighs, while all about it
Reel shadows of the indignant desert birds.
The darkness drops again; but now I know
That twenty centuries of stony sleep
Were vexed to nightmare by a rocking cradle,   20
And what rough beast, its hour come round at last,
Slouches towards Bethlehem to be born?

—WILLIAM BUTLER YEATS (1865–1939)

(Title) In Christian legend the prophesied Second Coming may refer either to Christ or to the An-
tichrist. Yeats believed in a cyclical theory of history in which one historical era would be replaced
by an opposite kind of era every two thousand years. Here, the anarchy in the world following
World War I (the poem was written in 1919) heralds the end of the Christian era. (12) *Spiritus
Mundi:* the racial memory or collective unconscious mind of mankind (literally, world spirit).

The Song of Wandering Aengus

I went out to the hazel wood,
Because a fire was in my head,
And cut and peeled a hazel wand,
And hooked a berry to a thread;
And when white moths were on the wing,   5
And moth-like stars were flickering out,
I dropped the berry in a stream
And caught a little silver trout.

When I had laid it on the floor
I went to blow the fire aflame,   10
But something rustled on the floor,
And some one called me by my name:
It had become a glimmering girl
With apple blossom in her hair
Who called me by my name and ran   15
And faded through the brightening air.

Though I am old with wandering
Through hollow lands and hilly lands,
I will find out where she has gone,
And kiss her lips and take her hands;   20
And walk among long dappled grass,
And pluck till time and times are done
The silver apples of the moon,
The golden apples of the sun.

—WILLIAM BUTLER YEATS (1865–1939)

The Wild Swans at Coole

The trees are in their autumn beauty,
The woodland paths are dry,
Under the October twilight the water
Mirrors a still sky;
Upon the brimming water among the stones   5
Are nine-and-fifty swans.

The nineteenth autumn has come upon me
Since I first made my count;
I saw, before I had well finished,
All suddenly mount   10
And scatter wheeling in great broken rings
Upon their clamorous wings.

I have looked upon those brilliant creatures,
And now my heart is sore,
All's changed since I, hearing at twilight,   15
The first time on this shore,
The bell-beat of their wings above my head,
Trod with a lighter tread.

Unwearied still, lover by lover,
They paddle in the cold   20
Companionable streams or climb the air;
Their hearts have not grown old;
Passion or conquest, wander where they will,
Attend upon them still.

But now they drift on the still water,   25
Mysterious, beautiful;
Among what rushes will they build,
By what lake's edge or pool
Delight men's eyes when I awake some day
To find they have flown away?   30

—WILLIAM BUTLER YEATS (1865–1939)

(Title) Coole Park, in County Galway, Ireland, was the estate of Lady Augusta Gregory, Yeats's patroness and friend. Beginning in 1897, Yeats regularly summered there.

PRACTICE AP® WRITING PROMPTS

W. H. Auden, "Musée des Beaux Arts" (pp. 356–357)

W. H. Auden's "Musée des Beaux Arts" alludes to paintings by Pieter Brueghel the Elder and describes one in detail. Read the poem carefully; then write an essay in which you discuss the speaker's response to the paintings, focusing especially on why he believes the Old Masters "were never wrong." In your analysis, explain how poetic elements such as diction, imagery, and allusion contribute to Auden's meaning.

Elizabeth Bishop, "Manners" (pp. 357–358)

Read Elizabeth Bishop's "Manners" carefully, including the epigraphic note immediately preceding the poem. Then write an essay in which you explore what the child in the poem learns about civility among humans as well as harmony between humankind and nature. In your essay, discuss how such elements as structure, selective details, and tone contribute to the poem's overall effect.

Amy Clampitt, "Witness" (p. 361)

Amy Clampitt's "Witness" captures a speaker's impressions of scenes that normally go unnoticed, viewed from a Greyhound bus on an "ordinary evening in Wisconsin." Read the poem carefully. Then, in a well-organized essay, analyze the poetic language that conveys the speaker's observations and insights as she recounts these moments.

Samuel Taylor Coleridge, "Kubla Khan" (pp. 363–364)

Literary critic Harold Bloom said of "Kubla Khan" that it is "a vision of creation and destruction, each complete." Read the poem carefully, paying close attention to its language and to the balancing of opposites. Then write a well-organized essay in which you show how poetic elements such as imagery, diction, and sound devices contribute to Coleridge's creation of this enchanted land.

Billy Collins, "Weighing the Dog" (pp. 364–365)

Read "Weighing the Dog," paying careful attention to the significance of determining the dog's weight. Write an essay in which you analyze the poet's analogy and symbolism.

Robert Frost, "Birches" (pp. 371–373)

Carefully read Robert Frost's "Birches," paying close attention to the shifts following lines 20 and 40. In a well-written essay, analyze the progression of the speaker's complex reflection. You may wish to consider devices of sound and rhythm as well as the elements of diction, syntax, and tone.

....

Thomas Hardy, "Channel Firing" (pp. 376–378)

Read "Channel Firing" by Thomas Hardy carefully, paying special attention to the interplay of speaking voices framed by the dramatic monologue. In a well-written essay, analyze how the author characterizes the contrasting attitudes of the various speakers in order to convey the complex meaning of the poem as a whole.

....

John Keats, "La Belle Dame Sans Merci" (pp. 388–389), William Butler Yeats, "The Song of Wandering Aengus" (p. 418)

Both "La Belle Dame sans Merci" by Keats and "The Song of Wandering Aengus" by Yeats draw deeply from Celtic folklore, particularly from recurrent tales involving troubling encounters with otherworldly temptation. Read both poems carefully. In a well-organized essay, analyze the similarities and important differences between the two poems, paying attention to the elements—such as point of view, structure, diction, syntax, and sound – that contribute to each poem's meaning and effect.

....

Archibald MacLeish, "Ars Poetica" (pp. 393–394)

Read "Ars Poetica" by Archibald MacLeish carefully. Then write an essay in which you show how the speaker develops a philosophy of poetry. Explain how such elements as figurative language, paradox, and sound devices support MacLeish's meaning.

....

Sharon Olds, "I Go Back to May 1937" (p. 402)

Read Sharon Olds's poem "I Go Back to May 1937" carefully. Then write an essay in which you discuss the impact of the speaker's complex perspective as both witness to and product of her parents' marriage. In your essay, analyze how literary elements such as paradox, diction, and imagery contribute to the poem's overall effect.

....

Christina Rossetti, "Up-Hill" (pp. 408–409)

Read "Uphill" carefully, paying close attention to the journey described. Then write an essay in which you analyze the conversation between the two speakers and explore the poem's allegorical significance. Support your essay with specific references to the poem's language and poetic techniques.

....

Edmund Spenser, "One day I wrote her name upon the strand" (pp. 409–410)

The sonnet form often encourages ironic contrasts. In the sonnet "One day I wrote her name upon the strand," Spenser repeats a word in line 5 both to emphasize its importance to his theme and to play different shades of the word's meaning against each other. Write a carefully detailed essay showing how the contrasting yet resonant senses of the word contribute to the complex meaning of the poem as a whole.

....

Jonathan Swift, "A Description of the Morning" (pp. 410–411)

Carefully read Swift's "A Description of the Morning." Then in a well-written essay, analyze how the author employs a selection of detail, structure, and tone to compose a complex depiction of eighteenth-century city life.

....

Thomas Wyatt, "My galley chargéd with forgetfulness" (p. 416)

Thomas Wyatt's sonnet "My galley chargéd with forgetfulness" describes a difficult interpersonal relationship almost entirely through an extended metaphor. After reading the poem carefully, write an essay in which you analyze how the author uses figurative language and the sonnet form to portray the complexities of the relationship between the speaker and his subject.

....

PRACTICE AP® MULTIPLE-CHOICE QUESTIONS

"A VALEDICTION: FORBIDDING MOURNING" BY JOHN DONNE

QUESTIONS 1–15. Carefully read the following poem before choosing your answers.

As virtuous men pass mildly away,
    And whisper to their souls to go,
Whilst some of their sad friends do say,
    The breath goes now, and some say no:

So let us melt, and make no noise,   5
    No tear-floods, nor sigh-tempests move;
'Twere profanation of our joys
    To tell the laity our love.

Moving of th' earth brings harms and fears;
    Men reckon what it did and meant;   10
But trepidation of the spheres,
    Though greater far, is innocent.

Dull sublunary lovers' love
    (Whose soul is sense) cannot admit
Absence, because it doth remove   15
    Those things which elemented it.

But we, by a love so much refined
    That ourselves know not what it is,
Inter-assurèd of the mind,
    Care less, eyes, lips, and hands to miss.   20

Our two souls, therefore, which are one,
    Though I must go, endure not yet
A breach, but an expansion,
    Like gold to airy thinness beat.

If they be two, they are two so   25
    As stiff twin compasses are two;
Thy soul, the fixed foot, makes no show
    To move, but doth, if th' other do.

And though it in the center sit,
Yet when the other far doth roam,   30
   It leans and harkens after it,
And grows erect as that comes home.

Such wilt thou be to me, who must,
   Like th' other foot, obliquely run;
Thy firmness makes my circle just,   35
   And makes me end where I begun

1. The poem employs the rhyme scheme that resembles
   (A) blank verse
   (B) ballad
   (C) terza rima
   (D) rhyme royal
   (E) ode

2. The poem suggests that Donne's love for his wife and hers
   for him is
   (A) sexual and lustful
   (B) physical, but not spiritual
   (C) intellectual as well as sensual
   (D) temporary but satisfying
   (E) consuming but unrequited

3. The poem as a whole exemplifies
   (A) a Petrarchan sonnet
   (B) a poetic parable
   (C) an Elizabethan pastoral
   (D) a metaphysical conceit
   (E) a stream of consciousness

4. In the opening, "As virtuous men pass mildly away, /
   And whisper to their souls to go" (lines 1–2), the speaker
   describes
   (A) a platonic love that ends with dignity
   (B) a hope that is eventually extinguished
   (C) a journey that reaches its destination
   (D) a peaceful death that happens without trauma
   (E) a good person's quiet struggle against death

5. In lines 7–8, "'Twere profanation of our joys / To tell the laity our love," the speaker asserts that the love shared by him and his beloved
   (A) would be cheapened by outward display of emotion
   (B) can never be understood because it is only spiritual
   (C) might be perceived as inappropriate by others
   (D) is largely a matter of physical infatuation
   (E) can exist only because it is platonic and chaste

6. In lines 9–12, the lovers are likened to moving planetary bodies that
   (A) seem random and chaotic
   (B) foretell natural disasters
   (C) move peacefully and calmly
   (D) appear to be out of their natural order
   (E) are irrelevant to human affairs

7. In line 16, the verb "elemented" most likely means
   (A) separated
   (B) removed
   (C) composed
   (D) expunged
   (E) eliminated

8. Beginning in line 17, the speaker suggests that the two lovers form their own self-sustaining universe because
   (A) they are not limited to physical attraction
   (B) they are made imperfect by their love
   (C) they are culturally "refined"
   (D) they have no need of anyone else
   (E) their separation is inevitable

9. In lines 22–23, the assertion that souls "endure not yet / A breach, but an expansion" suggests that
   (A) separation is likely to be unendurable
   (B) death will ultimately place them far apart
   (C) distance extends, rather than inhibits love
   (D) love will grow without regard to time
   (E) the breach between the lovers is certain to grow

10. In line 25, the speaker introduces the image of a compass in a(n)
    (A) extended metaphor
    (B) epic simile
    (C) archaic allusion
    (D) particular metonymy
    (E) equivocal paradox

11. By extending the image of the "twin compasses" (lines
    25–36), the author builds a simple figure of speech into
    (A) a complex synecdoche
    (B) a mournful valediction
    (C) an arrogant assertion
    (D) a metaphysical conceit
    (E) a sexual innuendo

12. In line 32, the pronoun "that" refers to
    (A) the "fixed foot" (line 27)
    (B) the speaker's lover
    (C) the "center" (line 29)
    (D) the "soul" (line 27)
    (E) the "other" (line 28)

13. Lines 33–34, "Such wilt thou be to me, who must, / Like
    th' other foot, obliquely run," suggest that the speaker is
    asking his lover
    (A) to bear his absence patiently
    (B) to go with him on a journey
    (C) to agree to a friendly separation
    (D) to follow his circular reasoning
    (E) to realize that separation ends a relationship

14. The poem's ending, "Thy firmness makes my circle just, /
    And makes me end where I begun" (lines 35–36), offers
    the concluding thought that
    (A) a compass provides a constant indication of true
        northerly direction
    (B) the steadfastness of the speaker's lover will bring him
        home again
    (C) in his intended departure, the speaker's is upright and
        justified
    (D) the extended comparison helps in understanding a
        decision to separate
    (E) the speaker's argument has brought him in a full circle

15. A major theme of this poem might be expressed as a sepa-
    ration that
    (A) must ultimately cause grief and despair
    (B) needs neither consolation or distress
    (C) is part of the nature and completeness of the lovers' world
    (D) holds no sacred significance or example
    (E) constitutes a mystical force of human emotion

See page 434 for the answers to this set of questions.

"AH, ARE YOU DIGGING ON MY GRAVE?" BY THOMAS HARDY

QUESTIONS 16–26. Carefully read the following poem before choosing your answers.

"Ah, are you digging on my grave
    My loved one?—planting rue?"
—"No, yesterday he went to wed
One of the brightest wealth has bred.
'It cannot hurt her now,' he said,   5
    'That I should not be true.'"

"Then who is digging on my grave?
    My nearest dearest kin?"
—"Ah, no; they sit and think, 'What use!
What good will planting flowers produce?   10
No tendance of her mound can loose
    Her spirit from Death's gin.' "

"But some one digs upon my grave?
    My enemy?—prodding sly?"
—"Nay: when she heard you had passed the Gate   15
That shuts on all flesh soon or late,
She thought you no more worth her hate,
    And cares not where you lie."

"Then, who is digging on my grave?
    Say—since I have not guessed!"   20
—"O it is I, my mistress dear,
Your little dog, who still lives near,
And much I hope my movements here
    Have not disturbed your rest?"

"Ah yes! *You* dig upon my grave . . .   25
    Why flashed it not on me
That one true heart was left behind!
What feeling do we ever find
To equal among human kind
    A dog's fidelity!"   30

428 PART THREE / POEMS FOR FURTHER READING

"Mistress, I dug upon your grave
        To bury a bone, in case
I should be hungry near this spot
When passing on my daily trot.
I am sorry, but I quite forgot   35
        It was your resting-place."

16. The poem might best be described as
    (A) a dramatic monologue
    (B) an ironic conversation
    (C) a satire on love
    (D) a pastoral elegy
    (E) a symbol of faithfulness

17. In line 5, "he" refers to
    (A) the first speaker, who is dead
    (B) the "loved one" (line 2)
    (C) "one of the brightest" (line 4)
    (D) the sexton of the cemetery
    (E) the first speaker's beloved

18. The first stanza implies that the first speaker
    (A) knows that her lover cheated on her when she was
        alive
    (B) knows what flowers are being planted
    (C) expected that her beloved would remain faithful after
        her death
    (D) enjoyed a prosperous, wealthy life
    (E) was jilted at the altar by a false-hearted lover

19. In the second stanza, the second speaker suggests that the
    relatives of the deceased are assuming that
    (A) tending her grave would be an unwelcome act
    (B) planting flowers would be pleasing to her spirit
    (C) planting rue would be preferable to planting flowers
    (D) visiting graves is too morbid an activity
    (E) cultivating flowers on a grave serves no practical purpose

20. In line 15, the first speaker implies that her "enemy"
    (A) might be expected to desecrate a grave
    (B) may have tried to steal her lover away
    (C) feels remorse for her previous jealousy
    (D) could suspect that the first speaker is really alive
    (E) still cares about her in spite of their differences

21. By capitalizing "Gate" (line 16) the author
    (A) makes it a reference to heaven
    (B) emphasizes that it is figurative
    (C) illustrates that death is inevitable
    (D) creates an example of synecdoche
    (E) attributes religious awareness to the "enemy"

22. The purpose of the fourth stanza might best be described
    as to
    (A) propose a hopeful explanation to the poem's recurrent
        question
    (B) offer a humorous interlude to a tragic story
    (C) eliminate the speaker's last chance at immortality
    (D) diminish the reader's sympathy for the second speaker
    (E) to create suspense by foreshadowing the poem's
        conclusion

23. The fourth stanza validates the deceased person's belief
    that
    (A) she is mourned by those she has left behind
    (B) her grave is being tended lovingly
    (C) she has not been forgotten by the living
    (D) her memory lives on in the people she cared about
    (E) love ultimately conquers death: life prevails

24. In line 30, the word "fidelity"
    (A) refers to the dog's forthright honesty, compared to the
        "sly" enemy in line 15
    (B) draws a contrast between the dog and the "loved one"
        in line 2
    (C) reinforces the first speaker's affection for her those left
        behind in line 9
    (D) mocks the ingenuousness of the second speaker in the
        poem
    (E) emphasizes the dog's willingness to answer the speak-
        er's questions

25. Lines 29–31 contain all of the following EXCEPT
    (A) personification
    (B) comparison
    (C) exclamatory statement
    (D) masculine rhyme
    (E) rhetorical question

26. The poem's rhyme scheme serves primarily to
    (A) make the poem easier to memorize
    (B) emphasize the relationship between the speakers
    (C) lend a generally sarcastic effect to the poem
    (D) build ironic tension before the last line of each stanza
    (E) imitate the speaker's natural speech patterns

See page 434 for the answers to this set of questions.

"MID-TERM BREAK" BY SEAMUS HEANEY

QUESTIONS 27–37. Carefully read the following poem before choosing your answers.

I sat all morning in the college sick bay
Counting bells knelling classes to a close.
At two o'clock our neighbors drove me home.
In the porch I met my father crying—
He had always taken funerals in his stride—   5
And Big Jim Evans saying it was a hard blow.
The baby cooed and laughed and rocked the pram
When I came in, and I was embarrassed
By old men standing up to shake my hand
And tell me they were "sorry for my trouble."   10
Whispers informed strangers I was the eldest,
Away at school, as my mother held my hand
In hers and coughed out angry tearless sighs.
At ten o'clock the ambulance arrived
With the corpse, stanched and bandaged by the nurses.   15
Next morning I went up into the room. Snowdrops
And candles soothed the bedside; I saw him
For the first time in six weeks. Paler now,
Wearing a poppy bruise on his left temple,
He lay in the four foot box as in his cot.   20
No gaudy scars, the bumper knocked him clear.
A four foot box, a foot for every year.

27. The likely effect of the poem's title is
    (A) satiric
    (B) ironic
    (C) realistic
    (D) naturalistic
    (E) romantic

28. The tone of the poem shifts from
    (A) matter-of-fact to ironic
    (B) foreboding to elated
    (C) reflective to reminiscent
    (D) happy to mournful
    (E) chagrined to relaxed

29. In line 2, the word "knelling" attaches to the college bells a connotation of
    (A) repetitive energy
    (B) fanciful whimsy
    (C) somber mourning
    (D) uncommon antiquity
    (E) archaic intellect

30. The arrangement of the poem's lines demonstrates
    (A) strict iambic meter
    (B) frequent enjambment
    (C) occasional polysyndeton
    (D) repeated slant rhymes
    (E) systematic assonance

31. In observing that "the baby cooed and rocked the pram" (line 7) the speaker
    (A) identifies with his younger sibling
    (B) foreshadows the dead person's age
    (C) offers a metonymy for the family's happiness
    (D) contrasts the gravity of the scene with innocence
    (E) illustrates an unwelcome distraction from the event

32. The selection of detail in lines 9–10, "old men standing up to shake my hand / And tell me they were 'sorry for my trouble'"
    (A) characterizes the awkwardness of such events
    (B) suggests the speaker's lack of trustworthiness
    (C) emphasizes the speaker's unaccustomed role
    (D) develops the contrast between the speaker and his father
    (E) reflects the increasing tension between appearances and underlying reality

33. The meaning of the statement in lines 12 and 13 that "as my mother held my hand / In hers and coughed out angry tearless sighs" is enhanced by
    (A) auditory imagery
    (B) metonymy
    (C) alliteration
    (D) metaphor
    (E) onomatopoeia

34. In line 17, the word "him" most likely refers to
    (A) the baby
    (B) the speaker's father
    (C) one of the old men
    (D) the corpse
    (E) the speaker's older brother

35. The simile in line 20
    (A) compares death to sleep
    (B) contrasts violence with peacefulness
    (C) suggests that the body was dismembered
    (D) evokes the image of an elaborate funeral
    (E) reveals affection for the deceased

36. The final line of the poem
    (A) celebrates the life of the deceased
    (B) provides a measure of the speaker's grief
    (C) confirms the age of the deceased
    (D) offers evidence of the number of children in the family
    (E) reveals the duration of the deceased person's suffering

37. It can be inferred from the poem that the deceased person died of
    (A) burns sustained in a fire
    (B) a disfiguring disease
    (C) a severe beating by an abusive adult
    (D) natural causes following a long illness
    (E) injuries suffered in a vehicle accident

See page 434 for the answers to this set of questions.

ANSWERS FOR THE AP®
MULTIPLE-CHOICE QUESTIONS

"A Valediction: Forbidding Mourning" by John Donne

1. B	6. B	11. D
2. C	7. C	12. E
3. D	8. A	13. A
4. D	9. C	14. B
5. A	10. A	15. B

"Ah, Are You Digging on My Grave?" by Thomas Hardy

16. B	20. A	24. B
17. B	21. B	25. E
18. C	22. A	26. D
19. E	23. C	

"Mid-Term Break" by Seamus Heaney

27. B	31. D	35. A
28. A	32. A	36. C
29. C	33. A	37. E
30. B	34. D	

GLOSSARY AND INDEX
OF LITERARY TERMS

The definitions in this glossary sometimes repeat and sometimes differ in language from those in the text. Where they differ, the intention is to give a fuller sense of the term's meaning by allowing the reader a double perspective on it. Page numbers refer to discussion in the text, which in most but not all cases is fuller than that in the glossary.

Accent   In this book, the same as *stress*. A syllable given more prominence in pronunciation than its neighbors is said to be accented. **(page 204)**

Allegory   A narrative or description having a second meaning beneath the surface one. **(page 100)**

Alliteration   The repetition at close intervals of the initial consonant sounds of accented syllables or important words (for example, *m*ap–*m*oon, *k*ill–*c*ode, *p*reach–ap*p*rove). Important words and accented syllables beginning with vowels may also be said to alliterate with each other inasmuch as they all have the same lack of an initial consonant sound (for example, "*In*ebri*a*te of *A*ir—am *I*"). **(page 187)**

Allusion   A reference, explicit or implicit, to something in literature or history. (The term is reserved by some writers for implicit references only, such as those in "in Just—" **[page 141]** and in "On His Blindness" **[page 142]**; but the distinction between the two kinds of reference is not always clear-cut.) **(page 135)**

Anapest   A metrical foot consisting of two unaccented syllables followed by one accented syllable (for example, ŭn-dĕr-stánd). **(page 208)**

Anapestic meter   A meter in which a majority of the feet are anapests. (But see *Triple meter.*) **(pages 208, 208n)**

Apostrophe   A figure of speech in which someone absent or dead or something nonhuman is addressed as if it were alive and present and could reply. **(page 77)**

Approximate rhyme (also known as *Imperfect rhyme, Near rhyme, Slant rhyme, or Oblique rhyme*)   A term used for words in a rhyming pattern that have some kind of sound correspondence but are not perfect rhymes. See *Rhyme.* Approximate rhymes occur occasionally in patterns where most of the rhymes are perfect (for example, *push–rush* in "Leda and the Swan" [page 148]), and sometimes are used systematically in place of perfect rhyme (for example, "Because I could not stop for Death" [page 106]). **(page 188)**

Assonance The repetition at close intervals of the vowel sounds of accented syllables or important words (for example, h*a*t–r*a*n–*a*mber, v*ei*n–m*a*de). **(page 187n)**

Ballad A fairly short narrative poem written in a songlike stanza form. Example: "La Belle Dame sans Merci"

Blank verse Unrhymed iambic pentameter. **(page 218)**

Cacophony A harsh, discordant, unpleasant-sounding choice and arrangement of sounds. **(page 233)**

Caesura A speech pause occurring within a line. See *Grammatical pause* and *Rhetorical pause.* **(page 205)**

Connotation What a word suggests beyond its basic dictionary definition; a word's overtones of meaning. **(page 41)**

Consonance The repetition at close intervals of the final consonant sounds of accented syllables or important words (for example, boo*k*–pla*q*ue–thi*ck*er). **(page 187)**

Continuous form That form of a poem in which the lines follow each other without formal grouping, the only breaks being dictated by units of meaning. **(page 250)**

Couplet Two successive lines, usually in the same meter, linked by rhyme. **(page 254)**

Dactyl A metrical foot consisting of one accented syllable followed by two unaccented syllables (for example, mér-r̆i-l̆y). **(page 208)**

Dactylic meter A meter in which a majority of the feet are dactyls. (But see *Triple meter.*) **(pages 208, 208n)**

Denotation The basic definition or dictionary meaning of a word. **(page 41)**

Didactic poetry Poetry having as a primary purpose to teach or preach. **(page 270)**

Dimeter A metrical line containing two feet. **(page 209)**

Dramatic framework The situation, whether actual or fictional, realistic or fanciful, in which an author places his or her characters in order to express the theme. **(page 30)**

Dramatic irony See *Irony.* **(page 120)**

Duple meter A meter in which a majority of the feet contain two syllables. Iambic and trochaic are both duple meters. **(pages 208, 208n)**

End rhyme Rhymes that occur at the ends of the lines. **(page 188)**

End-stopped line   A line that ends with a natural speech pause, usually marked by punctuation. **(page 205)**

English (or Shakespearean) sonnet   A sonnet rhyming *ababcdcdefefgg.* Its content or structure ideally parallels the rhyme scheme, falling into three coordinate quatrains and a concluding couplet; but it is often structured, like the Italian sonnet, into octave and sestet, the principal break in thought coming at the end of the eighth line. **(page 254)**

Euphony   A smooth, pleasant-sounding choice and arrangement of sounds. **(page 233)**

Expected rhythm   The rhythmic expectation set up by the basic meter of a poem. **(page 216)**

Extended metaphor   A figure of speech (usually metaphor, simile, personification, or apostrophe) sustained or developed through a considerable number of lines or through a whole poem. **(page 82)**

Extrametrical syllables   In metrical verse, extra unaccented syllables added at the beginnings or endings of lines; these may be either a feature of the metrical form of a poem (for example, "Is my team plowing" [**page 29**], ends of odd-numbered lines) or occur as exceptions to the form (for example, "Virtue," [**page 209**], lines 9 and 11). In iambic lines, they occur at the end of the line; in trochaic, at the beginning. **(page 209)**

Feminine rhyme   A rhyme in which the repeated accented vowel is in either the second- or the third-to-last syllable of the words involved (for example, *ceil*ing–ap*peal*ing, *hur*rying–*scur*rying). **(page 187)**

Figurative language   Language employing figures of speech; language that cannot be taken literally or only literally. **(page 73)**

Figure of speech   Broadly, any way of saying something other than the ordinary way; more narrowly (and for the purposes of this book), a way of saying one thing and meaning another. **(page 73)**

Fixed form   Any form of poem in which the length and pattern are prescribed by previous usage or tradition, such as *sonnet, villanelle,* and so on. **(page 252)**

Folk ballad   A narrative poem designed to be sung, composed by an anonymous author, and transmitted orally for years or generations before being written down. It has usually undergone modification through the process of oral transmission.

Foot   The basic unit used in the scansion or measurement of metrical verse. A foot usually contains one accented syllable and one or two unaccented syllables (the *spondaic foot* is a modification of this principle). **(page 207)**

Form   The external pattern or shape of a poem, describable without reference to its content, as *continuous form, stanzaic form, fixed form* (and their varieties), *free verse,* and *syllabic verse.* (page 250) See *Structure.*

Free verse   Nonmetrical poetry in which the basic rhythmic unit is the line, and in which pauses, line breaks, and formal patterns develop organically from the requirements of the individual poem rather than from established poetic forms. (page 206)

Grammatical pause (also known as *Caesura*)   A pause introduced into the reading of a line, usually by a mark of punctuation. (page 205)

Half-rhyme   A *feminine rhyme* in which either the accented syllables rhyme (as *lightly* and *frightful*) or the unaccented syllables do (as *maple* and *apple*). (page 188)

Heard rhythm   The actual rhythm of a metrical poem as we hear it when it is read naturally. The heard rhythm mostly conforms to but sometimes departs from or modifies the *expected rhythm.* (page 216)

Hexameter   A metrical line containing six feet. (page 209)

Hyperbole   See *Overstatement.* (page 115)

Iamb   A metrical foot consisting of one unaccented syllable followed by one accented syllable (for example, rĕ-heárse). (page 208)

Iambic meter   A meter in which the majority of feet are iambs; the most common English meter. (pages 208, 208n)

Imagery   The representation through language of sense experience. (page 57)

Internal rhyme   A rhyme in which one or both of the rhyme words occurs *within* the line. (page 188)

Irony   A situation, or a use of language, involving some kind of incongruity or discrepancy. (page 117) Three kinds of irony are distinguished in this book: verbal irony, dramatic irony, and irony of situation (or situational irony).

Irony of situation (or *situational irony*)   A situation in which there is an incongruity between actual circumstances and those that would seem appropriate, or between what is anticipated and what actually comes to pass. (page 121)

Italian (or Petrarchan) sonnet   A sonnet consisting of an octave rhyming *abbaabba* and of a sestet using any arrangement of two or three additional rhymes, such as *cdcdcd* or *cdecde.* (page 253)

Masculine rhyme (also known as *Single rhyme*)   A rhyme in which the repeated accented vowel sound is in the final syllable of the words involved (for example, d*ance*–p*ants,* sc*ald*–rec*alled*). (page 187)

Metaphor   A figure of speech in which an implicit comparison is made between two things essentially unlike. It may take one of four forms: (1) that in which the literal term and the figurative term are *both named*; (2) that in which the literal term is *named* and the figurative term *implied*; (3) that in which the literal term is *implied* and the figurative term *named*; (4) that in which *both* the literal and the figurative terms are *implied.* (page 73)

Meter   The regular patterns of accent that underlie metrical verse; the measurable repetition of accented and unaccented syllables in poetry. (page 206)

Metonymy   A figure of speech in which some significant aspect or detail of an experience is used to represent the whole experience. In this book the single term *metonymy* is used for what are sometimes distinguished as two separate figures: *synecdoche* (the use of the part for the whole) and *metonymy* (the use of something closely related for the thing actually meant). (page 78)

Metrical variations   Departures from the basic metrical pattern (see *substitution, extrametrical syllables*). (page 209)

Monometer   A metrical line containing one foot. (page 209)

Octave   (1) An eight-line stanza. (2) The first eight lines of a sonnet, especially one structured in the manner of an Italian sonnet. (page 253)

Onomatopoeia   The use of words that supposedly mimic their meaning in their sound (for example, *boom, click, plop*). (page 231)

Overstatement (or Hyperbole)   A figure of speech in which exaggeration is used in the service of truth. (page 115)

Oxymoron   A compact paradox in which two successive words seemingly contradict each other. (page 256)

Paradox   A statement or situation containing apparently contradictory or incompatible elements. (page 114)

Paradoxical situation   A situation containing apparently but not actually incompatible elements. The celebration of a fifth birthday anniversary by a twenty-year-old man is paradoxical but explainable if the man was born on February 29. The Christian doctrines that Christ was born of a virgin and is both God and man are, for a Christian believer, paradoxes (that is, apparently impossible but true). (page 114)

Paradoxical statement (or Verbal paradox)   A figure of speech in which an apparently self-contradictory statement is nevertheless found to be true. (page 114)

Paraphrase   A restatement of the content of a poem designed to make its *prose meaning* as clear as possible. (page 25)

Pentameter   A metrical line containing five feet. **(page 209)**

Personification   A figure of speech in which human attributes are given to an animal, an object, or a concept. **(page 75)**

Petrarchan sonnet   See *Italian sonnet.* **(page 253)**

Phonetic intensive   A word whose sound, by an obscure process, to some degree suggests its meaning. As differentiated from *onomatopoetic words,* the meanings of phonetic intensives do not refer explicitly to sounds. **(page 231)**

Prose meaning   That part of a poem's *total meaning* that can be separated out and expressed through paraphrase. **(page 151)**

Prose poem   Usually a short composition having the intentions of poetry but written in prose rather than verse. **(page 206)**

Quatrain   (1) A four-line stanza. (2) A four-line division of a sonnet marked off by its rhyme scheme. **(page 254)**

Refrain   A repeated word, phrase, line, or group of lines, normally at some fixed position in a poem written in stanzaic form. **(page 189)**

Rhetorical pause (also known as *Caesura*)   A natural pause, unmarked by punctuation, introduced into the reading of a line by its phrasing or syntax. **(page 205)**

Rhetorical poetry   Poetry using artificially eloquent language; that is, language too high-flown for its occasion and unfaithful to the full complexity of human experience. **(page 269)**

Rhetorical stress   In natural speech, as in prose and poetic writing, the stressing of words or syllables so as to emphasize meaning and sentence structure. **(page 205)**

Rhyme   The repetition of the accented vowel sound and all succeeding sounds in important or importantly positioned words (for example, *old–cold,* v*ane–reign, court–report, order–recorder*). The preceding definition applies to *perfect rhyme* and assumes that the accented vowel sounds involved are preceded by differing consonant sounds. If the preceding consonant sound is the same (for example, *manse–romance, style–stile*), or if there is no preceding consonant sound in either word (for example, *aisle–isle, alter–altar*), or if the same word is repeated in the rhyming position (for example, *hill–hill*), the words are called *identical rhymes.* Both *perfect rhymes* and *identical rhymes* are to be distinguished from *approximate rhymes.* **(page 187)**

Rhyme scheme   Any fixed pattern of rhymes characterizing a whole poem or its stanzas. **(page 251)**

Rhythm   Any wavelike recurrence of motion or sound. **(page 204)**

Run-on line   A line that has no natural speech pause at its end, allowing the sense to flow uninterruptedly into the succeeding line. **(page 205)**

Sarcasm   Bitter or cutting speech; speech intended by its speaker to give pain to the person addressed. **(page 117)**

Satire   A kind of literature that ridicules human folly or vice with the ostensible purpose of bringing about reform or of keeping others from falling into similar folly or vice. **(page 117)**

Scansion   The process of measuring metrical verse, that is, of marking accented and unaccented syllables, dividing the lines into feet, identifying the metrical pattern, and noting significant variations from that pattern. **(page 209)**

Sentimental poetry   Poetry that attempts to manipulate the reader's emotions in order to achieve a greater emotional response than the poem itself really warrants. (A sentimental novel or film is sometimes called, pejoratively, a "tearjerker.") **(page 269)**

Sestet   (1) A six-line stanza. (2) The last six lines of a sonnet structured on the Italian model. **(page 253)**

Shakespearean sonnet   See *English sonnet*. **(page 254)**

Simile   A figure of speech in which an explicit comparison is made between two things essentially unlike. The comparison is made explicit by the use of some such word or phrase as *like, as, than, similar to, resembles,* or *seems.* **(page 73)**

Situational irony   See *Irony*. **(page 121)**

Sonnet   A fixed form of fourteen lines, normally iambic pentameter, with a rhyme scheme conforming to or approximating one of two main types—the *Italian* or the *English.* **(page 254)**

Spondee   A metrical foot consisting of two syllables equally or almost equally accented (for example, trúe–blúe). **(page 208)**

Stanza   A group of lines whose metrical pattern (and usually its rhyme scheme as well) is repeated throughout a poem. **(page 251)**

Stanzaic form   The form of a poem written in a series of units having the same number of lines and usually other characteristics in common, such as metrical pattern or rhyme scheme. **(page 251)**

Stress   In this book, the same as *Accent*. But see page 204 footnote.

Structure   The internal organization of a poem's content. See *Form*. **(page 250)**

Substitution   In metrical verse, the replacement of the expected metrical foot by a different one (for example, a trochee occurring in an iambic line). **(page 209)**

Syllabic verse   Verse measured by the number of syllables rather than the number of feet per line. **(page 223)**

Symbol   A figure of speech in which something (object, person, situation, or action) means more than what it is. A symbol, in other words, may be read both literally and metaphorically. **(page 92)**

Synecdoche   A figure of speech in which a part is used for the whole. In this book it is subsumed under the term *Metonymy*. **(page 78)**

Synesthesia   Presentation of one sense experience in terms usually associated with another sensation. **(page 239)**

Tercet   A three-line stanza exhibited in *terza rima* and *villanelle* as well as in other poetic forms. **(page 255)**

Terza rima   An interlocking rhyme scheme with the pattern *aba bcb cdc,* etc. **(page 265)**

Tetrameter   A metrical line containing four feet. **(page 209)**

Theme   The central idea of a literary work. **(page 25)**

Tone   The writer's or speaker's attitude toward the subject, the audience, or herself or himself; the emotional coloring, or emotional meaning, of a work. **(page 165)**

Total meaning   The total experience communicated by a poem. It includes all those dimensions of experience by which a poem communicates—sensuous, emotional, imaginative, and intellectual—and it can be communicated in no other words than those of the poem itself. **(page 151)**

Trimeter   A metrical line containing three feet. **(page 209)**

Triple meter   A meter in which a majority of the feet contain three syllables. (Actually, if more than 25 percent of the feet in a poem are triple, its effect is more triple than duple, and it ought perhaps to be referred to as triple meter.) *Anapestic* and *dactylic* are both triple meters. **(pages 208, 208n)**

Trochaic meter   A meter in which the majority of feet are trochees. **(pages 208, 208n)**

Trochee   A metrical foot consisting of one accented syllable followed by one unaccented syllable (for example, bár-tĕr). **(page 208)**

Truncation   In metrical verse, the omission of an unaccented syllable at either end of a line (for example, "Introduction to *Songs of Innocence.*" **(page 209)**

Understatement   A figure of speech that consists of saying less than one means, or of saying what one means with less force than the occasion warrants. **(page 116)**

Verbal irony   See *Irony*. (page 117)

Verse   Metrical language; the opposite of *prose*.

Villanelle   A nineteen-line fixed form consisting of five tercets rhymed *aba* and a concluding quatrain rhymed *abaa*, with lines 1 and 3 of the first tercet serving as refrains in an alternating pattern through line 15 and then repeated as lines 18 and 19. (page 255)

COPYRIGHTS AND ACKNOWLEDGMENTS

GEORGE GORDON, LORD BYRON, "She Walks in Beauty" and "Stanzas" by George Gordon, Lord Byron.

AMY CLAMPITT, "Witness" from *The Collected Poems of Amy Clampitt*, copyright © 1997 by the Estate of Amy Clampitt. Used by permission of Alfred A. Knopf, a division of Penguin Random House.

LUCILLE CLIFTON, "good times" and "in the inner city" from *The Collected Poems of Lucille Clifton,* copyright © 1987 by Lucille Clifton. Reprinted by permission of BOA Editions. www.boaeditions.org.

HENRI COLE, "Mask" from *Pierce the Skin: Selected Poems, 1982–2007,* copyright © 2011 by Henri Cole. Reprinted by permission of Farrar, Straus and Giroux.

SAMUEL TAYLOR COLERIDGE, "Kubla Khan" by Samuel Taylor Coleridge.

BILLY COLLINS, "The Dead" and "Weighing the Dog" from *Questions About Angels,* copyright © 1991 by Billy Collins. Reprinted by permission of the University of Pittsburgh Press. "Divorce" from *Ballistics: Poems,* copyright © 2008 by Billy Collins. Used by permission of Random House, a division of Penguin Random House. "Sonnet" from *Sailing Alone Around the Room: New and Selected Poems,* copyright © 2001 by Billy Collins. Used by permission of Random House, a division of Penguin Random House. "Genesis" from *Horoscopes for the Dead: Poems,* copyright © 2011 by Billy Collins. Used by permission of Random House, a division of Penguin Random House. "Villanelle" from *Aimless Love: New and Selected Poems,* copyright © 2013 by Billy Collins. Used by permission of Random House, a division of Penguin Random House.

STEPHEN CRANE, "War is Kind" by Stephen Crane.

e.e. cummings, "Buffalo Bill's," "in Just–," "O Sweet Spontaneous," and "the Cambridge ladies who live in furnished souls" from *Complete Poems: 1904–1962,* edited by George James Firmage. Copyright © 1976 by George James Firmage and copyright © 1923, 1951, 1991 by The Trustees for the E.E. Cummings Trust. Used by permission of Liveright Publishing.

EMILY DICKINSON, "A little East of Jordan," A narrow Fellow in the Grass," "Because I could not stop for death," "Four Trees—upon a solitary Acre," "I died for Beauty—but was scarce," "I felt a Funeral, in my Brain," "I heard a fly buzz—when I died," "I taste a liquor never brewed," "If I can stop one heart from breaking," "It sifts from Leaden Sieves," "I would not paint—a picture," "Much Madness is divinest sense "There's been a Death in the opposite house," and "What soft—Cherubic Creatures" from *The Poems Of Emily Dickinson,* edited by Thomas H. Johnson. The Belknap Press of Harvard University Press. Copyright ©

1923, 1928, 1930,1939, 1969 by Henry Holt and Company. Copyright © 1936, 1944, 1951, 1956, 1958 by Robert Frost. Copyright © 1964, 1967 by Lesley Frost Ballantine. Reprinted with the permission of Henry Holt and Company.

LOUISE GLÜCK, "Cousins," "Labor Day," and "Lost Love" from *Ararat*, copyright © 1990 by Louise Glück. Reprinted by permission of HarperCollins Publishers. "Eurydice" from *Vita Nova*, copyright © 1999 by Louise Glück. Reprinted by permission of HarperCollins Publishers. "Primavera" from *Poems 1962–2012* by Louise Glück. Reprinted by permission of Farrar, Straus and Giroux. "Purple Bathing Suit" from *Meadowlands*, copyright © 1996 by Louise Glück. Reprinted by permission of HarperCollins Publishers.

RACHEL HADAS, "Ghost Yogurt," *The Yale Review*, July 2014, 102:34.

THOMAS HARDY, "Ah, are you digging on my grave?" "Channel Firing," "Hap," "The Darkling Thrush," "The Oxen," and "The Ruined Maid" by Thomas Hardy. "The Man He Killed" from *Thomas Hardy, Time's Laughingstocks and Other Verses,* copyright 1909 by Macmillan.

ROBERT HAYDEN, "Those Winter Sundays" from *Angle of Ascent: New and Selected Poems,* copyright © 1966 by Robert Hayden. Used by permission of Liveright Publishing Corporation.

SEAMUS HEANEY, "Digging," "Follower," "Mid-Term Break," "The Forge," "The Skunk," and "Villanelle for an Anniversary" from *Opened Ground: Selected Poems 1966–1996*, copyright © 1998 by Seamus Heaney. Reprinted by permission of Farrar, Straus and Giroux and Faber & Faber.

GEORGE HERBERT, "Love," "Peace," "The Pulley," and "Virtue" by George Herbert.

ROBERT HERRICK, "Delight in Disorder" and "To the Virgins, to Make Much of Time" by Robert Herrick.

GERARD MANLEY HOPKINS, "God's Grandeur," "Pied Beauty," and "Spring" by Gerard Manley Hopkins.

A.E. HOUSMAN, "Eight O'Clock" and "Is my team plowing" by A.E. Housman. "Loveliest of Trees," "Terence, this is stupid stuff," and "To an Athlete Dying Young" from *A Shropshire Lad* by A.E. Housman, 1896.

LANGSTON HUGHES, "Cross," "Harlem," "Suicide's Note," "The Weary Blues," and "Theme for English B," from *The Collected Poems of Langston Hughes*, edited by Arnold Rampersad with David Roessel, Associate Editor. Copyright © 1994 by the Estate of Langston Hughes. Used by permission of Alfred A. Knopf, a division of Penguin Random House.

TED HUGHES, "Hawk Roosting" from *Lupercal*, copyright © 2003 by the Estate of Ted Hughes. Reprinted by permission of Farrar, Straus and Giroux and Faber & Faber.

CLIVE JAMES, "Whitman and the Moth" from *The New Yorker*, November 22, 2010. Reprinted with permission of United Agents on behalf of Clive James.

RANDALL JARRELL, "The Death of the Ball Turret Gunner" from *The Complete Poems* by Randall Jarrell. Copyright © 1969, 1997 by Mary von S. Jarrell. Reprinted by permission of Farrar, Straus and Giroux.

BEN JONSON, "Still to be neat" and "To Celia" by Ben Jonson.

JOHN KEATS, "Bright Star," "La Belle Dame sans Merci," "Ode on Melancholy," "Ode on a Grecian Urn," "Ode to a Nightingale," "On First Looking into Chapman's Homer," "On the Sonnet," "O Solitude!" "This Living Hand," "To Autumn," and "When I have fears that I may cease to be" by John Keats.

GALWAY KINNELL, "After Making Love We Hear Footsteps" and "Blackberry Eating" from *Three Books,* copyright © 1993 by Galway Kinnell. Reprinted by permission of Houghton Mifflin Harcourt Publishing Company.

GRENVILLE KLEISER, "The Most Vital Thing in Life" by Grenville Kleiser.

PHILIP LARKIN, "A Study of Reading Habits," "Church Going," and "Toads" from *Complete Poems of Philip Larkin* by Philip Larkin, edited by Archie Burnett. Reprinted by permission of Faber & Faber and Farrar, Straus and Giroux.

D. H. LAWRENCE, "Piano" by D. H. Lawrence.

DENISE LEVERTOV, "To the Snake" from *Collected Earlier Poems 1940–1960*, copyright ©1960 by Denise Levertov. Reprinted by permission of New Directions Publishing.

GEORGE CABOT LODGE, "Lower New York: At Dawn" by George Cabot Lodge.

ARCHIBALD MACLEISH, "Ars Poetica" and "You, Andrew Marvell" from *Collected Poems, 1917–1982*, copyright © 1985 by the Estate of Archibald MacLeish. Reprinted by permission of Houghton Mifflin Harcourt.

CHRISTOPHER MARLOWE, "The Passionate Shepherd to his Love" by Christopher Marlowe.

ANDREW MARVELL, "To His Coy Mistress" by Andrew Marvell.

INDEX OF AUTHORS, TITLES, AND FIRST LINES

Authors' names appear in CAPITALS, titles of selections in *italics,* and first lines of poems in roman type. Numbers in **bold face** indicate the pages of the selection, and numbers in roman type indicate the pages where the selection is discussed.

A

About suffering they were never wrong, 356
Accounting, 49–50
A cold coming we had of it, 145
Acquainted with the Night, 251, 264–265
ADDONIZIO, KIM
   Sonnenizio on a Line from Drayton, 356
After Apple-Picking, 65–66, 250, 251
After Making Love We Hear Footsteps, 393
Ah, are you digging on my grave, 375, 427
"Ah, Are You Digging on My Grave?", 375–376, 427–430
A little East of Jordan, 149
All I know is a door into the dark, 64
All we need is fourteen lines, well, thirteen now, 159
ALVAREZ, JULIA
   Dusting, 51–52
Among School Children, 176–178
A narrow Fellow in the Grass, 167
And here face down beneath the sun, 104
Anecdote of the Jar, 410
Annabel Lee, 227–229
Announced by all the trumpets of the sky, 84
A noiseless patient spider, 93
An ordinary evening in Wisconsin, 361
Anthem for Doomed Youth, 241–242
Apartment Living, 397
A poem should be palpable and mute, 393
Apparition, The, 368–369
ARNOLD, MATTHEW
   Dover Beach, 179–181, 320
Ars Poetica, 393–394

A sight in camp in the daybreak gray and dim, 412
A slumber did my spirit seal, 124
A spirit moved, John Harvard walked the yard, 265
As the guests arrive at my son's party, 199
A sudden blow: the great wings beating still, 148
As virtuous men pass mildly away, 86, 423
A sweet disorder in the dress, 266
As You Like It, 193
AUDEN, W. H.
   Musée des Beaux Arts, 356–357
   That night when joy began, 188–189, 191
   Unknown Citizen, The, 126–127, 334
Aunt Jennifer's Tigers, 244
Aunt Jennifer's tigers prance across a screen, 244
Author to Her Book, The, 76–77

B

Barbie Doll, 119–120
Batter my heart, three-personed God, 124–125
Batter my heart, three-personed God; for you, 124
Bean Eaters, The, 14
Because I could not stop for Death, 106
Because I could not stop for Death, 106–107, 188
Before the war, they were happy, he said, 160
Behind him the hotdogs split and drizzled, 242
BEHN, APHRA
   On Her Loving Two Equally, 357
Behold her, single in the field, 415

Bells, The, 195–198, 230
Bent double, like old beggars under sacks, 6
Between my finger and my thumb, 96
Birches, 371–373
BISHOP, ELIZABETH
    Filling Station, 16–17
    Fish, The, 307–309
    Insomnia, 221–222
    Manners, 357–358
    One Art, 258–259
    In the Waiting Room, 52–55
Blackberry Eating, 244–245
Black Rook in Rainy Weather, 11–12
BLAKE, WILLIAM
    Chimney Sweeper, The, 120–122
    Garden of Love, The, 359
    "Introduction" to Songs of Innocence, 219–220
    Lamb, The, 162, 320
    Sick Rose, The, 95–96, 98
    Tiger, The, 162–163, 320
Blond, 411
Bloodline, Elegy: Su Qijian Family, Beijing,
    397–400
Blow, blow, thou winter wind, 193
Blow, blow, thou winter wind, 193, 251
Bop After Hip Op, 175–176
BRADSTREET, ANNE
    Author to Her Book, The, 76–77
Break, break, break, 226
Break, break, break, 226–227
Break of Day, 31–32
Bright Star, 77–78
Bright star, would I were steadfast as thou
    art, 77
BROOKS, GWENDOLYN
    Bean Eaters, The, 14
    Sadie and Maud, 360
    song in the front yard, a, 359–360
    We Real Cool, 193–194
BROWNING, ROBERT
    Meeting at Night, 58, 59, 75, 79, 252
    My Last Duchess, 151, 250–251,
        288–290, 333
    Parting at Morning, 59–60
    Porphyria's Lover, 151, 224–226
    Soliloquy of the Spanish Cloister, 130–133
Brushing out our daughter's brown, 50
Buffalo Bill's, 366
Buffalo Bill's defunct, 366
Busy old fool, unruly sun, 116

BYRON, LORD GEORGE GORDON
    She Walks in Beauty, 360–361
    Stanzas, 221

C
Cambridge ladies who live in furnished souls, the,
    366–367
Canonization, The, 281–283
Certainly it was possible—somewhere, 411
Channel Firing, 376–378
Chimney Sweeper, The, 120–122
Christmas Eve, and twelve of the clock, 173
Church Going, 181–183, 320
CLAMPITT, AMY
    Witness, 361
CLIFTON, LUCILLE
    good times, 362
    in the inner city, 127–128
COLE, HENRI
    Mask, 362
COLERIDGE, SAMUEL TAYLOR
    Kubla Khan, 363–364
Collection Day, 36–37
COLLINS, BILLY
    Dead, The, 364
    Divorce, 86
    Genesis, 147–148
    Introduction to Poetry, 19–20
    Sonnet, 159–160, 320
    Villanelle, 262–263
    Weighing the Dog, 364–365
Colonel, The, 161, 206, 320
Colossus, The, 129–130
Come bumble-footed ones, 403
Come live with me and be my Love, 394
Complacencies of the peignoir,
    and late, 301
Composed upon Westminster Bridge, September 3,
    1802, 275
Connoisseuse of Slugs, The, 402–403
Counting-Out Rhyme, 194–195
Cousins, 374–375
CRANE, STEPHEN
    War Is Kind, 365–366
Cross, 47–48, 317, 348
Crossing the Bar, 172–173
cummings, e. e.
    Buffalo Bill's defunct, 366
    Cambridge ladies who live in furnished souls,
        the, 366–367

in Just—, 141–142, 251
O sweet spontaneous, 157–158

D

Dalliance of the Eagles, The, 37–38
Dance, The, 248
Darkling Thrush, The, 378–379
Days Gone By, The, 276
Dead, The, 364
Death, be not proud, 260–261
Death of the Ball Turret Gunner, The, 387
Delight in Disorder, 266–267
Description of the Morning, A, 410–411
Desert Places, 48–49
Design, 156, 317
DICKINSON, EMILY
    Because I could not stop for Death,
        106–107, 188
    Four Trees—upon a solitary Acre, 155–156
    I died for Beauty—but was scarce, 367
    I felt a Funeral, in my Brain, 62–63, 231
    If I can stop one Heart from breaking, 277
    I heard a Fly buzz—when I died, 237–239
    I taste a liquor never brewed, 82
    It sifts from Leaden Sieves, 74–75, 280
    I would not paint—a picture, 276–277
    little East of Jordan, A, 149–150
    Much Madness is divinest Sense, 115–116
    narrow Fellow in the Grass, A, 167–169,
        320, 323
    There is no Frigate like a Book, 42, 44, 79, 344
    There's a certain Slant of light, 290–291, 334
    There's been a Death, in the Opposite House,
        32–33, 231
    What Soft-Cherubic Creatures, 128
Digging, 96–99, 318
Disillusionment of Ten O'Clock, 55–56
Divorce, 86
Does the road wind up-hill all the way?, 408
DONNE, JOHN
    Apparition, The, 368–369
    Batter my heart, three-personed God, 124–125
    Break of Day, 31–32
    Canonization, The, 281–283
    Death, be not proud, 260–261
    Flea, The, 174–175
    Good-Morrow, The, 369
    Hymn to God, My God, in My Sickness,
        107–109, 270
    Song: Go and catch a falling star, 367–368

Sun Rising, The, 116–117
Triple Fool, The, 13
Valediction: Forbidding Mourning, A, 86–88,
    423–426
Do not go gentle into that good night, 255
Do Not Go Gentle into That Good Night, 255–257
Do not weep, maiden, for war is kind, 365
DOTY, MARK
    Pescadero, 369–370
Dover Beach, 179–181, 320
DRAYTON, MICHAEL
    Since there's no help, 169–170, 235
Drink to me only with thine eyes, 388
Droning a drowsy syncopated tune, 305
Dulce et Decorum Est, 6–7, 80
DUNBAR, PAUL LAURENCE
    Sympathy, 370–371
    We Wear the Mask, 263–264
DUNBAR-NELSON, ALICE MOORE
    I Sit and Sew, 371
Dusting, 51–52

E

Each morning I wrote my name, 51
Eagle, The, 4, 59, 151
Earth has not anything to show more fair, 275
Eight O'Clock, 232–233
Elbows on dry books, we dreamed, 44
ELIOT, T. S.
    Journey of the Magi, 145–147
    Love Song of J. Alfred Prufrock, The,
        295–300, 318
EMERSON, RALPH WALDO
    Snowstorm, The, 84–85
Engraved on the Collar of a Dog Which I Gave
    to His Royal Highness, 183–184
Eros Turannos, 405–406
Eurydice, 140–141
Eurydice went back to hell, 140

F

Farewell, thou child of my right hand,
    and joy, 18
Fern Hill, 246–247
Filling Station, 16–17
Fire and Ice, 105–106
Fish, The, 307–309
Flea, The, 174–175
Follower, 380
Folly of Being Comforted, The, 261–262

FORCHÉ, CAROLYN
   Colonel, The, 161, 206, 320
Forge, The, 64, 231
For God's sake, hold your tongue, and let me love!, 281
For I can snore like a bullhorn, 393
For years, I wrote as if without stop—, 175
Four Trees—upon a solitary Acre, 155–156
Four Trees—upon a solitary Acre—, 155
From my mother's sleep I fell into the State, 387
FROST, ROBERT
   Acquainted with the Night, 251, 264–265
   After Apple-Picking, 65–66, 250, 251
   Birches, 371–373
   Desert Places, 48–49
   Design, 156, 317
   Fire and Ice, 105–106
   Home Burial, 291–295, 335–336, 339, 340
   Mending Wall, 373–374
   Nothing Gold Can Stay, 202
   "Out, Out—", 78, 136–137
   Road Not Taken, The, 91–93, 98, 116
   Stopping by Woods on a Snowy Evening, 153–154, 166

G

Garden of Love, The, 359
Gather ye rosebuds while ye may, 99
Genesis, 147–148
Ghost Yogurt, 85–86
Glory be to God for dappled things—, 272
GLÜCK, LOUISE
   Cousins, 374–375
   Eurydice, 140–141
   Labor Day, 14–15
   Lost Love, 170–171
   Primavera, 375
   Purple Bathing Suit, 102–103
Go and catch a falling star, 367
God's Grandeur, 191–192
God's Will for You and Me, 271–272
Good-Morrow, The, 369
good times, 362
Green Snake, when I hung you round my neck, 167
Gr-r-r—there go, my heart's abhorrence!, 130

H

HADAS, RACHEL
   Ghost Yogurt, 85–86

Had he and I but met, 24
Had I the Choice, 220–221
Had I the choice to tally greatest bards, 220
Had we but world enough, and time, 88
Hamlet, passages from, 116, 152, 192, 270
Hap, 378
Happy the man, whose wish and care, 404
HARDY, THOMAS
   "Ah, Are You Digging on My Grave?", 375–376, 427–430
   Channel Firing, 376–378
   Darkling Thrush, The, 378–379
   Hap, 378
   Man He Killed, The, 24–25, 28, 44
   Oxen, The, 173–174
   Ruined Maid, The, 379
Harlem, 73–74
Having been tenant long to a rich Lord, 100
Hawk Roosting, 33–34
HAYDEN, ROBERT
   Those Winter Sundays, 66–67
HEANEY, SEAMUS
   Digging, 96–99, 318
   Follower, 380
   Forge, The, 64, 231
   Mid-Term Break, 125–126, 188
   Skunk, The, 245–246
   Villanelle for an Anniversary, 265–266
Hear the sledges with the bells—, 195
He clasps the crag with crooked hands, 4
HERBERT, GEORGE
   Love, 381
   Peace, 381–382
   Pulley, The, 251–253
   Redemption, 100–101, 315
   Virtue, 209–219, 235
Here is the dawn a hopeless thing to see, 274
HERRICK, ROBERT
   Delight in Disorder, 266–267
   Upon Julia's Clothes, 35
   To the Virgins, to Make Much of Time, 99–100, 334
He saw her from the bottom of the stairs, 291
He stood, and heard the steeple, 232
He was found by the Bureau of Statistics to be, 126
His art is eccentricity, his aim, 272
History Lesson, 179
Home Burial, 291–295, 335–336, 339, 340

HOPKINS, GERARD MANLEY
   God's Grandeur, 191–192
   Spring, 60–61, 320
Hours continuing long, sore and heavy-
   hearted, 413
Hours continuing long, sore and heavy-hearted,
   413–414
HOUSMAN, A. E.
   To an Athlete Dying Young, 77, 385
   Eight O'Clock, 232–233
   "Is my team plowing," 29–31, 231, 319
   Loveliest of Trees, 152–153
   "Terence, this is stupid stuff," 118, 327,
     383–384
How dear to my heart was the old-fashioned
   hurler, 272
How strong does my passion flow, 357
HUGHES, LANGSTON
   Cross, 47–48, 317, 348
   Harlem, 73–74
   Suicide's Note, 17
   Theme for English B, 386
   Weary Blues, The, 305–306
HUGHES, TED
   Hawk Roosting, 33–34
Hymn to God, My God, in My Sickness,
   107–109, 270

I

I am four in this photograph, standing, 179
I am his Highness' dog at Kew, 183
I am silver and exact. I have no
   preconceptions, 36
I am two fools, I know, 13
I ask them to take a poem, 19
I caught a tremendous fish, 307
I died for Beauty—but was scarce, 367
I died for Beauty—but was scarce, 367
If but some vengeful god would call
   to me, 378
If by dull rhymes our English must be
   chained, 158
I felt a Funeral, in my Brain, 62
I felt a Funeral, in my Brain, 62–63, 231
If I can stop one Heart from breaking, 277
If I can stop one Heart from breaking, 277
I found a dimpled spider, fat and white, 156
I Go Back to May 1937, 402
I have been one acquainted with the night, 264
I have done it again, 309

I heard a Fly buzz—when I died, 237–239
I heard a Fly buzz—when I died—, 237
I know what the caged bird feels, alas!, 370
I leant upon a coppice gate, 378
I like watching you garden, 102
I love to go out in late September, 244
I'm a riddle in nine syllables, 81
I met a traveler from an antique land, 122
In 1965 my parents broke two laws of
   Mississippi, 412
In Breughel's great picture, The Kermess, 248
in Just—, 141
in Just—, 141–142, 251
Insomnia, 221–222
in the inner city, 127
in the inner city, 127–128
In the mud-colored Hai River a swirl of
   infant-girl bodies, 397
In the Waiting Room, 52–55
Introduction to Poetry, 19–20
"Introduction" to Songs of Innocence, 219–220
In Worcester, Massachusetts, 52
In Xanadu did Kubla Khan, 363
I placed a jar in Tennessee, 410
I sat all morning in the college sick bay, 125
I saw in Louisiana a live-oak growing, 67
I saw in Louisiana a live-oak growing, 67–68
I see them standing at the formal gates of
   their colleges, 402
I shall never get you put together
   entirely, 129
I shut my eyes and all the world drops
   dead, 259
I Sit and Sew, 371
I sit and sew—a useless task it seems, 371
I sit in the top of the wood, my eyes
   closed, 33
Is my team plowing, 29
"Is my team plowing," 29–31, 231, 319
I taste a liquor never brewed, 82
I taste a liquor never brewed, 82
I tied a paper mask onto my face, 362
It is awkward for me and bewildering for
   him, 364
It little profits that an idle king, 110
It's a year exactly since my father died, 14
It sifts from Leaden Sieves, 74
It sifts from Leaden Sieves, 74–75, 280
It's not easy living here, waiting to be
   charmed, 395

It was late, of course, 147
It was many and many a year ago, 227
I've stayed in the front yard all my life, 359
I wake to sleep, and take my waking
    slow, 189
I walk through the long schoolroom
    questioning, 176
I wandered lonely as a cloud, 414
I wandered lonely as a cloud, 414
I was angry with my friend, 273
I went out to the hazel wood, 418
I went to the Garden of Love, 359
I will arise and go now, and go to
    Innisfree, 416
I will not toy with it nor bend an inch, 262
I wonder, by my troth, what thou and I, 369
I would not paint—a picture, 276–277
I would not paint—a picture—, 276

J

JAMES, CLIVE
    Whitman and the Moth, 103–104
JARRELL, RANDALL
    Death of the Ball Turret Gunner, The, 387
JONSON, BEN
    To Celia, 388
    On My First Son, 18–19
    Still to be neat, 387
Journey of the Magi, 145–147
Just to be tender, just to be true, 271

K

KEATS, JOHN
    To Autumn, 69–70, 77
    Bright Star, 77–78
    *On First Looking into Chapman's Homer,
        253–254*
    La Belle Dame sans Merci, 388–389
    Ode on a Grecian Urn, 286–288
    Ode on Melancholy, 34–35
    Ode to a Nightingale, 389–391
    O Solitude!, 278
    To Sleep, 392
    On the Sonnet, 158–159, 320
    This living hand, 392
    When I have fears that I may cease to be, 278
KINNELL, GALWAY
    After Making Love We Hear Footsteps, 393
    Blackberry Eating, 244–245
Kubla Khan, 363–364

L

La Belle Dame sans Merci, 388–389
Labor Day, 14–15
Lady Lazarus, 309–312
Lake Isle of Innisfree, The, 416–417
Lamb, The, 162, 320
LARKIN, PHILIP
    Church Going, 181–183, 320
    *Study of Reading Habits, A, 25–27, 317,
        334, 349–351*
    Toads, 83–84, 188
Leda and the Swan, 148
Ledger, The, 51
Let me not to the marriage of true minds, 409
Let me not to the marriage of true minds, 409
Let us go then, you and I, 295
LEVERTOV, DENISE
    To the Snake, 167, 168–169, 320
Line a deep bowl with cheesecloth—or
    in my, 85
little East of Jordan, A, 149–150
Little Lamb, who made thee?, 162
Living in Sin, 63–64
Lost Love, 170–171
Love, 381
Love bade me welcome; yet my soul drew
    back, 381
Love is injustice, said Camus, 51
Loveliest of Trees, 152–153
Loveliest of trees, the cherry now, 152
Love set you going like a fat gold watch, 198
Love's Labor's Lost, passages from, 5, 192
*Love Song of J. Alfred Prufrock, The,
    295–300, 318*
Lower New York: At Dawn, 274–275

M

Macbeth, passages from, 80, 137–138, 317
MACLEISH, ARCHIBALD
    Ars Poetica, 393–394
    You, Andrew Marvell, 104–105
Mad Girl's Love Song, 259–260
Man He Killed, The, 24–25, 28, 44
Manners, 357–358
Mark but this flea, and mark in this, 174
MARLOWE, CHRISTOPHER
    *Passionate Shepherd to His Love, The,
        394–395*
MARVELL, ANDREW
    To His Coy Mistress, 88–90, 346

Mask, 362
MATHIS, CLEOPATRA
  Survival: A Guide, 395
Maud went to college, 360
May I serve you? This is delicious. Please sit
  anywhere. Please take off, 400
MCCKAY, CLAUDE
  White City, The, 262
MCCLATCHY, J. D.
  Ledger, The, 51
Meeting at Night, 58, 59, 75, 79, 252
Mending Wall, 373–374
Metaphors, 81–82
Midsummer Night's Dream, A, passages from, 77,
  192, 270
Mid-Term Break, 125–126, 188
MILLAY, EDNA ST. VINCENT
  Counting-Out Rhyme, 194–195
MILTON, JOHN
  On His Blindness, 142–143
Miniver Cheevy, 143–144
Miniver Cheevy, child of scorn, 143
Mirror, 36, 43, 75
Miscegenation, 412
Mr. Flood's Party, 406–408
MITCHAM, JUDSON
  Story, 396
  Stroke, 396–397
Morning Song, 198–199
Most Vital Thing in Life, The, 273–274
Moth, 403–404
Much have I traveled in the realms of
  gold, 253
Much Madness is divinest Sense, 115
Much Madness is divinest Sense, 115–116
Musée des Beaux Arts, 356–357
Music Lessons, 200–201
My Daddy has paid the rent, 362
My father worked with a horse-plow, 380
My galley chargèd with forgetfulness, 416
My galley chargèd with forgetfulness, 416
My grandfather said to me, 357
My heart aches, and a drowsy numbness
  pains, 390
My heart leaps up when I behold, 415
My heart leaps up when I behold, 415
My Last Duchess, 151, 250–251, 288–290,
  333
My long two-pointed ladder's sticking
  through a tree, 65

My mistress' eyes, 172
My mistress' eyes are nothing like the
  sun, 172
My old man's a white old man, 47
My Papa's Waltz, 128–129
My sister spent a whole life in the earth, 170
My son's very graceful; he has perfect
  balance, 374
My Son the Man, 144–145

N

narrow Fellow in the Grass, A, 167–169,
  320, 323
Nature's first green is gold, 202
Night and the Creation of Geography, 243–244
Nights too warm for TV, 49
No, no, go not to Lethe, neither twist, 34
Noiseless Patient Spider, A, 93–94, 95, 96, 318
Nothing Gold Can Stay, 202
Nothing is so beautiful as spring—, 60
Now as I was young and easy under the apple
  boughs, 246
Now hardly here and there a hackney-coach,
  410
Now this particular girl, 109

O

O, what can ail thee, knight-at-arms, 388
OATES, JOYCE CAROL
  Bloodline, Elegy: Su Qijian Family, Beijing,
    397–400
  Playlet for Voices, 206, 400–401
Ode on a Grecian Urn, 286–288
Ode on Melancholy, 34–35
Ode on Solitude, 404
Ode to a Nightingale, 390–392
Ode to the West Wind, 283–286
Oedipus Rex, 334
Oh, but it is dirty, 16
Old Eben Flood, climbing alone one
  night, 406
Old-Fashioned Pitcher, The, 272–273
Old Ladies' Home, 222–223
OLDS, SHARON
  Bop After Hip Op, 175–176
  Connoisseuse of Slugs, The, 402–403
  I Go Back to May 1937, 402
  My Son the Man, 144–145
  Rite of Passage, 199–200
  35/10, 50–51

OLIVER, MARY
  Music Lessons, 200–201
  Spring in the Classroom, 44–45, 59–60, 318,
    344, 348, 351–353
O 'Melia, my dear, this does everything
  crown!, 379
Once, two spoons in bed, 86
Once I am sure there's nothing going on, 181
One Art, 258–259
One day I wrote her name upon the strand, 409
One day I wrote her name upon the strand, 409–410
One must have a mind of winter, 68
One that is ever kind said yesterday, 261
On First Looking into Chapman's Homer,
    253–254
On Her Loving Two Equally, 357
On His Blindness, 142–143
On My First Son, 18–19
On the Sonnet, 158–159, 320
On the stiff twig up there, 11
O Rose, thou art sick!, 95
O'ROURKE, MEGHAN
  Apartment Living, 397
O soft embalmer of the still midnight, 392
O Solitude!, 278
O Solitude! if I must with thee dwell, 278
O sweet spontaneous, 157
O sweet spontaneous, 157–158
O the days gone by! O the days gone by!, 276
Othello, 317, 334, 335
"Out, Out—", 78, 136–137
OWEN, WILFRED
  Anthem for Doomed Youth, 241–242
  Dulce et Decorum Est, 6–7, 80
O wild West Wind, thou breath of Autumn's
  being, 283
Oxen, The, 173–174
Ozymandias, 122–123

P
Parting at Morning, 59–60
Passionate Shepherd to His Love, The, 394–395
PASTAN, LINDA
  To a Daughter Leaving Home, 223–224
Peace, 381–382
Pescadero, 369–370
Piano, 275–276
PIERCY, MARGE
  Barbie Doll, 119–120
Piping down the valleys wild, 219

Pitcher, 272
PLATH, SYLVIA
  Black Rook in Rainy Weather, 11–12
  Colossus, The, 129–130
  Lady Lazarus, 309–312
  Mad Girl's Love Song, 259–260
  Metaphors, 81–82
  Mirror, 36, 43, 75
  Morning Song, 198–199
  Old Ladies' Home, 222–223
  Spinster, 109–110
  Suicide off Egg Rock, 242–243
  Wuthering Heights, 139–140
Playlet for Voices, 206, 400–401
POE, EDGAR ALLAN
  Annabel Lee, 227–229
  Bells, The, 195–198, 230
Poison Tree, A, 273
POLLITT, KATHA
  Moth, 403–404
POPE, ALEXANDER
  Engraved on the Collar of a Dog Which I Gave
    to His Royal Highness, 183–184
  Ode on Solitude, 404
  Sound and Sense, 233–234
Porphyria's Lover, 151, 224–226
Primavera, 375
Pulley, The, 251–253
Purple Bathing Suit, 102–103

R
Redemption, 100–101, 315
Red Wheelbarrow, The, 15, 323
RICH, ADRIENNE
  Aunt Jennifer's Tigers, 244
  Living in Sin, 63–64
  Storm Warnings, 38–39
Richard Cory, 17–18
Rite of Passage, 199–200
Road Not Taken, The, 91–93, 98, 116
ROBINSON, EDWIN ARLINGTON
  Eros Turannos, 405–406
  Miniver Cheevy, 143–144
  Mr. Flood's Party, 406–408
  Richard Cory, 17–18
ROETHKE, THEODORE
  My Papa's Waltz, 128–129
  Waking, The, 189–191
ROGERS, PATTIANN
  Night and the Creation of Geography, 243–244

Romeo and Juliet, passage from, 260, 317
ROSSETTI, CHRISTINA
  Song, 408
  Up-Hill, 408–409
Round the cape of a sudden came the sea, 59
Ruined Maid, The, 379–380

S

Sadie and Maud, 360
Sailing to Byzantium, 300–301
Saturday morning, Motown, 36
Season of mists and mellow fruitfulness, 69
Second Coming, The, 417
SHAKESPEARE, WILLIAM
  Blow, blow, thou winter wind, 193, 251
  Hamlet, passages from, 116, 152, 192, 270
  Let me not to the marriage of true minds, 409
  Love's Labor's Lost, passages from, 5, 192
  Macbeth, passages from, 80, 137–138, 317
  Midsummer Night's Dream, A, passages from, 77, 192, 270
  My mistress' eyes, 172
  Othello, 317, 334, 335
  Romeo and Juliet, passage from, 260, 317
  Shall I compare thee to a summer's day?, 11
  Tempest, The, 84
  That time of year, 254–255, 280, 317, 319
  Twelfth Night, 300
  When my love swears that she is made of truth, 43–44
  Winter, 5–6, 189, 231, 251, 343, 348
  As You Like It, 193
Shall I compare thee to a summer's day?, 11
Shall I compare thee to a summer's day?, 11
Sharded in black, like beetles, 222
She fears him, and will always ask, 405
She had thought the studio would keep itself, 63
SHELLEY, PERCY BYSSHE
  Ode to the West Wind, 283–286
  Ozymandias, 122–123
She Walks in Beauty, 360–361
She walks in beauty, like the night, 360
Sick Rose, The, 95–96, 98
sight in camp in the daybreak gray and dim, A, 412–413
Silver bark of beech, and sallow, 194
Since I am coming to that holy room, 107
Since there's no help, 169–170, 235
Since there's no help, come let us kiss and part, 169, 356

Skirting the river road (my forenoon walk, my rest), 37
Skunk, The, 245–246
slumber did my spirit seal, A, 124
Snow falling and night falling fast, oh, fast, 48
Snow Man, The, 68
Snowstorm, The, 84–85
Softly, in the dusk, a woman is singing to me, 275
Soliloquy of the Spanish Cloister, 130–133
Solitary Reaper, The, 415–416
Some say the world will end in fire, 105
Something there is that doesn't love a wall, 373
Sometimes, in the middle of the lesson, 200
so much depends, 15
Song, 408
Song: Go and catch a falling star, 367–368
song in the front yard, a, 359–360
Song of Wandering Aengus, The, 418
Sonnenizio on a Line from Drayton, 356
Sonnet, 159–160, 320
SOPHOCLES
  Oedipus Rex, 334
Sorrow is my own yard, 61
So those despotic loves have become known to you, 397
Sound and Sense, 233–234
Southern History, 160, 320
SPENSER, EDMUND
  One day I wrote her name upon the strand, 409–410
Spinster, 109–110
Spring, 60–61, 320
Spring comes quickly: overnight, 375
Spring in the Classroom, 44–45, 59–60, 318, 344, 348, 351–353
STAFFORD, WILLIAM
  Traveling through the dark, 201–202
Stanzas, 221
STEVENS, WALLACE
  Anecdote of the Jar, 410
  Disillusionment of Ten O'Clock, 55–56
  Snow Man, The, 68
  Sunday Morning, 301–305, 333
Still to be neat, 387
Still to be neat, still to be dressed, 387
Stopping by Woods on a Snowy Evening, 153–154, 166

Storm Warnings, 38–39
Story, 396
Stroke, 396–397
Study of Reading Habits, A, 25–27, 317, 334, 349–351
Suddenly his shoulders get a lot wider, 144
Suicide off Egg Rock, 242–243
Suicide's Note, 17
Sunday Morning, 301–305, 333
Sundays too my father got up early, 66
Sun Rising, The, 116–117
Sunset and evening star, 172
Survival: A Guide, 395
Sweet day, so cool, so calm, so bright, 209
Sweet Peace, where dost thou dwell? I humbly crave, 381
SWIFT, JONATHAN
    Description of the Morning, A, 410–411
Sympathy, 370–371

T

Tempest, The, 84
TENNYSON, LORD ALFRED
    Break, break, break, 226–227
    Crossing the Bar, 172–173
    Eagle, The, 4, 59, 151
    Ulysses, 110–112, 216, 234–237, 250, 251
Terence, this is stupid stuff, 383
"Terence, this is stupid stuff," 118, 327, 383–384
That is no country for old men. The young, 300
That night when joy began, 188
That night when joy began, 188–189, 191
That night your great guns, unawares, 376
That's my last duchess painted on the wall, 288
That time of year, 254–255, 280, 317, 319
That time of year thou mayst in me behold, 254
The art of losing isn't hard to master, 258
The buzz-saw snarled and rattled in the yard, 136
The calm, 17
the Cambridge ladies who live in furnished souls, 366
The dead are always looking down on us, they say, 364
The first line will not go away, 262
The glass has been falling all the afternoon, 38
The gray sea and the long black land, 58

The horizons ring me like faggots, 139
The houses are haunted, 55
The instructor said, 386
The little goats like my mouth and fingers, 369
Theme for English B, 386–387
The moon in the bureau mirror, 221
The rain set early in tonight, 224
There is no Frigate like a Book, 42
There is no Frigate like a Book, 42, 44, 79, 344
There's a certain Slant of light, 290
There's a certain Slant of light, 290–291, 334
There's been a Death, in the Opposite House, 32
There's been a Death, in the Opposite House, 32–33, 231
The screeching cries, 243
The sea is calm tonight, 179
The starry night will still look good in black, 396
The time you won your town the race, 385
The trees are in their autumn beauty, 418
The whiskey on your breath, 128
The world is charged with the grandeur of God, 191
The world is too much with us; late and soon, 48
They eat beans mostly, this old yellow pair, 14
35/10, 50–51
This girlchild was born as usual, 119
This living hand, 392
This living hand, now warm and capable, 392
THOMAS, DYLAN
    Do Not Go Gentle into That Good Night, 255–257
    Fern Hill, 246–247
Those Winter Sundays, 66–67
Thou ill-formed offspring of my feeble brain, 76
Thou still unravished bride of quietness, 286
Tiger, The, 162–163, 320
Tiger! Tiger! burning bright, 162
'Tis true, 'tis day, what though it be?, 31
To a Daughter Leaving Home, 223–224
Toads, 83–84, 188
To an Athlete Dying Young, 77, 385
To Autumn, 69–70, 77
To Celia, 387
To His Coy Mistress, 88–90, 346
To Sleep, 392
To the Snake, 167, 168–169, 320

To the Virgins, to Make Much of Time,
     99–100, 334
Traveling through the dark, 201–202
Traveling through the dark I found
     a deer, 201
TRETHEWEY, NATASHA
     Accounting, 49–50
     Blond, 411
     Collection Day, 36–37
     History Lesson, 179
     Miscegenation, 412
     Southern History, 160, 320
Triple Fool, The, 13
True ease in writing comes from art, not
     chance, 233
Turning and turning in the widening gyre, 417
Twelfth Night, 300
Two roads diverged in a yellow wood, 91

U

Ulysses, 110–112, 216, 234–237, 250, 251
Unknown Citizen, The, 126–127, 334
Up, black, striped and damasked like the
     chasuble, 245
Up-Hill, 408–409
Upon Julia's Clothes, 35

V

Valediction: Forbidding Mourning, A, 86–88,
     423–426
Van Wyck Brooks tells us Whitman in old
     age, 103
Villanelle, 262–263
Villanelle for an Anniversary, 265–266
Virtue, 209–219, 235

W

Waking, The, 189–191
War Is Kind, 365–366
Weary Blues, The, 305–306
Weighing the Dog, 364–365
We Real Cool, 193–194
We real cool. We, 194
We Wear the Mask, 263–264
We wear the mask that grins and lies, 263
What happens to a dream deferred?, 73
What matters most is private and vast and
     can't be seen, 396
What passing-bells for these who die as
     cattle?, 241

What Soft—Cherubic Creatures, 128
What Soft—Cherubic Creatures, 128
When a man hath no freedom to fight for at
     home, 221
When as in silks my Julia goes, 35
When by thy scorn, O murderess, I am
     dead, 368
Whenever Richard Cory went down town, 17
When getting my nose in a book, 25
When God at first made man, 251
When I am dead, my dearest, 408
When icicles hang by the wall, 5
When I consider how my light is spent, 142
When I have fears that I may cease to be, 278
When I have fears that I may cease to be, 278
When I heard the learn'd astronomer, 158
When I Heard the Learn'd Astronomer, 158
When I see birches bend to left and
     right, 371
When I taught you, 223
When I was a connoisseuse of slugs, 402
When my love swears that she is made of
     truth, 43
When my love swears that she is made of truth,
     43–44
When my mother died I was very young, 120
When you feel like saying something, 273
White City, The, 262
WHITMAN, WALT
     Dalliance of the Eagles, The, 37–38
     Had I the Choice, 220–221
     Hours continuing long, sore and heavy-hearted,
          413–414
     I saw in Louisiana a live-oak growing, 67–68
     Noiseless Patient Spider, A, 93–94, 95,
          96, 318
     sight in camp in the daybreak gray and dim, A,
          412–413
     When I Heard the Learn'd Astronomer, 158
Whitman and the Moth, 103–104
Whose woods these are I think I know, 153
Why should I let the toad work, 83
Widow's Lament in Springtime, The, 61–62, 74,
     122, 151, 250, 320
Wild Swans at Coole, The, 418–419
WILLIAMS, WILLIAM CARLOS
     Dance, The, 248
     Red Wheelbarrow, The, 15, 323
     Widow's Lament in Springtime, The, 61–62,
          74, 122, 151, 250, 320

Winter, 5–6, 189, 231, 251, 343, 348
Witness, 361
WORDSWORTH, WILLIAM
I wandered lonely as a cloud, 414
My heart leaps up when I behold, 415
slumber did my spirit seal, A, 124
Solitary Reaper, The, 415–416
world is too much with us, The, 48, 77
world is too much with us, The, 48, 77
Wuthering Heights, 139–140
WYATT, THOMAS
My galley chargèd with forgetfulness, 416

Y

YEATS, WILLIAM BUTLER
Among School Children, 176–178
Folly of Being Comforted, The, 261–262
Lake Isle of Innisfree, The, 416–417
Leda and the Swan, 148
Sailing to Byzantium, 300–301
Second Coming, The, 417
Song of Wandering Aengus, The, 418
Wild Swans at Coole, The, 418–419
You, Andrew Marvell, 104–105